Courtship, marriage, and family:
American style

THE DORSEY SERIES IN SOCIOLOGY

Consulting Editor Charles M. Bonjean The University of Texas at Austin

Courtship, Marriage, and Family:
American Style

EVERETT D. DYER, Ph.D.
Professor of Sociology
University of Houston

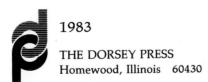
1983

THE DORSEY PRESS
Homewood, Illinois 60430

ISBN 0-256-02413-8

Library of Congress Catalog Card No. 82–72875

Printed in the United States of America

1 2 3 4 5 6 7 8 9 0 K 0 9 8 7 6 5 4 3

To my mother, Winnifred M. Dyer,
and my grandson, Lindsey Stuart Bannan.

Foreword

Authors of marriage and family textbooks assume a heavy responsibility. It is likely that the students who read these books will use the material to help them in their decisions about their lives—decisions which, in most cases, will affect their well-being and life satisfaction. Thus, the potential for both harm and benefit from these books is considerable.

All too often, in discharging their responsibilities, authors of marriage and family textbooks have resorted to sensationalism, oversimplification, and distortion to attract and hold students' interest. Some propagandize an ideological position. Many, in reflecting fads, become apologists for what they perceive as emerging social trends. Still others defend the traditional family patterns, refusing to consider the possibility that changes have been adaptive and functional. Even more frequently authors have been careless, often representing as proven facts generalizations which have little or no empirical support.

Marriage and family textbooks have generally not emphasized theory, but when they have, treatments have often been tedious, pretentious, pedantic, and of little value to students who attempt to apply them to their own family relationships. In short, the record of responsibility of authors of such textbooks is mixed, but overall not very good.

Everett Dyer has done an exemplary job of avoiding these deficiencies. The treatment of controversial issues in this textbook is unusually responsible and balanced. He has achieved a high level of clarity while maintaining intellectual integrity—rare in textbooks written for lower-division courses. Dyer's conclusions are tentative and qualified where appropriate; yet he does not imply that social scientists know little about marriage and the family. Although some of his values concerning family relationships are easily inferred, he does not try to impose them upon the reader. Dyer relates ideas and interpretations from other textbooks to primary sources for research findings. Further, he has selected as topics for discussion many of the important findings from recent research on marriage and family.

Dyer's book is theoretically eclectic, as are most marriage and family textbooks; but the eclecticism in this book is a strength. Differing theoretical perspectives are woven into the text in a way that should foster students' insights into their own family relationships and into relationships they observe. Theory is never presented in a pretentious or a pedantic manner.

As I read this book, I had the feeling that students should generally have more satisfying and socially responsible family relationships because they have read it. I have rarely had that feeling about a marriage and family textbook.

Norval D. Glenn
University of Texas—Austin

Preface

Young people, thinking of marriage and families in the future, are apt to feel some trepidation as well as some hopeful anticipation. They hear on the one hand that marriage and family are in trouble and may even be dying; on the other hand they are told that these basic social institutions are alive and well, even if they are undergoing changes and adjustments. So they are faced with dilemmas: Marriage, or not? Postpone marriage until the mid-20s—or even later? Perhaps try an up-to-date alternative to traditional marriage?

My aim in this book is to help young people prepare for future marital and family roles. I try to present the choices available, and point out some to the possible consequences of those choices. Accordingly, I have focused on some of the most salient issues, changes, and trends in male-female relations, both before and after marriage. These include premarital sexual attitudes and behavior, women's liberation and equality, dual-family earners, problems and issues confronting expectant and new parents, alternatives to conventional marriage and family living, and divorce and remarriage. I also show the social and historical contexts within which contemporary American mate selection, marriage, and parent-child relations—with their continuities and changes—have developed.

The organization of this book is in a developmental or life-cycle pattern. Part I presents the social context. Part II deals with premarital interaction and mate selection; Part III covers marriage, marital relationships, marital dissolution, and remarriage. Part IV moves on to family and kinship relations, embracing not only childrearing and parent-child relations, but also extended family ties, including in-law relations. The life cycle pattern is completed with a treatment of the middle and later years of family life. I conclude with some views on the future of marriage and family in America.

This book is intended for use in colleges and universities offering beginning- or intermediate-level courses in marriage and family, family life preparation, or sociology of the family. The book is appropriate for courses in marriage and family living in Home Economics Departments as well as in Sociology or Psychology Departments.

I wish to express my gratitude to all those whose research and interpretations have contributed to the preparation of this book. I would like to extend my warmest personal thanks for the guidance provided by Robin M. Williams, Jr., who served as an advisor to the Sociology Series of the Dorsey Press, throughout the development of this manuscript. My thanks to my sociology colleagues—Robert A. Clark, Gordon College; Irving Tallman, Washington State University; William J. Doherty, University of Iowa; and to Charles M. Bonjean, University of Texas-Austin, Consulting Editor to the Dorsey Press—who all read and criticized the various drafts, and whose suggestions have been gratefully followed. I owe a special debt to Norval Glenn, of the University of Texas-Austin, who meticulously reviewed the entire final manuscript and whose criticisms and recommended revisions have materially enhanced the book. And finally, my deepest thanks to my wife, Jacqueline L. Dyer, and my daughter, Janette Dyer Bannan, for their suggestions, research assistance, editing, and typing, always accompanied with unfailing encouragement and support.

Everett D. Dyer
University of Houston

Contents

xiii

Anthropological explanation of sex differentiation. MASCULINE AND FEMININE SEX-ROLE DEFINITIONS. Historical perspective on sex-role differentiation in America. Learning sex roles. *Sex-role stereotyping. Sexism.* Masculine and feminine subcultures in America. The subculture of the male. *Characteristics of the male subculture.* The subculture of the female. *Characteristics of the female subculture.* Some implications of the differences between male and female subcultures. CHANGES AND TRENDS IN SEX-ROLES. Changing sex-role definitions. *Decline in sex segregation. Increasing sex-role flexibility. Future trends in sex roles.* Significance of sex-role trends for dating and courtship.

PART THREE: MARRIAGE AND MARITAL RELATIONSHIPS

6. **Marriage: American style** **129**

TRANSITION TO MARRIAGE. Beginnings. *Readiness for marriage. The wedding: A rite of passage. The honeymoon.* Transition from single to marital status. *Developmental tasks.* College student marriages. MARRIAGE IN AMERICAN SOCIETY. *Sociolegal aspects of marriage. Age at marriage. Blood relationships. Void and voidable marriages. Some procedural aspects of marriage.* Marital relationships and processes. *Husband-wife interaction. Marriage as status and role transition. Marriage and role differentiation. Role choices in marriage.* Changes and trends in American marriage. *Some long-range trends. Some demographic trends and changes in marriage.*

7. **Marital adjustment: Getting along as marriage partners**. **153**

THE CONCEPT OF MARITAL ADJUSTMENT. FACTORS IN MARITAL ADJUSTMENT. Identification of factors and problem areas. *Socioemotional versus instrumental roles and relationships. Short-term satisfactions versus long-run goals and planning. Internal (family) commitments versus external (community) commitments. Parents versus children.* Marital adjustment and selected social and demographic factors. *Age and marital adjustment. Religion and marital adjustment. Race and marital adjustment. Education and marital adjustment. Social class and marital adjustment. In-laws and marital adjustment.* STUDIES IN MARITAL ADJUSTMENT. Pioneer studies in marital adjustment. *Early efforts to measure and predict marital adjustment. Critique of the early concept of marital adjustment.* Recent efforts to reconceptualize and study marital adjustment. *The dyadic adjustment scale. A typology of marriages: Marital adjustment in the upper middle class. Marital adjustment over the family life cycle. A national survey of marital happiness.* IMPROVING MARITAL ADJUSTMENT. Problem solving and conflict resolution. *Identifying the problem. Exploring alternative solutions. Selecting the best alternatives. Implementing the decision. Rebuilding the relationship. Reviewing the decision-making process.* Marriage counseling. Keeping the marriage alive and well.

8. **Sex and sexual adjustment in marriage**. **181**

MARITAL SEXUALITY. General overview. *Marital sexuality versus premarital sexuality. Unrealistic perceptions and expectations of sex in marriage.* Traditional conceptions of marital sexuality. Contemporary conceptions of marital sexuality. *Value conflicts regarding modern marital sexuality.* MARITAL SEXUAL ADJUSTMENT. Problems in marital sexual interaction and adjustment. *Some sexual problems of wives. Some sexual problems of the husband.* Sexual adjustment and marital adjustment. *Studies and interpretations. Some conclusions regarding sexual adjustment and marital adjustment.* EXTRAMARITAL SEXUAL BEHAVIOR. Reasons for extramarital sexual relations. Rates of extramarital sexual behavior.

9. **Marriage and occupational roles** **203**

OCCUPATION AND MARRIAGE AND FAMILY. The world of work and marriage and family. *Occupational involvement and marriage.* OCCUPATIONAL

ROLE OF THE HUSBAND. Importance of the husband's occupational role to the family. *Socialization for male occupational roles.* Conflict potential between husband's occupational role and his family roles. *Viewpoint of the wife. Differences in compatibility of jobs and family roles.* OCCUPATIONAL ROLE OF THE WIFE. Increased employment of married women. *Factors contributing to increased employment of married women.* Some consequences of the wife's employment on the marriage. Some possible consequences of the mother's employment on the children.

PART FOUR: FAMILY AND KINSHIP RELATIONS

hood and marital satisfaction. Gratifications of parenthood. Suggestions for potential parents.

PART ONE

Background and perspectives

CHAPTER 1

The social context of courtship, marriage, and family in America

Those who study and write about marriage and family find the task stimulating and rewarding, but in certain ways frustrating and difficult too. The subjects—husbands and wives, parents and children—are alive, varied, and changing. Moreover, most everyone is in a sense an "expert" on the family by virtue of lifelong experience as a family member. Each person normally starts out as a son or daughter in a parental family, then after growing up helps form a new family by getting married, and sooner or later most become parents.

This long and intense personal familiarity with the family can be both a help and a hindrance in the effort to study and understand the family in general in its larger social context. Personal familiarity is a definite help in providing basic insights and understandings of what marriage and family are all about. No one has to start from zero, as does the aspiring nuclear physicist. When one hears the word *marriage* that person normally envisions two people of the opposite sex joined together as husband and wife according to law or custom. The word *family* would probably mean to most Americans two parents with one or more children. Both of these terms may, however, have somewhat different meanings to people in some other societies, as indicated later in this chapter. Then, the very fact that everyone is so familiar with the family—with one's own family at least—makes it difficult to see the family in general, to see the family apart from the specific cases known from experience.

3

One's own family may or may not be typical of the majority of families in the United States. Whether it is or not, individuals tend to feel that the way their family is organized and does things is the right and probably best way, and that alternative ways of family life are probably not as good. Most everyone feels strongly about family life. For many people the strength of their beliefs and sentiments on matters of sex, marriage, and family is second only to the strength of their feelings on matters of religion. This again makes it difficult to be objective about the behavior of husbands and wives, parents and children.

The purposes of this introductory chapter are two: (1) to introduce the reader to the social context of courtship, marriage, and family in contemporary America, and (2) to introduce the reader to the sociology of marriage and the family.

The discussion begins with a look at what is happening to marriage and family today. Since the American culture is in a time of flux and change, and there are differing viewpoints as to what is happening and what the future may hold for marriage and family life, a glance at some of these different points of view is necessary.

In order to grasp what is happening to marriage and family today one needs to know something about the American family of the past, the American family heritage. An awareness of the many historical and cultural sources of marriage and family in the United States should make for an understanding of the complexities of courtship, marriage, and family living today. That Americans live in a time of social change is obvious, as is the fact that family life is in transition. The discussion will identify some of the significant trends and changes in marriage and family within the larger context of social change in America.

This brief introduction to what is happening to marriage and family today, its historical background, its trends and changes, is presented with the view of setting the stage for the more detailed treatment of courtship, marriage, and family relationships in the following chapters.

The remainder of Chapter 1 is devoted to a brief introduction to the sociology of marriage and family. The reader will be introduced to basic sociological terms and concepts to be used throughout the book in discussing and analysing courtship, marriage, and family relations.

INTRODUCTION

WHAT IS HAPPENING TO MARRIAGE AND FAMILY TODAY?

Many people today raise questions about the state of and changes in marriage and family life today. Is marriage on the way out? Will the family as we have known it soon pass away and be replaced by new

alternative lifestyles? Or will marriage and family be able to adapt successfully to the changing times and challenges confronting them today? There
are certainly differing points of view on what is happening to marriage
and family, viewpoints expressed in religious, political, and journalistic
circles as well as among social scientists. Let us look at two opposing
viewpoints.

Viewpoint: The American family is in trouble

Some fear for the future, seeing what they interpret as symptoms of
marital and familial disintegration in the rising incidence of premarital
sex, higher divorce rates, and widening gaps between parents and their
children. From these and other problems some people even predict the
demise of the family (Cooper, 1971). Others, while less pessimistic as
to the final outcome, are still concerned about the trends. They think
that many of the above-mentioned trends may be attributed to the weakening of marriage and family ties, which they see as brought on by reduced
family functions and by excessive individualism. Our obsession with the
rights of the individual, with "self-enhancement," has led us to the point,
it is argued, where each marriage partner, and each child in the family,
is mainly concerned with his or her own personal needs and interests
with little concern for the good of the whole (Zaretsky, 1976).

Bell (1976, p. 54) attributes the rise of excessive individualism to a
long-term shift in American values. He sees the old-fashioned values
of hard work, thrift, self-denial and responsibility being replaced or greatly
reduced by a newer "fun morality" stressing enjoyment and self-fulfillment. The Protestant work ethic has given way to a "new hedonism"
based on play, fun, and spending. In the past, it is argued, people lived
more for their children and for the well being of the family as a whole;
now one lives mainly for one's own self-fulfillment. This new hedonism
would seem to be incompatible with marriage and family stability—at
least if carried very far. Individuals who develop narrowly selfish orientations may come to treat human relationships in the same way they treat
cars or clothing, as things to be used for a short time and then replaced
by later models (Skolnick, 1978, p. 5).

Such an individualistic value orientation can make deep and lasting
marriage or family relationships hard to achieve. As Lasch (1976, p. 10)
points out, such a view "encourages people not to make too large an
investment in love and friendship, to avoid . . . dependency on others,
and to live for the moment."

The other point alluded to above—that the loss of many earlier family
functions is changing the family today and perhaps thereby undermining
family stability—has been heard for some time in sociological circles (Zimmerman, 1949). Most modern American families are no longer economic
productive units, and other institutions and agencies have taken over
many of the family's earlier educational, religious, ,and protective respon-

sibilities. Lasch (1976) sees the modern American family as the victim of the encroachment of the external world, of government and various other community agencies. The present-day family, it is argued, has been reduced to a few specialized functions, such as affection and companionship.

Viewpoint: The American family is alive and well

There are, of course, more sanguine views on what is happening to marriage and family today. While conceding that most modern families perform fewer functions than families in earlier periods of American history, more optimistic observers point out that marriage and family today still function to meet the deepest affectional, emotional, and identity needs of most Americans, as well as society's reproductive needs. The small independent family is well adapted to modern urban-industrial society. It is mobile, for example, and thus can follow the expanding economy with its various job markets without hindrance of traditional kinship ties (Parsons, 1959).

In a study of changes in the American family from 1870 to 1970 Uhlenberg (1978, pp. 94–95) found that over the span of a century an increasing proportion of women entered marriage, an increasing proportion of them bore children, and fewer women had their marriages disrupted by death before their childrearing years were completed. He also found that more men born in 1930 will be married and living with their first wife at age 50 than was true for men born in 1870; and that the percentage of men among the 1930 group who will never marry will be less than half of those in the 1870 group who never married. Uhlenberg (1978, p. 95) concludes that "in speculating on the family of the future, one should not ignore the remarkable stability and adaptability of the American family during the past century of vast social change."

Other sociologists, including Bane (1976a), express similar optimism regarding the condition of marriage and family today. In her *Here To Stay: American Families in the Twentieth Century,* she cites strong evidence that American men and women today still consider marriage exceedingly important. The vast majority of Americans marry at least once. More than 90 percent of the elderly have married, and about 95 percent of middle-aged people have too. Since so many young adults are now remaining single longer, the marriage rate for them may be lower. We'll have to wait and see. And although divorce rates are high, most divorced people remarry; and when divorce occurs there is a sense of great loss and grief on the part of both the man and the woman. Bane (1976a) also finds that even though many more mothers of young children are in the labor force now, the quality and the quantity of mother-child interaction has probably not changed much from earlier periods.

The author agrees with Bane and Uhlenberg that the American family is not going to disintegrate or be replaced by something else in the foreseeable future (Dyer, 1979). Despite the many difficult issues and problems confronting the institutions of marriage and family today, it is my judgment that they will survive the present period of change and adjustment, while moving toward a more flexible marriage and family structure which should provide greater opportunities and more freedom for all family members.

Many of the issues and problems raised here as to what is happening to marriage and family today will receive fuller discussion later. For example, how are changing sex codes and behavior affecting courtship and marriage, and contributing to divorce and remarriage? How is the employment of wives and mothers affecting relationships between husbands and wives and between parents and children?

If one hopes to understand this modern period of change and the related problems and issues confronting people today in marriage and family living, it is necessary to pause and look backward. What was family life like in the past? What is our American family heritage and how has this heritage affected marriage and family relationships today?

AMERICAN FAMILIES: PAST AND PRESENT

AMERICAN FAMILY HERITAGE: HISTORICAL BACKGROUND AND CULTURAL SOURCES

Historical background of present-day marriage and family

Family life in the American colonies represented in part a continuation of the customs and traditions colonists brought from Europe and in part modifications and new additions that the conditions of family life here in the New World shaped. The settlers generally came in immediate families or as single persons (mostly men), rather than in larger extended family groups (Goode, 1963). Thus the immediate or nuclear family, consisting of parents and their children, became the principal family unit in the colonies. As kinship ties weakened, individual choice in mate selection gained an early foothold in the American colonies, due partly to the preponderance of settlers from the lower classes in Europe and partly to new freedoms in the colonies and the operation of supply and demand. Since immigration from Europe was heavily weighted with males, females in the early colonies were often at a premium. Eager bachelors sought available women for wives, and women came to have more voice in the selection of their marriage partners (Calhoun, 1945, Vol. 1).

Although the shortage of women tended to enhance their value and improve their status in the colonies and on the frontier, the colonial

Greek family

David Bell

family continued to resemble its European ancestor quite closely in its structure. The family was still patriarchal, with the husband-father legally and socially head of the family. Women's roles were generally restricted to homemaking, childbearing, and childrearing. Children were definitely subordinate and were expected to do their share of the work in the family economy, on the farm or in the house. Neither the wife-mother nor the child had any separate legal status (Farber, 1964, pp. 106–109).

As families pushed westward during the long period of American expansion, various traditions and customs brought from Europe were modified still further. Frontier conditions favored early marriage and large families. Children were economic assets since they provided labor in clearing the land and working the farms. These frontier and rural conditions of life were conducive to strong family solidarity and loyalty, or familism (Calhoun, 1945, Vol. 1, p. 145).

While the frontier family tended to remain essentially patriarchal, the value of the labor of wife and children enhanced their status considerably. Thus it may well be that the seeds of equality between the sexes were planted on the American frontiers long before the 20th century (Cavan, 1953, p. 35). Frontier family organization became more flexible with more rights and prerogatives for women, and for children too.

Different sources of American families: Racial and ethnic origins

Except for those families that stem from native Indian stock, American families past and present are descendants of people from many different parts of the world; people migrated to the United States from Europe, Africa, Asia, and from other parts of the Americas. The United States is a truly heterogenous nation; its families stem from a rich variety of ethnic, racial, and national origins. The magnitude of these migrations

Chinese family

Barbara Van Cleve/Atoz Images, Inc.

is indeed staggering; more than 45 million people arrived on our shores between 1820 and 1970 (Dyer, 1979, p. 60).

The great majority of American families have a European origin. About 36 million Europeans migrated to the United States between 1820 and 1970, constituting about 80 percent of the total documented immigration for this period (Vander Zanden,1966, p. 23; Dyer, 1979, p. 61). During the colonial period most settlers arrived from the British Isles, France, Spain, and Germany, with a few from other western European countries. Until the 1880s the source of most American immigrants continued to be western and northern Europe, with the English, Irish, German, and Scandinavian peoples predominating. Then the ethnic constituency changed as people from southern, central, and eastern Europe outnumbered those from western and northern Europe. These "new immigrants" included Italians, Poles, Russians and other Slavic peoples, and Greeks and Portuguese. The culture—including family lifestyles—of these new immigrants tended to differ more widely from that of the majority of Americans than did the culture and family patterns of the "old immigrants" from western and northern Europe. The adjustment and assimilation of a great many new immigrant families was impeded by their strong patriarchal family traditions, which they tried to perpetuate in a new land that emphasized individual freedom and equalitarianism (Thomas & Znaniecki, 1958; Campisi, 1948).

Africa was another important source of American families during the colonial period and the early national period of American history. The first to arrive from Africa were 20 people landed at Jamestown, Virginia in 1619, with the status of indentured servants. As slavery developed in the colonies many thousands of African people were forcibly transported to the New World. By 1790 there were 757,000 blacks in the United States, about 19 percent of the total population (Vander Zanden, 1966, p. 26). By 1970 there were 22,673,000 black Americans, about 11 percent of the population.

It should be pointed out that while African-Americans stem from many different tribal and national stocks, their family patterns, past and present, probably reflect little of their African cultural background. This is due to the unusual nature of their migration to America—forceable capture in Africa, the separation of family members and friends in transport, and being sold into servitude as individuals in the American colonies. Under such conditions it became virtually impossible to keep alive and perpetuate African family customs and patterns (Frazier, 1957; Haley, 1974). Black American family life has been shaped largely by conditions and processes here in America.

Other sources of American families include Asian countries, especially China and Japan. Between 1820 and 1970 more than 500,000 immigrants arrived from China and some 365,000 from Japan. Others came from the Philippines, India, Korea, and Southeast Asia. (Vander Zanden, 1966, p. 26; Dyer, 1979, p. 61). Most of these Asiatic immigrants brought strong family traditions with them and have tended to cling tenaciously to their family customs even after several generations of residence in the United States.

Still other American families have come from Central and South America and Canada. From 1820 to 1970 Canada sent about 4 million immigrants and Mexico about 1.6 million. Immigration from Mexico has increased greatly in recent years and now includes as many or perhaps more undocumented entrants than documented or legal entrants each year (Dyer, 1979, p. 61).

In summary, American families today stem from a rich and varied past of racial, ethnic, and national stocks. Contemporary American marriage and family patterns owe much to these diverse cultural and historical sources. While the family life of most immigrants and their descendants inevitably became modified by experiences in America, certain patterns from their home lands tended to persist. Thus the family life of many Americans today consists of a mixture of the old and the new, as will be apparent in the chapters to follow.

From this brief historical background let us now turn attention to some of the social conditions and processes that have been important in shaping marriage and family life in contemporary America.

CHANGING TIMES: COURTSHIP, MARRIAGE, AND FAMILY IN TRANSITION

In many ways courtship, marriage, and family today are a far cry from what they were in earlier periods of American history. Whether the changes are judged good or bad may be largely a matter of opinion. In any event, we need to look at family change within the larger perspective of social change.

Family change within the context of social change

Changes in the ways men and women get together as marriage partners, organize their marriages and bear and rear their children have been influenced by a great many things—industrialization, urbanization, geographic and social mobility, and various ideological and social movements, including individualism, equalitarianism, feminism, and youth movements.

Industrialization-urbanization and family change. Most authorities agree that when a society undergoes industrialization its family patterns will change significantly from their preindustrial condition (Goode, 1963). Extended family ties and strong lineages normally found in earlier preindustrial, agricultural economies tend to weaken, and some form of a small nuclear family becomes more important. This nuclear family, consisting of the marriage partners and their children, fits the industrial economy better because it frees family members from restrictive ties with parents and other relatives so they can go where the industrial economy needs its workers (Parsons, 1959). Also, technological and industrial developments are generally accompanied by a number of interrelated social changes which themselves affect family life. For example, the industrial revolution brought about changes in transportation and communication, the growth of cities, the expansion of education and literacy, the rising expectations of the masses, and the spread of democratic and equalitarian ideologies (Goode, 1963).

With industrialization came the rapid growth of large cities where conditions of family life differed dramatically from those found in rural environments. Families moving from farms and rural villages into big American cities were confronted with dense populations, crowded neighborhoods, limited living space, and often little or no play facilities for children. By contrast with the rural community, the city was impersonal, full of strangers, and often hostile. Family members had to separate during the day, as one or both parents went to work for some employer and the children went to school (Wirth, 1938). Fischer (1975) contends that conditions of urban life contributed to the existance of varied subcultures and lifestyles. People of similar ideological, religious, or ethnic background tended to congregate in densely populated neighborhoods. This contributed to the continuation of family variations in urban America.

Ideological influences and family changes. In addition to the ideology of economic progress and technological development, the ideology of individualism has been important to the development of American society and to the emergence of the independent nuclear family (Goode, 1963). The ideology of individualism asserts the paramount importance of the individual and makes his or her well being and happiness the criteria for decisions and actions. Where this ideology prevails, the wishes of individual family members can come to be more important than traditional family goals or family solidarity. The acceptance of the ideology of individualism by a great many Americans has resulted in a greater tolerance of varied marital and family practices, and of divorce too (Udry, 1974, p. 14). Beyond a certain point, individualism can be detrimental to marriage and family stability.

The ideology of equalitarianism has also been a source of social and family change in modern America. Equalitarianism asserts the equal right of women and men to have a voice in decisions affecting their lives, including marriage and family decisions. Equalitarianism has challenged time-honored family traditions of masculine superiority and patriarchal family power. It has added impetus to the emergence of the independent conjugal family freed from control of the larger kinship group; it has been one of the driving forces in the women's liberation movement and in the push for equal rights and authority of the wife in modern marriage.

Significant trends and changes in marriage and family in America

How different are families today from what they actually were in the past? Many Americans have an idealistic notion of what family life used to be. Goode (1963) has aptly labeled this idealized image of the old-fashioned American family "the classical family of Western nostalgia." As Goode (1963, p. 6) describes this idealized picture:

> There are lots of happy children, and many kinfolk live together in a large, rambling house. Everyone works hard. Most of the food to be eaten during the winter is grown, preserved, and stored on the farm. . . . The family has many functions; it is the source of economic stability and religious, educational and vocational training. Father is stern and reserved, and has

the final decision in all important matters. Life is difficult, but harmonious because everyone knows his task and carries it out. All boys and girls marry, the couple lives harmoniously, either near the boy's parents or with them. . . . No one divorces.

Historians of the family doubt that there were many early American families that approximated this idealized old-fashioned model. Even though divorce was rare, it is not known how happy or harmonious most marriages were in the past. A lack of historical data plus the tendency to look back longingly to "the good old days" has resulted in a somewhat one-sided and unrealistic conception of marriage and family life down through the 19th century. In some ways life was simpler and maybe better back then; in other ways it is better now, considering labor-saving devices, more community resources, and better health care.

What are the significant changes in the American family since colonial days? Adams (1980, pp. 77–89) has attempted to identify the most important changes in the family since about 1800. In the case of courtship and mate selection, personal choice of a mate seems to have been well established in the colonial period, so the current pattern of each individual selecting a marriage partner does not represent a basic change. Romantic love was becoming a more common basis for mate selection throughout the 19th century. Until the early 20th century, however, courtship tended to be more restrictive, centered largely in the home or in chaperoned social gatherings. The post–World War I period brought much greater freedom for young people, particularly for young women; and this freedom, combined with the automobile, produced dating and a new type of courtship.

American nuclear family

E. D. Dyer

With the establishment of dating as the main pattern of premarital relations, some major transitions in premarital sex codes got under way (Adams, 1980, p. 79). The extent and significance of these changes will be examined in detail in Part Two of this book. Suffice it to note here that these sex-code changes are major and even revolutionary when viewed against the historical background of the Victorian era. Not only is there much greater freedom and openness in matters of sex today; it also may be argued that by mid-20th century America had become obsessed with sex, as evidenced by the movies, T.V., popular literature, pop music, and sex research and sex education.

In its internal organization and relationships the American family has undergone transitions ranging from moderate to great since 1800 (Adams, 1980, p. 81). Family size has declined, especially in the proportion of very large families. Birthrates declined steadily from 1860 to 1940. (See Figure 1–1.) The status of children in the family has changed significantly. Parental authority is no longer based mainly on tradition and on socializing the child to be a subordinate but important member of the family work team. The child today is thus freed from much of the earlier parental authority which a patriarchal father could assert. This change, combined with the decline in moral and religious absolutes in the 20th century, has increased parental permissiveness in childrearing and in parent-child relations. It should also be added that the 20th century has witnessed increasing parental concern for the child as a growing and developing

Figure 1–1

Birth rates, United States, 1860-1978

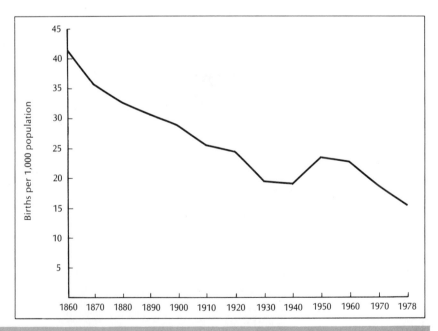

Sources: U. S. Bureau of the Census, *Current Population Reports,* 1965; *Recent Social and Economic Trends,* 1979.

human being. In general, the period has seen an increasing emphasis on the rights of the individual in the family circle, which has benefited women and children especially, since historically they have been in a subordinate position to men in the traditional family.

In the area of husband-wife relations, the lack of adequate historical data, plus the difficulty in accurately measuring power relations between husband and wife, pose problems in knowing what changes have occurred. In general, the traditional patriarchal authority pattern of the colonial family and the Victorian family have given way to more democratic or equalitarian patterns, especially apparent in middle-class families today (Dyer & Urban, 1958). Such changes are uneven across social class and ethnic lines, however. Ethnic families of more recent arrival tend to hold on to their traditional patriarchal patterns longer, as do many lower- and working-class native-born American families (LeMasters, 1975). As wives achieve higher education and pursue careers they become less dependent on their husbands and are in a better position to demand an equal voice in family matters.

Significant changes have taken place since colonial days in the status of women, affecting their lives inside and outside of the family. Over the last century or more women have gained politically, legally, and educationally. Women can now vote and hold public office. Married women now have the legal right of property ownership and of entering into business contracts. Females now generally have the same educational opportunities as males, and the 20th century has seen coeducation extended to virtually all institutions of higher learning. Economically, a great many women have become partially or entirely financially independent, as a majority of them now are employed outside the home.

These changes in the status of women have profoundly affected the roles of women in marriage and family, as will be discussed in detail in Part Three. Many of the problems and issues of husband-wife relations and marital adjustment today relate directly to the changes in statuses and roles of the wife and mother in modern families.

Other important transitions have been taking place in the relationship between the family and the community or the external world. For one thing, the 20th-century family tends to be considerably more mobile, moving more frequently and further as its economic interests dictate. As noted above, the mobile nuclear family seems to fit the needs of modern industrial economy, and probably has fewer dependent ties with kinfolk than earlier American families did. A somewhat related change is that the small mobile modern family has fewer functions than its earlier counterpart. Over the past century many traditional family functions have been transferred from the home to external institutions and agencies. With industrialization, the economic productive function was transferred from the home to the factory and office. Health care, recreation, and protective functions have departed the family in varying degrees, as have most educational and religious functions (Ogburn, 1933). Other important functions still remain in the family, however, including reproduction, care and socialization of children, and meeting the emotional and personal needs of family members.

With this brief overview of the American family heritage and of courtship, marriage, and family in transition, let us now pause briefly to review some of the terms and tools of the trade sociologists have developed for studying and analyzing marriage and family.

THE SOCIOLOGY OF THE FAMILY

WHAT IS THE FAMILY? SOME USEFUL TERMS AND CONCEPTS

Thus far, while making extensive use of such terms as *marriage* and *family*, we have not yet defined them precisely. It is necessary to pause here to do this, and to define other concepts and terms used throughout the book.

Definition of the family

While everyone knows what a family is through long experience as a family member, few could easily define the family in the abstract, or in a general way that would encompass other types of families beyond those in one's own society. Such a broad general definition of the family has been offered by a pioneer family sociologist, E. W. Burgess (1945, p. 8):

> The family may be defined as a group of persons united by marriage, blood or adoption; constituting a single household; interacting and communicating with each other in their respective roles of husband and wife, mother and father, son and daughter, brother and sister; and creating and maintaining a common culture.

This definition focuses on family membership and relationships. Family members include people who are marriage partners, those who are blood relatives, and those who have been adopted into the family. Burgess has thus identified the three universal criteria of family membership: marriage, blood or kin ties, and adoption. Members of a given family then normally share some kind of living quarters and relate to each other day in and day out in their respective family roles. This definition applies to the nearly universal immediate or nuclear family and does not specifically include secondary relatives, such as grandparents, or aunts and uncles, or cousins. In some societies the family may include such secondary kin, however (Murdock, 1949).

Since families may differ considerably from place to place and one time period to another, it will be helpful to look briefly at some different kinds or types of families found throughout the world.

Types of families

The nuclear family. This is the well-known family unit consisting of a married couple and their children. After studying family organization in 250 representative cultures from all over the world, Murdock (1949) concluded that this nuclear family was found throughout the world. (See Figure 1–2.)

The extended family. Nuclear families may exist as parts of larger kinship groups called extended families. The extended family normally includes three or more generations, grandparents, parents, and children. Thus an extended family would generally include at least two nuclear families belonging to different generations in a given kinship line. The grandparents compose one nuclear family, and the parents and their children make up a second. In ancient China the traditional gentry family might have four or more generations within the large, extended family group (Levy, 1949). (See Figure 1–2.)

Some societies emphasize the nuclear family and others emphasize the extended family. Where priority is given to the marital tie between husband and wife the nuclear family normally is predominant; where priority is given the kinship ties, such as the father-son or the mother-daughter tie, the extended family is usually more important than the nuclear. Modern American society tends to emphasize the marital bond, with the independent nuclear family relatively free of control by blood relatives. By comparison, the traditional Chinese extended family was based on strong blood ties and obligations with the parent-child bond (especially the father-son bond) much more important than the husband-wife bond (Hsu, 1967).

Family of orientation. This is the family into which one is born as a son or a daughter, It consists of one's father and mother, oneself,

Figure 1–2

Types of families

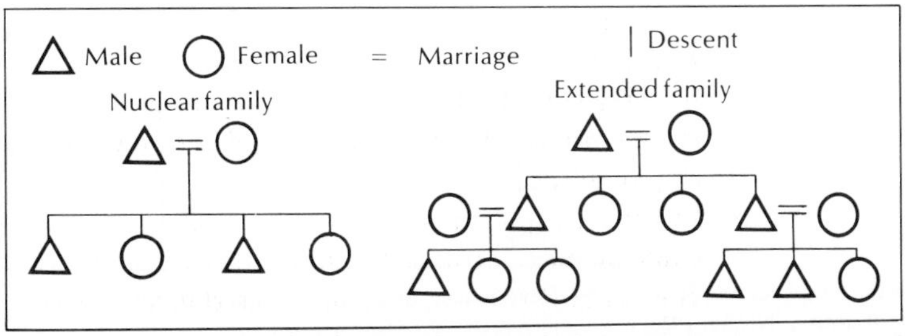

Source: *Social Structure* by G. Murdock, 1965.

Family life in Nepal is austere

Julie Heifitz

and one's brothers and sisters, if any (Warner, 1933). One normally grows up in the family of orientation. (See Figure 1–3.)

Family of procreation. Upon getting married, a couple creates a new family unit which may be called a family of procreation. In this new family the individual being used as a reference is a husband or a wife, and potentially or actually a father or a mother (Warner, 1933). So one's family of procreation consists of oneself, one's spouse, and any sons and daughters. It is the family group one normally lives in as an adult in such societies as ours. Americans are likely to think of it as "our own family." (See Figure 1–3.)

Figure 1–3

Families of orientation and procreation

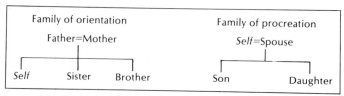

Source: "A Methodology for the Study of the Development of Family Attitudes" by W. L. Warner, Social Science Research Council, *Bulletin,* No. 18, 1933.

Types of marriage

For most purposes "marriage" is understood to be a part of "family." Burgess and Locke (1945, p. 1) identify marriage as one of the criteria for family membership and specifies the roles of husband and wife as parts of the family. Murdock (1949, p. 1) distinguishes marriage from family as a concept by defining marriage as a complex of customs which regulates the relationship between the marriage partners. Marriage defines how this relationship is established and maintained, and how it may be terminated. In a sense, marriage is a subsystem of the larger system known as the family. Americans generally think of marriage as a relationship in which two adults of the opposite sex make a personal and legal commitment to live together as husband and wife. Any offspring resulting from this marital relationship are socially and legally recognized as legitimate.

Anthropologists have found two major types of marriage throughout the world, monogamy and polygamy. Other minor variations, such as group or multilateral marriage, are rare by comparison, found here or there in such experimental communities as the Oneida community in New York State in the 19th century (Robertson, 1970). (See Figure 1–4.)

Monogamy.   This is the marriage of one man and one woman. It is the only legal form of marriage in many societies, including American society. Various societies and groups may differ in the way they interpret monogamy, however. There have been times and places where an individual has been allowed only one marriage partner in a lifetime, while elsewhere individuals are allowed to divorce current marital partners easily and immediately marry someone new. This has been called "serial monogamy." An interesting example was Tommy Manville, an American millionaire, who is reported to have had a succession of 14 different wives. Murdock (1949) found monogamy to be the only sanctioned type of marriage in 135 out of 554 societies around the world.

Polygamy.   This is the generic term for multiple marriage, and it has two logical subtypes, polygyny and polyandry. *Polygyny* is the marriage of one man to two or more women. *Polyandry* is the marriage of one

Figure 1–4

Types of marriage

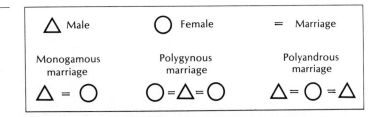

Source: *Social Structure* by George Murdock, 1965.

woman to two or more men. Of these two types of polygamy, polygyny is by far the most prevalent. In his comparison of types of marriage in a worldwide sample of 554 societies, Murdock (1949) found polygyny in 415 and polyandry in only 4.

The above figures on polygamy and monogamy need explaining. While in a strictly monogamous society no polygamy would generally be allowed at all, in most polygamous societies most marriages are in fact monogamous. Why is this so? Usually only the more affluent or high-status men in polygynous societies are in a position to support more than one wife; and since the sex ratio is approximately equal in most societies, if 50 men were to have two wives each in Utopia, another 50 men would probably be unable to have even one wife apiece.

Moslem societies have traditionally been polygynous, as the Koran permits a man up to four wives. On the other hand, most societies of the Judeo-Christian tradition are monogamous. Among the few people found to be practicing polyandry are the Tibetans in Central Asia and the Todas of India (Rivers, 1906).

The family as a social institution

In order to understand the nature and full significance of the family in human society, we need to look at it as both a social institution and

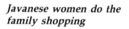

Javanese women do the family shopping

Julie Heifitz

a social group. The family is one of the basic social institutions found in human society, along with religious economic and political institutions.

A social institution may be defined as a set of customs and norms (folkways, mores, laws) organized for the purpose of carrying out certain "societal functions" (Davis, 1949, p. 71). A societal function is a kind of service that is performed or carried out for a society and its members. Such services are rendered to enable the society to "function" by having its basic societal needs met, such as the reproduction of new members, their care and socialization, and the production and distribution of goods and services (Bennett & Tumin, 1948). Failure to meet these basic societal needs, or "functional requisites" as they are sometimes called, can lead to the decline or even death of a given society. Social institutions are arrangements through which basic societal needs are met. Economic institutions, for example, organize the means for providing the goods and services necessary to sustain life and health of a society's members.

Viewing the family as a social institution enables one to see readily its importance and significance in human society. Goode (1963) maintains that the family is the most important of all social institutions, in that it is responsible for carrying out more basic societal functions than any other institution. Let us briefly identify some of these family functions.

Family functions. Among the many important functions the family has peformed for society and its members are (1) reproduction, or replacement of the members of a society; (2) maintenance, care, and nourishment of these new members during infancy and childhood; (3) socialization, or the upbringing of the young; and (4) social placement of these individuals in the community or society (Davis, 1949, p. 395). Also, the family usually serves as the main agency for transmission of property from generation to generation in most societies, including ours, where parents normally will their property to their children as heirs.

In addition to the above societal functions the family performs a number of closely related *individual-serving functions* which cater directly to the personal needs of family members (Winch, 1971). Through the marital relationship the family provides for satisfying the emotional and sexual needs of the marriage partners. Through both the marital relationship and the parent-child relationship the family provides for much of the love or affectional needs of its members. And in societies such as ours, the family may be expected to meet many of its members' companionship needs.

Family structure. Sociologically we connect family functions to family structure. Throughout the history of a given society its family structure has developed or evolved in ways which enable the family to fulfill its functions. The structure of the basic nuclear family may be said to consist of three fundamental relationships: (1) the marital relationship between the husband and the wife, (2) the parent-child relationship between the mother and father and their sons and daughters, and (3) the sibling relationship between brothers and sisters.

Each of these three sets of family relationships are defined by certain family statuses and roles. (A *status* is a position in a group, and a *role* is the performance of a person occupying a given status.) Thus the marital relationship is defined by the status and role of "wife" in reciprocity with the status and role of "husband." The parent-child relationship is defined by the statuses and roles of "mother" and "father" in relation to those of "daughter" and "son." And the statuses and roles defining sibling relationships are, of course, those of "sister" and "brother."

While the three fundamental relationships composing family structure are quite universal, the ways each relationship is defined and put into play may vary considerably from one society to another and from one period of history to another in a given society. In each society the family structure normally reflects the salient cultural values, norms, beliefs, and traditions, as well as adapting to the historical conditions and social processes that have shaped all the social institutions of that society. To illustrate, the predominant American family structure of today—the small, independent, nuclear family—makes sense or "fits" our urban, industrial, mobile society; whereas a large, sedentary, extended family structure would be more functional and appropriate in a more settled agrarian society. Also, in the latter type of society family structure is apt to be more patriarchal, with the authority residing in the status and role of the husband-father, while the wife-mother and the children are difinitely subordinate. In changing societies which emphasize freedom and equal rights, such as the American, the trend is toward an equalitarian family structure. The historical change from an earlier patriarchal family structure in America toward the emerging equalitarian family of today is one of the most significant lont-range trends in American family change, and is having a profound effect on marital relations today, as following chapters will show.

PLAN OF THE BOOK

This introductory chapter (which Part I comprises) provides a perspective for the remainder of the book by specifying the social and historical context within which present-day courtship, marriage, and family life have developed. Most of the problems, issues, and challenges which confront young people seeking marriage partners today, and those which face husbands and wives, parents and children and kinfolk, stem from the complexity of social, ideological, and technological conditions and processes that make up the American experience, past and present. This brief look into the past should help in understanding and contending with marriage and family living in the present.

The remainder of the book follows the family life cycle in a general way, starting with the period when boys and girls become interested in one another and moving through the various stages of dating, courtship, and mate selection. Then comes marriage, and eventual parenthood for most, followed by the middle and later years of marriage and family life.

Part Two, Pre-Marriage, Courtship, and Mate Selection. introduces the reader first to sex differentiation and sex roles in modern America, then follows with discussions of premarital involvement of young people as they develop love, dating, and then more serious courtship relationships. Special attention is given (Chapter 4) to diverse and changing premarital sex attitudes and behavior in the United States today. Chapter 5 deals with mate selection as a process, with a review of various theories of how one chooses a marriage partner.

Part Three, Marriage and Marital Relationships, is devoted to the nature of marriage itself, and the ways husband-wife relationships are defined and carried out in daily living. A good deal of attention is devoted to marital adjustment, the way husbands and wives get along as marriage partners (Chapter 7), and to sex and sexual adjustment in marriage (Chapter 8). Since today marital roles and relationships are so closely tied to external occupational roles and interests of both husband and wife, a full chapter is devoted to this (Chapter 9). As all marriages not only have a beginning, but also an ending—whether by death or divorce—Chapter 10 is devoted to marital dissolution and remarriage. Part Three concludes with a look at various alternatives to conventional marriage, such as remaining single and cohabitation (Chapter 11).

Whereas Parts Two and Three are devoted mainly to relations between the sexes prior to and during marriage, Part Four, Family and Kinship Relations, deals with the larger family group, starting with parenthood and parent-child relationships, then expanding the analysis to kinship and in-law relationships. Chapter 12, Transition to Parenthood, considers family planning, pregnancy, and childbirth, with special attention to the problems of adjustment of the wife and the husband to their new parental roles and responsibilities. Chapter 13 focuses on parenthood and various theories and methods of child care and rearing and on parent-child relations. The next chapter expands the discussion beyond the immediate or nuclear family to kinship relations in America, including the question of how extensive and important ties with relatives and in-laws are to most nuclear family members. Next, using the family cycle as the frame of reference, marriage and family life is viewed in the middle and later years, with emphasis on role changes and adjustments facing the husband and wife as their children grow up and leave home, and as the husband—and increasingly the wife too—face retirement from their occupational roles (Chapter 15). Part Four concludes with an attempt to assess the future of marriage and family in America.

PART TWO

Premarriage, courtship, and mate selection

The sexes and sex roles in America

There is often confusion about the meanings of various terms used in discussing the sexes and sex roles. Most human beings are born with a clearly identifiable gender, male or female, as indicated by certain physical characteristics. One's gender identity is genetically determined; only in cases of transvestites or transsexuals could this gender identity be changed.

One's sex role is not the same as one's gender identity. That is, sex role involves somthing more than gender. The relevant terms for sex roles are *masculine* and *feminine* while the terms *male* and *female* are strictly gender terms. Sex roles involve learned behavior. In any given society, males tend to display certain patterns of behavior defined as masculine, while most females tend to display another set defined as feminine. These learned attitudes and actions may be conceptualized as sex roles (Chafetz, 1974, p. 3).

SIMILARITIES AND DIFFERENCES BETWEEN THE SEXES

Most people, in our society and others, consider it natural for men and women to behave somewhat differently. In all likelihood, this has been true throughout human history. These different ways of behaving are not spontaneous or erratic, but rather have been found to be systematic and predictable. It seems that men do certain things because they are male and women do other things because they are female. Anthropologists and historians find such sex differentiation to be universal. For example, in the economic division of labor, certain typical or average sex differences exist in most cultures, even though the specific patterns of differences in men's work and women's work vary among them.

How may these behavioral differences between men and women be explained? Is it nature or nurture? Are the differences biologically determined and thus explained by genetic differences between females and males? Or do men and women behave differently because of differences in their conditioning, socialization, and experiences after birth as males or females?

Let us identify some of the principal theories that have been advanced to explain the why and how of sex differentiation.

BIOLOGICAL EXPLANATION OF SEX DIFFERENCES

There are, of course, some basic differences in anatomy and physiology between males and females. The sex of the individual is determined at the time of conception. A female is conceived if an X-bearing sperm unites with an X-bearing ovum, and a male is conceived if a Y-bearing sperm joins an X-bearing ovum (Hoyenga & Hoyenga, 1979, p. 25). Basic genetic differences between the male (X-Y) and the female (X-X) are influenced by the different male and female hormones that are produced in each sex beginning some months before birth (Hoyenga & Hoyenga, 1979, pp. 45–48). During the first three months of development in the uterus, the male and the female embryos look much alike. By the third or fourth month of prenatal growth the genital areas of the two sexes show different patterns of development. In the female fetus, the tiny labial swellings become the opening of the vagina. In the male fetus, the genital tubercle becomes the head of the penis, while the scrotum begins to form (Mahan & Broderick, 1969, p. 175). At birth these external genitals distinguish the sex of the baby.

Between birth and puberty, male and female hormones are at low levels in both sexes. The rapid growth at puberty is triggered by pituitary hormones that stimulate the sex glands (male testes and female ovaries) to greatly increase the hormone levels of estrogens in the girl and androgens in the boy (Hoyenga & Hoyenga, 1979, pp.50–57).

The maturing girls will increase in weight and height quite rapidly. Her breasts will develop and her hips broaden. Girls generally reach puberty a year or two earlier than boys. By about age 12, the girl will begin her cycle of monthly menstruation and ovulation, which continues until menopause. Maturing boys generally become taller and stronger, developing a larger chest and broader shoulders. The boy's voice will change to a deeper register during puberty. There are also, of course, many differences between individuals of each sex.

Both males and females may start functioning sexually and reproductively at puberty. Male sex cells (sperm) are produced in the testes and are ejaculated through the penis. Female sex cells (ova) develop at the rate of one each month and are released from the ovaries into the Fallopian tube and proceed to the uterus. During intercourse, the male sex cell can impregnate the female by fertilizing the ova or ovum—the only function of the male in the reproductive process. The female, however, not only ovulates; she also gestates and gives birth to the child. Following birth, she often breast-feeds the child.

Some biological explanations of sex differentiation emphasize the possible effects of sex hormones. Authorities generally agree that males and females have different amounts of the various sex-related hormones, and that sex hormones do enter the brain and affect its activity, but there is less agreement as to what the ramifications of these hormones may be for specific behavioral differences between the sexes (Chafetz, 1974, p. 24). Male hormones (androgens) are produced in both sexes early in prenatal development. Androgens stimulate the growth and maintenance of the male reproductive system; estrogens do the same for females. Unless it receives an adequate supply of the androgen called testosterone, the male fetus becomes female-like and fails to develop male characteristics (Money & Ehrhardt, 1972).

While more studies are necessary before it can conclusively be said how and to what extent sex hormones affect behavioral differences between the sexes, there is some evidence to suggest that they may predispose males and females differently. Money and Ehrhardt (1972) compared a group of 25 girls aged 4 to 16 (the patients), in whom a male androgen hormone had been introduced before birth for medical reasons, with 25 untreated girls (the control group). The control group was matched with the patients for age, IQ, race, and socioeconomic background. Although all 25 patients were raised as girls from birth, 20 of them showed definite masculine behavioral tendencies. They were regarded by their mothers, their playmates, and themselves as tomboys. Each girl expressed dissatisfaction at being a girl. They engaged in athletics and played rough games with boys more than the girls in the control group did. Only a statistically nonsignificant number of girls in the control group reported short periods of tomboyish behavior. Money and Ehrhardt (1972, p. 18) conclude that "human gender-identity differentiation . . . takes place . . . when a prenatally programmed disposition comes in contact with postnatal, socially programmed signals."

There are other authorities who think that environmental influences are probably more important than hereditary tendencies. Tiger (1970) and Chafetz (1974), for example, believe that sociocultural influences can be strong enough to overcome any such biologically based predispositions.

SOCIOCULTURAL EXPLANATIONS OF
SEX DIFFERENTIATION

Anthropological and sociological explanations of sex differentiation do not deny or ignore biological differences between males and females. However, they emphasize the interaction of the biological factors with the sociocultural factors in the individual's environment. The emphasis is on differential socialization and different kinds of experiences between girls and boys, or women and men. Since considerable attention will be paid below to how sex roles are learned, we will here look only briefly at a general anthropological explanation of sex differentiation.

Anthropological explanation of sex differentiation

Anthropologists emphasize the great cultural differences in the way the two sexes are defined throughout various societies around the world. If the behavioral differences between the sexes were biologically determined, they argue, one would expect to find the differences between the sex roles to be much the same in all societies. There is a good deal of anthropological evidence showing that this is not the case: sex roles may be very different from one culture to another. Mead's studies of various cultures in the South Pacific are relevant here.

Early in her career, Mead (1935) studied three small tribes in New

Greek boys and girls enjoy a summer afternoon

David Bell

Guinea and found remarkable differences in the way each group defined males and females. In the Arapesh tribe both sex roles involved personality traits that we would consider feminine. Both sexes were typically gentle, passive, nonaggressive, and emotionally warm and loving. Traits we generally identify with masculinity—such as competitiveness, aggressiveness, and acquisitiveness—were lacking in most areas. When it came to parenthood, there were few differences between the roles of mother and father. The main difference was that the mother bore the child and nursed it. In most other respects, the father was just as "maternal" as the mother in caring for and in "growing" the child.

By contrast, in the neighboring Mundugumor tribe, both men and women displayed personality characteristics we often associate with masculinity. Both sexes were typically competitive and aggressive, often to the point of hostility. Women dreaded becoming mothers, and displayed hostility toward their children, especially daughters. Mothers showed little evidence of what has been called the maternal instinct, or motherlove.

In the third tribe, the Tchambuli, there were pronounced differences between the sexes, but the sex roles were the reverse of what we would consider normal. The women were domineering, very energetic, and had many activities outside the home. In fact, women were the chief economic providers for their families. The men, on the other hand, were more "domestic," preferring to stay home with the children. The men tended to be more artistic than the women, spending a lot of time on artwork and gossip.

Mead concluded that sex traits such as these probably have no necessary connection with the biological differences between the sexes, but rather are shaped by the cultures within which males and females live. Subsequent studies by other anthropologists have generally supported Mead's position (Barry, Bacon, & Child, 1957; D'Andrede, 1966). This anthropological position, then, holds that sex roles are probably learned, not genetically determined. Some of the ways sex roles are learned are treated more fully below.

MASCULINE AND FEMININE SEX-ROLE DEFINITIONS

HISTORICAL PERSPECTIVE ON SEX-ROLE DIFFERENTIATION IN AMERICA

What did it mean to grow up in America before the 20th century? Early American views on the sexes and sex roles stemmed in large part from European and Judeo-Christian backgrounds. It was widely believed that God had ordained separate spheres of life for the sexes. Churches, schools, and families joined in teaching that boys should grow up to be the doers, thinkers, and movers in the world. Girls, on the other hand, were expected to grow up to be wives and mothers.

Boys and young men were admonished by parents, teachers, and preachers to study hard, work hard, and "dig for success." To pursue one's "calling" diligently was to act according to the will of God, and being successful was interpreted as having been blessed by God. Boys and men were admonished that "God makes the trees; men must build the house. God supplies the timber; men must construct the ship. God buries iron in the earth; men must dig it, smelt it, and fashion it." (Shannon, 1917).

Girls and young women were taught something quite different. "Female culture" books of the 18th and 19th centuries taught girls that nature intended them to be "vines" clinging to the "sturdy oak." To try to be assertive and independent like men would result in the loss of femininity and, what was worse, would ruin young women's chances for marriage (Sandford, 1834). Higher education for females was widely discouraged because it was believed that the required "brain activity" would drain off energies nature intended for maternity (Calhoun, 1945, Vol. 2).

These views on sex roles as divinely ordained were not universally accepted or unchallenged, however. Early feminists demanded greater freedom and variety in life for women (Wollstonecraft, 1792). By mid-19th century, some colleges, such as Vassar, began to provide women with an education somewhat comparable to that of college men; and one four-year college, Oberlin, became coeducational. Women began to enter professions and make themselves heard in politics. A good example was Lilla Day Monroe of Kansas, who, in 1895, passed her bar examination and became the first woman to be admitted to practice law before the Kansas Supreme Court. She went on to become a leader in the woman suffrage movement, which led to the passage of the suffrage amendment in Kansas in 1912 (Stratton, 1981).

However, in most circles the traditional sex-role definitions prevailed throughout the 19th century and well into the 20th. (See Figure 2–1.) The family, churches, and most media all reinforced these time-honored views of "natural" and God-ordained differences between the sexes. Boys and girls were taught to accept this and live their lives according to very different sex-role models. Boys were taught that one day they would be heads of families and breadwinners, and that they therefore must cultivate courage, strength, ambition, and leadership. Girls were taught that they would be wives and mothers, and so must cultivate qualities of gentleness, submissiveness, compassion, and dependency (Welter, 1966).

LEARNING SEX ROLES

While some questions remain unanswered as to how important genetic differences between males and females are in predisposing the two sexes toward different sex roles, there is little doubt that in every society girls

Figure 2–1

Male and female American and European college students favoring traditional male and female sex-role differentiation, 1969

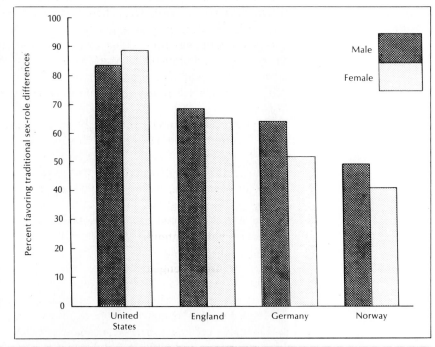

Source: "A Comparison of sexual attitudes and behavior in an international sample" by E. B. Luckey and G. D. Nass, *Journal of Marriage and the Family*, 1969, *31*, 364–79.

have to learn how to be feminine and boys have to learn how to be masculine, in accordance with social and cultural definition of these terms prevalent in their particular society. Thus, females and males are socialized into their respective sex roles.

Among the important agents and sex-role socialization in America are the family, the peer group, and the school. In the family, growing girls and boys normally have intimate day-by-day association with members of both sexes. Parents and older brothers and sisters consciously and unconsciously teach one how to behave in one's sex role. A girl may be reprimanded for "acting too much like a tomboy"; a boy may be praised for being "a big, brave boy—almost a man." Family traditions, customs, and rituals convey to the child, often in subtle and indirect ways, what is expected of members of one's sex. According to social-learning theorists, parents of the same sex provide the initial and continuous sex-role model for the growing child, and this sex-role behavior is expanded through imitations of a wide variety of sex-role models (Bandura, 1969). Duvall (1977, p. 13) describes this process of sex-role identification thus:

> Three-year-old Jane mirrors her mother's every move as the two "women" prepare a meal. A casual observer might say, "Isn't that sweet? Jane is

34

The beauty queen is a traditional sex role in America

U.S.D.A. photo by Roland Freeman

imitating her mother." Actually, Jane is working hard at *being* her mother in her food preparation roles and in all of her other activities and behavior. Jane's twin brother, Jim, meantime, lights his imaginary pipe and sits with one leg across the other scowling at the papers before him, just as his father does. Both children are identifying with the parent of the same sex, by internalizing what they see their parents doing. They talk over toy telephones in the same inflections and with the same words they hear their parents use. They play house and go through the same dialogues and routines their mother and father have modeled for them only hours before.

This sex-role identification process may be somewhat more difficult for boys than for girls. Girls, for instance, easily identify with their mothers, with whom they are in close daily association; boys tend to identify with a culturally defined male-role type which their fathers may or may not exemplify. The mother is at home more than the father, generally, and the father's main occupational activity is not only somewhere outside the home, but is also apt to be somewhat beyond the comprehension of young children. This makes same-sex identification somewhat easier for the girl (Lynn, 1966, p. 470).

In the learning of sex roles, a key cognitive event is believed to occur in very early childhood (between ages one and one half to three years) with the recognition that one is a male or a female (Kohlberg, 1966, p. 91). This major recognition then shapes the way the child perceives the rest of the world and his or her place in it. Gender identity becomes established and the child responds appropriately when called a boy or girl. Once children recognize their gender, they try to act like other males or females around them. Children find models of femininity or masculinity in their parents, brothers, sisters, playmates, and in stories and on television.

Sex-role stereotyping

When the conventional sex roles in a given society become so traditionally established that they are rigid and inflexible, it may be said that they have become stereotyped. The problem with this is that the society then expects males to conform to the stereotyped masculine model and females to conform to the stereotyped feminine model, without regard for individual differences in talents, interests, or motives. Such stereotyping also tends to separate and polarize the sex roles, making them mutually exclusive. This tends to arouse suspicions toward any girl who manifests any masculine traits or behavior, and toward a boy who shows any signs of being effeminate. For example, the boy who shows more interest in art and cooking than in sports or mechanics may be made to feel he is something less than a "real man." Similarly, the girl who shows more interest in mechanics than in "domestic arts" may be made to feel deviant.

Though sex-role stereotyping is still widespread in American society, there is a definite, opposing trend among certain well-educated young people who espouse equalitarianism and are critical of any traditional, restrictive sex-role stereotypes. This leads to another related topic, sexism.

Sexism

Sexism is closely related to the stereotyping and arbitrary dichotomizing of sex roles. Sexism goes beyond the categorical separation of sex roles in imposing prejudicial restrictions on one or both sex roles (Chafetz, 1974; Frieze et al., 1978). In American society (as well as in many other societies) such culturally imposed prejudicial limitations have been most apparent in feminine roles (see Figure 2–2). These sex-role restrictions have tended to cast females into roles inferior and submissive to men's, discouraging their participation in many of the more rewarding and prestigious areas of life, such as business, politics, and many professions.

The feminist movement of recent years, with its strong affirmation of the principle of equal rights for women, has helped reduce sexism in America somewhat. However, although some gains are being made, sexism survives—in many guises—in certain segments of our society. Studies

Figure 2–2

Freshmen male and female college students believing married women's place is in the home, 1970 and 1975

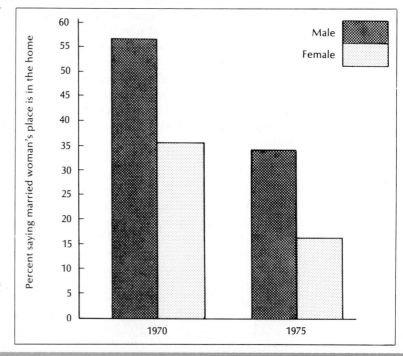

Percent saying married woman's place is in the home

Male
Female

1970   1975

Source: "This Year's Freshmen Reflect New Views of Women's Role" by B. T. Watkins, *The Chronicle of Higher Education,* January 12, 1976.

show that in the working classes strains and conflicts between husband and wife may result where the husband still has a strong sexist orientation (Komarovsky, 1962; LeMasters, 1975). For a good analysis of this kind of sexism in present-day America, see Lemasters's The Battle of the Sexes, in *Blue-Collar Aristocrats* (1975, pp. 80–92).

Sexism, like racism, can take many different forms, some overt and others covert. And, Frieze et al. (1978, p. 12) say,

> it need not necessarily imply conscious maliciousness on the part of the person or institution which exhibits it. Instead it may reflect that the differences between men and women are nonconsciously assumed to mean that women are less able human beings. The results of this assumption can be, and usually are, very insidious.

Overt instances of sexism are apparent in the discriminations against women in employment, promotions, and remunerations. As will be seen in a later chapter, women are underrepresented in the higher-paying and more prestigious business and professional occupations, and they are still apt to be paid less than men for the same work (Knudson, 1969; Stencel, 1977).

In fairness to men, it needs to be pointed out that some forms of sexism work to the disadvantage of men by reducing their options and activities. For example, men cannot stay at home and be "househusbands" without being stigmatized by people holding traditional values. And it is difficult for a man to be passive and dependent without incurring disdain from many people.

Since early 1970s there has been an increasing effort to reduce sexism and affirm equal rights of the sexes. Major textbook publishers now instruct their authors and editors to avoid terms, statements, and illustrations that may be construed as sexist, and to seek nonsexist alternatives. Examples are "salesperson" instead of "salesman," "human resources" instead of "manpower," "student" instead of "coed," and "the average person" instead of "the man on the street." Language usages, however, generally change slowly, and it will probably be a long time before sexist language and thinking are a thing of the past. Still, the accelerated efforts and pressures to reduce and avoid sexism in recent years is a hopeful trend.

MASCULINE AND FEMININE SUBCULTURES IN AMERICA

LeMasters (1957b) observes that in many societies, including our own, boys and girls spend most of the first 10 to 15 years of their lives in fairly distinct male or female social worlds, in which masculine or feminine ways of thinking, feeling, and acting become internalized in their personalities. These personality traits are reinforced through many years of daily associations with members of the same sex. Marriage may be the first exposure, for both the wife and the husband, to certain aspects of "how the other half lives." The husband is a product of one set of experiences and the wife the product of another, and the resulting differences in their habits, interests, and viewpoints will without question influence their marital adjustment.

While boys are learning one set of values, norms, and role definitions through long association with other males, girls are learning another set, and each sex will be excluded from the cross-sex group to a considerable extent. At about age five or six the youngster will normally begin this association with his or her same-sex group, and will be introduced over time to its well established customs, traditions, interests, and particular ways of looking at life. Stated more succinctly, Johnny joins the society of boys with its masculine subculture while Suzy joins the society of girls with its feminine subculture. This separation of the sexes, each with its own subculture, is found in almost all human societies. It is one of the accompaniments of sex-role differentiation (Stephens, 1963, pp. 270–271). Let us now look briefly at the male and female subcultures in American society, and how these subcultures influence sex-role development.

THE SUBCULTURE OF THE MALE

Male children generally enter the "world of boys" at about the beginning of grade school and from then on are normally immersed in it and its masculine subculture until the mid-teens, when they become involved with girls during early courtship days. Not that the teenaged boy's involvement with the all-male world ends here; in fact, his close association with "the boys" generally continues more or less throughout youth and, for many, well into adulthood. Many a wife has been heard to complain that her husband seems to prefer going hunting or drinking beer at the tavern with his male buddies to going out with her. (LeMasters, 1975, pp. 41–45). In the adult world, the male subculture may be seen in college fraternities, male work crews, hunting and fishing clubs, and professional ball teams. An extreme case would be a traditional military environment where males live and work together in isolation, such as on a destroyer or a submarine.

In the male peer group, the boy learns appropriate masculine behavior from older male role models. He is rewarded and gains acceptance as he exhibits proper masculine behavior, and is punished and ridiculed for unmasculine behavior. "Johnny's a sissy—go play with the girls!"—Johnny will probably come around pretty quickly under the sting of such sanctions as this. He will probably learn to use—at first with distaste, but maybe later with more relish—the rough and explicit male vocabulary, the "cuss words" of the guys.

Characteristics of the male subculture

Udry (1974, p. 69) notes that among the focal concerns of the masculine society and its subculture are "independence, emotional control, and conquest." These concerns are manifested in various kinds of interaction. Among the most obvious and salient are sex, sports, and a social life emphasizing male camaraderie. Let us examine these focal concerns in more detail as we look at some of the main characteristics of the male subculture.

Sex in the male subculture.

It has been argued that sex is probably the most pervasive interest in the masculine subculture (Udry, 1974, p. 69). Few would disagree that one's acquired attitudes toward sex will have ramifications for one's relationships with members of the opposite sex in courtship and marriage. Many of the average boy's predispositions and much of his knowledge about sex comes from the all-male subculture. Early in grade-school years, the boy will become aware of the general interest in sex pervading the male peer group. With variations according to social class, ethnicity, and religion, he will probably be exposed to a traditional vocabulary including the four-letter words for sexual anatomy and acts. He will learn that this language is generally forbidden outside the peer group. While he may or may not use it extensively, he may perhaps admire those who are highly proficient with this vocabulary. Long before most parents get around to discussing "the facts of life" with Johnny, he has already picked up a good deal of information, and has likely had a variety of experiences with his male peers.

According to Kinsey, nearly half of all preadolescent boys become involved in sexual exhibition or sex play with other boys. (Kinsey, 1948, p. 168). Preadolescent boys seem to be more interested in sex itself than in girls and thus heterosexual activity is probably less frequent than sex play with other boys (Kinsey, 1948, p. 173). By adolescence, however, the interest will normally become heterosexual. Status among male peers results from the adolescent boy displaying his sexual knowledgeability and convincing his friends of his heterosexual activity. In bull sessions there is considerable exaggeration and not infrequently outright fabrication of sexual experiences. Not only do male peers judge masculinity by sexual sophistication and activity, but these things also become important in the youth's assessment of his own masculinity as well. As Ehrman (1959, p. 361) observes:

> Our culture, in innumerable ways . . . instills in the male the all-important idea that eroticism is essential to maleness, and that it is the mark of a man both to make sexual advances and to have some reasonable expectations of success.

As LeMasters (1957b, p. 489) points out, the importance of sex to the male and to his self-image has been rather difficult for the average American woman to comprehend. While this may be less true of today's more liberated woman, the female subculture is probably still different in its orientation toward sex. Thus the girl will probably develop somewhat different attitudes and expectations than the boy. During courtship these subcultural difference may become apparent to some degree; after marriage they may become very apparent, requiring adjustment on behalf of wife and husband both.

Sports. Participation in sports is an important part of the lives of many American males of all ages. Starting in early grade school with playground activities, the boy is introduced to sports—baseball, basketball, football, track, and so on. As a focus of masculine interest and identity, sports may become as important as sex for a great many male youths. The boy who is a successful athlete in high school (or earlier) attains status not only among male peers but among adults also. An example of adult approval would be parents proud of a Little League baseball star. For the adolescent and the college student, athletic success also leads to probable success with girls. The boy who does not display interest in sports may be thought to be deviant in some way; he may come to see himself as lacking in masculinity (Udry, 1974, p. 72)

On reaching adulthood most American men no longer look to athletic achievement as an important source of masculine status. Still, they generally have a continuing interest—often passionate—in the world of sports, both amateur and professional (LeMasters, 1975). When men get together, sports will often be the main topic of conversation; and spectator sports, either at the stadium or in front of the television set, are many a man's principal recreational interest. Baseball and football widows now greatly outnumber hunting and fishing widows.

In recent years more American wives have probably moved closer to their husbands in their interest in and appreciation of the world of sports. Television is partly responsible for this trend, along with the middle-class concern about husband-wife companionship and shared recreational interests.

Camaraderie. Male competition for females, jobs, and athletic success, rather than being a divisive factor, seems to represent a set of common interests and experiences which tend to cement males together in a social world somewhat apart from females. As Udry (1974, p. 72) puts it:

> There is among young males a sense of camaraderie which is an important part of the feeling of masculinity, and which manifests itself in numerous subtle ways. This characteristic is nearly absent from female groups and might be thought of activity peculiar to male solidarity. Loyalty to the male groups is a distinctive part of maleness which really has no counterpart among females.

Though homosexuality is strongly tabooed in the male subculture, deep personal friendships, and even affection, exist in a number of acceptable ways among boys. These include horseplay and wrestling; the camaraderie implied verbally in kidding, exchanging insults, and swapping stories, and, of course, in drinking together. Newcomers may be "put over the ropes," or "hazed," before being accepted as full-fledged buddies in the male group.

Many examples of the all-male social world where this kind of close camaraderie persists may be found. Most taverns or saloons have traditionally been men's worlds. There are also various fraternal organizations, such as the American Legion, the Elks, the Moose, and the Masons—although some have women's auxiliaries, such as the Masons' sister group, the Eastern Star. There are male athletic clubs, hunting and fishing clubs and, of course, the age-old male world of the military which with a few execptions and until quite recently has generally been closed to women. As LeMasters (1957b, p. 491) says, it is a rare wife who can fully appreciate what it has meant to her husband to spend three or four years of his life in the armed forces, working and living only with men. Attachments can become strong and endure for years. Comparable same-sex attachments may develop among women too, of course (Willmott & Young, 1960; Gans, 1962).

While courtship and marriage can, and generally do, disrupt the all-male relationship patterns, such relationships often continue on a reduced or sporadic basis after marriage, in such events as stag parties, the "night out with the boys," poker games, hunting trips, and so on. It should be noted that there are significant social class differences here. Today most middle-class married men probably spend less time with their male buddies than their fathers or grandfathers did. Working-class men, however, are still more apt to continue the traditional all-male leisure time activities. This can be a source of conflict between the husband and the wife who may at times feel that her husband's male buddies have first priority in his life (LeMasters, 1975, pp. 37–45).

THE SUBCULTURE OF THE FEMALE

The world of women is characterized by concerns for such things as personal attractiveness, popularity, sociability, courtship and marriage, and, for many women, motherhood. These concerns are manifested in the interest and attention girls and women give to clothing, cosmetics, and diets; in their close associations with other females; in their interest in boys or men; and in mothers' concern for their children.

Characteristics of the female subculture

Personal attractiveness.
Attractiveness has long been a focal concern in the feminine subculture. Early in life, girls become aware of whether or not they are considered pretty or perhaps even beautiful in the eyes of others. By adolescence the typical American girl has learned how to make the most of her natural facial and other physical attributes by the way she dresses, styles her hair, and uses cosmetics. Girls less blessed by nature are likely to turn more to cosmetics and other commerical products to enhance their attractiveness. Until recently at least, most adolescent girls realized that the future depended in a large part on their ability to attract the "right kind" of man as a marriage partner—a man who would truly love her and be able to support her in the lifestyle she desired. Her personal attractiveness could be crucial to her whole future. Americans have long been "beauty conscious"— witness the endless series of beauty contests—and to be considered beautiful gives a girl a competitive advantage in mate selection, brings prestige in most female groups, and enhances her self-image. There is evidence that the most attractive women have the widest choice of marriage partners; they get the "highest quality" husbands and they generally marry first (Holmes & Hatch, 1938; Elder, 1969). Taylor and Glenn (1976) found that female attractiveness is related to the occupational status of the husband, but more so for women of low-status than of high-status origin. Udry (1977) found that for a white woman, attractiveness has a strong bearing on whether or not she gets a high-

E. D. Dyer

status husband if she does not go to college, but not if she does go to college. For a black woman attractiveness plays an important part in getting a high-status husband whether or not she goes to college.

There is evidence that the physical attractiveness of the male is important too in dating and mate selection. Males as well as females may be concerned about their physical attributes, since females may be more drawn to physically attractive males (Walster et al., 1966).

Clothing, jewelry, hairstyles, and other items of personal adornment have come to be basic concerns in the feminine subculture because of their association with the value attached to personal attractiveness. One has only to look at the attention the media pay to these female accoutrements. LeMasters (1957b) observes that, while men are partly to blame for this hectic pursuit of beauty by women, few men prior to marriage have much of an idea of the amount of time, effort, and money it takes for a woman to maintain the desired standard of grooming and dressing. New husbands are apt to be in for some surprises when they first see their wives' department store and beauty parlor bills. Still, since most men want and appreciate attractive wives, "it follows that only the most ungrateful husband would fail to understand that feminine beauty demands a price." (LeMasters, 1957b, pp. 500–501)

Sex. Compared to the world of preadolescent boys, the feminine world of the preadolescent girl traditionally has been largely lacking in sexual conversation and figures of speech. Various pieces of research have shown that girls' and women's attitudes toward sex differ from those of boys and men. Kinsey (1953) found females to be less easily aroused sexually and to regard sex as an integral part of love rather than in the more physical terms of many males. According to Ehrmann (1959, p. 340), when American women talk about sex they are apt to be voicing concerns about how to handle male sexual aggression in dating situations, expressing regrets or guilt feelings for going too far sexually, justifying sexual activity as an expression of love. More recently, Reiss (1976, p. 157) found that young women in America still emphasize love and affection as important prerequisites for sexual behavior.

Today, with the women's movement and the general trend toward sexual equality, it is probable that more girls and adult women are becoming more explicit and candid with each other about sex. It seems likely that sex as a topic of conversation is more acceptable among females today than in earlier generations.

Marriage and motherhood. According to Udry (1974, p. 75), "The one emphasis of the female subculture which dominates everything else is the orientation toward attracting males and, eventually, getting married." Most other concerns have been secondary by comparison and have been viewed as contingencies against not getting married, or against the possibility of needing to work after marriage or, perhaps, after a divorce. Occupational or career considerations once had to be accommodated to marriage expectations; however, this is now changing as more young women are postponing first marriages, more widowed and divorced women are postponing remarriages, and more married and single women are placing greater emphasis on work and careers.

The female subculture has traditionally included much folklore on motherhood. Many women derive a large part of their feminine identity from motherhood. For women anticipating motherhood, traditions, customs, and practices surrounding pregnancy, childbearing, and childrearing have constituted sizeable concerns, from which men have been largely excluded. The mother is, of course, more directly and personally involved in gestation, childbirth, and infant care than the average father, so it is natural that women would be more intensely concerned with these matters than would men. Recently, however, some men have begun to assist in the delivery of their offspring.

The new mother's intense preoccupation with her child may be a source of strain or even conflict between wife and husband. In a study of the effects of the first child on the marriage, the author found that many husbands felt somewhat neglected by their wives, who had become completely immersed in their roles as mothers (Dyer, 1963). The new father needs continued emotional and marital support from his wife after the birth of their child, just as the new mother needs continued emotional support from her husband (Wanderman, et al., 1980).

SOME IMPLICATIONS OF THE DIFFERENCES
BETWEEN MALE AND FEMALE SUBCULTURES

LeMasters (1957b, p. 481) observes that for most young women and men "marriage is the first point at which [each] attempts to really live (or try to live) intimately in the world of the other sex." A girl who has brothers and a father present has probably shared in their *male* world only in a limited way. Similarly, boys normally have only a marginal exposure to the feminine world of their sisters and mother. Thus after having spent a good part of one's childhood and youth immersed in the subculture of one's sex group, marriage brings each marriage partner into contact and interaction with the subculture of the other in a new, much more intimate way. Good marital adjustment requires that each partner make an effort to understand that the other is largely a product of the social world and subculture of the opposite sex.

The sex subcultures can produce some differences in basic value orientations between men and women (Didato & Kennedy, 1956). Where sex-role differentiation is greater—as it is in traditional rural America and in some immigrant groups—the greater the likelihood of differences in values and interests between the sexes; thus, a smaller basis for mutual understanding and companionship exists between them. On the other hand, where sex-role differentiation is diminishing somewhat—as it appears to be doing in urban America today—there will likely be a parallel lessening of the value differences between the male and female subcultures, making it easier for the wife and husband to understand and adjust to each other. An example would be the current change from the traditional division of labor between husband and wife (he the sole family provider; she the sole homemaker) toward more flexibility of roles and sharing of these activities. This sharing is conducive to a deeper, reciprocal understanding and a more rewarding companionship. Such trends suggest a possible diminishing of the long-standing sex subcultures.

CHANGES AND TRENDS IN SEX ROLES

CHANGING SEX-ROLE DEFINITIONS

Throughout most of American history—in fact, until quite recently—sex-role differentiation has been well marked. Both outside the family and within it, "woman's place" and work were clearly distinct from "man's place" and work. Boys grew up learning how to do men's work; girls grew up learning how to do women's work. These traditional patterns are changing today under pressure from many sides, including the women's rights, equalitarianism, and secularism movements.

Most authorities agree that sex-roles have been undergoing some re-definition in recent years. Mead (1953) sees male and female sex roles becoming more alike through the increased masculinization of the female role. She sees the convergence of sex roles as a result of the increasing heterosexual togetherness resulting from the breakdown of sex segregation. In her own words:

> In coeducational schools, girls and boys are educated alike, and taught to be individualistic, assertive, active, to want to make something of themselves. . . . The boy wants the girl to be independent, to have something to say for herself, to be able to make her own living. . . . Girls have become more like boys and their goals as human beings have steadily approached each other (Mead, 1953, pp. 14–18).

As early as the 1940s, Komarovsky (1946) found that many college women were already moving away from the traditional "feminine" role toward a "modern" role which "partly obliterates the differentiation in sex. It demands of the woman much the same virtues, patterns of behavior, and attitudes that it does of the men of a corresponding age." (Komarovsky, 1963, p. 127). College women, of course, could be expected to be pioneers in this trend. Changes in sex-role definitions may be seen in the decline of sex segregation and in recent movements toward unisex and sex-role transcendence.

Decline in sex segregation

Traditional segregation by sex is declining today. Most schools and colleges are now coeducational. Old-fashioned men's clubs which histori-cally excluded women have largely disappeared since the 40s, as have many exclusive women's organizations. As American courtship processes become longer and more elaborate, heterosexual interaction begins earlier in life. Studies show that high-school aged youth may be spending as much or even more of their free time with dating partners as with friends of the same sex (Udry, 1974, p. 78). Sex segregation still appears to be the case among many grade-school boys and girls; boys especially are under considerable pressure from the guys to learn and conform to proper masculine norms and actions. However, for the middle class at least, there are many indications of a trend away from single-sex association toward more heterosexual association, beginning in junior high school or earlier (Hoult, et al., 1978).

While there may be resistance to them in all social classes, many of these changes appear to be slower in the working and lower classes. There is evidence that in these circles the male and female subcultures are still strong and many men and women continue to live a good deal of their lives in somewhat separate worlds (Shostak, 1969; Mindiola, 1970). This may be especially true for the men, who in some cases still strongly

Boys and girls share more playground activities today

Julie Heifitz

resist changes they feel threaten their masculine prerogatives and traditional privileges (LeMasters, 1975).

Increasing sex-role flexibility

It is apparent that sex roles are becoming less rigid than in the past, that women and men share more responsibilities, interests, and activities. Many Americans are making conscious efforts to get away from traditional sex-role stereotypes and anything that suggests sexism. These concerns have led to some interesting efforts to redefine sex roles along the following lines.

Androgyny. The term *androgyny* is derived from two Greek words, *andro* (male) and *gyn* (female), and thus literally means male-female. The term has recently been adopted to refer to persons who have both male and female personality characteristics rather than mixed male-female physical characteristics, such as hermaphrodites possess. Androgyny connotes the capacity of a person of either sex to embody the full range

*Today, both girls
and boys participate in
rodeo events*

U.S.D.A. photo by Duane Dailey

of human characteristics, even though some are labeled "feminine" and others "masculine." An androgynous person could be gentle or tough, yielding or assertive, and so on, and thus be better able to cope with a wider variety of social situations than one who is limited to being either masculine or feminine. (Bem, 1975). Many young people in the 1960s and 1970s moved away from the conventional male-female polarized roles toward some degree of unisex in clothing, grooming, and behavior. Just how far this trend may go is not clear as yet, but androgyny could mean a more uniform and unisexual integration into society.

Sex-role transcendence. The difference between sex-role transcendence and androgyny is that the latter means the masking or possible elimination of differences between the sexes, while the former "implies flexibility. . ., plurality, personal choice, and the development of new or emergent possibilities once we move away from the present oppressor-oppressed sex-roles" (Hefner, Meda, & Oleshansky, 1975, p. 10). Conventional sex roles would be transcended, allowing each person to do what is appropriate or satisfying without the strictures of masculine or feminine labeling. In the family the wife, for example, may pursue a career and provide the family income, while the husband may stay home and do the housework, if that is what both want. The sex-role transcendent person may become more productive and "self-actualized," according to some theories, but may also be in danger of missing out on other potential growth and satisfactions related to one's sex (Feldman & Feldman, 1975a, p. 6).

Future trends in sex roles

Historically, the family is entering a stage which calls for greater sex-role flexibility and perhaps some amount of sex-role transcendence. Up to now most families have been supported by productive work done outside the home by the husband-father, with the wife-mother caring for the home and children. The new stage finds more and more wives and mothers joining their husbands in the family provider role, with the couple pooling their incomes and other personal resources and sharing more in the home maintenance roles (Sawhill, Ross, & MacIntosh, 1973). (See Figures 2–3 and 2–4.)

While the general trend toward more role flexibility and sharing of roles is apparent, it is not uniform from group to group, and many individ-

Figure 2–3

Labor force participation of married women with husband present, 1950–1978

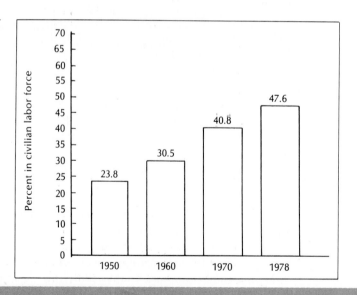

Source: "American Families and Living Arrangements," U.S. Bureau of the Census, *Current Population Reports* (Series p-23, no. 104), May 1980.

Figure 2–4

Percent of family income earned by the wife, 1960–1978

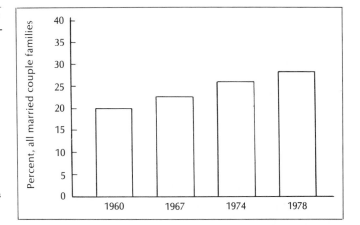

Source: "American Families and Living Arrangements," U.S. Bureau of the Census, *Current Population Reports* (Series p-23, no. 104), May 1980.

uals show signs of ambivalence (Komarovsky, 1973; Mindiola, 1970). We have previously mentioned the resistance found in some working-class circles to changes in traditional sex-role patterns. While this same kind of resistance can be expected to continue there and in other tradition-bound ethnic and religious groups, there are signs of its weakening. (Mirande, 1977; Mindiola, 1970). Parent-child conflicts may be expected in many families where parents are trying to socialize sons and daughters into conventional sex roles and the young people are pushing for greater freedom and flexibility. Highly educated middle-class families will probably continue leading the way in trends toward greater flexibility. Many parents in these families are now consciously working toward the reduction or even elimination of conventional sex-role typing in their own children (Scanzoni & Scanzoni, 1976, p. 49). As more parents begin to see traditional sex-role norms as restrictive rather than rewarding, ". . . we may expect to see a movement away from gender typing and an emphasis on human qualities and experiences desirable for all persons regardless of sex" (Scanzoni & Scanzoni, 1976, p. 52).

SIGNIFICANCE OF SEX-ROLE TRENDS FOR DATING AND COURTSHIP

If the Scanzonis (1976) are correct that more parents—especially middle-class parents—are now making efforts to reduce sex-role typing and sexism in the upbringing of their children, then we may expect these children to be freer of traditional sex-role stereotypes and accompanying attitudes at an early age. Of course the male and female childhood peer groups may counter these family teachings to some degree, but probably less so now than before since, as we have seen, the youth male and female subcultures are on the decline, especially in the middle classes. With the reduction of sex-role typing starting in the family circle, boys and girls will be less prone to settle into traditional segregated sex groups on the playgrounds and at school. There is some evidence that segregation by sex is also on the decline, as are probably the traditional sex subcultures. Since World War II enrollments in women's colleges have declined, most traditionally all-male colleges have opened their doors to women, and coeducational college enrollments have increased sharply. Memberships in many traditionally all-men's clubs and all-women's associations have declined greatly, also (Udry, 1974, p. 77). The apparent decline of clear-cut sex subcultures in recent times is likely a manifestation of changing attitudes about sex roles, with the emerging view that the human qualities and concerns common to both sexes are more important than sex differences.

If Mead (1970) is correct that the trend is toward a converging of sex roles due to a breakdown in sex segregation, the opposite is also true; that is, that the increased association of boys and girls engendered by the breakdown of sex segregation can also lead to reductions in sex-role distinctions and sexism. The processes here are cyclical. At any rate, the upshot is that boys and girls apparently are now becoming more like each other in interests and viewpoints than earlier. And it seems likely that as they become more similar they will be more comfortable with each other and find their relationships more companionable and rewarding.

What do these trends portend for dating and courtship? Dating will likely start earlier and the processes of courtship thus become extended over a longer period of time. As boys and girls share more goals and interests, there will be more cross-sex interaction and earlier heterosexual involvement—a practice which, in fact, has been under way for some years now and will in all likelihood spread further. A few generations ago, dating was largely a college and senior high school pattern; by the 1950s it had filtered down to junior high school. We now find heterosexual activities of at least a quasi-dating nature among many preadolescents in the elementary schools (Udry, 1974, p. 78). A study by Rowe (1966) of 11-year-old elementary-school children showed that a sizable minority of them had already begun to date and to become involved in various activities with members of the opposite sex. Among the 11-year-old girls attending an urban grammar school, about 30 percent had dated or gone steady with a boy, about 22 percent had "kissed seriously," and nearly 50 percent had "been in love."

At the other end of the courtship spectrum the impact of the changes in sex roles may be of a different order. As sex roles become more flexible, and women find more opportunities and wider options open to them, many single young women will be less apt to feel the need to rush into early marriage, either for security reasons or to prove themselves as women. More women will continue their education and pursue various kinds of extrafamily activities, including careers. This trend became apparent by the mid-1970s as many more young women were postponing their first marriages until their early or mid-20s. While some may postpone marriage longer—perhaps indefinitely—while sampling alternative marital lifestyles, it is very likely that the majority of these women will sooner or later get married.

It should be noted again that these trends are more apparent in urban, middle-class circles than elsewhere in the population. While some breakdown of sex differentiation and sexism is underway in the lower and working classes (and in the upper classes too), traditional sex-role differences and the subcultures of the male and the female still persist in these classes, and sex segregation continues as a pattern. However, middle-class equalitarian influences are now being felt there, with younger women especially pressing for more rights and greater freedom of choice. These demands may be expected to produce more tension and conflict in the relations between equalitarian-oriented young women and their more traditionally minded men friends, both before and after marriage.

CHAPTER 3

Premarital involvement:
Love and dating

In America, love and sexual attraction are probably the most important factors impelling young people toward heterosexual involvement. At a certain age, a young boy's fancy will begin to be taken by young girls in new and exciting ways. Where earlier he generally scorned female company in favor of his male friends, he now somehow feels strongly attracted to girls. He will probably not withdraw entirely from the all-male world; still, once he starts dating—and especially once he "really falls in love"—his male buddies may consider him lost to them. Although the growing girl will experience something quite similar as she becomes interested in and involved with boys, she is more likely than the boy to continue in close communication with her girlfriends regarding her developing romances. The young adolescent girl matures quite rapidly both physically and socially. She tends to pay increasing attention to her appearance and to physically attractive and interesting boys. The sexes now seek out and enjoy each other's company, and the stage is set for the development of personal and emotional involvement between them.

This chapter will focus on the development of love and dating relationships, and the following chapters will deal more directly with sex in premarital involvement.

LOVE: ITS MANY SPLENDORS AND DIMENSIONS

In discussing the sentiment of love, Waller and Hill (1951, pp. 107–108) make the observation that there is probably "no more difficult nor thankless task than that of treating the sentiment of love in a scientific manner." We all have probably felt its sway, its power over us. We know love as one of the main sources of beauty and happiness—and possibly bitterness and unhappiness—in our lives. We have heard the poet sing the best, and the cynic say the worst, about love. But what has the scientist said about love that anyone ever listened to?

The sentiment of love is, however, at the heart of many issues and problems in premarital involvement and mate selection, as well as in marriage and family living, and thus is a matter of deep interest to the social scientist. As Waller and Hill (1951, p. 107) note, marriage for love is one of the taken-for-granted things in American culture. It is customary for people to get married because they are in love, and most Americans probably still believe it is somewhat unnatural to marry for any other reason. Love is a big thing in American culture, and it may not exist in exactly the same way in other cultures.

ROMANTIC LOVE

The sentiment of love in America has been closely connected with certain traditions and practices often referred to as the romantic complex, or romantic love. This idea has been a dominant theme in American society for many years. It has been a compelling force in the lives of millions of young people. A generation ago it was described this way by Waller and Hill (1951, p. 114):

> According to the prevalent mythology, the young man or young woman usually arrives at the marriageable age with his heart undamaged, and then a mysterious thing happens: he falls in love, and of course, he marries the girl and lives happily ever after, or for quite a while. Romantic love, as Americans understand it, is an ungovernable impulse, a wholly normal and even sought-for state of grace in which one is unable to think of anything but the loved person—and a striving toward her sometimes attended by extravagances of jealousy and morbid despair if one does not prosper in his suit.

While times have changed and the idiom of love is expressed in somewhat different terms today, one wonders if the basic sentiment has changed much.

The concept of romantic love is neither new nor an American invention, of course. In Europe, romantic love has been traced back to the 13th century troubadours, stricken young men who expressed their feelings in song or verse for some unattainable lady of higher station with whom marriage was impossible. Anthropologists note that many societies recognize the existence of strong emotional attachments between persons of the opposite sex but are apt to view such feelings as afflictions or abberations. America is one of the few societies that have—until quite recently—made these emotional sentiments the main basis for marriage (Linton, 1936, p. 175).

American society has traditionally been saturated with the notion of romantic love, as evidenced by our literature, popular songs, movies, and the mass media. From early childhood, youth have been socialized to believe in and seek out romantic love. They have been conditioned to expect to fall in love, to actively love and be loved, and to marry for love. While this is still the case for many youth today, there are indications of some decline or modification in traditional romantic love in recent years, as will be discussed later in this chapter.

As well as being a many-splendored thing, love may be said to have many facets or dimensions. Waller and Hill (1951, pp. 110–113) suggest that the sentiment of love comprises a number of components, including sexuality, pride, security in the love relationship, and economic motivations. Bell (1967, pp. 115–116) believes that in American society love includes the elements of idealization, fantasy, strong emotions, exclusiveness, and often jealousy. In American folklore, romantic love may be expressed in the idea of the "soul mate," that unique, very special person who is meant to be one's only true love; in the idea of love at first sight which may strike one suddenly "some enchanted evening across a crowded room"; and in the idea that true love conquers all (Bell, 1967, pp. 116–118).

Of course, since love is such a personal, subjective experience, these descriptions would not apply to everyone's love experience. For most Americans, however, the essence of romantic love would normally include elements of physical attraction, emotional feelings, and idealization of the loved one—poets and songwriters are not so very wrong, after all. When it comes down to personal experience, most people seem to be able to recognize what love is. In a recent study of 1,079 college students, they were asked whether they thought they knew what love was. About 85 percent of the men and 90 percent of the women answered in the affirmative (Kephart, 1977, pp. 284–285).

It has been argued that the experience of falling in love is without equal in human experience. The love-stricken couple know that something wonderful and soul stirring is happening to them. In his essay "On Falling In Love," (1925) Robert Lewis Stevenson described it eloquently:

> This simple act of falling in love is as beneficial as it is astonishing. It arrests the petrifying influence of years, disproves cold-blooded and cynical conclusions, and awakens dormant sensibilities. Hitherto the man had found it a good policy to disbelieve the existence of any enjoyment which was out of his reach; and thus he turned his back upon the strong, sunny parts

of nature, and accustomed himself to look exclusively on what was common and dull. . . . And now, all of a sudden, he is unhorsed, like St. Paul, from his infidel affection. His heart, which has been ticking accurate seconds for the last year, gives a bound and begins to beat high in his breast. It seems as if he had never heard or felt or seen until that moment; and . . . he must have lived his past life between sleeping and waking. . . . He is practically incommoded by the generosity of his feelings, smiles much when he is alone, and develops a habit of looking rather blankly upon the moon and the stars. . . . The lover begins to regard his happiness as beneficial for the rest of the world and highly meritorious to himself. . . . The presence of the two lovers is so enchanting to each other that it seems as if it must be the best possible thing for everybody else. They are half inclined to fancy that it is because of them and their love that the sky is blue and the sun shines.

LOVE AND COURTSHIP IN AMERICA

Some theoretical implications of love for courtship

Granting the importance of love in bringing men and women together and providing new meaning and zest to their lives, we now need to ask if romantic love is beneficial or "functional" for society. Does it possibly lead to hasty or ill-advised marriages? To mismatched mates? To too many marriages perhaps? While evidence could probably be marshalled to support an affirmative answer to each of these questions, other evidence and arguments may be made that love serves societal as well as individual needs.

The Waller and Hill (1951) viewpoint suggests that romantic love may be dysfunctional in that it can lead to ill-advised marriages. Romantic love is seen as a highly subjective sentiment which tends to overcome objectivity in those possessed by it. Inherent in the development of romantic love is idealization: Without being aware of it, each partner strives to be like the dating partner's idealized image of what he or she should be. Both thus tend to assume statures and qualities not ordinarily characteristic of them. They are caught up in a powerful flow of emotion which makes it difficult to exercise rational judgement. Love in this view may be seen as a powerful force which can sweep a romantic couple into a marriage for which they are really unsuited. The early stages of marital adjustment may be difficult for such couples as they are forced to "come down to earth" and face reality. High separation and divorce rates in the early stages of marriage suggest that this viewpoint has some validity.

There are those, however, who argue that love is functional in various ways, both for individuals and for society.

Kolb (1950) maintains that love can benefit both the individual and the community. Love gives the individual a voice in selecting a marriage partner and stimulates personality growth and creativity in interpersonal

Deeply in love

Julie Heifitz

relations. Furthermore, love provides protection against the development of completely endogamous norms in mate selection in the community. If people were always to marry according to the wishes of their parents, the result would be extreme conventionality and a stifling of personal growth and creativity.

Romantic love is also defended by Beigle (1951), who sees it as an expression of a "socio-psychological process that aims at the reconciliation of basic human needs with frustrating social conditions" (Beigle, 1951, p. 326). In a society where the institutional supports for the permanency of marriage may not always be strong, love is a positive force in helping couples adjust to the inevitable frustrations they will encounter in their relationship. Love also has done much to raise the status of women and promote the equality of the sexes.

Greenfield (1969) argues that love functions by compelling young people toward marriage. Love induces them to overcome many obstacles, to put aside other interests, to reduce rational reluctances and to take the not always logical step of getting married right away. As Greenfield (1969) puts it, love operates as a special mechanism to induce generally rational people to do what is not necessarily in their immediate personal interest to do—to go ahead and get married.

> Somehow they must be induced—we might almost say in spite of themselves—to occupy the positions of husband-father and wife-mother. . . . What we are suggesting is that the romantic love complex in middle-class America serves as the reward-motive that induces individuals to occupy the structurally essential positions of husband-father and wife-mother (Greenfield, 1969, p. 360).

People who fall in love and get married generally feel they are doing the right thing; they normally also have strong support from their families and friends and from the community in general. From this perspective, romantic love may well be functional by inducing individuals to become husbands and wives and fathers and mothers, thereby creating the new round of nuclear families needed each generation.

Foote and Cottrell (1955) argue that, in spite of the presence of idealization and "emotion over reason," the love relationship is generally highly conducive to the optimum growth of each partner. People deeply in love commit themselves to one another; and as marriage partners they provide each other with mutual trust and support, which is conducive to individual development and increased competency in interpersonal relations.

Goode (1959) has presented another theoretical implication of love. He sees it as being potentially disruptive to the established social structure. Unless love is controlled and channelled along socially acceptable lines, it may result in marriages that weaken established lineage patterns or undermine the social class system. Goode argues that to permit completely random possibilities of love and mating would probably result in drastic changes in the existing social structure. Thus many societies have sought to prevent the potentially disruptive consequences of love by such steps as child betrothal and arranged marriages, rigid norms of social class endogamy, the isolation of young people from ineligible partners, and strict chaperonage. In our society, which has relatively open courtship systems and in which young people may date across class lines, we still depend on parents and friends to influence one's choice of a socially acceptable marriage partner. How is this done? According to Goode (1959, p. 45), parents

> seek to control love relationships by influencing the informal contacts of their children. . . , by making their children aware that certain individuals have ineligibility traits (race, religion, manners, taste, clothing, and so on). Since youngsters fall in love with those with whom they associate, control over informal relationships also controls substantially the focus of affection. . . . Most marriages take place between couples in the same class, religious, racial, and educational levels.

The extent of such family control over love and mate selection varies, of course, from society to society and, in societies like ours, from group to group. Families in the upper social stratum will exercise stricter control over love and courtship than families in the middle and lower strata. And in various segments of contemporary American society which espouse equalitarianism and individualism, such traditional family controls are rapidly weakening. The effects of these trends—increasing marriage across class, ethnic, racial, and religious lines—will be considered more fully elsewhere.

DATING AND COURTSHIP

THE AMERICAN COURTSHIP SYSTEM: THE DATING STAGE

LeMasters (1957b, p. 70) defines courtship as "the process by which the individual moves from the single status of the adolescent to the married status of the adult." This process includes various experiences and relationships with members of the opposite sex, from casual encounters to deeper and more durable relationships with potential marriage partners. In American society, where one has both the freedom and the responsibility to choose one's own mate, the courtship process is of vital importance both to the participant and to society at large. Courtship in America—especially in the middle classes—has become an elaborate and long drawn-out process. Dating has come to play a vital role in the total courtship process in the 20th century. Let us look briefly at the way dating has developed, and its relevance to courtship and mate selection.

Emergence of dating in America

Dating is not a 20th century invention. In fact, dating of one kind or another can be traced back to colonial America. As individuals and nuclear families migrated from the Old World many of the conditions of life became conducive to greater freedom for young people. This was especially true under frontier conditions as the population moved westward (Calhoun, Vol. 2, 1945).

Young men and women could find ways of spending time together in spite of unfavorable conditions, such as poor roads, long distances between farms or villages, and in the northern colonies, long cold winters. One kind of dating custom which seemed to be well established in the 18th century northern colonies was "bundling," which was widely approved in spite of its hazards because it so often led to marriage. This practice allowed a young man to visit a young lady in her parent's home in the evening, after work and often after a trip of many miles on a cold winter night. They would have little privacy until the daughter's parents and siblings went to bed. By then the day's supply of fire wood was exhausted, so in order that the couple might continue their courting

60

Dating couple

Fredrik D. Bodin/Stock, Boston

and not freeze in the process, they were permitted to retire to the daughter's bed together, fully clothed, but under covers to keep warm. The honor system was supposed to operate in this kind of dating. Sex codes were very strict, especially in New England, and the bundling couple were expected to refrain from any sexual intimacy and, of course, from sexual intercourse. To what extent the honor system worked is a matter of dispute. Calhoun (1945, Vol. 1) believes there were breakdowns, and points to evidence that there was a high percentage of pregnant brides in New England at this time. The church records in Groton, Massachusetts show that out of 200 weddings performed between 1761 and 1765, 66 of the couples confessed the indiscretion of committing fornication (Calhoun, 1945, Vol. 1, p. 133). Despite such problems, the bundling practice was supported by most parents in the lower socioeconomic groups where it prevailed, because it did lead to marriage. It fit the needs of courtship during the long, harsh, New England winters, and apparently was not practiced during the summer (Reiss, 1976, p. 76). As living conditions improved the bundling custom diminished. In the 19th century the young man courted his lady love in the heated parlor rather than the bedroom. By the 20th century the automobile put courtship on wheels, affording the young couple a new kind of privacy as well as much greater mobility.

One of the best-known studies and analysis of emerging 20th-century dating was done by Waller (1938), who observed the dating patterns of American college students in the late 1920s and early 1930s. He found a kind of casual dating among college youth which he thought did not have much relevance for true courtship and mate selection. This casual dating differed from older forms of courtship whereby young men and women would move in a fairly predictable progression from their initial interest in each other to emotional involvement to commitment and marriage. In place of this older type of courtship, Waller found a "rating-dating" system on the college campuses, consisting of casual and competitive dating oriented toward thrill seeking and often exploitation rather than toward engagement and marriage. Accordingly, Waller advanced his thesis that this new kind of dating was essentially a "dalliance relationship" rather than true courtship. Unlike true courtship, which is a means toward the future goal of marriage, the new dating was only present oriented, with the "fun and games" of the date itself as its main purpose. The rating-dating system was especially apparent among fraternities, where one of its functions was to allow a member to establish or reassert his status. Success in dating depended on such things as money, access to cars, dancing ability, personal popularity, and the ranking of one's fraternity. Such factors, Waller believed, were not too important in most marriage-oriented courtships.

When social class lines were crossed, the new, competitive, status-oriented dating could lead to exploitation of the lower-status partner. This led to Waller's concept of the "principle of least interest" (Waller, 1938), which states that in a dating relationship, the partner who has the least interest in maintaining that relationship will normally control it. This person has less to lose if the relationship is ended, so he or she can dictate the terms under which it will continue. The other person, desiring to hold onto the dating partner, will yield to the other's terms, often to the point of being used or exploited. Exploitation was also possible when one dating partner held to older norms which defined increasing intimacy through dating as progressive commitment toward engagement and marriage, while the other held the new dalliance view of dating and intimacy.

Waller's work has provoked a good deal of reaction from family social scientists. Studies of dating on college campuses since Waller's time have not supported all of his interpretations (Smith, 1952; Lowrie, 1951; Blood, 1955; Christensen & Johnson, 1971). Out of these studies have come the following criticisms of Waller: (1) he overemphasized the exploitative and prestige-seeking aspects of dating; (2) he failed to see the role dating actually played in mate selection; and (3) he did not recognize the importance of dating as a support of social class homogamy (Gordon, 1978, pp. 178–179). In fairness to Waller, however, it is quite likely that the dating patterns on college campuses of the 1950s and later were somewhat different from those he had found 20 or more years before. Studies made in the 1970s suggest this is probably so.

Krain et al. (1977) recently investigated the dating patterns of Greek fraternity members on a midwestern college campus. The investigators attempted to test some of Waller's ideas about the existence of prestige hierarchies and the tendency of fraternity members to date within their ranks. A randomly selected sample of 21 Greek organization members validated a scale of prestige ranking of the Greek organizations on campus; and another randomly selected sample of 97 Greek organization members showed that "prestige homogamy" in dating was clearly evident within the differently ranked fraternities. But no evidence was found to support the idea of a rating-dating complex on the campus. The findings indicate more relaxed and humanistic patterns of modern dating, in contrast to the more competitive and materialistic type Waller observed. Another recent study (Hansen, 1977) of high-school students suggests that dating is now seen by most adolescents not just as a form of recreation, but as a type of courtship and a prelude to mate selection.

There is also evidence that dating behavior is becoming quite uniform among black and white youth in America. In a study of black and white adolescents, Dickinson (1975) found that since school desegregation the dating behavior of black youth has changed in the direction of that practiced by whites, so that today there is a good deal of homogeneity in their expectations and behavior.

Going steady

While casual and random dating continued on into the mid-20th century, the practice of going steady was on the increase and appeared to be the preferred kind of dating for many high school and college youth in the post–World War II era. In his study of students attending the University of Wisconsin in the mid-1950s, Herman (1955) found that going steady was not only the preferred form of dating, but was also likely to be oriented toward marriage. Random or casual dating served only to tide one over between more durable relationships. The students saw going steady as providing greater security, as less competitive, and as providing enough time for getting to really know each other. Going steady, they believed, was also conducive to personal growth, and the emotional involvement could lead to engagement and eventual marriage.

A decade later, Reiss (1965) did a study of campus dating at a college in Virginia. He was interested in differences between casual and serious dating and relationships between dating and the social class identity of the daters. He found a campus class system that affects whom one dates on both a casual and a serious basis. This class system—differentiated by high-ranked fraternities, low-ranked fraternities, and independents—reflected the parental social class background of the students. In certain ways, casual dating as well as serious dating functioned as "true court-ship." Casual dating helped one select a "field of eligibles" from which one then went on to select a partner with whom one wished to become more serious. While casual dating tended to be intraclass rather than interclass, this was even more true for serious dating. That is, students got serious mostly with dating partners from their own social class. There was not much evidence that casual dating was mainly a dalliance relation-ship. Reiss concludes:

> In any case, it seems clear that casual dating is on the main track of a marriage-destined type of dating system. Even though the couple involved is not aiming at marriage, the very fact that they come from compatible (class) groups increases their chances of finding someone with whom they will become serious.

How does casual dating develop into serious dating? How does a dating couple become increasingly emotionally involved and committed? In his Wheel Theory of Love Reiss (1960) has attempted to conceptualize the processes through which emotional involvement develop between two people. This development of love entails four consecutive processes: (1) rapport; (2) self-revelation; (3) mutual dependency; and (4) need fulfill-ment. First, upon meeting, the young man and woman make a quick assessment of the *rapport* they feel. Do they feel at ease together? Do they communicate freely? Similarity in social background and ideology, and so forth help establish rapport. Insufficient rapport generally stops the development of further relationships. However, when good rapport exists, this can lead to a relaxed and easy state conducive to *self-revelation*. One is now more likely to confide one's hopes, dreams, ambitions, and so on. Here also, one's social background is important in influencing what one thinks should be revealed to the other. And at this stage, male and female subcultural differences in orientation often enter the relationship, with the male more likely to think that sexual intimacies are now proper. As self-revelation unfolds, "interdependent habit systems" are built up. *Mutual dependence* develops as each partner gets used to doing things that require cooperation from the other to accomplish. One comes to need the other to confide in, to share a success with, to listen to one's jokes, to make love with, and so on. These deepening relationships come to produce *personality need fulfillment*. That is, the relationship now functions to fulfill such basic personality needs as the need for someone to love and confide in, who will stimulate one's ambitions and assuage one's ego wounds.

Reiss has labeled this explanation of progressive emotional involvement the Wheel theory of Love because the four processes are interdependent and operate in a circular manner. Rapport leads to self-revelation, which leads to mutual dependency, which in turn results in personality need fulfillment. However, the wheel may also turn in the other direction, with the resulting reduction of emotional involvement. As Reiss (1976, p. 96) explains it:

> I chose this label because . . . the processes are interdependent, and a reduction of any one of them will affect the development or maintenance of a love relationship. For example, if one reduced the amount of self-revelation through an argument or by means of a competing interest, that would affect the dependency and need fulfillment processes, which would, in turn, weaken the rapport process, which would, in turn, tend to lower the revelation even further. Thus, the processes flow into one another in one direction to develop love and can flow the other way to weaken a love relationship.

Krain et al. (1977) examined the ways communication developed between dating partners as they progressed from casual dating to more serious stages of their relationship. Using university student couples ranging from those just starting to date to those only weeks from marriage, Krain found that over the three stages of dating described by Reiss, communication tends to progress qualitatively in ways that strengthen the relationship. In the late stage couples become more adept at talking out their differences and patching up difficulties than in the earlier stages.

Collins (1974) was also interested in the progression of the dating experience. Focusing on the changing norms and expectations of girls and boys during the different stages of dating, Collins (1974) found that the intimacy expectations and behavior of males was generally more permissive than that of females during initial dating. But as their commitment to the affectional relationship increased, female dating behavior came to resemble more closely that of the male. A subsequent study of university students corroborated this finding (Collins, et al., 1976). Males, regardless of age, expected more intimacy from their partners, starting in the early stages; females expected less intimate behavior during early dating, but increasing intimacy in the later stages of going steady and when marriage is being considered. Also, older females expected more intimacy than younger ones.

Functions of dating

Let us now try to stand back and look at the whole range of dating behavior with the objective of finding the various purposes it serves, or the functions it performs. Dating may be said to include behavior and relationships ranging from casual and random contacts through the more serious intimacies of going steady, "going with" and "engaged to be engaged" (Delora, 1963, p. 83). The purposes or functions of dating will normally differ according to which dating phase one is in. Also, of course, persons date for different reasons at different times, and dating objectives and norms may vary from group to group (Skipper & Nass, 1966).

Dating as recreation.   As noted above, casual or random dating, as well as some kinds of going steady, provide young people with enjoyable relationships and activities that may be considered ends in themselves. That is, the date in and of itself is the end or purpose of their getting together, with no future obligations nor commitments implied. The immediate enjoyment of doing something together is the reason for going to a movie or a dance. This recreational function of dating corresponds closely to Waller's idea of dating as a dalliance activity. For some, of course, such dates may lead to more durable and serious relationships.

Dating as status-seeking.   Recall Waller's notion of rating and dating. Dating may function for participants as a means of status or prestige pursuit and validation. This seems to have been an especially salient function of dating on college campuses over the years (Rogers & Havens, 1960; Skipper & Nass, 1966). A student's status on campus is enhanced by dating "people who count." Thus students tend to date and be seen with others of similar rank or status. Fraternity men generally date sorority women. By dating a man who is highly rated by one's peers, a woman may raise or at least validate her status on campus. By dating a beauty queen a man may enhance his status.

Dating as socialization.   The early periods of the dating process function especially to help one get acquainted with members of the opposite sex, and to see oneself through their eyes (McDaniel, 1969). One is learning sex roles and how to relate to a number of different types of persons of the opposite sex, and in the process developing a broader self-image by "taking the role" of these various "opposite-sex others" toward oneself. One is learning the norms of heterosexual interaction. Thus dating experiences contribute to personal growth. Viewed developmentally, the earlier, casual dating experiences provide valuable "anticipatory socialization" for the following, more serious dating which precedes mate selection. As LeMasters (1957b, p. 105) expresses it, random dating functions "to prepare young people for courtship—that is, to launch them into the [courtship] system."

Dating and ego needs.   As seen above in our discussion from Reiss (1976) on the development of emotional involvement, serious dating especially contributes to important ego-need fulfillment. All people need understanding, sympathy, affection, recognition, and so forth. Young people especially may feel insecure and unimportant at times, and need the kind of ego bolstering a sympathetic and affectionate dating partner can provide. Dating can help meet the ego needs of adolescents during the difficult years of growing up and finding themselves.

Dating as a type of courtship.   For many young people, dating certainly functions as "real courtship," as the main process through which one selects a marriage partner (McDaniel, 1969; Skipper & Nass, 1966; Reiss, 1976). To some degree, most dating entails a consideration of the dating partner as a potential spouse. For lower- and working-class youth, there is a greater likelihood that most dating is marriage oriented than is the case for middle- and upper-class youth (LeMasters, 1957b, pp. 127–128). Regardless of social class, dating does provide opportunities for unmarried youth to associate with each other with a view of narrowing the field of prospective marriage partners to the point where a final selection is made.

ISSUES, PROBLEMS, AND ADJUSTMENTS IN DATING

In his analysis of random dating, LeMasters (1957b, pp. 113–116) found that certain types of young people adapt more readily than others to this kind of relationship. Shy and introverted youth seem to have more difficulty with casual dating than more open and outgoing youth. Also, some have greater difficulty than others in controlling their emotions; they are prone to fall in love quickly and are more vulnerable to exploitation, or at least to being hurt by their "less interested" casual dating partner. Skipper & Nass (1966, pp. 413–414) found that the greater the disparity between the emotional involvement of the partners, the greater the chance that conflict and distress will occur in the relationship, with the partner most emotionally involved usually suffering the greatest distress. Also, the greater the difference between the partners in their "instrumental orientation" toward dating (where dating is seen as a means toward some larger goal, such as marriage) the more likely the relationship is to produce stress and conflict. Stated a little differently, if one partner has an "expressive orientation" (viewing dating as a recreational end in itself) while the other has an instrumental orientation (viewing dating as a means to marriage), it is likely the latter at least will suffer some distress and the relationship may be conducive to conflict. The former may or may not feel some guilt.

Other related issues and problems associated with dating have been observed, including the following.

Earlier dating

American youth appear to be dating earlier in life now, often in their early teens (Bayer, 1968; Place, 1975). While such early dating may be beneficial in the long run, it also exposes boys and girls to emotional and sexual adjustment problems while they are very young and immature.

Lack of clear codes of conduct

Since dating as we know it appears to be a recent American innovation, its codes and norms are not yet well established. Without established and agreed-upon standards of conduct, dating couples are not always sure of what is right or wrong, and may have to work out their relationship more or less by trial and error (Collins, 1974; Krain et al., 1977). This can be hard on the young people, as well as on their parents, who are responsible for them.

Parent-child conflict

Parents understandably wish to influence and protect their children in their dating choices and activities, as responsible parents should. Sussman (1953a) found that in a midwestern sample of parents, 81 percent admitted that they had either persuaded or threatened their children with withdrawal of support when their sons or daughters were dating persons of whom the parents disapproved. Bruce (1976) found that mothers became increasingly involved in their daughter's dating as they became more seriously involved. Today many teenagers tend to consider this as interference or intrusion. In a study of 1,079 college students, Kephart (1977, p. 274) found that 50 percent of the females and 40 percent of the males reported instances of conflict with their parents over persons they dated. Interreligious and cross-class dating were sources of such conflict, with older, more conservative parents objecting to the desires of their liberal-minded sons and daughters to date across these lines.

The issue of physical attractiveness

In a society that exalts romantic love, physical attractiveness looms large in the business of attracting dating partners. The mass media floods our society with images of beautiful women and handsome men. Good looks have become something of a fetish in America. Young women especially find their beauty or lack of it a vital factor in their ability to attract dates and be popular. Therefore, lack of physical attractiveness may be one of the most serious problems in the American dating and courtship systems. Unfair though it is, the homely, as well as the socially awkward, have the fewest options, and some get left out entirely (Klemer, 1971).

Walster, et al. (1966) found that in college dating, physical attractiveness was an overriding determinant, especially in men's reaction to women. Mathes (1975) found that physical attractiveness was not only a "triggering mechanism" for the first date, but continued to be an important factor over the first five dates.

The problem of sexual involvement

The issue of premarital sex is a potential or actual problem for dating couples. As Kephart (1977, p. 277) observes:

> Although many adults have succeeded in closing their eyes to the fact, sex has become an important part of the general dating pattern. While the goal of dating may not be primarily sexual, it is probably safe to say

that there are relatively few dates wherein the sex problem does not make itself felt in one way or another. . . . If the couple indulge in some sort of sexual activity, there may be feelings of remorse and guilt. If they abstain altogether, there may be feelings of frustration. If they have intercourse, there is always the possibility of pregnancy. Verily, it would seem that all roads lead to some sort of conflict.

The parent-child generation gap is certainly a factor here, especially in these times of the alleged sexual revolution. Many parents still find it difficult to communicate with their sons and daughters on matters of sex. In a study of adolescents aged 13 to 19 Sorensen (1973) found that over 70 percent of their parents were unable to talk freely about sex with them. Sex norms have been undergoing changes in recent years, moving toward greater freedom and permissiveness (see Chapter 7). Many parents dislike and even fear these changes, and even those who are trying to understand the changing norms are not always sure how best to counsel their sons and daughters as they become involved in dating.

Problems of superficiality and insecurity

LeMasters (1957b., p. 105) notes that the criteria often used in choosing dating partners may be quite superficial. The tendency to emphasize such things as physical appearance, clothes, car, and ability to dance well is somewhat inevitable due to the nature of casual dating. Each partner is trying to make a good impression on the other, and is out to have a good time. He tries to impress her with his car, his "line," and his machismo; she tries to impress him with her beauty and charm (Skipper & Nass, 1966). Either or both may be insecure to some degree as they try to impress the other, and they may possibly try to convince one another that they are more serious than they really are. Mathes (1975) found that due to high expectations and numerous uncertainties, dating partners tended to exhibit high levels of anxiety during their first few dates. Waller and Hill (1951, pp. 217–220) argue that such superficially oriented, random dating could be detrimental to courtship in that it does not reveal the traits that are important for a good marriage. This can be true for those who cut short the courtship process; for example, for those who fall in love quickly and elope before they really know each other. The author tends to agree with LeMasters that, even though the criteria for partner selection and much of the behavior in random dating are scarcely sufficient to prepare a couple for marriage, they are not really meant to do so. Casual or random dating prepares the participants for more serious stages of courtship where the deeper testing and probing of self and other takes place.

Problems of breaking up

In our free-choice dating and mate selection system it is inevitable that break-ups occur. There are all kinds of reasons for breaking off a dating relationship: cessation of love, development of stress or conflict, inadequate communication, realization of mismatched interests or values, parental pressures, one partner more serious than the other, and of course, falling in love with someone else.

In a study of dating relationships of college students over a two-year period, Hill et al. (1976) studied the break-up of 103 couples. Factors contributing to these break-ups included: unequal involvement in the relationship, differences in age, differences in educational aspirations, discrepancies in intelligence, and differences in physical attractiveness. The desire to break up was seldom mutual. The women were more likely to perceive problems in the relationship, and were somewhat more likely to precipitate or initiate the break-up. It seemed easier for women to fall out of love. There were two sides to every break-up, hers and his. There was a general tendency for the reactions of the two partners in a break-up to be inversely related: the freer the one partner felt on breaking up, the less free the other felt. Each partner also tended to say that it was he or she, rather than the partner, who wanted the break-up. It was apparently easier to cope with if one viewed it as a desired outcome (precipitated by oneself or mutually agreed to), rather than something imposed against one's will.

Dating among adults

Dating is not limited, of course, to the very young. Although the bulk of social science literature deals with dating and mating among adolescents and youth in high school and college, the dating needs and practices of the divorced, the widowed, and never-married persons beyond their early 20s also deserve attention. Dating of divorced men and women will be treated in Chapter 10, and dating of the widowed is discussed to some extent in Chapter 15.

The increasing number of singles in the United States does not necessarily mean that single women and men are avoiding relationships with members of the opposite sex. Actually, the possibility of exploring a variety of relationships is often seen as one of the major attractions of singlehood today. However, once out of school or college, meeting potential partners can become difficult for many (Starr & Carnes, 1972). Since in conventional circles adult life is apt to revolve around married couples, single adults may feel somewhat uncomfortable, and may also be viewed as a threat by those who are married.

Places such as singles bars may provide sources of new associations for some men and women. For others, however, the false glamor, hyped-up stimulation, and socially enforced role playing tend to obstruct the development of meaningful relations in such settings (Stein, 1976). Other sources of dating partners are singles clubs and singles housing complexes. Again, such sources may not meet the needs of everyone: Proulx (1973) found that patrons or tenants tended to focus on the sexual aspects of singlehood; those who desired something more, such as friendship or a lasting relationship, found little appeal in these places.

For many middle-class men and women, work is often a source of personal association and dating partners. This may be less true for blue-collar workers and lower level white-collar workers whose work groups are more apt to be sex segregated (Jacoby, 1973; Stein, 1976). Stein believes that the future will see the development of new formal structures to meet the needs of single women and men for friendship and intimacy.

THE FUTURE OF LOVE AND DATING IN COURTSHIP

THE FUTURE OF LOVE IN MATE SELECTION

Some authorities believe that romantic love is on the decline in America today and will probably decline further as people become more sophisticated and as premarital (and extramarital) sexual permissiveness increases (Blood, 1952; Wilkenson, 1978). This view is based, in part, on a theory that there is a relationship between romantic love and "sexual blockage" or the blocking of sexual expression before marriage and outside of marriage (Freud, 1922). Wilkenson, while noting that romantic love certainly has more than one cause, found a strong correlation between romantic love and sexual restrictiveness in 24 cultures around the world—evidence, he believes, of empirical support for the theory. He also finds some evidence that romantic love is declining in America as sexual freedom and permissiveness increase. Some other investigators, however, think there is no necessary incompatibility between romantic love and greater sexual freedom (Udry, 1974, pp. 140–141). Wilkenson and others caution against predicting a significant decline in romantic love and the role it will probably continue to play in courtship and mate selection (Wilkenson, 1978; Kephart, 1977).

How good—or how functional—is love as a basis for mate selection? Does love produce the kinds of marriages that we want? Or does it produce mismatched partners and problem marriages? Unfortunately, the research data are not adequate to allow clear answers to these questions. One of the difficulties lies in the ambiguity of the word *love*. Some kinds of love seem to be more functional than other kinds for marriage. Lantz and Snyder (1962) find that "mature love" is a good basis for marital success but "immature love" is not. When love is defined as purely physical or emotional attraction, most authorities agree it is not a sufficient basis upon which to build a good marriage. When love is more broadly defined to include also companionship, communication, consensus, and common interests, the authorities tend to think it is good for marriage.

Differences of opinion have been expressed about the consequences of the love basis for marriage as an institution. Some, like DeRougemont (1959) argue that the marriage institution is damaged by basing marriage, a lasting relationship, on love, a passing fancy. Others, including Spanier

Love will continue to be important in mate selection

Jeff Albertson/Stock, Boston

(1972), Beigel (1951), and Kephart (1977), see mainly beneficial consequences of love as a basis for marriage. The author is inclined to agree with this position. Given our history and cultural values, which emphasize individual rights, freedom of choice, and personal growth and enhancement, love—including romantic love—will probably continue to play an important role in sorting young American men and women into marriage partners, and helping them get started in marriage.

THE FUTURE OF DATING IN MATE SELECTION

As noted in this chapter, 20th-century dating has become a thoroughly established, multipurpose aspect of premarital cross-sex relationships in America. Dating, says Adams (1975, p. 185), "has become so pervasive as to virtually embody the current mate-selection processes in the United States." If this is true, it would seem safe to predict that dating will continue on into the foreseeable future. Undoubtedly there will be modifications in dating practices and attitudes. Some observers see a trend toward greater informality in dating, along with a decline in casual pair dating and an increase in loosely defined heterosexual group dating (Reiss, 1976, p. 87; Gordon, 1978, pp. 184–185).

Vreeland (1972) studied changing dating patterns among college students at Harvard University during the 1960s and early 1970s. She concluded that dating is becoming less formal and less exploitative. "Students . . . have begun to treat their dates as persons and potential friends rather *than as competitors or candidates for marriage"* (Vreeland, 1972, p. 66). She believes that the most important dating motive for today's male student is finding a friend who is female and who will be a good companion. This differs in emphasis from earlier times when the recreational role of dating was more important (for freshmen in the 1960s), and when learning about another's personality and establishing one's own identity were also important (for seniors of the 1960s and freshmen of the 1970s). Young people get together more informally now, especially where former sex barriers have fallen, such as in coed dormatories or in hiking and skiing clubs.

Reiss (1976, p. 86) suggests that the very term *dating* may be too formal and stiff for the 1970s. Also, the term *going steady* is used less in some groups today because it implies too much of a commitment. The looser term *going with* seems to be preferred now. This allows more latitude and can apply to a high school couple who go with each other for only a few weeks as well as to a more serious college couple who may go with each other for a year or more before getting married. Also, a good deal of the casual dating of the 1970s is not just couple dating, but a kind of casual group dating, somewhat reminiscent of group dating in earlier decades (LeMasters, 1957b, pp. 96–97), where a group of several males and females get together, often quite informally, to go on an outing, attend a party, or go to a ballgame. This kind of loosely arranged heterosexual group activity is often simply called going out instead of dating or going with (Reiss, 1976, p. 87). Such mixed group get-togethers may, of course, lead to pairings, which then go on to the going with stage of dating.

Assessment of dating as courtship

We have discussed the nature of dating, its variations and changes, its functions, and some of its problems for participants and for society. Is it possible now to make any general assessment of dating as courtship, as it functions in mate selection?

There seems to be a pretty good fit between our dating patterns and the American cultural emphasis on the heterosexual pair relationship with its expectation of emotional and sexual gratification. This emphasis is increasingly apparent in the marital relationship, in which partners expect to share mutual love and sexual gratification. The conjugal bond has become more important than other family bonds and relationships. It is through dating that the younger generation is socialized and initiated into these highly valued pair relationships and begins to participate in them. Dating thus functions as important, anticipatory socialization for normal, adult, heterosexual, emotional relations in America. As Udry (1977, p. 100) puts it: "There can be little question that the young people of today come into marriage with more extensive and initimate experience with the opposite sex than their parents did." It can be argued, of course, that the present American emphasis on emotional and sexual gratification has gone too far, and that a better balance between these and other values and relationships should be sought, perhaps with more emphasis on parent-child relationships or on same-sex friendships. This, however, is a larger issue that cannot be resolved simply by altering existing dating practices. So, given the current cultural valuation Americans accord love and emotional and sexual gratification in marriage, it may be argued that dating is functional in preparing young people for these aspects of marriage.

Furthermore, there is evidence that dating does more than just sort young people into compatible love-sex partners. Studies show that young people are still looking for traditionally valued and approved personal characteristics in dating partners whom they are considering as prospective

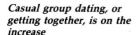

Casual group dating, or getting together, is on the increase

Linda Perry-Shafer

mates. In a comparison of such characteristics, Kephart (1977, p. 279) found a remarkable similarity among college men and women over a period of 35 years (from 1939 to 1975). For both men and women, the most desired personal characteristics were: (1) a dependable character and emotional stability; (2) a pleasing disposition, and (3) mutual attraction. The author concludes that there has probably been less change in what young people are seeking in their marriage partners than many parents and other elders have feared; and that, in effect, dating is probably "working" as well now as earlier in helping young people find good marriage partners.

From a societal viewpoint, it may be argued that dating seems to benefit our free-choice marriage market by fulfilling the societal need of getting generally compatible males and females sorted out into marriage partnerships. This is evidenced by the continuing high marriage rates. Of course, divorce rates are also high, and while this may be partly due to dating practices, it also has to be explained by the complexity of changing conditions and processes associated with our urban, secular, mobile, individual-oriented society.

CHAPTER 4

Premarital sexual attitudes and behavior

All human societies are concerned about the sexual behavior of their members. Anthropologists find that the social control of sexual behavior is a universal feature. While societies vary a great deal in how they control sexual behavior and in what they define as normatively acceptable, all societies do exert some kinds of restrictions as to who may do what with whom under what conditions. Such sex codes pertain to premarital as well as marital behavior.

America is no exception, obviously. From the days of the Puritans in colonial America down through the Victorian era of the 19th century to the present-day "enlightened" late 20th century, our history is replete with various sex codes. Today there is a good deal of disagreement as to what is proper and acceptable concerning premarital sex. While such differences of opinion are not new, they are certainly more openly expressed and widely discussed than earlier. This chapter will first review American attitudes and viewpoints on premarital sex, past and present, and then look into trends in premarital sexual behavior itself. Some of the ramifications of premarital sexual involvement for American youth will be discussed.

AMERICAN VIEWPOINTS TOWARD PREMARITAL SEX, PAST AND PRESENT

IS THERE A SEXUAL REVOLUTION?

The term *sexual revolution* has become part of the current American vocabulary, due primarily to the mass media and, to a lesser degree, to the research and writings of behavioral scientists since World War II. Authorities do not all agree, however, that there really is a sexual revolution. The term itself may, of course, have different meanings to different people. And there are questions as to what exactly is being "revolutionized." Is it attitudes and beliefs, mores and laws? Is it the actual sexual behavior, the incidence of premarital sexual intercourse, or what? Also, what time periods are being considered? Changes just since the 1960s, or since World War II? Since the turn of the 20th century? Or perhaps since Victorian or even Puritan times? And just how extensive or drastic must the changes be to qualify as revolutionary?

Young men and women now enjoy freer relationships

Luis Medina Photo

A top authority on sex in America, Reiss (1976), sees 20th-century changes toward increasing premarital sex as significant, but really more gradual than sudden or revolutionary. Bowman and Spanier (1978, p. 84) tend to agree. They believe that the term *sexual evolution* more accurately identifies what has been happening in American society. They see changes occurring in sex attitudes, codes, and behavior as related to changes in other areas of American society and culture, such as the trends toward equalitarianism, individualism, feminism, and greater freedom of choice in personal conduct. Other authorities, including Cuber (1971, p. 176), think that changes taking place in sex codes and related behavior are great enough to constitute a real sexual revolution. Cuber points out that whereas in earlier generations in American youth those who broke the strict premarital chastity codes experienced a good deal of guilt, many who today indulge in premarital sex feel little or no guilt because they no longer believe in the old restrictive sex code. The evidence on this point is not clear-cut, however. There are indications that some who engage in premarital sex today do still feel guilty about it. This question will be discussed more fully later.

Few would argue that significant changes are not taking place today in premarital sexual standards and behavior. Let us now try to get a better perspective on the current scene by looking at early American attitudes toward premarital sex, and then at changes that have occurred recently.

THE PAST: TRADITIONAL AMERICAN ATTITUDES TOWARD PREMARITAL SEX

Historical background to attitudes toward sex

There are indications that premarital sexual behavior was more prevalent in colonial America than is generally believed (Gordon, 1978, p. 188). Smith (1973) finds evidence that rates of premarital sex relations rose in the 18th century, turned downward under Victorian influences in the 19th century, and then upward again in the 20th century, with at least two sharp upswings, in the 1920s and later in the 1960s. Overall, American premarital sexual behavior appears to have gone through a number of cycles.

Another factor should be kept in mind as we look at the historical background to current American attitudes toward premarital sex, and that is the differences in attitudes toward male sexuality as opposed to female sexuality. Traditionally, men have had more sexual freedom than women—the time-honored double standard—and thus female sexuality has generally been more strictly regulated throughout our history. One of the quite recent and perhaps truly revolutionary changes has been the sexual liberation of American women, which represents a belated effort to catch up with the longstanding, greater freedom of American men (Reiss, 1976; Zelnick & Kantner, 1972; Bell & Coughey, 1980).

Traditional American viewpoints toward premarital sex

In the traditional, patriarchal American family of our rural past, the male had more rights and greater freedom than the female in many areas of life, including sex. It was argued that men had stronger sex needs than women. Sex was thought to be of considerably less interest to women, who acquiesced mainly for the purpose of satisfying their husband's needs, and for purposes of reproduction. Premarital chastity was considered much more important for a woman than for a man. In the Judeo-Christian religious tradition, a bride was supposed to be a virgin. According to the Old Testament, a nonvirgin bride could be put to death. In sacred societies the value of a daughter in the marriage market was greatly reduced if she were a nonvirgin.

Early American attitudes toward premarital sex for men were often somewhat contradictory. Since 19th-century Victorian attitudes toward sex in general tended to be negative, ideally the man as well as the woman should abstain from premarital sex. In practice, however, there was a good deal more premarital sexual freedom—as well as extramarital sexual freedom—for men than for women. In other words there was a definite sexual double standard which allowed a certain amount of sexual freedom for men while imposing heavy restrictions on women (Udry, 1974, p. 105). The contradiction inherent in this double standard is that the man wanted a sexually chaste woman for marriage while also desiring a sexually available woman as a premarital partner and perhaps as an extramarital sexual partner too. Men subscribing to the double standard often resolved this contradiction by dividing women into two categories, "good women" and "bad women" (Bell, 1979, p. 160). To such men, the latter were fair game for purposes of satisfying their sexual needs, while the former were off limits for carnal purposes. While the 20th century has brought a definite decline in the double standard, there is evidence that it was still accepted to some degree in contemporary America, at least into the 1960s. Reiss (1976) found that among high school and college students nearly one third of the males and about one fourth of the females believed in the double standard of sexual behavior.

A number of studies conducted up until the mid-1960s suggested the continued existence of the sexual double standard. These showed that about 60 percent of college men had experienced premarital sexual behavior as compared to only about 20 percent of college women (Ehrman, 1959; Freedman, 1965; Reiss, 1976). However, research conducted since the late 1960s suggests a decline in the double standard. While the percentage of college males reporting premarital intercourse has remained about the same as before, the percentage of college females has about doubled, increasing to about 40 percent (Kaats & Davis, 1970; Cannon & Long, 1971). Bell and Coughey (1980) found that in a sample of 328 college women at one university in 1978, one half had had premarital sex while dating, two thirds while going steady, and three fourths while engaged.

THE PRESENT: CHANGING SEXUAL ATTITUDES

There is little doubt that attitudes toward sex and sexual activity, including premarital sex, have become more liberal or permissive in recent times. This trend is not uniform, however, as many people still adhere to earlier, restrictive sex codes and values. Numerous studies and surveys attest to a rapid trend toward permissiveness, though, in many segments of the American population. In a study of college students, Robinson, King, and Balswick (1972, pp. 191–192) found that both male and female students were considerably more permissive toward premarital sex in 1970 than in 1965. In the 1965 sample, 33 percent of the men and 70 percent of the women believed that premarital sex is immoral, while in 1970 only 14 percent of the men and 34 percent of the women felt that way. Studies by Reiss (1976) also show that the number of Americans who are becoming more tolerant of premarital sex are increasing considerably. He found that the percentage of American adults who accept premarital intercourse as proper under some conditions had increased from 21

Clowning around

William S. Nawrocki

percent in 1963 to 52 percent in 1970. Most studies show that men are still more permissive than women, but the latest studies show women in the process of catching up.

As might be expected, young people are more permissive than their elders. A Gallup Youth Survey of American teen-agers aged 13 to 18 conducted nationwide in 1978 (*Houston Post,* 1978) found 59 percent of the respondents saying that premarital sex is all right as opposed to 30 percent saying it was wrong, with 11 percent undecided. For the boys in the sample, the ratio in favor of premarital sex—66 percent approving and only 22 percent disapproving—was greater than for the girls, who were more closely divided, with 52 percent approving and 38 percent disapproving. The older teenagers (aged 16–18) of both sexes were more tolerant than the younger ones (aged 13–15), with 64 percent of the older and 54 percent of the younger approving. For those who still believe that premarital sex is wrong, the prevailing view is that marrying a virgin is important. Those who approve of premarital sex believe it is not important to marry a virgin.

Using data from seven independently drawn national samples taken during the 1970s, Glenn and Weaver (1979) found that standards concerning extramarital and homosexual relations remained highly restrictive, but standards concerning premarital sex were much more permissive and still rapidly changing in the direction of permissiveness. The survey data showed that in 1972, 49 percent of the respondents thought it not wrong at all or wrong only sometimes for a man or a woman to have sexual relations before marriage; by 1978, 57.5 percent felt the same way.

Why has this rather dramatic change in attitudes toward premarital sex come about? Let us examine some influential sociocultural factors.

Factors affecting premarital sexual attitudes

In the 20th century, American society has experienced a pronounced increase in secularization and individuation as the United States has become a huge urban-industrial nation (Dyer, 1979). This general societal change has meant a loosening of traditional family restraints on sons and daughters, including a weakening of sex codes. More young people are becoming emancipated from the historical family and religious moral restrictions, enabling them to date earlier and more freely and to let their emotions carry them to greater heterosexual intimacy before marriage than would have been morally acceptable earlier.

Other factors influencing premarital sexual attitudes are feminism and the women's liberation movement. A weakening of the patriarchal traditions has meant more freedom for women and a drive toward equal rights and opportunities. Women want control of their personal lives, including their sex lives. Technological and scientific advances have helped this trend. The ready availability of such birth control devices as the Pill has reduced, but not yet entirely removed, the age-old fear of unwanted pregnancy.

As young American women become emancipated from traditional family bonds and community restrictions, as they get more educational and occupational opportunities and so on, they come increasingly under the influence of modern secular educational, peer, and work groups. It is in such extrafamilial groups that the old morality is no longer in vogue and the new morality of permissiveness is popular. Single young women today are not only freer from traditional family moral restrictions than in earlier generations; they are less apt now to be financially dependent on men. As they get additional higher education and better jobs, more young women are becoming financially self-supporting and able to stay single if they wish. Also, when women had no other means of financial support except men, it was to their advantage to keep the sources of sexual gratification in short supply. Now that they can support themselves, women have less reason to use sex in exchange for financial support. In sum, premarital sexual attitudes are changing, due in part to the growing emancipation of women and to the equalitarian point of view that women as well as men have the right to control their personal lives.

Another factor contributing to increasing premarital sexual permissiveness is a belated acceptance of the view that women's sexual needs are as important as men's. This position provides strong support to the argument that women should have the same rights and freedom as men to seek sexual satisfaction and fulfillment. More married women now expect sexual satisfaction in marriage. This expectation has led to more tolerant attitudes about sex in general for women, contributing to the permissive view that sex before marriage may be justified for women as well as for men under certain conditions. Also contributing to increasing premarital sexual permissiveness and to the breakdown of the traditional double standard is the development of effective contraceptive methods. Ethnographic materials show that in the past there have been no known societies in which sexual standards have not been somewhat stricter for women than for men, for the basic reason that women get pregnant and men do not. With effective contraceptives, that is no longer a crucial issue, and a single standard becomes practical.

Reiss (1976) finds the explanation of increasing premarital sexual permissiveness related to the fact that in America today young people have greater freedom to date privately and have an important voice in choosing their marriage partner. According to Reiss (1976, p. 164),

> the participant-run courtship institution leads to values and pressures that promote the acceptance of permissiveness . . . , [and] to the extent that a particular group has an autonomous, free courtship system, to that extent their likelihood of accepting high degrees of sexual permissiveness is increased.

The level of sexual permissiveness in a given courtship system will vary from group to group according to the general level of permissiveness prevalent in each. For example, among the Mormons, whose religious, family, and educational institutions show a very low tolerance of sexual permissiveness, community influences can be expected to strongly inhibit any permissive tendencies which might develop in their courtship system. Again, the extent to which such "outside" adult-centered influences are felt inside the courtship system varies considerably among different religious, ethnic, and social class groups. In middle-class, urban, secular circles the greater autonomy of young people from adult and traditional social controls would likely promote higher levels of permissiveness, as compared to, for instance, a rural, Mexican-American community where strong Catholic traditions and strict family codes still prevail.

Changes in premarital sexual attitudes need to be seen in the larger context of changing values and beliefs. During the 1960s there emerged a set of values, beliefs, and related norms often referred to as the New Morality, which gives considerable impetus to the trend in premarital sexual permissiveness (Reiss, 1976). This New Morality assumes a situational ethics which says that one should judge human actions in terms of the extent to which such actions promote love between the actors. This code would justify intimate premarital relations between a young man and a young woman, including sexual relations under affectional conditions. Premarital sex would be viewed as right and good, providing the presence of genuine love or affection. Thus, in recent years, "permissiveness with affection" has emerged as a new sex code among young people who generally subscribe to the New Morality. Reiss (1976, p. 157) found that for American girls and young women particularly, love and affection have become important justifications for premarital sex. Most studies show very little indication of any major trend toward sexual permissiveness without affection (Hunt, 1974; Davis, 1973). However—though empirical evidence is lacking—one has the impression that permissiveness without affection may be increasing in recent years, such as may exist among divorced men and women in their late 20s and 30s.

PREMARITAL SEXUAL BEHAVIOR

In examining the actual incidence of premarital sexual behavior in America, studies show two quite distinct periods of marked increase in the 20th century. The first occurred about the time of World War I and shortly thereafter; the second began in the mid-1960s. There is evidence of little increase in premarital sex during the four decades or so between the early 1920s and the mid-1960s. (Bowman & Spanier, 1978, p. 92). Both periods of rapid increase were times of rapid social change and considerable upheavel in major social institutions.

A study done in the 1930s, comparing premarital coitus rates of men and women by the decade of their birth, gives an indication of the increases in the post–World War I period (Terman, 1938). For males born before 1890, 49.4 percent had engaged in premarital sex as compared to 67.4 percent of those born between 1900 and 1909. For females born before

1890 only 13.5 percent had premarital sexual experience as compared to 48.8 percent of those born between 1900 and 1910 (Terman. 1938, p. 321). After reviewing available data, Reiss (1976, p. 183) concludes that the proportion of females who were nonvirginal at marriage had doubled in the period (1915–1920) from 25 percent to 50 percent. In the second period (1965–1970) the proportion of nonvirginal females at marriage increased "from 50 percent to a current rate of about 75 percent" (Reiss, 1976, p. 183). These and other findings suggest that, with changing sexual attitudes and codes, women are in the process of catching up with men, who have been freer from restrictions longer.

A review of many studies of premarital sexual behavior reveals some key findings. Among the studies reviewed are those by Kinsey (1948; 1953), Ehrmann (1959), Reiss (1960; 1976), Christensen (1966), Levitt and Klassen (1974), Zelnick and Kantner (1972), Simon, Berger, and Gagnon (1972), Carnes (1973), Sorensen (1973), Hunt (1974), and Walsh et al. (1976). The following represent some of the main findings from these studies.

1. While premarital sex is increasing among American women, there are still significant differences between the rates for males and females, with the males still the more active. The woman's sex partner is more apt to be someone she is in love with and to whom she feels a serious commitment. Males generally have more sex partners than women do before marriage; and men report fewer guilty feelings than women do about having premarital sex (Carnes, 1973).

2. There are significant differences between black and white people in premarital sex behavior. Blacks begin sex earlier, and rates of premarital sex are higher for both black men and women than for white men and women (Zelnick & Kantner, 1972; Levitt & Klassen, 1974).

3. While some earlier studies show that premarital sex began sooner and rates were higher among the lower social classes (Kinsey, 1948; 1953; Ehrmann, 1959), other, more recent studies suggest that the rates among the more educated middle classes are on the increase and may soon catch up with those of the lower classes (Levitt & Klassen, 1974; Simon, Berger, & Gagnon, 1972).

4. Most studies indicate the importance of love and a feeling of commitment between most premarital sex partners. This is especially true for women, who emphasize affection as a precondition for sexual relations. Also, most women have few premarital sex partners; a great many women experience premarital sex only with a fiancé.

5. Premarital sex is not only on the increase among teenagers, it is also starting at earlier ages. However, sexually experienced young women are not generally promiscuous. One nationwide study showed that at least half have intercourse only with the men they intend to marry (Zelnick & Kantner, 1972).

6. Despite liberalized attitudes and sex codes, and despite the importance of affection as a precondition for most premarital sex, there is still evidence of some guilt, regrets, and qualms on the part of many young

people—especially females—who engage in premarital sex (Soronsen, 1973; Hunt, 1974).

7. The more religious a person is, the less likely he or she is to engage in premarital sexual intercourse. The highest proportion of youth with premarital sexual experience is found among those who subscribe to no religion at all (Zelnick & Kantner, 1972; Spanier, 1973).

8. A major increase in premarital sex occurred in the late 1960s and early 1970s. Walsh (1976) found that the proportion of unmarried college students who had experienced premarital sex during college jumped from 36 percent for the class of 1971 to 69 percent for the class of 1974. Bauman and Wilson (1974) found the proportion of college students who had experienced premarital sex in 1968 to be 56 percent for men and 46 percent for women. Four years later the percentages had increased to 73 percent for both men and women. In a national sample of adults, Hunt (1974) found that 95 percent of the men and 81 percent of the women had experienced premarital sex.

Summing up, we can say that in 20th-century America there were two periods of great increase in premarital sexual relations; the first occurring around the time of World War I and the second originating in the mid-1960s. These increases have occurred during periods of changing sexual attitudes and norms, which today are approaching a normative position of approval of individual choice in sexual matters, a "legitimation of sexual choice" as Reiss (1976, p. 183) defines it. There is more open discussion of sex today, and taboos regarding sex in books and mass media have all but departed. In fact, books, magazines, and movies now display explicit sex in ways that would not have been tolerated a generation ago. And the joys and healthiness of sex are extolled by such popular writers as Comfort and Hefner. Today an increasing number of American youth believe they have as much right to choose their own sexual style of life as they do to choose their religion and politics.

THE COURSE OF PREMARITAL SEXUAL INVOLVEMENT

The foregoing discussion shows that more American young people are becoming sexually involved before marriage, and that certain changes in attitudes and sex codes tend to sanction this premarital sexual involvement. Under what conditions or circumstances does such involvement generally occur? How long and how well do a young man and a young woman generally have to know each other before becoming sexually intimate?

Blood and Blood (1978, pp. 41–42) found that in the dating phases of courtship young people are apt to differ greatly in their readiness to become emotionally involved. For those who are not overly inhibited, the sexual aspects of dating are apt to develop rather spontaneously.

For those more inhibited, often from families where demonstrations of affection are infrequent, it may be more difficult to respond affectionately to a dating partner. One function of dating thus can be to help one overcome inhibitions and learn how to be more affectionate and responsive.

Komarovsky (1974), in a study of male college students, found that there was a significant relationship between self-disclosure and premarital sexual involvement. Those men who were willing and able to reveal more about themselves—their feelings, their personalities—to their female partners tended to become both more affectionately and more sexually involved. Their female partners were the chief confidantes of these men. Thus there is evidence that premarital sexual involvement appears to be related to one's ability to disclose one's inner self to a member of the opposite sex.

Readiness for premarital sexual involvement is naturally related to the prevailing beliefs and norms of reference groups, and conformity to these norms affects how one feels about oneself. In conservative groups with premarital abstinence norms, women who refrain from premarital sex generally have high self-esteem, while those who engage in sex relations tend to have low self-esteem. On the other hand, in liberal circles where premarital sexual involvement is approved, those women who achieve the desired involvement have higher self-esteem than those who are less able to achieve such involvement (Perleman, 1974, p. 472).

As dating continues, a couple normally progress sooner or later toward greater emotional and physical intimacy. In his study of people who had completed their courtship and gotten married, Hunt (1974) found that in recent years petting has become for an increasing number of Americans merely a stage in progressive sexual involvement. In his nationwide survey Hunt (1974) found significant differences in the extent of male and female premarital sexual involvement. The typical man who participated in sex relations before marriage had had six different partners, while a slight majority of the sexually experienced women had had only one partner. The longer the man or woman remained single, the greater the number of sex partners. The male–female differences in premarital sexual involvement reflect in part the fact that women marry earlier, and men therefore have two or three more years of being single. In general, the earlier they marry the fewer the number of premarital sexual partners single men and women have had; and for a woman there is a greater probability that the sex partner is the man she will marry.

Men and women seem to differ also in the degree of emotional or affectional build-up needed before they are ready to become sexually involved. Most men appear to require less emotional preparation than do women. Burgess and Wallin (1953, p. 330) found that about 45 percent of the engaged couples in their sample had premarital sexual relations with each other. About one half of the engaged men had also had premarital sex with someone else, while only about one eighth of the engaged women had become sexually involved with anyone else. By the 1970s there were indications of a significant increase in the number of women becoming sexually involved with other men in addition to their fiancés. Hunt (1974, p. 153) found that 43 percent of the engaged women reported having premarital sex with their fiancés only, but another 35 percent reported having premarital sex with men other than their fiancés.

It is generally true that the longer a relationship lasts the more intimate it tends to become. Intimacy is progressive: The longer a couple go together, the greater the likelihood they will become sexually intimate. Burgess and Wallin (1953) found that 50 percent of the couples who had been engaged for more than 15 months had had premarital sex, while only 39 percent of those engaged less than 9 months had gone this far. How extensively one participates in dating also appears to be related to the probability of physical intimacy before marriage. Bell and Chaskes (1970) found that girls who started their dating careers in their early teens were more apt to engage in premarital sex than those who started later. Also, the more men they dated and had gone steady with the more likely they were to have gone all the way at some time.

SOME POSSIBLE CONSEQUENCES OF PREMARITAL SEXUAL INVOLVEMENT

While premarital sexual relationships may bring physical and emotional gratification, they also entail various risks—physical, social, and psychological. Physically, there is the ever-present risk of an unwanted pregnancy, and the possibility of contracting a venereal disease. Psychologically, many who engage in premarital sex may still feel varying degrees of guilt or anxiety. Socially, the consequences of premarital sex on the total relationship of the couple appears to be harmful to some couples and helpful to others. Let us examine briefly some of the possible effects of premarital sexual relations.

Potential physical consequences

Premarital pregnancy. For a couple whose relationship has advanced to the point of sexual relations, there is the continual risk of pregnancy. Over the years, in fact, this has been a fairly common consequence. Kinsey (1953) found that almost 20 percent of sexually experienced women had had at least one premarital pregnancy. More recently, Bower (1975) found that about 25 percent of sexually active single young women, mostly students, had experienced at least one accidental pregnancy. The existence of more reliable contraceptives and more widespread knowledge about birth control apparently has not significantly reduced the incidence of premarital pregnancies. As Bowman and Spanier (1978, p. 107) emphasize:

It is not sufficient to point out that pregnancy is a possible unintended consequence of sexual intercourse. We must emphasize that among unmarried persons it is an extremely common consequence.

A nationwide study in the 1970s showed that about 80 percent of the sexually experienced, single females aged 15 to 19 had sometimes engaged in sex relations without using any contraceptive, and that about 3 in 10 of these teenagers had become pregnant (Shah, Zelnick, & Kantner, 1975). Studies on various college campuses indicate that between 30 and 65 percent of sexually experienced female students either used no contraceptive at all, or used one of the least effective methods. Why don't more sexually active youth use available birth control methods? Based on many years of premarital counseling, Bowman and Spanier (1978, p. 107) have come to this conclusion:

> Generalizing, we can make the conclusion that many young women feel that it is awkward, presumptious, and unromantic to be contraceptively prepared for sexual intercourse. In short, sexual intercourse is something that is supposed to happen "naturally" in a romantic context. . . . A woman does not want it to appear that she was presuming to have coitus, even though she perhaps was.

There are, of course, a variety of reasons why premarital sex may take place without adequate contraceptive protection, as many studies show. Among the reasons are (1) lack of knowledge as to what contraceptive methods are safe and effective and how to get them; (2) objections to contraceptive use on religious or moral grounds; (3) denial that any contraceptive method really works; (4) desire for evidence of one's virility or fertility; (5) immaturity and irresponsibility; (6) greater sexual pleasure without using contraceptives; (7) availability of abortion services; and (8) the feeling that "it can't happen to us."

When an unmarried woman becomes pregnant, she has three alternatives: to get married and have her baby; to have an abortion; or to have her baby even though she is unmarried. In the last case, she may either keep the baby or place it for adoption. An investigation by Jaffe and Dryfoos (1976) of unmarried adolescents aged 15 to 19 who become pregnant showed that 14 percent of the pregnancies ended in marriage, 38 percent in abortion, 20 percent in miscarriages, and 29 percent in out-of-wedlock birth.

While the heaviest burden of premarital pregnancy is on the female, there are also potentially serious consequences for the male. He may be faced with the expenses for the abortion. He may face a "shot-gun" marriage, or at least marriage sooner than planned. He may be faced with child support costs. If the couple's relationship had progressed to a really serious stage (such as engagement) before the pregnancy, the problem may be solved by moving up the wedding date, though this can still mean serious disruption of their educational or occupational plans, as well as distress for their families. A more serious situation is that in which the couple had no plans to marry and are not well suited to each other, but are pressured into a premature marriage to camouflage the pregnancy and give the child a legal father. The potential here for damage to the man, the woman, and the child is great. Just how many speeded-up, forced, or premature marriages take place each year is unknown, but some evidence suggests they may be numerous. Christensen (1966) found that in a sample of married people, about 20 percent of all the first births were the result of pregnancies that must have occurred before the wedding. In 1977, the Department of Health and Human Services estimated that about 20 percent of first babies were born to women who had been married fewer than eight months. When babies born out of wedlock are added, it is estimated that close to one third of all first babies were conceived premaritally or extramaritally.

Risk of venereal disease. There are a number of common infections of the genital tract which may be transmitted from infected persons to their sex partners, commonly called venereal diseases. Three of the most serious are syphilis, gonorrhea, and venereal herpes. Of these, syphilis is the most dangerous disease. Syphilis can be cured in the early stages of infection, but if left untreated it can spread to virtually every system of the body, and may even lead to death. Gonorrhea, while less dangerous, infects the genitourinary tract and may result in sterility. It may also enter the blood stream and cause inflammation of the joints and arthritis.

Although less well known than syphilis or gonorrhea, genital herpes is another serious venereal disease that is on the increase today. It is caused by a virus known as Herpes Simplex Type 2. Symptoms, which may show up within a week after contact with an infected person, consist of sores and blisters on the genitals, similar to cold sores and fever blisters. Herpes infection triples the chance of miscarriage in women, may cause brain damage or even death to babies carried to full term, and may be related to cancer of the cervix (Subak–Sharpe, 1975). As yet there is no known cure for this disease, and outbreaks may go on in an infected person for months or even years.

By mid-20th century it had been thought that penicillin would bring venereal diseases under control, and in fact the disease rates declined until about 1970, when an unexpected upturn occurred. This trend reversal was due partly to some strains of gonorrhea becoming partially resistant to penicillin, partly to the onset of Herpes Simplex, and partly to the increase in sexual activity in recent years. The only contraceptive that is effective at all in preventing venereal disease is the condom, and fewer men are using the condom these days due to the increasing use of the pill and IUDs by women. The World Health Organization now ranks gonorrhea as the second most prevalent communicable disease after the common cold (Bowman & Spanier, 1978, p. 110). The United States Public Health Service figures for 1974 showed that there were 469 cases of gonorrhea and 38 cases of syphilis per 100,000 population in the United States (Blood & Blood, 1978, p. 51).

Possible psychological and interpersonal consequences

The possible psychological or emotional consequences of premarital sexual intimacy are more difficult to assess than the possible physical effects. Some efforts have been made in this direction, however. From a study of college students in Iowa, Reiss (1976) found that the greater the degree of sexual intimacy, the more likely the students were to feel guilty about their behavior. This was true for both men and women, but especially so for women. More than twice as many women as men reported feeling guilt after engaging in sexual relations. Guilt was universally felt by those who had violated their own sexual standards. Even among those espousing the most permissive sexual standards, a majority reported having felt guilt after engaging in sexual relations. It is possible that verbalized permissive or liberal philosophies may mask deeper inhibitions which may be related to earlier family or religious teachings (Reiss 1976).

How may premarital sex affect the total relationship between a young man and a young woman? Does this full physical intimacy strengthen or weaken their relationship? Does it increase the probability they will get married? If they do marry, does their previous sexual intimacy affect their marital adjustment in any significant way?

In their study of engaged couples, Burgess and Wallin (1953) found that those who had become sexually intimate were more likely to end in a broken engagement than were those who abstained. It should be kept in mind that this study was done several decades ago when premarital sex, even among engaged couples, was widely viewed as deviant behavior. Other studies show that the quality of the relationship, including the intensity of their love, their commitment to each other, and their mutual agreement about entering into a physical relationship, are all important in determining how premarital sex will affect a couple. For example, sexual intimacy forced on a reluctant or unready partner can certainly hurt or even destroy a relationship. Kirkpatrick and Kanin (1957) found that many university women became angry or offended when their male partners pushed aggressively for sexual intercourse. They felt anger and disillusionment toward the man and guilt or shame for their own involvement. Some engagements were broken off when the man pushed the woman faster and further than she wished to go.

On the other side, there is evidence that under certain favorable conditions premarital sex may have more positive effects on interpersonal relations. Kanin and Davidson (1972), in a study of college students, found that where the partners professed deep love for each other, the effect of premarital sex was generally beneficial, intensifying their love still further. It is, however, difficult to distinguish cause and effect here. Were these young people essentially rationalizing or justifying their behavior after the fact? Studies show that both those who engage in premarital sex and those who abstain until marriage tend to justify their behavior (Burgess & Wallin, 1953). Ard (1974) found that couples who abstained from premarital sex believed strongly that having waited until marriage for full sexual intimacy was definitely beneficial to their marriage.

Blood and Blood (1978. p. 60) think that the affects of premarital intercourse depend on the quality of the relationship between the partners. The more loving the relationship, the greater the chance that premarital intimacy will be beneficial.

Beyond various possible effects of premarital sex on the premarital relationship, does having engaged in premarital sex help or hurt a couple who go on to marriage? Evidence here is varied and inconclusive. Terman (1938) found greater marital happiness among couples who abstained until marriage as compared to those who had engaged in premarital sex. In a comparison of happily married couples and divorced couples Locke (1951) found that more divorced couples had engaged in premarital sexual relations than had happily married couples. Burgess and Wallin (1953) found that the more frequently a couple had engaged in sexual relations before marriage the lower their subsequent marital satisfaction. Perhaps the negative effects of premarital sex were greater when these studies were made than they are since the liberalization of sexual attitudes and codes in recent years.

After reviewing the available recent evidence, Blood and Blood (1978, p. 61) conclude: "As of this writing, there is no firm evidence that becoming involved sexually before marriage generally benefits the marriage, but on the other hand, most of the negative effects seem to have disappeared."

Reiss (1976) observes that much of the research and analysis of premarital sex until quite recently, has emphasized the "costs" and neglected the "rewards," such as physical pleasure, emotional satisfaction, or any benefits in general sexual abilities. Today a more scientific and objective approach indicates that there are a variety of types of premarital sexual relationships with different meanings and consequences. As Reiss (1976, pp. 283–84) expresses it:

> In short, we are now aware of the fact that there is no single type of premarital sexualty, and there is no single set of consequences that follow from premarital intercourse. Much depends on the quality of the relationship and on the values of the participants. Very few people today contend that all those who engage in premarital coitus will have poor marriages, for it is apparent that the variety of people and relationships involved make any one outcome most difficult to predict.

More studies of contemporary couples are needed, focusing on the varieties of premarital sexual relationships and the possible mixes of effects, both positive and negative.

PREMARITAL LIVING TOGETHER

It is appropriate to discuss premarital living together, or cohabitation in this chapter dealing with premarital sexual behavior and attitudes. However, present treatment will be limited since living together will also be discussed in a later chapter on alternatives to marriage. Cohabitation may be defined in several ways. It may be seen as a temporary matter of convenience that appeals to those who have no present interest in marriage. For others, it may be defined as a "trial marriage," a testing period to see if they are suited for marriage. For a very few, cohabitation may be viewed as a permanent alternative to marriage. There is evidence to suggest that while living together is on the increase as a substitute for marriage, a good deal of present-day cohabitation among the unmarried—especially among college students—is really a premarital relationship rather than a more permanent alternative to marriage itself. Population reports for 1979 show that many more women are remaining single in their early 20s as compared to those reported in the 1960 and 1970 censuses (U.S. Bureau of the Census, 1980b). However, the 1979 figures also show that these young women are virtually as likely to get married as were those in the earlier group, but at a later age. (See Table 4–1). While it is likely that many of the single young women reported in the 1970 census are cohabiting, the census data suggest that they were delaying marriage, not rejecting it.

In the context of deepening emotional and physical involvement of a couple before marriage, let us consider briefly some recent trends in living together, and the possible significance of these trends for those involved.

There are no comprehensive statistics on how many couples are living together outside of marriage, but evidence suggests that the number is large and growing larger each year. United States census data gives some indication of the incidence on the national level. In the 1960 census, only about 17,000 people reported that they were unmarried and living with a member of the opposite sex. In the 1970 census, about 143,000 people reported the same situation (Glick, 1977). Census data for 1976 showed that unrelated adults of the opposite sex who were sharing quarters represented about 1 percent of all household heads (U.S. Bureau of

Table 4–1

Percentage of single never-married women, by age, 1960, 1970, and 1979	Age	1960	1970	1979
	20–24	28.4	35.8	49.4
	25–29	10.5	10.5	19.6
	30–34	6.9	6.2	9.5
Source: U.S. Bureau of the Census, *Current Population Reports* (Series P–20, No. 349), 1980.	35–39	6.1	5.4	6.5
	40–44	6.1	4.9	5.1
	45–54	7.0	4.9	4.4

the Census, 1977). It has been estimated that less than 1 percent of all couples who are living together are unmarried (Glick, 1977, p. 12).

A nationwide study of selective service records of young American men who registered between 1962 and 1972 showed that about 18 percent had lived with a woman outside of marriage for a period of six months or longer (Clayton & Voss, 1977, p. 275). Another nationwide study of American women in the mid-1970s found that about 3 percent of the 18,000 women surveyed had lived with a man outside of marriage (Bell, 1979).

Many of the best studies of cohabitation have been localized, often centering on university campuses. One such study in 1971 found that about 20 percent of the 762 students queried at a large urban university in the Northeast were then living together with a member of the opposite sex (Arafat & Yorburg, 1973). Another study at a large southwestern university found that about 29 percent of male and about 18 percent of female students from a sample of 300 had lived together with a member of the opposite sex (Hudson & Henze, 1973). These and other studies suggest that there probably are not many important regional differences in cohabitation.

These increases in the incidence of cohabitation before marriage seem to be a logical accompaniment of the permissive trend in codes for sexual behavior. That this kind of cohabitation should be widespread among college students on large secular college campuses is not surprising. Many students have become disenchanted with traditional dating patterns, and some with conventional marriage. Also, many universities have now removed the once prevalent regulations which had restricted relations between male and female students—the old *in loco parentis* model—on campus, thus enabling students who are so inclined to live together. Other factors contributing to increases in cohabitation on campuses are the greater availability of contraceptives and abortion services.

There is evidence that personal motivations for living together may vary considerably between men and women. Arafat and Yorburg (1973) found that 36 percent of the male students said their primary motivation was sex, while few female students admitted to this motive. About 30 percent of the women said their primary motivation was marriage, while few men gave this as a reason for cohabiting. Evidence from a number of sources shows that for both men and women some of the most frequently given reasons for living together are strong emotional attachment, a desire for security, and a need for companionship (Bowman & Spanier, 1978, p. 40).

College campus studies show that many students appear to drift into cohabitation, often without being sure of their original motives. In a study conducted at Cornell University, Macklin (1972) found that once couples had become involved sexually they often began staying together one night at a time at first, then began spending weekends together, and sooner or later added one or more nights during the week. This frequently ended in one of them, most often the woman, moving in with the other. The woman usually keeps her own living quarters, where she receives her mail and eats some meals. This gives her a refuge if things do not go well with her partner, and also helps conceal the cohabitation arrangement, especially from her parents. About one half of the women felt their relationships were strong and exclusive, based on affection and mutual respect. Another one third, however, said they were still interested in dating other men. Many of the women thought they might ultimately marry their live-in partners, but were unwilling yet to make a definite commitment. While most felt their relationships to be rewarding and maturing, many also admitted to having problems. A major emotional problem was the tendency for one or both partners to become overinvolved or overdependent on the relationship. Some women felt trapped, and some felt they were being used by their partners. Nearly two thirds of these women reported having sexual problems. Fluctuation in sexual interest was most frequently mentioned, followed by lack of satisfaction in sexual intercourse, and fear of pregnancy. Despite these problems, about three fourths of the women reported that their relationships were satisfying sexually. This study—and most other campus studies—show that relationships with parents are a real problem for cohabitators, especially for women. More than two thirds of the Cornell women tried to conceal from their parents the fact that they were living with a man. Guilty feelings over deceiving their parents, and fear of the consequence should their cohabitation be discovered, were commonly reported.

Our discussion thus far has focused mainly on temporary or convenient cohabitation. Just a word now on cohabitation as a preliminary test of marital compatibility. Some evidence suggests that while many young cohabitators may not be explicitly looking forward to marriage, they may be doing so implicitly or covertly. In such cases, one of the results or by-products of living together is a kind of testing of the couple's possible marital compatibility. "Living together is a kind of quasi-marital experience, a preview of what marriage would be like" (Blood & Blood, 1978, p. 76).

It has been argued earlier that the more thoroughly a couple know each other before marriage, the fewer the surprises and adjustment problems they are likely to encounter after marriage. If this is true, cohabitation may function for some as a new screening device to help reduce marital mismatches, and perhaps help reduce the divorce rate. There is insufficient evidence at present to know whether this is true or not. Olday (1977) found that cohabitation was not a more effective screening device than traditional courtship patterns in mate selection. Newcomb (1979), after reviewing all empirical research available on premarital cohabitation, concluded that cohabitation does not seem to increase the quality of the mate-selection process. More studies are needed before we can answer the question of whether or not premarital cohabitation prevents many marital failures.

Before living together can ever become an established and fully accepted part of the American courtship system, our emancipation from traditional premarital sexual taboos will have to advance much further and become more uniform throughout the land. Given the present position of a great many of our religious leaders and other moral custodians, such uniformity is not likely to come about in the immediate future. This means that premarital cohabitation will continue to be looked upon as deviant and morally unacceptable to a large proportion of Americans in spite of its prevalence in secular circles.

Further discussion of cohabitation will be left for Chapter 11, in which it will be considered as an actual substitute for marriage.

THE FUTURE: TRENDS, ISSUES, AND IMPLICATIONS OF PREMARITAL SEX FOR INDIVIDUAL CHOICE

There can be little doubt that America has been experiencing a trend toward greater premarital sexual permissiveness since the 1960s. The large majority of those who have accepted the permissive standards, however, have not accepted sexual promiscuity; rather, they have come to associate sex with affection and personal commitment to one's partner. It should also be emphasized that the permissive trend is far from universal in America, and that many traditionally conservative groups are still strongly resisting the increases in premarital sexual activity and the permissive code which sanctions it. However, nationwide surveys show that in the 1970s the percentages of Americans approving premarital sex increased gradually in a wide range of age, educational, racial, and religious groups. (Singh, 1980).

It seems that America is still divided on the issue of premarital sex, and that this schism is not likely to be resolved in the immediate future. There are those who still cling to the traditional-sacred value orientations associated with the Puritan and Victorian eras of our past, who abhor premarital sex as sinful and immoral; and there are those who hold the most modern-secular value orientations, who see premarital sex as good and as a matter of private individual choice. Between these extremes lie various intermediate value positions.

Rubin (1965) identified six-value-positions on premarital sex ranging along a continuum as follows.

1. *Traditional repressive asceticism* defines premarital sex as completely wrong. This traditional orientation is still reflected in the laws of many states which make premarital sex illegal, with fines up to $500 and prison sentences of up to three years for violations of the law.

2. *Enlightened asceticism* opposes the slackening of traditional sex codes on a rational basis. The argument here is that premarital sex can have harmful consequences for individuals involved and for the whole society. Sexual controls are needed to safeguard American society against the

softness and weakness that can result from lack of discipline and overindulgence. Premarital self-control is advocated to help prevent these negative consequences.

3. *Humanistic liberalism* holds that morality inheres in one's responsibility for the consequences of one's actions, rather than in the commission or omission of the act itself. The position of "permissiveness with affection and commitment" comes close to this viewpoint.

4. *Humanistic radicalism* also emphasizes a concern for the human being, but sees a need for basic changes which would free the individual from those traditional sexual restraints which induce guilt among those who engage in premarital sex. Sex, in or out of marriage, should be viewed as a natural act, not a moral issue.

5. *The fun morality* takes the view that sex is pleasurable and that the more pleasurable and guilt-free sex one has the more psychologically healthy one is apt to be. Thus premarital sex is advocated for well-informed and well-adjusted people. This fun orientation is essentially that advocated in magazines such as *Playboy*.

6. *Sexual anarchy* represents the end of the continuum opposite traditional repressive asceticism. It advocates the removal of all sexual taboos and controls, with full and universal availability of sex, the only restriction being the prohibition of sexual violence.

The distribution of these various value orientations among the American population is unknown. Neither Rubin nor anyone else has as yet attempted to find out what percent of Americans accept each of these six positions. After reviewing available evidence, Adams (1975, p. 207) estimates that humanistic liberalism is probably the most prevalent, followed by traditional asceticism. These would be followed by the fun morality and enlightened asceticism. Sexual anarchy and humanistic radicalism would have few advocates.

SOME IMPLICATIONS OF PREMARITAL SEX FOR AMERICAN YOUTH

Whether strict prohibitions against premarital sex were ever a "cultural universal" in America, even in Victorian times, is debatable. However, there is no question that no such universal prohibition exists today. As we have just seen, attitudes and values vary greatly on the subject. It may be argued, as Adams (1975, pp. 207–212) has, that premarital sex has now become a "cultural alternative" in American society. A cultural alternative is some practice or belief on which the people have divided viewpoints and feelings, which is certainly true in the case of premarital sex.

What are some of the implications of this cultural alternative situation for American youth? Do the divided viewpoints and debates create problems or dilemmas for young people as they become involved in dating

Are today's premarital sexual guidelines adequate?

Julie Heifitz

and courtship? For one thing, the often conflicting positions of parents and peers can be a source of strain and anxiety for many youths. The value-position of parents may cause one to feel guilty if one engages in premarital sex, while peer group pressures may make one feel guilty or old fashioned if one does not. Also, where older norms and guidelines have been rejected by youth, often there have not as yet emerged any clear-cut new norms to replace those discarded. This can induce feelings of insecurity and vulnerability to exploitation. Blau (1964, p. 80) points out the possible sexual dilemma facing a young woman in such a normatively ill-defined situation. She may possibly increase her young man's love for her by granting him premarital sexual favors; but by so doing she may depreciate their value and their power to produce a deeper commitment or attachment. Adams (1975, pp. 208–209) notes that the problem of insincerity is especially acute in the area of premarital sex.

> How can the female know *for sure* that the male's intentions are serious? The answer is simple: she can't. She can only take, or avoid taking, a calculated risk—without knowing whether either her indulgence or her abstinence will increase or decrease his interest. (Adams, 1974, p. 208)

Another aspect of the problem facing American youth is that the widespread publicity given the so-called sexual revolution has made it appear that American society has moved completely away from the traditional, premarital abstinence norms all the way to the opposite position of premarital indulgence. Hadden and Borgatta (1969, p. 219) describe how it is possible for the changes to be so overstated or exaggerated on college campuses that students get the impression that premarital sex is now completely normative. Students may read in a college newspaper that "sex on the campus is so commonplace as to be a part of the mores." This kind of statement does not distinguish between permissive patterns and normative patterns at another level (Hadden & Borgatta, 1969, p. 219). Such "indulgence norms," while likely as out of step with actual behavior as the older, total abstinence norms, can make young people feel deviant or "not with it" if they are not sexually active.

On a more positive note, the changing premarital sex codes probably have helped remove some of the strains associated with the discrepancy between verbal norms and actual behavior which often existed before and the hypocrisy inherent in such situations. For example, years ago a man who publicly espoused abstinence might visit "a woman of light virtue" on the sly. At least behavior is more open now. And, in this same vein, the new open orientation toward sex has meant a decline of the old double standard of higher morality expected of women than of men, often associated with the Victorian era. Young women now are insisting more and more on equal rights in the matter of sex. Reiss (1976, p. 185) sums up the current situation this way:

> In the sexual sphere we have moved away from a formal culturally decreed sexual code of abstinence and an informal double standard to a variety

of sexual codes from which individuals must learn to choose. The element of risk and mistake is much higher, but the potential satisfaction is also much higher. . . . It is most fundamentally the search . . . for equity in all spheres that has altered . . . our sexual relations. We are developing new and more flexible male-female role models both in and outside of marriage, and this is leading to a reaffirmation of the value of an intimate dyadic two-person relationship in and outside of marriage.

It would seem that we are moving toward a position of individual choice in the matter of premarital sex. As we have seen, the guidelines for choosing are not always clear, with the result that the individual has the burden of choice thrust on him or her more than ever before. There certainly are risks here, as well as potentials for personal satisfaction and growth. There are a number of different value-positions or "cultural alternatives" upon which to base one's choice, but many of the ramifications for the individual in choosing one alternative over another are not as yet clearly discernible.

CHAPTER 5

Selecting a mate

Every human society has some kind of mate selection procedure which functions to sort out males and females as marriage partners. The methods and processes for doing this—generally called courtship—differ from society to society, and from time to time in a given society.

Since American society has opted to let its young people select their own marriage partners, a number of questions and issues loom large, such as what criteria to use, how to go about finding suitable prospects, and how best to make the final selection. It can be argued that the single most important choice an individual makes in his or her lifetime is the selection of a marriage partner. We prize highly the right and the freedom to make our own decisions; with this, however, goes the heavy responsibility of making sound, wise choices. Throughout history, most societies have not considered young people mature or wise enough to make this all-important choice themselves. With current high divorce rates and evidence of a good deal of marital discontent, it can be argued that choices made by many American youth are neither sound nor wise. On the other hand, the question of whether parents could do a better job of selecting suitable and compatible mates for their children is debatable, as will be seen below.

BARGAINING AND THE MARRIAGE MARKET

Hypothetically, any single adult in America has the freedom to approach any other single adult of the opposite sex as a prospective marriage partner. There is, however, a big gap between this hypothetical marriage market and the actual pool of eligibles for any given individual. Combinations of personal, social, cultural, and demographic factors always limit the field of possible candidates. All societies impose numerous restrictions and requirements which limit the field of eligibles. Family, friends, community, church, and so forth exert pressures on the young woman or man to make a suitable choice from their various points of view.

As Goode (1970, p. 8) points out, our mate-selection process operates very much like a market system.

> *All* courtship systems are market or exchange systems. They differ from one another with respect to *who* does the buying and selling, which characteristics are more or less valuable in that market, and how open or explicit the bargaining is.

Each candidate brings various things of value into the bargaining process. Personal qualities, such as love and mutual attraction, are very important in our conjugally oriented marriage system where the husband-wife relationship has primacy, as compared to a kinship-oriented family system where economic and social class characteristics would be more important in the bargaining. Such economic and social factors do, however, affect the bargaining process in America by affecting the actual pool of eligible candidates, as we shall see shortly.

DEFINING THE FIELD OF ELIGIBLES

The pool of candidates eligible as marriage partners are defined in most societies in terms of such factors as age, race, ethnicity, religion, education, and social class or caste. Thus for a given individual many categories of persons of the opposite sex are screened out of the eligible pool because they do not belong to a given race or ethnic group, a particular social class, a religious group, or an age group. To illustrate, an upper-class young lady from Beacon Hill in Boston would be unlikely to consider an unskilled Italian immigrant worker from South Boston as an eligible; nor would a devout Catholic be likely to consider an avowed atheist. In courtship young people learn to view each other through an initial screening process which delineates the field of acceptable eligibles according to the groups they belong to and the norms and traditions of those groups. True—as will be discussed more fully later—for many young Americans today the field of eligibles is expanding as some of the older restrictions are weakening under the impact of equalitarian and individualistic values. But for most, the traditional restrictions and limitations still operate to a significant degree.

Accordingly we find in our society, as in others, various *endogamous* and *exogamous* norms or rules of mate selection. An *endogamy* rule is a requirement that a marriage partner be selected from *within* a particular group or category to which one belongs, such as one's racial or religious group. An *exogamy* rule requires that one's marriage partner be selected from *outside* a certain group or category one belongs to, such as one's close kin. This particular exogamous rule—the well-known incest taboo— is virtually universal. Exogamous norms encourage alliances between certain groups, such as kinship groups or clans, while endogamous norms discourage alliances between other groups, such as races or religious groups.

In a sense, the field of eligible candidates is circumscribed or bounded by the rules of endogamy on one side and by those of exogamy on the other. When one of these rules is ignored, a misalliance has taken place from the viewpoint of that given society. In societies where marriages of sons and daughters are arranged by parents, few such misalliances can take place. In societies such as modern America, where the individual has great freedom to make his or her own choice and secular trends are challenging traditional values and norms, marriages across religious, class, and even racial lines are more likely to take place.

Let us now look in more detail at some of the specific social and demographic factors that influence the process of mate selection.

The incest taboo

The incest taboo excludes close relatives from the field of eligible marriage partners. This prohibition applies almost universally to members of the immediate or nuclear family (forbidding marriage between siblings and between parent and child); but in many societies it also extends to other blood relatives, such as cousins, aunts, and uncles, and may extend to various in-laws and others related by marriage or adoption. Many attempts have been made to explain the pervasiveness of the incest taboo. The Freudian concept of the Oedipus complex, which emphasizes the need to repress sexual attraction between parent and child; the genetic concern that marriage between close blood relatives increases the probability of defects in offspring; and the confusion in family statuses that would result from intermarriage between parent and child. Davis (1960, p. 401) points out that if a father were to marry his own daughter, their child "would be a brother of his own mother, i.e., the son of his own sister; a stepson of his own grandmother; possibly a brother of his own uncle; and certainly a grandson of his own father."

Exchange theory offers a further explanation against incestuous marriages. According to the anthropologist Levi-Strauss (1956), the incest taboo reinforces the interdependent ties between separate families. The incest taboo states that families can only marry between each other and not inside themselves. And futhermore, the taboo implies a reciprocity or exchange between the family of the bride and that of the groom. "It means: I will give up my daughter or sister if my neighbor will give up his also. . . . The fact that I can obtain a wife is, in the last analysis, the consequence of the fact that a brother or a father has given up a woman." (Levi-Strauss, 1949, p. 75).

Building on the original ideas of Levi-Strauss, Scanzoni and Scanzoni (1976) suggest that the incest taboo has functioned "as a means of insuring an institutionalized pattern of gains through exchanges. Couples who married within their own families would only be sharing what they already possessed. . . . But to marry *outside* one's family opened the way to bring other resources in " (Scanzoni & Scanzoni, 1976, p. 122). This theory can also help explain the few historical exceptions to the incest taboo. While marriage outside the family would typically bring the above-mentioned gains, there could be situations where such gains would be minimized and it would be better for family members to marry within the family itself. A classic historical example would be the brother-sister and father-daughter marriages found in the royal families of ancient Egypt. Such incestuous marriages kept the crown safely in the family, preserved the sacred bloodlines (the pharaohs were believed to be gods and goddesses), and kept the family property intact from generation to generation. But such exceptions to the incest taboo are rare indeed.

To return to the main point, the incest taboo normally functions to exclude close blood relatives from the pool of eligible candidates for marriage. This ensures that marriage will take place between members of two different families.

Age as a factor in mate selection

Another factor which tends to limit the range of eligible candidates is age. Over the years most Americans have married within their age range, and this tendency may be on the increase. In addition, it is customary for men to date and marry women who are a few years younger than themselves, on average about two or three years younger. While this small age difference would not appear at first to be too limiting a factor, upon further examination it is seen to reduce significantly the number of eligibles for both sexes. If, for example, the age range were 3 years in either direction, a 22-year-old person could choose a mate in the 19 to 25 age bracket, provided it made no difference whether the male or the female was older. But since the norms prescribe that the man be older than his wife, this hypothetical 19 to 25 year age span is cut almost in half. For the man it becomes 19 to 22 and for the woman 22 to 25 (Kephart, 1977, pp. 239–240). On college campuses students may become well aware of these age differentials. As a freshman, a college woman can date virtually any college man; but by the time she is a

Table 5–1

Median age at first marriage, by sex, 1900–1979	Age at first marriage	
Year	Female	Male
1979	22.1	24.4
1975	21.1	23.5
1970	20.8	23.2
1960	20.3	22.8
1950	20.3	22.8
1940	21.5	24.3
1930	21.3	24.3
1920	21.2	24.6
1910	21.6	25.1
1900	21.9	25.9

Source: "Marital Status and Living Arrangements: March 1979," U.S. Bureau of the Census, *Current Population Reports* (Series P–20, No. 349).

senior the eligible male dating partners have been reduced to about one quarter of the college male population. For men, the situation is just the reverse. The reduction in the field of eligibles due to age is greatest among young males and older females. This has important ramifications, especially when considered in relation to the surplus of older women in the population.

Another age-related factor affecting courtship and mate selection in America is the pattern of early marriages. From 1900 to 1960 the trend each decade was for earlier marriages for both sexes. In 1900, the median age at first marriage for women was 21.9 and for men 25.9; by 1960, the median age for women had declined to 20.3 and for men to 22.8 (U.S. Bureau of the Census, 1972). Since 1960 this downward trend has stopped, and in the 1970s the age at first marriage has increased. In 1970 the median age at first marriage for women was 20.8 and for men was 23.2; in 1979, the comparable ages were up to 22.1 for women and 24.4 for men (U.S. Bureau of the Census, 1980b). (See Table 5–1.) However, when compared to the populations of other urban, industrialized nations such as England, France, Sweden, and Japan, Americans still marry at a younger age.

Is there an optimum age for getting married? This is a difficult question to answer in the affirmative; but if we rephrase the question and ask at what age marriage is least likely to result in a successful and lasting marriage, the answer is quite clear. One of the few dependable statistics concerning marital stability is the fact that marriages of very young couples have higher separation and divorce rates (Monahan, 1953; Burchinal, 1965; Glick, 1975; Bumpass & Sweet, 1972). Teenage marriages rank lowest in both marital satisfaction and stability. The most stable and enduring marriages appear to be those contracted in the mid to late 20s. In her study titled "Is There a Best Age to Marry? An Interpretation," Lasswell (1974) concluded that

From the standpoint of marital stability, then, men who marry between 27 and 31, and women who marry at about 25 seem to have waited long enough to maximize their chances at a durable relationship. This is more than three years, for both men and women, past the average age at first marriage in the United States currently (Lasswell, 1974, p. 240).

Propinquity as a factor in mate selection

Another factor which influences the practical pool of eligible candidates is physical proximity, or propinquity. Some years ago a popular song expressed the idea this way: "When the one I love's not here, I love the one that's near." This suggests the potential role of proximity or propinquity in courtship and ensuing mate selection. It has become a sociological truism that young people tend to choose a marriage partner from among those who live near them. In his original study of propinquity, Bossard (1932) found that out of 5,000 marriages in Philadelphia, one third of the couples lived within 5 city blocks of each other and more than one half within 20 city blocks of each other. Since Bossard's study, many other researchers have reported essentially the same findings, that the closer to each other a young man and woman live, the more likely they are to become "eligibles" to each other.

Why is propinquity such a definite factor in mate selection? Beyond the obvious points that one is unlikely to marry someone he or she has not met and interacted with, and that one is more apt to meet and interact with a person who lives nearby, how does propinquity operate? To try to answer this question, it is necessary to find the relationships between physical proximity and other social and normative factors such as endogamy and homogamy (the tendency of "likes" to marry). Katz and Hill (1958) have attempted to show these relationships in what they call a "norm-interaction theory" of propinquity, which includes these three propositions:

1. That marriage is normative; i.e., mate selection is restricted by cultural considerations. Every individual has a field of eligibles among whom he or she selects a marriage partner.
2. That the cultural groups (nationality, social class) that comprise the field of eligibles are residentially separated.
3. That within the field of eligibles, the probability of marriage varies directly with the probability of interaction (Katz & Hill, 1958, pp. 27–35).

While the role of propinquity in mate selection may not be fully understood yet, it seems clear that people of the same social and cultural backgrounds and identities tend to live together in American communities and neighborhoods. They interact more frequently, and with the help of endogamous norms and in-group pressures, tend to marry each other. This brings us to the related topic of homogamy.

Homogamy as a factor in mate selection

Homogamy refers to the general tendency of like to marry like. The term has been most frequently used to apply to social and cultural "likes," for example, persons belonging to the same race, nationality, religion, or social class. The term *homogamy* has also been applied to similar physical and psychological traits, such as height, weight, intelligence, and "personality."

We have already discussed homogamy by age. Let us briefly examine homogamy by race, nationality, religion, and social class.

Race. In America endogamous norms have traditionally been very strong with respect to race; and, at least until quite recently, there has been little racial intermarriage. While the data have not always been adequate or reliable, various estimates have indicated that about 99 percent of all marriages in the United States have been racially endogamous (Eckland, 1968, p. 79). It has been estimated that, in spite of a slight increase in interracial marriage in recent years, less than 1 percent of marriages in America in the 1970s were between blacks and whites. The out-marriage rate for Orientals, particularly for Japanese-Americans, is increasing more rapidly. Tinker (1973) found that of all marriages of Japanese-Americans living in Fresno, California in 1959, 7 percent were racial intermarriages; by 1971, intermarriages had increased to 49 percent. A complete survey of marriages of people with Japanese surnames in San Francisco showed that, in 1958, 25 percent were racial intermarriages; for 1971 the figure had risen to 58 percent. (See Table 5–2.)

What does the future hold? Will traditional racial homogamy continue to limit the field of eligible marriage candidates largely to one's own racial group? There is evidence that in some circles people are taking a much more tolerant view of interracial marriage, especially between Orientals and whites. However, the evidence does not suggest any widespread move in this direction for black and white Americans.

Table 5–2

Racial intermarriage of Japanese-Americans, Fresno County, California, 1959–1971	Year	*Percent racial intermarriage*
	1971	49
	1968	38
	1965	36
	1962	14
	1959	7

Source: "Intermarriage and Ethnic Boundaries: The Japanese-American Case" by J. N. Tinker, *Journal of Social Issues,* 1973, *29,* 55.

Nationality, or ethnicity. With more than 50 million immigrants coming to the United States in the past 200 years, nationality or ethnicity has been a significant factor in American social life, including citizenship and mate selection. Social forces pressing for the assimilation of the new-comers were generally impeded by strong ethnocentrism on behalf of both native Americans and the immigrants themselves. Thus many national groups tended to maintain their ethnic identity in America through the decades. Central to this tendency was the persistence of strong endoga-mous marriage norms within these national groups. Data from the 1930s into the 1960s showed that strong national endogamy prevailed among such groups as the Irish-Americans, Italian-Americans, Polish-Americans, Scandinavian-Americans, and others. Even in the 1970s, long after mass immigration had ceased, nationality was still apparently a significant factor in mate selection, even though a current trend toward more dating and marrying across national or ethnic lines exists among some American populations, such as in heterogeneous college student populations.

Social class. To what extent does social class homogamy limit the field of eligible marriage candidates in America? Do young men and women still tend to choose a marriage partner from within their social class or status group? Or are they more apt to marry across class lines today than in earlier generations?

While the criteria for social class identification and differentiation are not always clear nor uniformly applied by social scientists, among the criteria most frequently used are occupation, income, education, and residential area. Eckland (1968, p. 79) found that most studies in the United States show a moderately high rate of social class homogamy, ranging from 50 percent to 80 percent. The 80 percent figure is based on studies making a broad division of the population into middle class and working class; the 50 percent figure came from other, more exacting studies using six or seven social class or socioeconomic status divisions.

While most of the earlier studies (from the 1930s into the 1950s) generally supported the principle of social class homogamy, some of the subsequent studies suggest that this principle is now weakening. Dinitz and his associates (1960) found some decline in endogamous social class marriages; and Leslie and Richardson (1956) found relatively little evidence of social class endogamy among college students who met and married while in college. They concluded that the college campus situation, by encouraging interaction of persons of different social class backgrounds, and by emphasizing democratic norms and values, tends to favor heterogeneous courtship and marriage. They believe that social class homogamy may be on the decline today, especially in some circles, such as among college students. While this would appear to be consistent with the long-range trend toward social democracy and secularism, evidence from other studies shows that social class homogamy still continues, even among college students. Eshleman and Hunt (1965, p. 32) found pronounced social class endogamous norms among married college students. Men from high-status families were most likely to marry women from the same social class background. The same was true for middle-class and working-class men. And the same pattern was found for married college women. Eshleman (1974, p. 299) thinks that these findings may be interpreted in terms of exchange theory, whereby individuals and families "attempt to achieve the best possible bargain for themselves and their children by weighing marital resources and alternatives." This tends to be a countervailing force to social democracy, which encourages marriage across class lines.

Rubin (1968) asked the question, "Do American women marry up?" He sought the answer by comparing the wife's father's occupation with the husband's father's occupation, using a large nationwide sample of white married couples. He concluded that there is no overall tendency for American women to marry up—the only exception being those women whose fathers had white-collar occupations. These women tended to marry men whose fathers were in professional and managerial occupations. Rubin's study lends additional support to the principle of social class endogamy in America, rather than to the principle of social class hyperogamy, or marrying up.

Using U.S. Census Bureau data, Winch (1971, p. 281) found socioeconomic homogamy in 71 percent of the marriages of 25,000 men. Rawlins (1978) found that most people marry those whose education is quite similar to their own. Data from the 1970 census showed that out of every 100 married couples, 39 husbands and wives were at the same educational level, and another 37 percent were only one, two, or three years apart educationally. And the great majority of college educated men and women select mates who have college education. (See Table 5–3.) However, for those who do not marry within their educational

Table 5–3

Educational homogamy in mate selection, United States 1977 percentages

	Education of wife					
	Elementary	High school		College		
Education of husband	1–8 years	1–3 years	4 years	1–3 years	4 years	5 years or more
Elementary:						
1–8 years	49.3	22.9	23.5	3.2	0.8	0.3
High school:						
1–3 years	13.6	37.3	42.0	5.3	1.4	0.3
4 years	5.4	14.5	65.2	10.5	3.2	1.0
College:						
1–3 years	3.0	7.0	49.8	28.9	8.6	2.7
4 years	0.9	2.4	33.5	27.4	28.9	6.8
5 years or more	0.8	1.5	20.8	22.8	31.0	23.1

Source: "Perspectives on American Husbands and Wives," U.S. Bureau of the Census, *Current Population Reports: Special Studies* (Series P–23, No. 77), 1978.

group, there is a greater tendency for women to marry more highly educated men than vice versa (Rockwell, 1976).

The conclusions drawn by Dinitz and his associates (1960) appear to still have validity. They found that with the passage of time there are not only fewer maximally endogamous social class marriages; there are also few widely exogamous marriages. That is, while higher education, democracy, and mobility has increased the tendency for youth to select marriage partners from a broader social class spectrum, this range is still somewhat restricted at both extremes. Stated differently, while there appears to be more intermarriage among young people within the broadening middle ranges of the social class system, there is still little evidence of intermarriage among people from the extremes, such as among upper-class and working- or lower-class young men and women. In this way, at least, the principle of social class homogamy continues.

Religion.   Does religious homogamy still operate to limit the field of eligibles in America? Are endogamous norms showing signs of weakening in the various religious groups?

Americans are highly diverse religiously. This diversity is seen not only in the variety of religious denominations and groups, but also in the salience religion has in the lives of people. Thus the way religious endogamy operates depends a good deal on the particular religion or denomination being considered. While religious endogamy would be virtually 100 percent among the Old Order Amish, quite a different situation would be found among various Protestant denominations, such as the Methodist or Presbyterian, where interdenominational marriage is not at all unusual.

Important issues and problems involving religious homogamy most often involve the major religious groups—Jews, Catholics, and Protestants—and their traditions and norms pertaining to marriage. While all three of these religious groups have long-standing endogamous norms, Jews and Catholics have traditionally been much stricter than most Protestant groups in forbidding their members to marry out. Things are changing now, however. There is ample evidence that the rates of marrying out are increasing for both Catholics and Jews. After reviewing many current studies, Kephart (1977, p. 246) estimates that in America today about 30 percent of Jewish marriages are mixed and one third or more of Catholic marriages are mixed. Traditionally, Jewish endogamous requirements have been strong, especially for Orthodox and Conservative Jews. Most rabbis will not marry a Jew and a Gentile. But today the increased marrying out of Jewish youth attests to the weakening of these traditional norms. Secularization, increasing mobility, and the decreasing salience of religion and religious differences in the lives of many youth are a part of the explanation. Also, Jews compose only about 3 percent of the American population, and a strict adherence to religious endogamy would automatically exclude the other 97 percent from their pool of eligibles. Monahan

(1973) found that the proportion of Jewish intermarriage varies widely from place to place in America, from as low as 5 percent in Rhode Island to as much as 50 percent in Indiana.

Increases in Catholic marrying out can be attributed, in part, to the same changing social conditions and influences affecting Jewish marrying out. Important changes are apparent within the Catholic Church. Many of the traditional doctrines and norms are being challenged today, including prohibitions against artificial birth control, divorce, and marrying non-Catholics. Young people especially are taking what they consider more enlightened views on these kinds of issues. Religious differences have less meaning to them than to earlier generations. There is evidence that those who marry out have weaker religious ties, and often weak family ties too (Heiss, 1960).

Using data from six national surveys conducted from 1973 to 1978, Glenn (1982) compared interreligious marriages in the mid-1970s with those of the mid-1950s. He found that there was still a fairly high degree of religious homogamy in terms of religious preference, even though there had been a substantial decrease since 1957. However, the present level of religious homogamy was due largely to the fact that so many persons change their religious preference to agree with that of their spouses, either in anticipation of marriage or after marriage. The apparent fact that many

Sharing the same religious faith can strengthen a relationship

Julie Heifitz

women and men are now willing to marry a person of a different religion and to change their own religion suggests that religious institutions are exerting only weak influences on marital choices today in America.

What does this all add up to? What does it mean for the individual seeking a marriage partner to have his or her field of eligibles defined and circumscribed by homogamy, propinquity, and so on? For most, it means that one's choice of a mate is massively, although often quite subtly, influenced by a wide range of social factors and processes, many of which one is quite unaware at the time. Only a small minority of people avoid or overcome these pervasive influences. As Udry (1974, p. 168) points out, anyone who picks a mate who is not socially homogamous usually makes a deliberate decision and effort to do so, and often has some special motivation to marry across some conventional religious or racial line. Udry (1974, p. 168) concludes that in America today one is still

> most likely to marry someone who is pretty much like himself in most of his social characteristics. This represents a considerable departure from the romantic myth and from American values of individualism and equalitarianism, but these are apparently values which are compromised when it comes to making individual decisions.

THEORIES OF MATE SELECTION

Many of the various, early theories of mate selection were simplistic and reductionistic in nature. One such theory, which holds that a man is guided to a particular woman by some kind of genetically determined instinct, was held by the psychologist Carl Jung (Evans, 1964). Jung maintained that a man carried a mental image of a particular woman in his genes, and that when the right female came along the man would immediately recognize her. Today few social scientists would put much faith in such genetic determinism.

We have seen that mate selection in our society is circumscribed by many social and demographic factors, including age, kinship, propinquity, race, social class, religion, and ethnicity. Within the actual field of eligibles, however, the question of who will marry whom is difficult to answer. Scientifically, it is difficult to accept either Jung's genetic theory or the romantic theory that there is a one-and-only waiting in the wings for each of us. Let us then review some of the most current and promising mate selection theories offered by today's social scientists.

ROLE THEORY

Sociologists use the concept *role* to mean a set of culturally defined behavioral expectations that are appropriate for a given position or *status*

(Linton, 1936). Each of us has various roles defined for us as we move through our life cycle—son, daughter, student, employee, husband, wife, parent, and so on. Through socialization processes one learns these role definitions and normally comes to want to behave in the way expected of a son or daughter, a student, an employee, and so on. In societies such as ours, where there are heterogeneous cultural backgrounds and where many roles are undergoing considerable change, significant differences in role definitions may exist from group to group. Differences in role definitions or expectations have been used in analysis of marital adjustment (as will be seen in Chapter 7), but only recently has this idea been applied to analysis of mate selection.

According to role theory, it would be unlikely that a man and a woman with widely discrepant definitions of the husband role or the wife role would select each other as marriage partners. Interpreted positively, role theory says that people tend to seek marriage partners whose marital role definitions or expectations are in agreement with their own. For example, a man with a traditional-patriarchal orientation who believes that the husband should be the sole family provider and the boss in the family would tend to select a wife who expected to be a conventional housewife and mother rather than a career woman or a woman's liberation activist. So according to role theory it is the anticipated compatibility of future marriage and family roles that is important in mate selection. At the appropriate stages in the courtship process a couple can, if they will, check their agreement-disagreement on many of the dimensions of marital and familial roles, such as division of labor and division of authority between husband and wife in matters of employment, family financing, housework, recreation, childrearing and so on.

VALUE THEORY

Values define what is good or bad, right or wrong, moral or immoral in a given society. Thus values are central to a person's mode of conduct, including one's goals in life and the means one adopts to pursue these goals. Coombs (1961) has attempted to develop a value theory of mate selection. He suggests that one's values or value system is so important to the individual that one will seek out a marriage partner who shares similar values. Homogamy enters the picture here, since persons with similar social backgrounds tend to learn and share similar values. As courtship partners, a young man and woman who find they share many values are apt to find interaction rewarding and communication easy. This leads to feelings of satisfaction with each other and a desire to continue and deepen the relationship. Such a relationship with a member of the opposite sex who shares one's values helps validate one's own beliefs and promotes emotional satisfaction and security. As Coombs (1961, p. 166) says:

The thesis is that value consensus fosters mutually rewarding interaction and leads to interpersonal attraction. It is reasoned that the sharing of similar values is, in effect, a validation of one's self which promotes emotional satisfaction and enhances communication ease.

Coombs found empirical support for his theory of value consensus among a sample of dating college couples (Coombs, 1966, pp. 166–173). Whether or not such value consensus or similarity is a determining factor in final mate selection remains to be seen.

EXCHANGE THEORY

In our initial discussion of bargaining and the marriage market, it was suggested that a courtship system is in one sense a system of exchange, where a male or a female seeking a marriage partner eventually strikes a bargain with a member of the opposite sex, or perhaps has it done by one's parents.

Exchange theory holds that social relationships are regulated or shaped by the desire of each participant to derive maximum gain or profit at minimum cost or pain. As applied to courtship and mate selection, the theory holds that participants are most apt to be attracted to members of the opposite sex who offer the highest ratio of marital rewards to costs. Elaborating on this idea, Edwards (1969, pp. 518–519) says that

> individuals are impelled to enter into association with one another in order to accomplish their desired ends and to fulfill those expectations their positions demand. Since it is necessary for individuals to exchange, the attainment of one person's goals entails an investment and cost on the part of the other. . . . It is further assumed that each party to a transaction attempts to maximize his gains and, thereby, minimize his cost. Over the long run this means actual exchanges tend to become equalized, particularly in view of the operation of the principle of reciprocity.

This theory of mate selection—as was also true of the value theory—fits well with the general theory of homogamy. An exchange theory of homogamous mate selection is suggested by Edwards (1969, p. 525):

> 1. Within any collectivity of potential mates, a marriageable person will seek out that individual who is perceived as maximizing his rewards.
> 2. Individuals with equivalent resources are most likely to maximize each other's rewards.
> 3. Pairs with equivalent resources are most likely to possess homogamous characteristics.
> 4. Mate selection, therefore, will be homogamous with respect to a given set of characteristics.

Edwards does not always specify the kinds of resources participants may bring into the bargaining process, or how they may be judged as equivalent, but it may be assumed that such things as the man's earning power and his career prospects and the woman's domestic skills and potential as a mother would be involved. Other resources would include the ability of each to provide for the other's emotional and companionship needs. The exchange theory helps explain how and why homogamous tendencies operate in mate selection. This leads to another, somewhat related theory involving reciprocal or complementary needs in mate selection.

COMPLEMENTARY NEEDS THEORY

This theory of mate selection, with its notion of the "attraction of opposites," has sometimes been juxtaposed against the theory of homogamy, which emphasizes the attraction of similars or likes.

Winch (1955) developed the theory of various complementary needs of men and women operating in the mate-selection process. He hypothesized that while one chooses a marriage partner one feels will provide maximum need-gratification, this gratification occurs best when the personality characteristics of the man and the woman are *complementary* rather than similar. If, for example, the male is basically submissive, he will seek a woman who can dominate him. Or if a woman is a "nurturant" person who needs to have things done for her, she will be attracted to a "succorant" man who gains satisfaction from doing things for others.

While Winch's own research revealed the presence of such complementary needs among married college students (Winch, 1958), subsequent studies have generally failed to provide much corroboration (Burr, 1973). Though the theory has attracted a good deal of interest, and numerous efforts have been made to test it empirically, relatively little empirical support exists so far. Winch himself conceded the need for some reformulation of the theory (Winch, 1967).

SEQUENTIAL THEORIES OF MATE SELECTION

While each of the preceding theories has focused on the role of one particular factor in mate selection, such as values, roles, or personality needs, there are other theories which have attempted to combine or place in sequence several factors as they come into play at different points during the courtship process. We will briefly review three theories of this type.

The filter theory

This theory, advanced by Kerkhoff and Davis (1962), holds that mate selection is not just a matter of the marrying of "likes" in social background (homogamy), nor of the marrying of "unlikes" in personality needs (heterogamy). Rather, social background, group memberships, values and interests, and complementary personality needs may all come into play at various stages of a given courtship, from its beginning to the ultimate marriage. For example, agreement on values and similar social background may be important at an early stage of courtship, while complementary personality needs may become more crucial at a later period in the relationship.

The filter theory points to a sequence or series of screening or filtering processes which operate in courtship and mate selection. In the initial stage, such factors as race, religion, and social class have normally restricted the field of eligibles. At this early stage, dating involves doing enjoyable things together. Many relationships do not survive this stage, since the enjoyment can wear off. Those relationships which do survive this early and often idealized stage may lead to the discovery of shared, compatible values. Deepening involvement may now entail complementary personality needs and their satisfaction. Thus in the later stages of courtship a much stronger personality-based bond develops, which can lead to marriage.

Kerkhoff and Davis (1962) found some empirical support for their filter theory in a sample of university students who were seriously involved in courtship. They found that value consensus appeared in the earlier stages of courtship while need-complementarity was more apparent in the later stages.

The process approach to mate selection

Advocates of this sequential approach argue that mate selection is not merely a function of values, interests, needs, and the social backgrounds of the couple. Rather, the actual selection of a mate is a developmental process during which increasing commitment pushes the couple toward marriage. One of the originators of this approach, Bolton (1961, p. 235), explained it this way:

> Perhaps, mate selection must be studied not only in terms of the variables brought into the interaction situation but also as a process in which a relationship is built up, a process in which the *transactions between individuals* in a certain societal context are determinants of turning points and commitments out of which marriage emerges.

This process approach to mate selection does not ignore social backgrounds or personality factors. It does attempt, however, to put such factors in the context of the developing relationship of a courting couple, as the relationship gathers momentum and escalates toward a final commitment to marry. In his study of married couples, Bolton (1961) found at least five different kinds of apparent developmental relationships or processes, including "personality meshing," "identity clarification," "relation centered," "pressure centered," and those that are "expedience centered."

Stimulus-value-role theory (SVR theory)

Another sequential approach has been advocated by Murstein (1970), who sees mate selection as a three-stage sequence involving stimulus-value-roles (SVR). He believes that in such an essentially free-choice society as the United States, most couples pass through these three stages before coming to the final decision to marry. Murstein uses exchange theory to explain the dynamics of the developing relationship of the couple.

The stimulus stage. Initially a man may be attracted to a woman (or vice versa) because of his perception of her personality or her physical or social attributes, and also "his perception of his own qualities that might be attractive to the other person" (Murstein, 1970, pp. 466–467). If there is sufficient mutual stimulus attraction between the man and the woman they then enter the second stage of "value comparison."

The value comparison stage. Here the couple "sit down and talk." As Murstein (1970, pp. 468–469) explains this stage:

> Unlike the "stimulus" stage in which attributes of the partner are evaluated without any necessary interpersonal contact, the value comparison stage involves the appraisal of value compatibility through verbal interaction. The kinds of values explored through discussion are apt to be much more varied than those possible in the "stimulus" stage. The couple may compare their attitudes toward life, politics, religion, sex and role of men and women in society, and marriage.

Increasing interaction permits more continuous and closer scrutiny of physical appearance and other factors, such as temperament, and ability to relate to others. Sharing similar values should be a definite factor in drawing two people together.

Some couples may decide to marry on the basis of initial stimulus attraction and verbalized value similarity. But for most couples being able to *function* in compatible roles before reaching the final decision to marry is important.

The role compatibility stage. Here the couple begins to test their role compatibility in areas of life relevant to marriage. According to Murstein (1970, p. 469):

> as the couple's relationship ripens, the members increasingly confide in each other and, thus, become aware of a broader range of each other's behavior than heretofore. They may also become more cognizant of what they desire in a future spouse, and more consciously compare their expectations with their perception of the partner.

The mutual "role fit" is mutually rewarding, and the desire to continue this highly satisfying relationship can lead to a decision to get married.

Murstein tested his theory on two samples of couples engaged or going steady and found that all of his hypotheses received at least moderate support. This theory is insightful and deserves further development and empirical testing.

SUGGESTED GUIDELINES FOR SELECTING A MATE

Are there any practical suggestions that can be offered with any degree of confidence to the person seeking a mate, or to the young couple anticipating marriage? Professional opinion, backed by research findings, suggests the importance of a thorough courtship which enables the couple to really get to know each other and to test their compatibility in many ways before making the final decision to marry.

IMPORTANCE OF A THOROUGH COURTSHIP

Many family authorities believe that the American courtship system can do a pretty good job of sorting out men and women into compatible marriage partners, if the system is given a proper chance to work. That is, it is necessary that those seeking a mate make adequate use of the successive phases of the system before arriving at a final choice. High divorce and separation rates are in part the consequences of inadequate courtship, which increases the chance of ill-advised or hasty marriages and poor choices of partners. There are many reasons for poor choices of marriage partners, of course, and while not all could have been prevented by a more thorough or truly functional courtship, a good many could have been.

Reasons for poor choice of marriage partner

Bowman and Spanier (1978, p. 130) cite some factors contributing to a poor choice of a mate:

> Confusing infatuation with love; hoping to reform the other party; judging by too few qualities; marrying before tastes and attitudes are well understood; overemphasizing money; acting under the stimulus of rebound, spite, habit, pity, and similar attitudes—these obviously contribute to errors in judgment.

In our society, which emphasizes freedom of choice, youth, and romantic love, it is little wonder that some young people make poor choices by marrying in haste. Strong sex urges and the euphoria of new love may impel an immature couple into a hasty marriage. While love and sex are certainly important in marriage, to marry the first person one falls in love with or feels strongly attracted to sexually without giving the relationship time to broaden and be tested on other important grounds is risky.

There are other young people who get married before they have had time to learn what marriage is really all about, what its requirements and responsibilities are. They don't yet fully understand that there are, indeed, serious responsibilities that go with the privileges and pleasures of marriage. The very high divorce rates among those who marry very young speak to this point.

Others may marry out of a sense of duty or to please their family. This is not unusual in traditional societies which emphasize familism, and under such cultural conditions these marriages may work well. But in America today, where personal factors are so important in marriage and the couple will live as an independent, nuclear family, the final choice of one's mate should be a matter of careful and serious decision.

Some ill-advised marriages result from the need or desire of a person to escape from an unhappy or unpleasant home situation, or from an unsatisfactory school or work situation. Tensions or conflicts with parents, the boredom of schoolwork, or the drudgery of an unrewarding job, may be sufficient cause for a young person to succumb to the temptation of an early or ill-advised marriage with someone who promises to "take you away from all this."

Role of parents in mate selection

In their study *Engagement and Marriage,* Burgess and Wallin (1953, pp. 560–564) found that parents could predict with some accuracy the probable marital success or failure of their sons or daughters—especially the latter. Such findings suggest that it would be advisable for a son or daughter to pay some attention to the views and reactions of their parents when it comes to seeking a mate. Parents may, of course, raise various kinds of objections to the marriage or the specific choices of their sons or daughters, objections that range from relevant and rational to nonrelevant and irrational. When parents and their children disagree on the choice of a marriage partner, the children tend to disregard parental opinions. One factor here is the generation gap. Parents belong to an earlier generation and their experiences and norms tend to be somewhat different from those of their children. In a study of Wisconsin college students, Prince (1961) found that the parents wanted their sons and daughters to find a marriage partner of the same religious faith, from a good family background, and possessing a good disposition. For the daughter, the marriage partner should have good financial prospects; for the son, the prospective mate should be a good wife and homemaker. Parents, in general, seem to place less emphasis than their children on the values of love and companionship.

In spite of such differences between the experiences and outlooks of parents and their children, there are still sound reasons for a son or daugh-

A father and his daughter's fiancé get acquainted

Robert E. Potter III

ter to listen to their parent's reactions to a prospective mate. Parents are normally less emotionally involved than their sons or daughters, and can see aspects of the relationship or personal characteristics of the prospective partner which their children may be unable to see. Parents also have a broader time perspective and have had more experience with people. A daughter deeply in love may ignore or shrug off selfishness and unreliability on the part of her partner, though her parents may recognize these flaws as serious danger signals long before she does. Parents may also have a sharper awareness of the needs, strengths, and shortcomings of their children than the children do; thus, they realize what kind of a mate is suitable.

On the other hand, there is no question that parental objections can sometimes be irrelevant or irrational and based on the emotional needs and problems of a parent. A parent who is very emotionally dependent on a son or daughter may be unable to let the child go no matter how suitable the prospective marriage partner is. An unhappily married or neurotic mother, for example, may be fearful of her "baby" marrying anyone. However, all but the most intransigent parental opposition can generally be resolved by patience, effort, and mutual respect, providing the mate choice is basically sound and lines of communication remain open between the child and the parents. From their experience in premarital and marital counseling, Blood and Blood (1978, p. 112) offer their insight on this matter.

> Although marrying in the face of parental opposition strains parent-child relationships, anguish can be minimized by mutual consideration. Secret

marriages or living together in secret bypass hostile parents, but alienate them even more when discovered. Most parents want to attend the wedding even if they aren't enthusiastic about the match. They appreciate being kept informed of their child's plans, even when they disagree with them. Sensitive handling of parental opposition may not dissolve it immediately, but can pave the way for better relationships in the long run.

Ryder et al. (1971) found that parents may play a separative role during certain stages of the courtship of a daughter or a son, and then a supportive role at other stages. In the early "latency" stage, parents may be supportive of the new girlfriend or boyfriend; but when the daughter or son shows definite signs of becoming serious, and the friend is seen by the parents as a potential future spouse, the parents' attitudes may shift to opposition. It is during this "precommitment" stage that "the full panoply of parental opposition activities emerges, if it emerges at all." (Ryder et al., 1971, p. 454). If the courting couple persist and move on to the next stage of "commitment," another reversal in parental attitudes may occur. When the parents recognize that the marriage is probably inevitable, "they arrange a peace treaty with their child's fiancée," and will likely begin to participate in the plans for the wedding.

The value of engagement

For many of today's youth, engagement represents a less formal or explicit stage in the courtship process than was true for earlier generations of Americans. There may never be a formal proposal of marriage, the couple may just gradually arrive at an understanding that they will sooner or later get married. At some point in the relationship, however, this private understanding is generally followed by a more formal or public announcement of some kind.

Engagement is understandably considered by many as one of the most important stages or periods in the whole courtship process (LeMasters, 1957b). For the couple, the engagement period represents important transitions and shifts in statuses and roles, during which each partner is undergoing anticipatory socialization for upcoming marital roles. Specifically, engagement involves a shift from one's parental family to one's marital family, with the anticipation of shifting from a son or daughter role to a new husband or wife role and from a single status to a marital status. With engagement, the couple make an explicit and more serious commitment to each other and to marriage. They are now fiancés and this label brings a change in their self-concepts and in their relationship. They will very likely learn many things about each other not known before.

In his *Modern Courtship and Marriage,* LeMasters (1957, pp.157–164) discusses the importance of engagement for the couple. He sees a number of functions of a successful engagement.

1. During engagement, the couple experiences a wider and deeper exploration of each other. Much of the earlier dating experience can be quite superficial, limited to fun, recreational activities. Even people deeply

in love do not find it easy to reveal their most intimate selves to each other. More of this self-revelation normally takes place during engagement than in the previous stages of courtship. The couple who are dating or going-steady tend to see each other in more limited and segmented roles and situations. For many, engagement expands the relationship and social interactions, so that more of the whole person is revealed. For example, how does he react under stress or in a crisis? How does she react to disappointment or frustration? Marriage is going to require living with the whole person, not just his most charming or her most enticing self. As LeMaster's (1957b, p. 161) observes:

> In a sense, this function of broader and deeper exploration during engage-ment has as its ultimate purpose the reduction of the element of *surprise* after marriage, the elimination of the phrase so well known to marriage counselors: "But I didn't know he (or she) was like that."

2. Engagement also helps bring about a more thorough knowledge of each other's family. Anthropologists say we marry not only the other person but, in a sense, the other person's family as well. If one has not come to know one's prospective in-laws prior to engagement, now, rather than after marriage, is the time to do so. This advance knowledge will prove valuable in the inevitable relationships with and adjustments to one's in-laws following marriage, and will probably help the couple in their own marital adjustment, as will be seen in Chapter 7.

In many ways a person's fiancé is the product of her or his family experiences and relationships over the past 20 years, more or less. Consid-erable insight into the personality of one's prospective mate can be gained from observing the family customs, traditions, and lifestyles, as well as the personalities, of his or her parents. Visits to each other's homes, vaca-tion trips together, dropping in unexpectedly, all can be educational and revealing.

3. Engagement helps clarify and make public the relationship between the couple. There is frequently some ambiguity in the relationship in the earlier stages of courtship. As Waller (1938) has shown, the man may define the relationship and degree of commitment one way while the woman has a quite different definition. This can be true for a couple who are living together as well as for couples dating or going-steady (Macklin, 1972). Engagement, however, will normally clarify the situation for all concerned. "Yes, we are going to get married. Probably next June. It will be announced in the Sunday paper." This making the commitment to marry public lets the whole community—families, friends, relatives, former boy and girl friends—all know the score. It is also likely to have a sobering and maturing effect on the couple—they are now approaching the point of no return.

In sum, engagement functions as an important learning and preparatory period for many couples. It formalizes their commitment to each other, and helps clarify the situation for family and friends. Engagement helps a couple test their compatibility and their prospects for a successful marriage. However, it is recognized that in these days of increasing informality in courtship, many young people marry without ever being formally engaged. Many who subscribe to the New Morality may live together for a period before deciding whether or not to get married.

Let us look next at some suggestions and guidelines that a couple who are contemplating marriage may follow in testing their compatibility and assessing their prospects as marriage partners.

TESTING FOR COMPATIBILITY

As noted earlier, a person in love has a tendency to idealize the partner. Seeing the loved one through rose-colored glasses can lead to self-deception, making a realistic assessment of the relationship difficult. Blood and Blood (1978, pp. 102–110) believe that such problems can be overcome by varied and sufficient compatibility testing. (The following discussion follows Blood and Blood quite closely.)

One of the ways a couple can put their compatibility to a test is to engage in many different kinds of activities together. Movies, concerts, discos, sporting events—both spectator and participant—offer opportunities not only to test shared and compatible interests, but also to learn each other's likes, dislikes, strengths, weaknesses, and tolerances. As noted earlier, the subculture of the male may have predisposed him toward more intensive involvement in sporting activities, while the female may be more interested in spending time dancing and listening to music. Of course, as a married couple they will not always have to share all of each other's activities, but there is currently a strong trend toward husband-wife companionship in most walks of life, especially in the middle class. The important thing in this kind of compatibility testing is that each partner experiences those activities which are most salient or important to the other.

While all kinds of activities provide opportunities for a couple to test their compatibility, it is also important for them to engage in ample conversations, to have full and frank discussions which reveal feelings, sentiments, personal aspirations, and so on. Past and present interests, experiences, and friends can be discussed—at least up to a point. While open and honest communication leads to mutual understanding, there is evidence that discretion should be the rule in revealing or "confessing" past relationships with members of the opposite sex. Burgess and Wallin (1953) found that, during engagement, talk about former men or women friends provoked more "reticence, tension, or emotion" between couples than any other topic of conversation. In general, however, there is a trend today toward more open conversation about more topics than ever. Koller (1951) found that college-graduate couples now were talking a good deal more and about more serious topics before marriage than did their mothers and grandmothers. Topics most frequently discussed (in descending order) were: (1) having children, (2) place to live, (3) man's occupation, (4) woman's occupation, (5) religion, and (6) handling money in marriage (Koller, 1951, p. 369).

Couples can also test their compatibility in decision making and in problem solving. Starting with early dating, couples have decisions to make, such as what to do, where to go, and how much money to spend on the evening's activities. In earlier times he would probably make most of these decisions; today they are likely to share them. Solving these and more important problems, such as how to deal with sex before marriage, can put the compatibility of the couple to some crucial tests. Working out religious or political differences, or deciding whether to have an "open marriage," may determine whether or not a couple feel compatible enough to go ahead with marriage.

A good look at the friends of one's prospective mate can tell one a good deal. That is, the company one keeps may be quite revealing, since common interests and views of life are generally shared among friends. LeMasters (1957b) emphasizes that one should make an effort to meet *all* of the other's friends, or at least a representative sample of different kinds of friends. For a couple who met each other in a church group, the woman may be acquainted only with the man's church-going friends. He may be reluctant to introduce her to his poker-club crowd or his beer-drinking buddies. Or take the example of a college man who "pinned" a coed whose steadiness and domesticity attracted him. Soon, however, the man was complaining about her "arty" friends who, he believed, had a bad influence on her—"a bunch of long-hairs who I think are nuts" (Blood & Blood, 1978, p. 105). The probability of wooing one's partner away from such friends—in effect reforming him or her according to one's wishes—is not very good. Better to learn about any such incompatibilities before marriage than after.

The functional value of becoming thoroughly acquainted with each other's parental families has already been mentioned. Suffice it here to reiterate that getting to know the family of one's prospective mate can be even more revealing than getting to know his or her close friends. Sons and daughters may resemble their parents in many ways.

Also, how well does one's prospective mate get along with his or her parents and siblings? Are they compatible and well adjusted or do they always seem to be at cross-purposes? And how well adjusted are the parents as marriage partners? Burgess and Cottrell (1939) found that one of the factors predictive of good marital adjustment for a couple was the marital happiness of their parents. Luckey (1960) found that less satisfied husbands saw their fathers as being less loving, cooperative, and responsible than themselves. Whitehurst (1977) found that full and satisfying childhood experiences in one's parental family are critical to one's marital happiness.

Compatibility testing takes time. Just to do the numerous things suggested above would take many hours together over a period of months. After the initial period of euphoria and idealization have worn off, does the couple still get along well, or do they seem to be getting on each other's nerves, maybe finding less in common than they thought earlier? Enough time is needed for each to see the other in mundane situations and even in crisis situations, not only in "best-foot-forward" situations on dates. The question of how much time is enough has intrigued sociologists. Burgess and Wallin (1953, p. 286) found that the longer the prior acquaintance before the couple became engaged, the greater the proportion of engagements that resulted in eventual marriage. After reviewing the evidence on this question, Blood and Blood (1978, p. 109) conclude:

> Other things being equal, the longer people know each other prior to committing themselves, the more likely they are to have a lasting and happy relationship. Given time to discover their incompatibility, those without such happy prospects are more likely to opt out of the relationship.

Common sense tells us that this principle applies only up to a certain length of time. One doubts that a ten-year acquaintance is better than a five-year acquaintance.

Questions are frequently raised as to whether or not premarital sexual relations are useful as a test of a couple's compatibility. Since the most important factors in sexual compatibility are psychological rather than physical it is not really necessary for a couple to test out how well they are matched anatomically. Human beings of various sizes and shapes can relate well sexually. But the social and psychological aspects of premarital intercourse differ in important ways from those of marital intercourse. The latter has social approval while the former generally does not. Couples who feel guilty or anxious about engaging in premarital sex may find the experience less than satisfactory, and thus one or both partners may have questions about their sexual compatibility. This could be unfortunate and misleading since they could very likely function satisfactorily sexually in the more relaxed, secure setting of marriage. However, there is also evidence that couples who are satisfied with their sexual experience before marriage can expect their sexual compatibility to continue after marriage (Burgess & Wallin, 1953). On the other hand, couples who abstain before marriage can assume that, with a little time and patience, they will be able to initiate and maintain a perfectly normal and satisfactory sexual relationship after marriage.

For some couples professional premarital counseling may be helpful or even advisable in assessing their compatibility or suitability as future marriage partners. Blood and Blood (1978, p. 113), who have many years of experience as professional counselors, point out some of the advantages of this kind of service:

> A skillful premarital counselor can help couples of doubtful compatibility. Any man and woman who find themselves in conflict within themselves, between partners, or between themselves and their parents would do well

124

to seek professional counsel. Parents can usually be counted on for feedback, but a professional person is more dependable. Parents have little knowledge to draw on save their own marriage experience and the marriages of their immediate circle. Counselors have the double advantage of scientific knowledge about marriage and experience in counseling other couples, so their perspective is broad. For the couple themselves, discussing their situation with a neutral party is likely to yield new insights and objectivity.

MAKING THE FINAL DECISION

At some time the outcome of the various compatibility tests must be added up, assessed, and a decision made. The couple may decide they are, indeed, compatible and plan to go ahead with marriage; or they may decide they are not compatible or well enough suited to go ahead and thus break up; or they may postpone the decision for a while longer. The final decision is one of the most important a person will be called on to make in one's lifetime. It is not always easy or unambiguous. Most choices entail degrees of uncertainty and risk. There are few, if any, universal standards for compatibility between a man and a woman; nor is it really known how much compatibility is enough for a good marriage. If after many months of association a man and woman continue to have persistent doubts about their compatibility, it may be unwise for them to go ahead with marriage. Burgess and Wallin (1953, p. 565) found that for engaged women especially, doubts as to the probable success of the

Bounds of mate selection are influenced by family norms

Bohdan Hrynewych/Stock, Boston

marriage often foretold a broken engagement, or a divorce if they went ahead with the marriage.

Blood and Blood (1978, pp. 116–117) point out that choosing a marriage partner involves two kinds of risks: (1) One must decide sometime if one wants to marry a particular person in spite of the fact that there are many other prospects "out there" who may be even more desirable than this person. (2) The decision to marry this particular person has to be based on what he or she is now, without knowing what this person will be like in the future. In the first instance, one has to choose between a visible prospect and invisible alternatives, between going ahead today or finding someone even more suitable tomorrow. The second risk is of a different nature. Both partners will develop and change, of course. But how and in what direction? Together, or in divergent paths? Here the thoroughness of the courtship and the extent of compatibility testing should help each partner judge the probable future growth and stability of the other.

Choosing a marriage partner is only the beginning of marriage, and marriage means a good many serious commitments. It means committing oneself to a particular person and turning one's back on other, possibly better, prospects. It also means a commitment to a particular person without advance knowledge of whether or not that person's needs, values, and interests will continue to be compatible with one's own in later years. Risks, yes; but the vast majority of American youth still seem willing to take them, and eager to make their final choice of a marriage partner in their early 20s.

PART THREE

Marriage and marital relationships

Marriage: American style

The transition from the single state to the married state is one of the most significant changes experienced in one's lifetime. One is no longer primarily a son or a daughter in one's family of orientation. One has become, rather abruptly, primarily a husband or a wife in a newly created family of procreation.

In this chapter we will examine the transition to marriage, starting with the wedding and the honeymoon, and following with a review of various developmental tasks confronting the marriage partners as they assume their roles of husband and wife. Then, since so many young people today are starting married life while in college, we shall look briefly at some special conditions and adjustments associated with college marriages. Next will be an analysis of various sociolegal aspects of marriage, and the way marital interactive patterns develop and become established. Finally, some trends and changes in marriage in America will be reviewed.

TRANSITION TO MARRIAGE

BEGINNINGS

Readiness for marriage

There are many personal and social factors that bear upon an individual's and a couple's readiness for marriage. A young couple, for example, who may be emotionally and economically ready for marriage may have to postpone the wedding due to strong family obligations, or perhaps to occupational commitments that keep them separated. And of course socioemotional factors are important in one's readiness to marry. Is one emotionally and socially mature enough to accept the heavy responsibilities that marriage brings? Is one's partner also mature and really ready for marriage? Has the couple's courtship been thorough enough to test their compatibility for a lifelong marriage partnership? Have they had ample premarital experiences to prepare them for a life together? Can they communicate well on serious and difficult subjects as well as on pleasant subjects? Can they argue constructively and resolve their differences in a way that benefits their relationship rather than damages it? Are they economically and financially ready to support themselves after marriage?

Assuming that a young couple who are deeply in love have decided that they are ready for marriage, their plans for getting married will logically move ahead to the point of setting a date for the wedding.

The wedding: A rite of passage

In the transition to marriage the wedding serves as a rite of passage symbolizing to the couple and to their relatives, friends, and all concerned that they have now entered a new state or condition as a married couple. Throughout the world the importance and seriousness of these status changes are attested by the near universality of some kind of wedding ceremony, and by the solemnity attached to the ceremony, often couched in religiously, as well as legally, defined forms.

The wedding has a personal as well as a social function for each partner. It is an explicit public expression of mutual commitment on the part of the couple. It makes clear the meaning and purpose of their new relationship "I . . . , take you . . . , for my lawful wife (or husband), to have and to hold, from this day forward, for better, for worse, for richer, for poorer, in sickness and in health, until death doeth us part." Such vows, repeated publicly by each partner, tend to reinforce their mutual commitment.

The importance of marriage as one of mankind's most basic social institutions is seen in the public and formalized nature of the wedding ceremony. Most weddings are performed by an official representative of society, religious or civil, and generally require official witnesses also. Usually relatives and friends of both bride and groom attend. In addition, public announcements of the forthcoming wedding are traditionally made, orally or in writing. In some religious groups today the traditional custom of publishing the banns still prevails. (This is a public announcement during church service of the couple's intention to marry.) The public's concern with the marriage is often represented in the wedding ceremony by the clergyman's statement: "If anyone can show just cause why this

Outdoor wedding

Jean-Claude Lejeune

man and woman may not be lawfully joined together, let him speak, or else hereafter forever hold his peace."

Of course, wedding customs and ceremonies vary from group to group and also may change over a period of time. A Catholic high-mass marriage ceremony may take two hours or longer and includes an elaborate series of rituals and impressive trimmings and decorations, with participants in traditional costumes and garb; while a civil wedding before a justice of the peace and two witnesses may take only a few minutes for a young couple dressed in ordinary street clothes. Legally and socially this latter couple are just as truly married as are the Catholic couple. (The reader might like to speculate on the comparative likelihood of these two marriages lasting.)

Some young couples today are revising or even entirely rewriting their wedding vows, while others adhere to the traditional vows found in the ceremonies of their particular religious group. The wedding may take place in a church or in the home of the bride or groom, or perhaps in some favorite outdoor spot, such as a meadow or on a mountainside. The bride may wear a traditional wedding gown and veil or a simple dress, while the groom may wear a tuxedo or a regular suit—or both may wear blue jeans. Most conventional church or home weddings are followed by a reception of some kind. It is understandable that in a culturally varied, changing society like America there would be many different kinds of wedding practices. But even couples who tend to reject the traditional and conventional practices still usually look upon the wedding, whatever its form, as a symbol of their commitment to each other as husband and wife and a celebration of their love. Bowman and Spanier (1978, p. 179) express this idea thus:

Wedding reception

David S. Strickler/Atoz Images, Inc.

Off for the honeymoon

George W. Gardner/Stock, Boston

Perhaps the central point of emphasis and significance is that, regardless of social changes that have occurred in recent years, increased sexual permissiveness, unconventional living arrangements, and the inclination of some young people to discard tradition and the trappings of traditional ways, many of these young people, in their own way, seek to express publicly their love and commitment. This need for a public expression of commitment upon which an enduring relationship may be founded seems to be personally and culturally persistent, suggesting that it must involve deep meaning and value.

The honeymoon

The honeymoon has represented an important step in the transition to marriage for a great many newlyweds, especially those with a traditional orientation to marriage. Many modern couples, particularly those who have been sexually involved before their wedding, dispense with the honeymoon (Kanin & Howard, 1958; Blood & Blood, 1978). A conventional honeymoon would in all likelihood be viewed as an anachronism by most couples who had cohabited for any length of time before getting married. For the less-emancipated or the inexperienced, the honeymoon helps facilitate the transition to marriage in certain ways. For many couples, this trip will be the first extended period alone together, away from

Hawaiian honeymoon

The photography of H. Armstrong Roberts

family and friends, in a socially approved intimate relationship. The honeymoon functions to give the newlyweds privacy and is also a respite from other roles and responsibilities, such as their jobs. Freed from other demands and distractions, they can concentrate on each other and on the new joys of marriage. In this new, pleasant setting they also begin to practice such marital competencies as considering each other's wishes in making plans, respecting each other's feelings, and learning about each other's personal habits and idiosyncracies.

For the inexperienced, the honeymoon helps each partner develop those personal qualities which are important in married life, such as patience, tolerance, and the ability to withstand disappointments. It also helps weld the newlyweds into a married dyad. The happy memories of the honeymoon can help bolster morale in the following months, when the couple are contending with the everyday, mundane demands of setting up housekeeping and sorting out their various roles. For many, the honeymoon is a time to adjust to the new meaning of being husband and wife; a time to celebrate their commitment and love; a time to symbolize their transition to marriage.

TRANSITION FROM SINGLE TO MARITAL STATUS

Developmental tasks

Duvall (1977) conceptualizes the transition from singlehood to marriage in terms of *'developmental tasks'* connected with the new statuses and roles of husband and wife. Developmental tasks are defined as "tasks that arise at or near a certain time in the life of an individual, the successful achievement of which leads to . . . happiness and . . . success with later tasks—whereas failures leads to unhappiness in the individual, disapproval by society, and difficulty with later tasks" (Havighurst, 1972, p. 2). This concept may be applied to any stage of the family cycle, and it is most appropriate for the transition from single statuses and roles to the marital statuses and roles of husband and wife. While recognizing that there are apt to be variations in developmental tasks and in their priorities from group to group and from one family to another, efforts have been made to identify some of those most salient for Americans (Havighurst, 1972; Duvall, 1977; Aldous, 1978). Duvall (1977, pp. 191–192) describes some of the main developmental tasks confronting the new husband and wife:

> Some of these (tasks) are: (1) realigning loyalties so that the spouse comes first; (2) participating in all that is involved in establishing a new home; (3) assuming his or her share of responsibilities of being married; (4) becoming a more satisfied and satisfying sexual partner; (5) acquiring a self-image as a wife or husband and learning to interpret the appropriate conjugal roles in action; (6) relating to parents as a married son or daughter; and (7) outgrowing earlier dependencies for more mature and appropriate interdependence within marriage.

While these tasks are clearly appropriate for white middle-class couples, they are relevant in varying degrees for couples in other classes and ethnic groups too.

It will be worthwhile to discuss in more detail some of the developmental tasks which are central to the transition to marriage.

Realigning loyalties so the spouse comes first, while retaining satisfactory relationships with parents and other relatives. According to Matthew 19:5, Christ said that a man should leave father and mother and cleave to his wife. This is not so easily done, however. Up to the time of their marriage, the man and the woman have been primarily a son and a daughter in their parental families, and cannot be expected to become primarily a husband and a wife overnight. This transition will take time and patience, especially where one (often the bride) or both have always lived at home with parents. For those who have become more independent of parents and kin before marriage, the transition will probably be easier. As the newlyweds move into their own home they find themselves identified now with three families instead of just one: the wife's family of orientation, the husband's family of orientation, and their own new family of procreation. Relatives on both sides are now considered to be a part of their larger kin group, and must be remembered appropriately on special occasions, such as birthdays and holidays. Each marriage partner has the developmental task of working out his or her relations with the spouse's family. Problems of in-law relations are generally most pronounced in the earlier periods of marriage, as will be discussed further in a later chapter. Young couples today generally see their in-laws as "friendly allies" who can be counted on to help when needed (Duvall, 1954; 1977, p. 201).

Each marriage partner assuming a share of the responsibilities of marriage and of establishing their new home. It may now require more effort by couples to work out an equitable and mutually satisfactory division of responsibilities than in earlier periods, when marriage roles were more clearly defined and divided according to sex. Also, the modern husband and wife may enter marriage with somewhat differing role-expectations. The new husband may not, for example, be prepared to accept the idea that present-day marriage and homemaking require more of him than just earning the living. He may enter marriage expecting to be waited on after coming home from work the way his mother waited on his father. His wife, of a different generation than his mother, may not expect to do this. With the wife probably continuing her outside employment after marriage and thus sharing with her husband the family provider role, it is only equitable for the husband to assume a larger share of the various housework and homemaking responsibilities. Since no well-established norms exist to guide the couple here, each married pair has to work out more or less by trial and error their own way of sharing the various responsibilities of marriage and of establishing their home.

Establishing mutually satisfying emotional and sexual roles. This is a continuous developmental task for the marriage partners. It takes continuous effort, especially in the early months of marriage, to work out a mutually acceptable and satisfying sexual relationship. In a sense the couple have the objective of becoming as one, emotionally and sexually. Deep emotional involvement—love—as we have seen earlier, is probably the most important criteria for marriage, and husbands and wives expect to give and receive love in marriage. Sex is generally considered a concommitant to love, and newlyweds normally have high expectation for achieving sexual satisfaction in marriage. However, the transition from the premarital sexual pattern is not always a simple one. For many persons, especially for many women, marriage involves a transition from premarital chastity, or at least infrequent or incomplete premarital sexual experience, to a marital relationship of regular, complete, and unrestrained sex. This transition normally takes some time, requiring the woman to redefine her sexuality and sexual objectives from premarital abstinence or reluctance and self-protectiveness to marital acceptance and enjoyable sharing. For the man the transition may be one of changing from a premarital orientation of giving first consideration to his own sexual satisfaction to now giving at least equal consideration to the sexual satisfaction of his wife. As a married couple they are called upon to change their premarital attitude toward sex, with its limitations and anxieties, to a new attitude of full and free acceptance of sex as an important, integral part of their lives.

Changing from a premarital single identity to a marital or couple identity.

Marriage partners undergo certain changes as they leave behind their respective single statuses and come to be identified as a married couple. In our society, with its patrilineal vestiges, these changes are most noticeable for the woman, who normally assumes her husband's surname at marriage. She changes from Miss to Mrs. though he keeps his name as before and continues to be Mr. Some modern women may combine their maiden names with their husband's name to make a hyphenated married name, such as Farrah Fawcett-Majors. With the woman's liberation movement has come the practice of more married women using Ms. rather than Mrs. Some women find this abrupt identity change at marriage difficult or perhaps even traumatic. After being Miss Barbara Harcourt for more than 20 years the new bride suddenly finds herself Mrs. Joe Dumple.

The groom generally doesn't experience the identity crisis at marriage to the same degree as the bride since he keeps his original name, and is more often thought of as the head of the household. If his wife is more socially prominent, or perhaps more highly successful in her career than he is, the man may feel threatened (being viewed as, say, "Mr. Grace Rockefeller").

There are many ways the identity of the newlyweds as a couple may be expressed or symbolized. The wearing of wedding rings is one traditional way, and more men are wearing bands now than earlier. Some subcultures, such as the Amish, symbolize the changes by the bride discarding her white apron for a solid-colored one, while the new groom grows a beard. He changes his open buggy for a new closed-top buggy, and the newlyweds withdraw their association with single young people and take up with those who are married (Kollmorgen, 1942).

Other developmental tasks confronting the married couple include finding and furnishing a suitable dwelling place, establishing adequate and mutually satisfying ways of economic support, establishing themselves in the community, and for most, sooner or later planning for the advent of children (Duvall, 1977, p. 195). Many of these tasks will be considered further in the chapters immediately following.

COLLEGE STUDENT MARRIAGES

Since increasing numbers of young American's start their marriages while attending college, it is appropriate to discuss college marriages at this point. While student marriages are not new, they have been quite rare until recent years, especially for undergraduates. Factors contributing to the upswing in student marriages include the surge in female enrollment, the increases in older students, and increase in part-time students. United States census data for 1974 showed that 11.2 percent of male and 12.5 percent of female college students were married with spouses present. Of the married male students, 61.7 percent were enrolled full-time and 38.6 percent part-time, while 50.8 percent of the married female students were enrolled full-time and 49.2 percent part-time (U.S. Bureau of the Census, 1975; 1976b).

What are some of the special conditions confronting married college students? What kinds of adjustments do college couples have to make as they start out in married life? For one thing, how does being married seem to affect a student's academic performance? Some studies show that married students earn higher grades than unmarried students (Riemer, 1947; Busselen & Busselen, 1975). Being married in college may give the student a sense of security and purpose, as well as more freedom from the hectic pressures of dating and courtship activities. On the other hand the added responsibilities of marriage may cause the grades of some college students to suffer (Samenfink & Milliken, 1961).

Another consideration is the views parents take of the marriage of their son or daughter while in college. Some traditionally oriented parents who would likely approve of the young couple's marriage if they were through college might not approve when one or both are still students. Being of an earlier generation, parents may think that their child should finish college before assuming the responsibilities of marriage. The college couple may have to adjust to such parental disapproval, or at least reluctance. Another consideration is the financial support of the married college couple. Parents who fully expect to help support a single son or daughter attending college may be reluctant to subsidize the same son or daughter

College student weddings are now quite frequent

U.S.D.A. photo by Bill Marr

after marriage. There is a rather well-established American cultural norm that a married couple should be self-supporting. The young couple may feel this way themselves and be reluctant to seek or accept continued financial support from parents after getting married. On the other hand, there is evidence that many middle-class American parents do continue providing various kinds and amounts of economic aid for their married children (Sussman, 1953b). It would be expected that parents who feel this way would probably be more willing to continue contributing to the support of a married son or daughter who is still going to college. This area represents a still rather new and not well-defined aspect of parent-child relations in modern America. Each married student couple has to work it out with the two sets of parents. Open communication is obviously important in doing this successfully.

In most student marriages one or both of the partners will normally be employed at least part-time. In order to expedite the husband's pursuit of his degree and his occupational objectives thereafter, the wife may be the primary breadwinner. While they both may accept the wife's employment as a practical expediency while he is devoting full time to his studies, still one or both may feel uneasy about such a role reversal, even though it is only temporary. The husband may feel some what guilty at having to depend on his wife for financial support, and the wife may feel resentment at having to support them with her job. She is probably also doing most of the housework. The husband may feel he should be helping more with the housework in light of his wife's occupational demands, and he may try to do so, but the demands of his studies on his time and energy as he pursues that all-important college degree may be so great that he leaves the bulk of the housework to his wife. Role reversal problems are apparently present to some degree in many student marriages (Hepker & Cloyd, 1974).

Not only are role reversals a consideraton in student marriages; there may also be problems of multiple roles for one or both partners, and for the student wife especially there may well be an overload of roles. Stated simply, she may assume too many responsibilities. As we have just noted, she may be employed and carrying the main responsibility of the financial support, and also will probably carry the main responsibility for caring for the home; as a wife she is expected to be emotionally and sexually responsive to her husband and to encourage him in his studies and pursuit of his degree. And if she is also a student she is expected to find time for her own studies. Also, if she becomes pregnant she must plan for having and caring for their child (with the help and support of her husband, of course).

Both husbands and wives may be overloaded in student marriages. An increasing number of career-oriented student-wives need their husband's financial support and help at home while they finish their degrees and then pursue their careers. In equalitarian marriages—and college-educated people generally lead this trend—her degree and career are viewed as equally important to his, and he is expected to make as many sacrifices as she does.

As Bowman and Spanier (1978, p. 190) point out, for a college marriage to be successful the young couple need to recognize several things. First, they need to realize that a college marriage is not the same as an ordinary marriage. In addition, there are a number of special conditions and pressures to be contended with, such as the strong academic pressures on one or both, and the need for the wife to assume multiple roles, often including that of family provider.

MARRIAGE IN AMERICAN SOCIETY

Up to now we have focused on the transition to marriage the newly married couple experience. Now we will expand the discussion to look at the broader social context within which marital relations take place in America. What cultural and legal norms and traditions limit and direct the way a man and a woman relate to each other as marriage partners? How are the statuses and roles of husband and wife defined and acted out in daily living?

Chapter 1 indicated that marriage may be structured differently from one place to another and from one time to another. In terms of the number of marriage partners, marriages may be monogamous or polygamous; in terms of authority or power, marriages may be patriarchal, matriarchal, or equalitarian. There may be a strict division of labor between husband and wife or there may be an equal sharing of most roles and responsibilities. Variations in the ways husband and wife statuses and roles are defined and enacted may be seen in contemporary America to some degree between ethnic groups, from one social class to another, and from rural to urban settings (Dyer, 1979). Such variations in the way marriage is defined is understandable in light of the heterogeneous cultural origins of the American population, as well as the variety of value orientations and lifestyles in today's rapidly changing society. Over the generations there has been a general trend away from the more traditional patriarchal structuring of marriage toward an equalitarian structuring of husband-wife roles and relations, and an emphasis on fulfillment of the individual needs of each marital partner. While this trend is most pronounced in middle-class groups, equalitarian norms are also increasingly influencing marital relations in the working class and in many ethnic groups (Le Masters, 1975; Mirande, 1977; Lalli, 1969).

SOCIOLEGAL ASPECTS OF MARRIAGE

Marriage has always been defined and circumscribed by various social customs, traditions, and norms, formal or informal. In complex societies it is generally agreed that marriage laws are needed to assure that a marriage is valid and that individuals meet certain minimum requirements before getting married. Laws also protect those who marry from exploitation or misrepresentation, provide legitimacy for offspring, and provide responsibility for care of the offspring. In the United States each state (and the District of Columbia) has its own set of marriage laws. While there are many similarities in marriage laws from state to state there are also some differences, such as the legal age for marriage and the grounds and procedures for terminating marriage. Let us now examine briefly some of the marriage laws found throughout the United States.

Age at marriage

For the purpose of preventing persons who are too young or too immature from getting married, each state has set minimum ages for marriage. There is normally an age below which one may not get married. There are also ages specified at which a male or a female may marry with consent of parent or guardian, and other ages specified for marriage for each sex without such consent. For example, Alabama law specifies that a man must be 17 years old and a woman 14 years old in order to marry with parental or guardian consent, but the man must be 21 years old and the woman 18 years old to marry without such consent (Bowman

& Spanier, 1978, p. 450). The difference in age for male and female is based on a traditional view that females mature earlier than males. In recent years many states are doing away with such age differentials.

Blood relationships

In America, as in most societies, the incest taboo has resulted in laws prohibiting marriage between a man and a woman who are closely related by blood. All states forbid marriage of father and daughter, mother and son, brother and sister, grandfather and grandaughter, grandmother and grandson, aunt and nephew, and uncle and niece. In addition, about half of the states forbid the marriage of first cousins, and some states prohibit the marriage of second cousins. In addition to all these restrictions, which are based on direct blood ties or consanguity, about half of the states have other restrictions based on affinity, which denotes a relationship through marriage rather than a blood or kinship tie. Such affinity-based restrictions would forbid marriage between a stepparent and stepchild, or between a mother-or father-in-law and a son-or daughter-in-law. (One may wonder if or when such matters would ever become issues.) Some of these affinity prohibitions would appear to be carrying the incest taboo rather far.

Void and voidable marriages

Some marriages may be null and void from the time they are entered into because they are in violation of the requirements of the law. An example would be the marriage of first cousins in a state prohibiting such marriages. No court action is needed to void such a marriage. There are other situations in which a marriage is voidable through a court action initiated by one of the parties concerned; until such action is taken, however the marriage remains legal and binding despite having been entered into illegally. Examples of voidable marriages would be those in which fraudulent claims were made by one of the parties before marriage, or where coercion was used to get one of the parties to agree to the marriage, such as in the shot-gun marriage. The aggrieved party has to bring court action to have the marriage declared void. In such cases the judge grants an annulment, and it is legally assumed that the marriage never existed. Thus an annulment differs legally from a divorce, which terminates a marriage that has actually existed. After a divorce the man and woman become ex-husband and ex-wife; after an annulment they are simply single.

Some procedural aspects of marriage

There are certain legal requirements which must be met before an individual may marry, and others that must be met before a man and woman may marry one another. Each person normally must have a physical examination, the couple must obtain and record their marriage license, and there is generally a waiting period before they may get married. Let us look briefly at these procedural legal requirements.

Physical examination.

In the early 20th century some states began to require premarital physical examinations for men to assure that they were not infected with a communicable venereal disease. Since World War II premarital blood tests for both sexes have become required by law in a majority of states. The law generally says that the couple must furnish a medical certificate specifying that neither party has syphilis. A marriage license will not be granted without this certificate. However, there is evidence that such laws are not always strictly or uniformly applied. A couple can often get around such laws by getting married in a nearby state where no such blood test is required.

Waiting period.

Most states now have a waiting period between the time the couple applies for a marriage license and the time the license is actually issued. Waiting periods vary from one to five days, with a three-day rule in most states. Such waiting period laws serve as advance notice of the impending marriage and impose a "cooling off" period to enable the couple to pause and think again before taking the final plunge. Such laws have prevented many spur-of-the-moment or "quickie" marriages. Estimates are that as many as 20 percent of all couples applying never use the marriage license or do not even return to pick it up after the waiting period (Kephart, 1977, p. 331).

Marriage license and authorized marriage officiant or official.

A couple desiring to get married must obtain a marriage license, except in those few states where common-law marriage is still legal. The marriage license, normally obtained from the county courthouse, certifies that the couple have met the requirements of the law and are legally free to marry. It also serves as a public record of the marriage.

State laws also generally specify who is officially authorized to perform a marriage ceremony, usually including such religious authorities as a minister, a priest, or a rabbi, and such civil authorities as a judge or a justice of the peace. The law also requires witnesses to verify that the marriage took place. Within these broad limitations set by law a given couple is free to choose the type of marriage ceremony they prefer, and may even write their own marriage vows. So long as the man and woman mutually affirm and declare that they take each other as husband and wife, and make this declaration before an authorized officiant or official in the presence of witnesses, the ceremony is valid and they are legally married.

Common-law marriages.

A common-law marriage is one that is entered by mutual consent of the partners without being solemnized by a wedding ceremony. The couple live together and present themselves to the community as husband and wife. Today common-law marriages are a kind of anachronism or holdover from the past. Well into the Middle Ages in Europe, marriage was generally considered a private affair, thus a spoken pledge of matrimony between the man and the woman was often all that was required. The Christian Church in the Middle Ages recognized such "self-marriage," but preferred good Christians to be married in a religious ceremony. In fact, this position became the official Church ruling in 1563 at the Council of Trent, which required Catholics to be married by a priest in the presence of two witnesses. Protestants, however, continued to recognize the older common-law marriage. Common-law marriages continued in colonial America, partly on the basis of the old European tradition and partly on the basis of expediency and the conditions of marriage and family life in the new world (Calhoun, 1945: Vol. 1, pp. 44–45). Under pioneer and frontier conditions it was often impractical, if not impossible, to find an official to perform a wedding ceremony. Rather than wait, a couple who were ready to marry would often enter into a common-law marriage, which was considered legal and binding and which legitimized any children born to the couple. Many who entered such common-law marriages had every intention of having a wedding ceremony later when an officiant or official—such as the circuit-rider preacher who might visit the remote frontier settlement only once every few months—could be found.

Thus the traditional legal right of common-law marriage has been passed on down to the present day even though the rationale for it has ceased to exist. As might be expected, common-law marriages are being increasingly challenged today. Only about a dozen states still permit them, and another dozen or so still recognize the validity of such marriages if they were entered into prior to a given date, generally the date when the state outlawed all subsequent common-law marriages.

Common-law marriages entail a number of legal and personal problems for the partners. Such a marriage enables them to bypass many of the legal qualifications and requirements for marriage, such as the blood test, the marriage license, and the waiting period. While a conventional marriage, with a license and an official court record of the wedding, provides the state as well as the couple with an authorized legal record of the marriage, such is generally not the case for a common-law marriage. Questions of property rights of the partners, of inheritance rights, and even of the validity of the marriage itself are frequently found in the dockets of courts in states where common-law marriages exist. Widows of these marriages often have legal difficulties in establishing their insurance benefits, property inheritance rights, or social security benefits. With the decline in common-law marriages in the United States it would seem that many of these problems would diminish. However, with the increase in couples living together as an alternative to marriage, the reciprocal rights and responsibilities of men and women who cohabit without benefit of legal marriage will likely continue to be problematic and subject to different interpretation by the man and the woman, as the highly publicized Lee Marvin "palimony" case of 1979 well illustrates.

MARITAL RELATIONSHIPS AND PROCESSES

Now let us turn our attention to the marriage relationship itself, to husband-wife interaction patterns, marriage role transition and differentiation, and role choices in present-day marriages in America.

Husband-wife interaction

Soon after their wedding the newlyweds normally begin to settle down into some kind of daily routine as married couple. Their new relationship as man and wife and their love for one another will normally suffuse the early months of marriage with euphoria and enthusiasm. There will be some experimentation in working out their daily and weekly routines. While the emotional "high" of the honeymoon and early marriage period will recede as the couple are confronted with daily home and job demands, their love and enthusiasm will be beneficial in the early stages of marital adjustment and in helping them establish viable routines and mutually satisfactory divisions of labor and authority.

Regardless of how thorough their courtship and how well the marriage partners think they know each other, every marriage includes unknowns and undefined situations. This state of affairs has been aptly expressed by Waller and Hill (1951, p. 254):

> Strictly speaking . . . , every new marriage is an undefined situation, just as every new status involves undefined elements for the neophyte. Each individual begins tentatively to explore the behavior possibilities of the situation. Each tries to find out what he can do and should do and begins to form habits, but neither can stabilize his habits at once, because the other person is also carrying on an exploratory process.

Marriage as status and role transition

Marriage statuses and roles entail reciprocally related norms and expectations (Linton, 1936). The status, or position, of "husband" consists of a bundle of duties, rights, obligations, privileges, and so on that are in reciprocity to those of the status of "wife." For example, the husband's traditional duty to support his wife financially is reciprocally tied to her right to receive this support; she in turn has the duty to provide a home for him to return to after work, which becomes one of his rights as her husband.

Since the marital roles of husband and wife are reciprocally intertwined, the attitudes and actions of each partner affect the role performance of the other. Successful marriage requires much give and take between a man and a woman who are continuously taking into account each other's roles, attitudes, interests, and other personality characteristics.

Marriage and role differentiation

All societies differentiate between the roles of husband and wife in the marriage and family system. For example, in many societies the role of the husband includes the main responsibility for the economic support of the family (the breadwinner role), while the role of the wife includes the responsibility of caring for the home (the homemaker role). In earlier periods of American history such sex-role differences were more distinct than in more recent years. In fact, there is much more role-flexibility and role-blurring in a great many American marriages today, with the result that husbands and wives are now more apt to have to work out their division of responsibilities and authority in a continuous dialog, as Scanzoni (1972) emphasizes in his *Sexual Bargaining*. These issues will be dealt with in detail in the following chapters.

The trend toward greater role-flexibility and sharing of roles by husband and wife is especially apparent in middle-class American families (Zeldich, 1955; Dyer, 1979). Such trends mean greater potential in modern marriages for more varied and richer experiences, but they also require additional effort in working out a mutually satisfactory division of labor and authority. Add to this the increasingly high expectations each partner brings into marriage and it becomes clearly apparent that a successful marriage today requires continuous effort.

Role choices in marriage

In marriage each partner not only has to think out and make choices as to his or her own marital roles; each also has to seek out and understand the role-expectations of the other. How well each partner perceives, understands, and essentially agrees with the role definitions and expectations of the other is most important in marital adjustment. Studies show that in marriage the role desires and expectations each partner holds for one's spouse and oneself are among those crucial aspects of marriage which require continuous adjustment and good communication (Stuckert, 1963a; Luckey, 1960).

Here are some of the areas of married life upon which role decisions will have to be made:

1. Will the husband be the main or sole family provider, or will the wife share this role?

2. Will the wife be the main or sole homemaker, doing the housekeeping, cooking and cleaning, while he earns the living, or will he share the homemaking role?

3. How will the career-oriented husband divide his time and energies among his career, his family, and other community interests?

4. If the wife is employed outside the home, how will she divide her time and energies between her occupation or career and her marriage and family roles?

5. For both husband and wife, when—or even if at all—should they start having children? This decision is indeed important and needs to be made in light of adjustments and sacrifices required of their other roles and interests, both as marriage partners and as employees. Studies show that the arrival of the first child often produces crises, expecially in middle-class marriages where the wife has been employed (Dyer, 1963; Rossi, 1968).

Many of these questions and the related choices that husbands and wives have to make in present-day marriages will be addressed again in the following chapters on marital adjustment.

CHANGES AND TRENDS IN AMERICAN MARRIAGE

Now let us turn from the more specific aspects of marriage roles and relationships to a brief look at the larger picture of social and demographic trends and changes which provide the setting within which married couples will have to work out their own patterns of roles and relationships.

Some long-range trends

In his work *The American Family: Variety and Change*, the author attempts to sum up some of the salient changes and trends in marriage in America (1979, p. 278):

> The outstanding change (in marriage) has been the trend toward greater equality in relations. This relates directly to the long-term trend toward emancipation of women. . . . Such trends, however, have been felt unevenly up and down the social-class structure. Husband-wife equalitarianism is more advanced in middle-class families than in working-class families. . . . While equal status for women has yet to be fully realized, predominant middle-class values and norms, supported by trends in law and the economy, are pushing for such equality in marriage and family relations. Internally, this equalitarian trend has been manifest in the emergence of the companionship family . . . and in the increasing flexibility in the division of labor in the family. These changes have been accompanied by attitudes questioning the traditional family role definitions, and in some circles by an outright rejection of stereotyped views of men's work and women's work in the family. Both marital and family adjustment now focus on the welfare and personal satisfaction, happiness, and growth of all family members. Thus the emergence of interpersonal criteria of success in marriage.

The extent and significance of the changes and trends in American marriage over the years may be seen by contrasting the "Traditional-Patriarchal" family type predominant in early American history to the

148

"Modern-Equalitarian" family type toward which we appear to be moving today (Loomis & Dyer, 1976, pp. 39–78). In the Traditional-Patriarchal family consanguine or kinship bonds were emphasized, whereas in the Modern-Equalitarian family the conjugal bonds between husband and wife are stressed. The Traditional-Patriarchal was highly familistic and multifunctional, while the Modern-Equalitarian has only limited functions and emphasizes individualism. In the former type there was a strict sex division of labor and masculine authority, while in the latter type there is great role-flexibility, varied and experimental division of labor between the marriage partners, and equalitarian authority patterns. In the former there was male dominance and special masculine privileges, while in the latter there are equal rights and privileges for the husband and the wife. In the Traditional-Patriarchal family the wife had status and rank subordinate to the husband, while in the Modern-Equalitarian family there is equal status or rank between the marriage partners. In the former, marriage was considered a religious and social obligation and understood to be relatively unbreakable, while in the latter marriage is viewed as something one is free to undertake or not, and if chosen is defined as an interpersonal relationship of compatibility and satisfaction of personal needs. Divorce is approved if one feels such personal needs are not being met or if the marriage is considered a failure.

These "ideal" or "constructed" family types enable us to span the range of possible variations in marriage and family structure and relationships, and by comparing actual families against the types in different periods of our history we can see how much change has taken place. It should be pointed out that few families even in colonial times, actually fulfilled the Traditional-Patriarchal type 100 percent, and today there are few families in urban, secular America that fit the Modern-Equalitarian type 100 percent. But the evidence is clear that the direction of marriage and family change today is toward the latter.

Some demographic trends and changes in marriage

In his study of the life cycle of marriage and family, Glick (1977) sees certain trends in the age of men and women at marriage, the age of women when they have their children, and the age of the parents when their last child marries and leaves home.

Women entering marriage during the decade of the 1970s were expected to marry at about the same age (21.2 years) as did women entering marriage during the first decade of the 20th century (21.4 years). But the women marrying in the 1970s will have one and two fewer children, will end their childbearing period three years sooner, and will have about 11 more years of married life after their last child marries, as compared to the women marrying in the first decade of the present century (Glick, 1977, p. 5).

A woman entering marriage in the 1970s has a median age at first marriage of 21.2 years; she is 22.7 at the birth of her first child, and 29.6 at the birth of her last child; she is 52.3 at the marriage of her last child, and at the death of one of the spouses she is 65.2 years of age (Glick, 1977, p. 6). Instead of the marriage of the couple being dissolved by the death of a spouse (generally the husband) less than 2 years after their last child marries, as was the case in the first decade of the 20th century, a couple entering marriage in the 1970s has the prospect of living together 13 more years after their last child marries. These 13 more years represent about one third of the total years of married life normally expected. This additional time together following the departure from home of their last child, called the "empty-nest" period of the family cycle, is due partly to the improvement of the survival rates among adults in the 20th century, and partly to the earlier completion of childbearing. In the 1970s the average number of children born per married woman was 2.3, compared to 3.3 for those married in the first decade of the century. This difference reflects a long-term decline in birth rates which—aside from the baby boom right after World War II—has followed a general downward path to the present. With fewer children and with more years of the empty-nest stage married couples today can expect to spend more years of their total marriage as a twosome. Some of the research on marital adjustment shows that these child-free years are among the most satisfying in the whole marriage (Feldman, 1971).

One of the more striking demographic changes in the 1960s and 1970s was the increasing proportion of young people who postponed their first marriages. Men and women in their 20s, which is the age when most people who marry do so, were putting off entry into marriage until they were about one and a half years older than young people two decades before. In 1978, the median age at first marriage for men was 24.2 years and for women 21.8 years. In 1956 the comparable figures were 22.5 for men and 20.1 for women (Glick, 1979b, p. 2). (See Figure 6–1.)

The proportion of young women in their early 20s who were not yet married increased by more than 50 percent between 1960 and 1977. In 1977, 45 percent of all women aged 20 to 24 years had not yet married as compared to 28 percent in 1960. One factor that helps explain this upswing in postponement of first marriage of young women is the unbalanced sex ratio found in those most marriageable years. In those age groups when most first marriages occur—18 to 24 years for women and 20 to 26 years for men—there has been a 5 to 10 percent excess of women in recent years. This imbalance in the sex ratio is due largely to past fluctuations in the birth rate. For example, women born in 1947, at the time of the post–World War II baby boom, were ready to marry at age 20 in 1967, but the men that were most likely to marry were born in 1945–46, when the birth rate was still low. So men of marriageable age were in short supply in the late 1960s and early 1970s. Glick (1979b, p. 2) calculates that marriageable men were about 8 percent less numerous than the 20-year-old women then. While these figures show a pattern

Figure 6–1

Median age at first marriage, by sex, 1890–1978

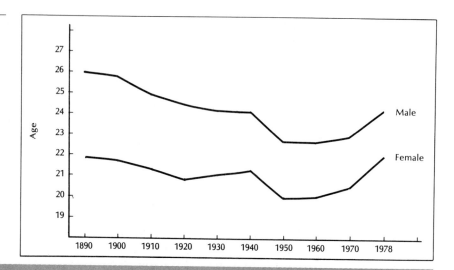

Source: U.S. Bureau of the Census, Current Population Reports, and decennial censuses.

of postponing first marriage among young adults, this does not necessarily mean a significant increase in the incidence of lifelong singleness.

Demographic data underline the fact that Americans still believe in marriage. As Glick (1979b, p. 3) points out, in spite of the increases in divorce (92 per 1,000 married persons in 1979 versus 47 per 1,000 in 1970) and in various nonmarital living arrangements during the past 10 to 15 years, the large majority of American people continue to live in nuclear family households centering on the husband and wife. In 1977, about 77 percent of the 213 million persons in the noninstitutionalized American population were living in husband-wife households, with another 10 percent in one-parent households; thus 87 percent were living in nuclear family households. Of the remainder, 7 percent were living alone as one-person households, 1 percent were living together as unmarried couples, and 5 percent were living in various other alternative living arrangements (Glick, 1979b, p. 3). (See Table 6–1.)

Table 6–1

Household types and living arrangements, U.S. population, 1977*

Household type or arrangement	Percentage of population
Husband-wife households	77
One-parent households	10
One-person households	7
Unmarried couple households	1
Various other living arrangements	5

* Noninstitutional population. About 1 percent of all persons were living in institutions.

Source: "The Future of the American Family" by Paul Glick, U.S. Bureau of the Census, *Current Population Reports: Special Studies*, January 1979, p. 3.

The purpose of this chapter has been to introduce Part Three. Many of the topics discussed will be elaborated in the following five chapters. In this chapter we have attempted to acquaint the reader with the nature of marriage in contemporary America, with what the transition from being single to being married means for women and men, and with some of the changes are that are taking place in marriage in our time. Chapters to follow will examine marital adjustment—including sexual adjustment in marriage—marriage and occupational roles, broken marriage and remarriage, and various alternatives to conventional marriage.

Marital adjustment: Getting along as marriage partners

Why do some married couples get along so much better than others? Why are some wives and husbands happy together while others are not? Why are some marriages clearly more successful than others? Why are some marriages stable and enduring while others are unstable and short lived? As usual, it is far easier to raise such questions than to find the answers; but these, and other questions and issues relating to the general topic of marital adjustment, will be the focus of the present chapter. Actually, all the chapters in this section (Chapters 6 to 11) treat selected aspects of marital adjustment in one way or another. This chapter is devoted to the concept of marital adjustment, to various factors related to it, to research studies on the subject, and finally, to efforts and suggestions toward improvement of marital adjustment.

THE CONCEPT OF MARITAL ADJUSTMENT

Marital adjustment is a term that has been widely used by marriage and family specialists, but has not been clearly defined. In implies various processes and adjustments in the relations of the marriage partners—processes of accommodating to daily situations, of balancing each individual's needs, interests, role-expectations, and viewpoints, and adapting to changing conditions of marriage and family living.

The Dictionary of Modern Sociology (Hoult, 1969, p. 192) defines marital adjustment as "changes in the marital partners' attitudes and behaviors such that the partners may mutually fulfill their marriage expectations and hopes; sometimes operationally defined as a complex of factors (for example, shared activities, degree of role complementarity, amount of conflict, etc.) believed to be associated with the happiness or success of given marriages." Much of the literature on marital adjustment focuses on these latter points; that is, on the happiness, satisfaction, or perceived success of a marriage in relation to a variety of personal and social factors. There is almost always an implicit or explicit qualitative dimension to the concept of marital adjustment. Marriages where the partners are happy or satisfied have good marital adjustment, while marriages dominated by tensions and conflict have poor marital adjustment. Such a concept always carries the danger of hidden or implied value judgments as to what a good or a bad marriage is—judgments biased in favor of one particular kind of marital adjustment. Later in the chapter, in reviewing some of the criticisms of the concept, we will show how the biases and viewpoints of some researchers have slanted the theory and research findings on marital adjustment.

In his *Modern Courtship and Marriage*, LeMasters (1957b, p. 229) says that "marital adjustment can be conceptualized as the *capacity for adjustment* or adaptation, as ability to *solve* problems rather than *absence* of problems." Marital adjustment is always a matter of degree, so any marriage at a given time would occupy a point on a scale ranging from poor adjustment to very good adjustment. Adjustment, in or out of marriage, is a continuous and changing process. Situations change and people change. Consider this example. A young couple get married while they are college students. She quits college to help earn their living so he can study full-time and earn his degree quickly. Their goals and their enthusiastic cooperative efforts keep them close emotionally; they are happy and their marital adjustment is very good. Some years later, as he becomes absorbed in his career and she is bearing and caring for their children, their interests and views may diverge—the personal happiness of both may lessen, and their marital adjustment may diminish. Then, after their children have grown up and left home, the husband and wife will have more time for each other, and their marital adjustment may improve again. Such changes in marital adjustment may be inferred from cross-sectional studies of the family life cycle, as will be discussed later in the chapter.

The total adjustment of any married couple at a particular time may be viewed as a balance of many different factors, a composite of a large number of elements and conditions influencing their relationship. Over the years, many social scientists have attempted to identify the salient factors which affect marital adjustment. Let us turn now to what has been discovered.

FACTORS IN MARITAL ADJUSTMENT

IDENTIFICATION OF FACTORS AND PROBLEM AREAS

A perusal of the literature on marital adjustment reveals a variety of social, psychological, personal, and demographic factors which relate to marital adjustment and have some bearing on the relative success or failure of the marriage. A good deal of research and writing has been devoted to this area over several decades, as will become apparent.

LeMasters (1957b, p. 236) identifies nine sets of factors associated with marital adjustment: (1) personality factors, (2) family background, (3) social class background, (4) sexual factors, (5) in-law relationships, (6) attitudes toward money, (7) religion and basic values, (8) children, and (9) male and female subcultures. Udry (1974, pp. 240–257) concurs with LeMasters that social class background and social mobility are important in marital adjustment. He also sees other factors affecting the adjustment or marital success of the couple as including (1) age at marriage, (2) relative age of the mates, (3) propinquity, (4) education of the spouses, (5) religion of the spouses, and (6) race of the spouses. Nass (1978, pp. 289–308) identifies major areas of marital adjustment to include (1) adjusting to in-laws, (2) adjusting to youthful marriages, (3) work-role adjustments, (4) gender-role adjustments, (5) leisure activities, and (6) adjusting to the family at home. It is quite clear that these authors agree to a considerable extent on many of the factors and areas of marriage and family living wherein adjustments have to be worked out—or worked on—by married couples.

Using a slightly different approach, Farber (1964, pp. 285–320) sees a number of predicaments or problem areas confronting married people which require cooperative effort for resolution and viable marital adjustment.

Socioemotional versus instrumental roles and relationships

Each married couple has to work out a satisfactory balance between needs and demands of a personal and emotional nature and others of an instrumental nature. The former involve values and expectations relating to emotional and affectional need-satisfaction, companionship, and personal development; the latter involve values and norms pertaining to economic and financial security, physical health and well being, and the family's position in the community. Traditionally the statuses and roles of the wife have emphasized the socioemotional area (home, children, and kin), while the statuses and roles of the husband have been predomi-

A young couple starts married life in a mobile home

U.S.D.A. photo by Bill Kuykendall

nant in the instrumental areas (breadwinner, representative of the family in the community, and so on). However, with the advent of feminism, equalitarianism, and individualism, traditions have now weakened. Many married couples today are faced with predicaments in sorting out their roles and responsibilities along these lines.

Short-term satisfactions versus long-run goals and planning

Time is one of the important conditions of social interaction (Loomis & Dyer, 1976). In their daily living a married couple may emphasize the here and now, concentrating on current family problems and interests and on immediate personal gains and gratifications, giving little thought to the future or to possible long-term consequences of their immediate actions and choices. Conversely, a couple may be essentially "future oriented," giving maximum consideration to long-range planning and to organizing their present activities with the attainment of future goals in mind, often at the expense of some more immediate gratifications. Middle-class couples have at times shown a greater tendency toward such deferment of gratification while lower-class couples have been more apt to adopt the short-term view (Kahl, 1957).

Internal (family) commitments versus external (community) commitments

The predicament here is how much time and energy the couple should devote to or invest in home and family activities as compared to outside and nonfamily activities. This predicament is greater in our contemporary, individual-oriented, multiinterest society than in earlier times when familism was stronger and male and female interests were more segregated. In our present secular, urban society there is greater competition between the outside community and the family. Equalitarianism and feminism have both opened the outside world to married women and put pressure on them to have more extrafamily interests and activities, including careers. Correspondingly, there are some signs of counter-pressures on husbands and fathers to devote more time to home and family. These issues and predicaments come into sharp focus in many two-career marriages today. The process of marital adjustment for such couples is a far cry from that of most traditional 19th-century rural marriages.

Parents versus children

As conceptualized by Farber (1964, p. 317) the predicament here is whether to give priority to the needs and gratifications of children or of parents. Since a majority of married couples have children this is a general problem. American parents have traditionally been expected to sacrifice or subordinate many of their personal or conjugal needs and desires to those of their children (Duvall, 1946). This familistic viewpoint has suffered some with the trend toward individualism and the emphasis given to conjugal relations in some modern circles. Studies have shown that the arrival of the first child can put a serious strain on the marital relations of a couple. Effort and maturity—especially on the part of the husband—are required to get the marriage back into good adjustment (Dyer, 1963).

How a given couple work out—or continuously work on—these four interrelated predicaments will depend on their particular marriage and family orientations. In these times of social change and ambivalence many couples will have to work harder and longer at resolving such predicaments and issues.

MARITAL ADJUSTMENT AND SELECTED SOCIAL
AND DEMOGRAPHIC FACTORS

As indicated above, many specific social and demographic factors have been found to be associated with marital adjustment. Let us now see how some of them have been found to affect marital adjustment.

Age and marital adjustment

Most studies investigating age as a factor show that marital adjustment is lower when the partners marry at a very young age, that is, when the man is under age 20 and the woman is under age 18 (Udry, 1974; Schoen, 1975). The studies suggest that, in their immaturity, they tend to romanticize marriage and are less well-prepared for the responsibilities of marriage than those who marry later. The very young, confronted by the demands and burdens of marriage, may rather quickly become disappointed, discouraged, and unhappy (DeLissovoy, 1973). Divorce rates can be high among prematurely married very young people. (See Table 7–1.) Not only are those in this group more apt to be immature and less well-prepared for marriage, they are also more likely to come from a lower-class background, and are thus more prone to suffer additional deprivations which make marital adjustment even more difficult (Roth & Peck, 1951). Youth from lower socioeconomic groups are apt to have less education and fewer resources to use in pursuing socially valued goals, such as prestigious and high-paying jobs. Lower-class youth who quit school to marry jeopardize their ability to get high-income jobs in the future. These problems and frustrations can produce dissatisfactions which make marital adjustment more difficult for them than for the better-educated, better-off middle-class youth.

Is marital adjustment affected by age differences between the spouses? Findings of studies dealing with age differences and marital adjustment have not been conclusive. Some have found it beneficial for the spouses to be of the same age (Locke, 1951; Blood & Wolfe, 1960); while others have found that age differences have no significant effect on marital adjustment (Udry, Nelson & Nelson, 1961). After reviewing the evidence on age differences and marital success, Udry (1974, p. 242) concluded that there is as yet no conclusive evidence of any significant relationship between them; that whatever difference might be created by husband-wife age differentials, their effect on the success of the marriage appears to be negligible.

Religion and marital adjustment

The relationship between religion and marital adjustment has been investigated over the years. Here also, the various findings have not always

Table 7-1

Mean divorce rates by age at first marriage, California, 1969		Mean divorce rate*	
	Age at first marriage	Females	Males
	16	3.03	—
	17	2.72	—
	18	2.37	2.82
	19	1.81	2.59
	20	1.55	2.22
	21	1.33	2.02
	22	1.13	1.65
	23	1.08	1.52
	24	.91	1.34
	25	.91	1.20
	26	.90	1.16
	27	.89	1.19
	28	—	.99
	29	—	.94
	All	1.55	1.55

* Arithmetic mean of 36 age-duration-specific divorce rates (0–35 years of marriage). Divorce rate = number of divorces and annulments granted to persons at specified age at first marriage and duration of first marriage per 100 persons in the population at that age at first marriage.
Source: "California Divorce Rates by Age at First Marriage and Duration of First Marriage" by R. Schoen, *Journal of Marriage and the Family,* 1975, *35,* 553.

been consistent nor in agreement. Terman (1938) concluded that the religious background of the spouses was a relatively insignificant factor in their marital happiness. Burgess and Cottrell (1939) found that, though disagreements between husband and wife over religious matters played only a small part in marital unhappiness, agreement on religious matters was positively correlated with marital happiness for their sample of 526 middle-class couples. Locke (1951), in a comparison of 200 divorced couples and 200 happily married couples, found that the happily married couples were more religious than the divorced couples. But he also found that marriages in which the husband was of one religious faith and the wife another were just as frequently found in the happily married group as in the divorced group, and that marital happiness was no greater for the intrafaith marriages than for the interfaith marriages.

More recent studies on mixed religious marriages (Christensen & Barber, 1967; Glenn, 1982) found evidence that, for men at least, interfaith marriages between Catholics, Jews, and Protestants are somewhat less happy than are intrafaith marriages for these three major religious groups. Glenn (1982) found that the effects on marital happiness of interreligious marriage involving combinations of Protestants, Jews, and Catholics indicate a moderate negative effect for white males but no effect for white females. As America becomes more and more secular, and traditional religious faiths lose their hold on more people, a greater frequency of interfaith marriages can be expected, and their marital adjustment will probably show little or no difference from that found in other marriages.

Race and marital adjustment

Although the overall incidence of interracial marriage in the United States is very small—probably less than 2 percent of all marriages—it is rising and will likely continue to do so (Monahan, 1976). So far there have been no major studies of marital adjustment in which racial intermarriage was a variable. Although there is a widely held popular opinion that interracial marriages are hazardous, there is actually little statistical evidence to support this view (Udry, 1974, p. 254). A study by Golden (1954) of 50 black-white marriages in Philadelphia showed that in spite of severe premarital pressure from their families to discontinue the relationships, these marriages had a high probability of surviving because the couples had given much more forethought to their marriages than most couples do. Another study of black-white marriages by Smith (1966) found essentially the same thing. The family and community pressures and obstacles that these interracial couples faced required more joint effort to overcome and thus actually tended to strengthen and enhance their marriages. In a study of interracial marriages in Iowa, Monahan (1970) found that black-white marriages were more stable than black-black marriages; he also found that marriages where the husband was black and the wife white had the lowest divorce rates of all, being actually lower than divorce rates in white-white marriages.

In Hawaii, where interracial marriage rates (mostly between Orientals and Caucasians) are several times higher than on the mainland, the divorce rate is no higher than it is on the mainland, according to one study (Cheng & Yamamura, 1957). It seems likely that many of the difficulties experienced by couples in interracial marriages are related to the degree of social and cultural separation of the two racial groups represented, and to the tenacity of the endogamous norms within each racial group. Where social and cultural separation is still considerable and the taboos against intermarriage are still strong—as in most mainland states—those who defy the taboos and marry across racial boundaries are subject to strong negative sanctions from their racial groups. In spite of such opposition to mixed racial marriages, scientific evidence does not support the position that interracial marriages today are less stable than intraracial marriages (Udry, 1974, p. 255).

Education and marital adjustment

There is a good deal of evidence that the more education the marriage partners have the greater the probability of good marital adjustment and the lower the probability of divorce. This may be due partly to the fact that the more education one has the older one will probably be at marriage (Bumpass & Sweet, 1972).

Studies focusing on marital satisfaction show that for both wife and husband higher education is positively associated with marital satisfaction. Women with more education are more satisfied with their love and affectional relations with their husbands (Blood & Wolfe, 1960) and have more satisfying sexual relationships (Terman, 1938; Kinsey, 1953). An item bearing on the relationship between education and marital adjustment is that some men and women with less education are more apt to remain unhappily married, whereas college-educated men and women are more apt to get divorced if their marriages are unhappy (Landis & Landis, 1963).

Data from recent national surveys suggest that education may no longer be a very important factor in marital adjustment. Glenn and Weaver (1978) found no significant correlation between the number of years of education and marital happiness. For men, there was a small positive correlation between the number of years of schooling and marital happiness. This suggests that education is conducive to the success of marriage for men. For women the picture is less clear. The most highly educated women are more likely to have been divorced than are those with no more than a high school education (Udry, 1966; Bumpass & Sweet, 1972). Highly educated women are more apt to be economically self-sufficient and less reluctant to end an unsatisfactory marriage.

The relationship between educational differences between the partners and marital adjustment is not entirely clear. Studies generally support the position that the more similar the husband and wife are in education level the more satisfied they are in their marriage. Some of the early studies using middle-class samples showed little or no relationship between husband and wife differences in education and marital adjustment (Terman, 1938; Burgess & Wallin, 1953). Had their sample been less educationally homogeneous, their findings might have been different. Blood and Wolfe (1960), using a broader, more representative sample, found that married women were more satisfied with marriages in which both partners had equal education. If divorce is taken as a consequence or poor marital adjustment, then there is evidence that a less educated husband may contribute to marital adjustment problems. Scanzoni (1968) found that marriages in which the husband had less education than the wife were more apt to end in divorce than marriages in which the husband had as much or more education than the wife. In general, similar education of the spouses seems to be conducive to marital adjustment. Where differences in educational achievements exist, the most potentially disruptive difference is probably where the wife is college-educated and the husband is not.

Social class and marital adjustment

Sociologists generally agree that social class differences exist in America, despite our equalitarian ideology. Social class differences in customs, values, and beliefs are reflected in marriage and family attitudes and behavior. Studies generally support the position that marital adjustment and stability are greater in the middle and upper ranges of the social class spectrum than in the lower ranges (Roth & Peck, 1951; LeMasters, 1975). This appears to be partly due to the fact that lower class subcultures and conditions of life do not support marital stability and a smooth adjustment between wife and husband as well middle- and upper-class subcultures and life conditions do. Lower-class marriages are subject to chronic stresses and strains related to menial jobs, low income, unemployment, poor housing, and health problems, among others. The "culture of poverty" within which the partners have been born and brought up contribute to feelings of disenchantment, apathy, and low self-esteem (Lewis, 1965; Kahl, 1957).

Life under these conditions affects marital relations in many ways, mostly unfavorable. The husband is aware that his failure to support his wife and children is bound to effect his relations with them (Leibow, 1967). He is likely to spend more time with other men—and often other women—outside the family. His wife is likely to turn to female relatives (especially her mother) and friends for companionship and security. Traditionally the bonds between women in the lower class have been very strong, and husbands may be merely tolerated in this close family circle. Duberman (1976, p. 127) sums up this situation:

> In lower class marriage then, there is a vicious circle. The husband and wife expect to be emotionally isolated from each other, and this expectation forces the wife to turn to her mother, which in turn arouses the husband's resentment and further estranges the couple.

It would, however, be incorrect to leave the impression that most lower-class marriages are maladjusted. There is evidence that in spite of their disadvantages and problems, lower-class marriages and families in America tend to be remarkably resilient and demonstrate many strengths (Billingsley, 1968; Hill, 1971).

The comparative disadvantages of lower-class marital adjustment vis-à-vis middle- and upper-class marital adjustment may also be partly due to the fact that the criteria of marital success and the methods by which marital adjustment are measured are apt to be somewhat biased toward middle-class definitions of what a successful, well-adjusted marriage is (Kolb, 1948; Rodman, 1964). Some recent survey data relating marital happiness directly to class-related variables, such as income and occupational prestige, show only modest relationships (Glenn & Weaver, 1978).

If the marriage partners come from different social class backgrounds, does this affect their marital adjustment? There is still very little empirical data upon which to base an answer to this question. Roth and Peck (1951) found that cross-class marriages generally show lower marital adjustment than same-class marriages, and that marital adjustment was lowest where the husband and wife were more than one social class apart at the time of their marriage. While such differences in social class background can affect the attitudes and behavior of the marriage partners in ways that make their adjustment difficult, it may well be that their social class identity at the time of marriage is less important than what the social class orientation of each partner is as the marriage progresses. The upwardly mobile person with a lower-class background can expect to have a better adjusted marriage with a middle-class mate than with a lower-class mate who is not also upwardly mobile. Thus while Roth and Peck found that while cross-class marriages may be lower in adjustment than same-class marriages in the middle class, the cross-class marriages are generally better adjusted than are marriages in which the husband and wife were both from the lower class. This is consistent with the general finding that middle-class marriages have better adjustment than do lower-class marriages, although here only one of the partners has a middle-class background while the other, even though of lower-class background, is upwardly mobile and thus has a middle-class orientation.

In cross-class marriages it makes a difference whether the husband or the wife has the higher class background. A number of studies have shown that when the husband is from a lower class than his wife, the marriage is less likely to succeed than when the wife is from a lower class than her husband (Roth & Peck, 1951; Blood, 1960; Scanzoni, 1968). Sociological theory, which helps to explain these findings, points to the fact that the social class status of the nuclear family in America has traditionally been determined by the occupational status of the husband-father; therefore, if a middle-class woman marries a lower-class man she will lose status and the couple will be defined as lower class. This can mean a difficult downward adjustment for the wife which creates strains in her relationship with her husband. (As noted above, if he is upwardly mobile, these problems may diminish as the marriage progresses.) When the wife is lower class and the husband is middle class the situation would probably be less potentially stressful. She would be moving up and joining her husband in the middle class.

Another reason for lower marital adjustment between a middle-class wife and a lower-class husband is that it is quite likely he will have been brought up with a traditional cultural orientation emphasizing patriarchal family authority and other masculine prerogatives. The middle-class wife, in addition to possessing superior social class identity, is likely to have been socialized to believe in equalitarianism and feminism, which may clash with her husband's male dominance viewpoint.

Some of the current research on marital conflict and social class differences of the spouses sheds further light on marital adjustment in cross-class marriages. In some situations, a social class difference between the spouses was definitely associated with low marital adjustment and conflict, but not so in other situations. Pearlin (1975) attempted to explain the inconsistencies by showing that one kind of social class intermarriage is especially likely to produce marital conflict, that is, where a person who marries down also places a high value on upward social mobility and achievement. Such a person may be expected to experience a keen loss of social status. The data from Pearlin's study generally supported this view. Jorgensen (1977) attempted to test Pearlin's findings on a sample representative of the social classes in Minneapolis-St. Paul. He found that Pearlin's explanation was essentially valid for the wives, but not for the husbands. Jorgensen offers this explanation of why a combination of marrying down while striving to move up leads to a greater perception of marital conflict for wives than for husbands: for husbands, marrying up or down is of less consequence than for wives since the social class status of the family depends primarily on the husband's occupation, and males are less dependent on their wives for their social class placement than vice versa. However, since the social status of the wife is still largely dependent on her husband's career aspirations and achievements, her perception of his progress will be an important factor in their marital adjustment, especially when she is upwardly mobile and values social status advancement.

In-laws and marital adjustment

Marriage creates in-laws, and in societies such as ours where the in-law statuses and roles are not clearly defined, each married couple has to work out, often by trial and error, their relationships with their in-laws. (We don't even know how to address our mother-in-law, do we?) In addition, each husband and wife has to adjust to the other's family of orientation. One of the developmental tasks facing newlyweds is how to handle continuing relationships with parents and other close kin after marriage. Society expects the couple's new marital bond to be stronger than the much older bond linking them to their parental families, but such deep and long-standing bonds are not always easily relegated to second place. Parents often find it difficult to let their adult son or daughter go. And each spouse may, while desiring to continue close ties with one's own relatives, view as a potential threat to the marriage bond the other spouse's continuing relation with his or her relatives (Duvall, 1965a).

The few studies we have on in-laws indicate that in-law problems are more likely to involve women than men (Duvall, 1954; Komarovsky, 1963). Mother-in-law and daughter-in-law are more apt to be the center of in-law clashes than father-in-law and son-in-law. The points of friction more often involve the activities and roles of women, such as housekeeping and child-rearing. Men are not immune from in-law frictions, however, as Komarovsky (1962) found in her study of working class marriages. These working class husbands often bridled at what they considered interference in their family life by their wife's female relatives. The husband's problems with his in-laws surfaced when a man felt his status or self-respect was being threatened by members of his wife's family.

Close ties with mother-in-law help strengthen a marriage

Fredrik D. Bodin/Stock, Boston

According to LeMasters (1957b, pp. 316–319), some of the social and cultural factors contributing to in-law tensions and problems are: (1) the emancipation problem in American families, that is, the difficulty many American parents have in letting their children go, in "cutting the apron strings"; (2) marriage takes the child away from his or her parents, thus disrupting the larger family system; (3) the new marital partner, "displacing" the parents in our conjugally oriented marriage system. These interrelated factors certainly can contribute to difficulties in marital adjustment, especially in the early years of marriage. On the more positive side, the American independent nuclear family system may contribute to a reduction of in-law problems by allowing the couple to set up housekeeping in a new place away from both sets of in-laws, thus freeing them to develop their marital relationship with less interference from relatives than is possible in societies with extended family systems and patrilocal or matrilocal residence.

Social change in recent years has brought on a general reduction of negative myths and stereotypes of in-laws, such as the old mother-in-law jokes. Newlyweds today are thus less apt to enter marriage with negative preconceptions of in-laws. As Duvall (1977, p. 201) observes, in-laws today are more apt to be counted on as "friendly allies" by young married couples, rather than being seen as potential interferers in their marriages.

STUDIES IN MARITAL ADJUSTMENT

There has been a long, fascinating history of efforts to study marital adjustment, dating back to the 1930s. We will start with a review of some pioneer studies by University of Chicago sociologists and by social scientists in California. These early studies involved efforts to measure marital adjustment: To seek personal, social, and demographic variables associated with marital adjustment and predict marital adjustment based on the findings. We will present a critique of these early efforts to conceptualize and measure marital adjustment. Finally, we will look at some of the more recent attempts of social scientists to reconceptualize and continue the study of marital adjustment.

PIONEER STUDIES IN MARITAL ADJUSTMENT

Early efforts to measure and predict marital adjustment

One of the most ambitious pioneer efforts to study marital adjustment was undertaken by Burgess and Cottrell in Chicago in the 1930s. Their study was published in a monograph entitled *Predicting Success or Failure in Marriage* (1939). Their sample consisted of 526 couples who had been married from one to six years. Couples were asked to rate the happiness of their marriage on a 5-point scale ranging from very unhappy to very happy. A marital adjustment scale was then developed based on selected aspects of marriage relationships which were shown to be positively correlated with marital happiness, including husband and wife agreement on important issues, shared interests and joint activities, frequent demonstrations of affection, lack of dissatisfaction with marriage, and lack of feelings of unhappiness or loneliness. This measure of marital adjustment made it possible for each respondent to be assigned a marital adjustment score. The next stop was to seek correlations between these marital adjustment scores and numerous personal, social, and demographic factors present in the marriages.

Burgess and Cottrell found some significant factors associated with marital adjustment. Foremost among them was the fact that the more similar the spouses were in family background, the higher their marital adjustment. The domestic happiness of the parents of both husband and wife was also correlated with good marital adjustment. Marital adjustment, in a way, seems to run in the family, and children of happily married parents seem to have a head start toward good adjustment in their own marriage. Other assorted background factors associated with good marital adjustment included: spouses being between 22 and 30 years of age at time of marriage; a long period of premarital association; an active social life, with friends of both sexes; higher education for both spouses; security and stability in occupation (this was more important than income level); and the desire to have children.

Terman (1938) conducted another pioneer study in marital adjustment at about the same time in California, published in a monograph entitled *Psychological Factors in Marital Happiness.* Terman got his data from 792 middle-class couples in the Los Angeles area who had been married an average of 11 years. As the title indicates, Terman was mainly interested in the part that personality factors play in marital adjustment. He developed a composite adjustment or marital happiness measure by combining a number of separate scores from the couples' responses, to questions on shared common interests, agreements and disagreements, how disagreements were handled, the number of complaints each spouse had about their marriage, frequency of regretting the marriage, contemplation of divorce, whether one would marry the same person again, the length of periods of unhappiness, and their self-rating of the happiness of their marriage. Based on their composite scores, the sample was divided into 2 groups: 300 happily married couples and 150 unhappily married couples. Then these two groups were compared as to their personality characteristics and on certain social background factors.

How did the happily married differ from the unhappily married? Terman compiled general "portraits" along these lines. A happily married wife is kindly, cooperative, methodical, meticulous, conservative, conventional, self-assured, and optimistic; an unhappily married wife is emotionally unstable, insecure, feels inferior, is overactive, radical, and egoistic. A happily married husband is emotionally stable, cooperative, extroverted, responsible, methodical, conservative, and equalitarian in ideals; an unhappily married husband is moody, neurotic, domineering, radical, and feels insecure and inferior.

Unlike Burgess and Cottrell, Terman explored the relationship between marital happiness and various sexual attitudes and experiences. Good sex education in the parental home, with frank parental responses to the son's or daughter's curiosity about sex, was favorable to marital happiness. Marital happiness was highest where the spouses were equal or the husband slightly higher in sexual desire; and marital happiness for both spouses was highly correlated with the wife's capacity for orgasm. Social background factors associated with marital happiness included long engagement or long acquaintance before marriage, happy childhood and strong emotional attachment to parents, and happy marriage of parents.

It is interesting to note that, although the Burgess and Cottrell study and the Terman study were done in different parts of the country using different methods, their findings are remarkably similar. Both studies found that couples who score high in marital adjustment or happiness tend to be well-adjusted people; they are mature, stable, quite conventional, and come from conventional families where the parents are happy and well adjusted. Quite a number of subsequent studies have generally confirmed the findings of these two early studies (King, 1952; Locke, 1951; Karlsson, 1951; Burgess & Wallin, 1953).

Many of the early researchers (including those just reviewed) hoped to eventually be able to predict marital adjustment or marital success or failure. The predictions were to be based on data on the personal or background factors of married couples which had been found to be highly correlated with marital happiness, such as the length of engagement or the marital happiness of parents. A methodological weakness in some of these efforts at prediction is illustrated by Terman (1938), who attempted to infer marital adjustment from data on personality and family background of the marital partners obtained at the same time that marital adjustment was being measured by other items. Cause and affect in such situations are difficult to untangle, and accurate knowledge of personality and family factors *prior* to the time of the study were not really known, as should be possible in good longitudinal studies.

Burgess and Wallin, in *Engagement and Marriage* (1953), present one of the few longitudinal studies of marital adjustment. Their findings were based on both premarital and postmarital information on marital adjustment. They studied 1,000 engaged couples and followed up with a study of 666 of these couples after they had been married from 3 to 5 years. The premarital factor they found to be most predictive of marital success was "success in engagement," as measured by an Engagement Success Inventory. Other factors predictive of marital success were self-ratings of happiness in childhood and a desire on the part of both partners to have children. One interesting finding was that a combined prediction, or more accurately a forecast, of the likelihood of the success of the marriage could be made by the fiances themselves, their parents, and their close friends. Critics of social scientists' marital prediction efforts say that such subjective assessments are about as good as the more elaborate, scientific method of predicting marital success or adjustment. In his review and critique of the marital prediction studies, Kirkpatrick (1963, pp. 394–404) found that the scientific correlations achieved up to then were quite low and could not yield very reliable predictions. He believed that simpler, common-sense methods of forecasting might be about as good. Due to problems of measurement and prediction, as well as to problems related to the concept of marital adjustment itself, more recent studies have paid less attention to marital prediction.

Critique of the early concept of marital adjustment

Although efforts to measure and study marital adjustment still go on, they have been dampened not only by problems of measurement but also by various criticisms of the concept itself, especially as it was used by some of the early researchers, including Burgess and Cottrell and Terman. Their definitions of marital adjustment have been accused of containing various biases—middle class and "functionalist"—because they emphasize conformity, conventionality, and homogamy and contain an implicit disapproval of nonconformity, unconventionality, and heterogamy in mate selection and marriage.

One of the most outspoken critics of the marital adjustment concept has been Kolb (1948), who argues that there are implicit value judgments in most of the criteria used to define and measure marital success or "good" marital adjustment. Kolb believes that the early marital adjustment studies present a composite picture of a successful marriage that is bland and generally static. "Well-adjusted" spouses describe themselves as happy, safisfied with their marriage, in agreement on decisions and leisure-time preferences and interests, and affectionate and confident. In a sense, this conventional concept of marital adjustment is negative because it defines a good or successful marriage in terms of an absence of conflict. A positive concept takes into consideration the development and pursuit of new and stimulating goals. Kolb contends that new experiences and personality development, as well as contentment and conformity to conventional community norms and expectations, should be part of the test of a successful marriage. Such criticisms of the concept of marital adjustment as it was used by many early researchers led to efforts to rethink and reconceptualize the concept.

RECENT EFFORTS TO RECONCEPTUALIZE AND STUDY MARITAL ADJUSTMENT

In spite of criticisms and problems related to definition and measurement, the concept of marital adjustment continues to hold a prominent place in the study of marriage and family relations. According to Spanier (1976) marital adjustment is probably the most frequently studied dependent variable in the field of marriage and family. With this sustained interest, marriage-life specialists are trying to sharpen and improve the concept and develop theoretically relevant, reliable measures which may be used in new studies of marital adjustment. Some of these efforts will be discussed below.

The dyadic adjustment scale

Spanier (1976) has made a valuable contribution toward an improved measure of dyadic, or couple, adjustment, including marital adjustment.

His Dyadic Adjustment Scale "proceeds from the pragmatic position that a new measure, which is theoretically grounded, relevant, valid, and highly reliable, is necessary since marital and dyadic adjustment continue to be researched" (Spanier, 1976, p. 15). The scale produces a total adjustment score, derived from self-rating on 32 items which fall into 4 general categories: (1) dyadic satisfaction—the extent to which the partners are satisfied in their relationships; (2) dyadic cohesion—the feelings of togetherness the partners have; (3) dyadic consensus—the extent of agreement between the partners; and (4) affectional expression—the extent to which each partner expresses feelings of love and affection. Spanier believes that the total adjustment between the married partners is an ongoing process, which at any given time represents a composite or balance between the above four sets of elements. Spanier (1976, p. 17) describes it thus:

> We have accepted the idea that dyadic adjustment is a *process* rather than an unchanging state, but that the most heuristic definition would allow for a measure which would meaningfully evaluate the relationship at a given point in time. . . . Thus, we subscribe to the notion that adjustment is an ever-changing process with a qualitative dimension which can be evaluated at any point in time on a dimension from well-adjusted to maladjusted.

Spanier thinks that his Dyadic Adjustment Scale represents an improvement over other measures of marital adjustment, but that there are still some troublesome methodological issues, such as the relative weights to be assigned the different items in the scale.

A typology of marriages: Marital adjustment in the upper middle class

Cuber and Harroff (1963) made another effort to redefine and make more dynamic the concept of marital adjustment. They interviewed 437 upper-middle-class men and women in the 35 to 55 age range, described by the authors as highly educated, financially successful, and articulate. They discovered a fascinating variety of marital relations and adjustments among their respondents, which offer some revealing insights into the modern upper middle class. Cuber and Harroff identified at least five general types of marital relations and adjustments in this sample of people.

Conflict-habituated relationships.

In certain marriages there seems to be a state of chronic and continuous tension and conflict, although the partners mostly keep it "controlled." At worst the spouses quarrel and nag in private and sometimes before other family members or even before friends, but generally they are more discreet and polite to each other when in the company of outsiders. Both husband and wife are aware that their incompatability is pervasive and conflict is ever-potential. Although such a conflict-habituated relationship may sometimes be considered "dead," this is not really the case. Something subtle but very active permeates the lives of the married couple. The vital force in these marriages seems to be the tension and conflict per se and how to handle same, day after day. This condition seems to be the basis for continuing the relationship; it is perhaps the main cohesive factor in the marriage, ensuring its continuity and endurance—in some cases, even for a lifetime.

Devitalized relationships.

These marriages, which used to be more lively and vital, now are typically lacking in zest or enthusiasm, but are not marked by conflict. There are some aspects of these marriages which are still satisfying to the partners, such as a mutual interest in their children, family traditions, or property. There is no really serious threat to the marriage, but the interplay between the husband and wife has come to be bland, somewhat apathetic, or even lifeless, as compared to what it was when they were starting out in marriage. Such marriages tend to be perpetuated by habit, legal requirements, and often by religious beliefs and expectations.

Even though these relationships lack their earlier vitality, there is still *something* there—occasional companionship, memories of earlier times of sharing, a recognition of each other's good qualities. The author's believe that this kind of marital adjustment is quite common. In fact, many respondents who have such devitalized marriages assert that "marriage is like this— except for a few odd balls or pretenders who claim otherwise" (Cuber & Harroff, 1963, p. 142).

Passive-congenial relationships.

This mode of marital adjustment is found about as frequently as the preceding one. The typical relationship is one of "comfortable adequacy." While the couple may claim to share and enjoy a number of common interests, it is more apt to turn out that these interests are not vital, nor do they involve much actual joint husband-wife participation. Their daily interaction is typically congenial, but rather low-keyed, and shows little evidence of enthusiasm. The authors judge that this has been the prevailing situation in most of these marriages from the beginning. While the spouses are not disillusioned, as in the preceding type, their relationship lacks the vitality found in the next type of marriage.

Vital relationships.

Here the husband-wife relationship typically exudes a vitality and excitement which is often manifested through their sharing of some important experience. It may be some shared creative enterprise, or sex, or childrearing, or a hobby. "The clue that the *relationship is vital* and significant derives from the *feelings of importance about it* and *that that importance is shared*" (Cuber & Harroff, 1963, p. 143). The partners will readily sacrifice other things for it. It is apparent to others that the partners are living for something which is exciting and vital.

Total relationships. A total relationship is like the vital relationship with the addition of its being multifaceted. A wider and more varied sharing of interests and activities exists in these marriages. While such total relationships are rarely found, occasionally one will turn up in which husband and wife share and participate in virtually all important aspects of life. Some marriages may approximate a total relationship for a period of time but are unable to sustain totality as circumstances change.

While Cuber and Harroff did not attempt to count the number of people in their sample who fell into each of the five classifications, they make it clear that the majority would be found in the first three types. While few marriages achieve or sustain total relationships, it is presumed that vital relationships are more common.

Cuber and Harroff's study is thought-provoking. In contrast to many of the earlier researchers of marital adjustment, who found a high incidence of marital happiness or satisfaction, these authors suggest that a majority of marriages—at least in the upper middle class—may actually be routinized and unexciting, something less than stimulating and vital.

Marital adjustment over the family life cycle

There are very few good longitudinal studies of marital adjustment which follow a sample of married couples over the years from the time of marriage through the middle and later years of life. Most of the studies are cross-sectional, that is, they use different samples of couples, each in a different period of married life, and there are methodological difficulties in using cross-sectional data to arrive at conclusions about developmental change (Spanier, Lewis, & Coles, 1975). Due to such shortcomings, care must be exercised when assessing some of the conclusions of a number of cross-sectional studies on marital adjustment throughout the life cycle.

Numerous studies have consistently shown that marriages tend to become less satisfying and that problems of marital adjustment arise over

Family camping trip contributes to marital adjustment

U.S.D.A. photo

the years as couples move from the preparenthood stage of marriage into the parenthood stages. This period of lower marital adjustment is then frequently followed by increases in marital adjustment after the children grow up and leave home. This pattern suggests a curvilinear relationship between marital adjustment and the family life cycle. Not all studies show a curvilinear relationship, however. Blood and Wolfe (1960) and Luckey (1966) did not find much, if any, increase in marital adjustment in the later periods of marriage. Spanier, Lewis, and Coles (1975) question the methodology of some other studies which did find a curvilinear relationship. However, there is little disagreement that marital adjustment tends to drop off rather sharply with the arrival of the first child (LeMasters, 1957a; Dyer, 1963; Rossi, 1968; Russell, 1974), and continues to decline during the children's early years, or for about the first 10 to 15 years of marriage (Blood & Wolfe, 1960; Luckey, 1966; Rollins & Feldman, 1970; Spanier, Lewis, & Coles, 1975).

In a study of 799 middle-class couples, Rollins and Feldman (1970) found that the proportion of couples who rated their marriages as "very satisfying" declined through the early stages of the family cycle down to a low point at the time they were launching their grown children from the home. They also found that after the children were grown and had departed, both the wife and the husband showed substantial increases in marital satisfaction through the "retirement stage." (See Figure 7–1.)

Figure 7–1

Percentage of husbands and wives in each stage in the family life cycle reporting that their marriage is very satisfying

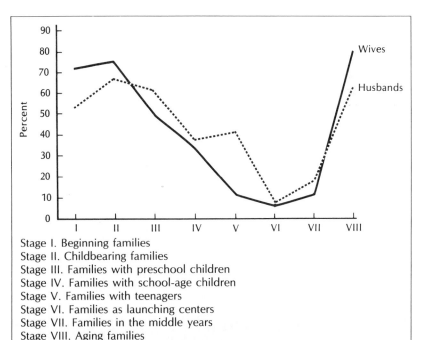

Stage I. Beginning families
Stage II. Childbearing families
Stage III. Families with preschool children
Stage IV. Families with school-age children
Stage V. Families with teenagers
Stage VI. Families as launching centers
Stage VII. Families in the middle years
Stage VIII. Aging families

Source: "Marital Satisfaction over the Family Life Cycle" by B. C. Rollins and H. Feldman, *Journal of Marriage and the Family*, 1970, *22*, 26. Reprinted by permission of the National Council on Family Relations. Copyright by the National Council on Family Relations.

Feldman (1971) also reports elsewhere that parenthood tends to have a pervasive influence on marital relations, and that differences between wife and husband in childrearing attitudes and expectations appear to have a definitely negative affect on marital happiness. Feldman (1971) also reported that couples with children had a significantly lower level of marital satisfaction than those without any children. Further study is needed, especially of a longitudinal nature, to test the findings of Rollins and Feldman (1970) as to the curvilinear relationship between marital adjustment and the family life cycle.

A national survey of marital happiness

In an analysis of data from three recent U.S. national surveys (1973, 1974, and 1975), Glenn and Weaver (1978) attempted to estimate the direct affects on marital happiness of a number of independent variables, including husband's occupation and family income, years of school completed, age at marriage, presence of children, church attendance, and the wife's employment outside the home. Statistical analysis was used to estimate the effects of these variables on the reported marital happiness of married white males and females ranging in age from 18 to 59. The investigators found that, contrary to predictions based on theory and other studies, most of the estimated direct effects of these variables on marital happiness were weak or nil. Only two variables showed direct affects on marital happiness, both negatively, and for wives only. One was the presence of very young children, and the other was being middle aged. The authors believe that at least part of the explanation for the differences between their findings and those of many other researchers lies in the methods they used—a single, rather global measure of self-reported marital happiness, and a complex, multivariate method of analysis of large national samples. Also, they think that some of the differences in their findings reflect recent changes associated with the increase of marital stability since the 1960s. Distinctions between the success of marriages and the marital happiness of individuals may be crucial in explaining the weak relationship between marital happiness and so many of the independent variables, Glenn and Weaver believe (1978, p. 280). Their study deals only with reported marital happiness of individuals in *intact* marriages. In their own words:

> The prediction of the success of marriages and of marital happiness of individuals are not necessarily the same, since terminated unsuccessful marriages no longer contribute to unhappiness in the married population. If, as we suspect and as some evidence suggests . . . , the persons most likely to enter into unsuccessful marriages are generally the same people who are most likely to terminate unsatisfactory marriages, then even the strongest predictors of success of marriage may bear little or no relationship to the happiness of individuals in intact marriages. In other words, to the extent that marital "mistakes" are quickly rectified by divorce, they may contribute little in the long run to marital unhappiness.

The author agrees with Glenn and Weaver that the trend in recent years for unsatisfactory marriages to end in divorce has contributed considerably to the rise in divorce rates, while at the same time reducing the range of differences in marital happiness in intact marriages.

IMPROVING MARITAL ADJUSTMENT

Given the various human and social conditions surrounding marriage and marital relationships—differences in attitudes, interests, and needs; differences in perceptions and expectations; constant changes in life circumstances and in people—some disagreement and conflict between most husbands and wives is inevitable. How may serious differences be successfully resolved? Are there any tested ways of improving marital adjustment when they arise? Family life educators and marriage counselors answer in the affirmative. Some of their recommendations follow.

PROBLEM SOLVING AND CONFLICT RESOLUTION

In their *Communication, Conflict, and Marriage,* Raush, Barry, Hertel, and Swain (1974) emphasize that problem solving involves a series of steps or stages. They identify six such steps that, if properly followed, would enable the couple to solve the problem, resolve any related conflict, and help restore and solidify their marital adjustment. Let us quickly run through these six successive steps.

Identifying the problem

Some problems are easier to identify and bring out in the open than others. Sex problems have often been difficult for many married people to talk about freely. Another difficulty lies in misleading cues as to what the problem really is. A wife who nags about her husband's spending too much time and money at the tavern may really be indicating her resentment of his not spending more time at home with her. Raush and his associates (1974) say it is not enough to realize that something is wrong; it is necessary to clarify the problem so the couple can grasp it and deal with it. Even when a clearly identified problem is not immediately resolved, the partners at least know where the other stands, and the way is opened to the next steps.

Exploring alternative solutions

When the problem or issue has been clearly identified, and the feelings of each partner have been expressed and heard, it is time for each to offer some kind of a solution. Each, in turn, says what she or he would like, and what seems to her or him to be a good solution. Neither one should feel threatened, because each has the opportunity to express views and propose solutions. As soon as one possible solution is suggested, they can discuss the pros and cons. Raush and associates (1974) note that incompleteness is often a difficulty here. Instead of seeking all possible alternatives, only a few may be considered. Seeking and discussing a variety of alternatives gives each partner a sense of involvement in reaching a final decision.

Selecting the best alternatives

After considering a range of alternative solutions to the problem, the couple can begin looking for the one or two best choices. This means evaluating each proposal on its own merits, and then eventually finding one solution on which they can agree. On some complex, ambivalent problems, decision making may be expedited by drawing up a list of pros and cons, or gains and losses, resulting from making a certain choice. An example could be one in which the partners have to decide whether or not to accept a job offer in another city. Will the gains of a higher salary and opportunities for promotion offset the loss of friends, the trials of changing schools for the children, and higher living expenses?

At some point the weighing of alternative solutions must come to a halt and a decision made. Raush et al. (1974) say that a danger here is that one or both partners may not be disclosing their true feelings because they may be tailoring their proposals too much to what they think the other partner wants. It is difficult to find the best solution if each partner has not candidly expressed her or his real preference. If they are lucky, they may discover that they both prefer the same thing and thus arrive at a consensus. If this is not possible, further discussion and postponement may be in order. "Sleeping on it" often gives both a new perspective, and once the tensions have relaxed, agreement may appear, perhaps unexpectedly. The final decision will probably require an accommodation of each partner to the feelings and desires of the other, and usually some degree of compromise between the preferences of each.

Implementing the decision

Once the choice has been made it has to be carried out. Implementation of a decision is not automatic. An advantage of a jointly made decision over a unilateral one is that in the former both partners feel some responsibility for its implementation. No matter how thoroughly the partners agreed on their decision, difficulties may crop up in putting it into operation. If deeply embedded habits have to be altered, the agreed-upon solution to the problem will take time and effort to implement, even with the best of intentions. For example, in marriages in which the wife has taken a full-time job the husband may agree that he should compensate by doing more of the housework, but his long-standing habits of doing other things on evenings and weekends may be hard to change.

Rebuilding the relationship

Except in cases when husband-wife consensus has been reached in making the final decision, one partner may probably feel like the "loser," to some extent at least. Raush et al. (1974) found that the "winner" was often aware of the bad feelings of the loser, and took steps to relieve these feelings. Such efforts may include expressions of sympathy and reassurances of love. The old expression "kiss and make up" pretty well expresses these efforts toward rebuilding the relationship following a difficult decision in which one partner has been put in the position of a loser, or at least feels that way. The whole experience may bring the couple into a fresh or renewed relationship.

Reviewing the decision-making process

Raush et al. (1974) found that many of the couples in the study took time to review what they had done, particularly after a strenuous struggle. They would take pride in the way each had "fought fair" in the give and take of working toward a solution to their problem. They felt satisfaction in improving their problem-solving skills. Couples found it stimulating and provocative to rehash the whole experience. The struggle they had shared helped them discover and understand things about themselves that would be valuable in their future relations. Various other studies have shown that joint husband-wife decision making is highly correlated with marital satisfaction (Dyer, 1959; Blood & Wolfe, 1960; Pratt, 1972).

MARRIAGE COUNSELING

Marriage counseling may be considered an emergency resource available to a married couple who are themselves unable to resolve marital conflict. In situations where the conflict has become chronic, it is better to seek outside professional help than to let the conflict continue unabated and perhaps escalate to the point of no return, at which the marriage will be destroyed.

Couples with marital difficulties are apt to take their problems first to relatives and close friends. These people are more readily accessible and certainly less expensive to consult than trained professionals. However, no one really knows just how effective such "informal counselors" really are. Blood and Blood (1978, p. 382) believe that even if their success rate is low, their aggregate service to married couples in need of help is enormous. Today, however, more couples are willing to seek professional help when their marriage is in serious trouble.

Marriage counselors represent a broad range of professional training and experience today; counseling is practiced by many social workers, psychologists, family sociologists, by some ministers and doctors, and by a few lawyers. The main organization concerned with marriage counseling is the American Association of Marriage and Family Counselors. Marriage counseling services are also available from staff members of the Family Service Association of America, whose agencies are found throughout the United States. Although these agencies are not limited to marriage counseling, their staff of social workers are an important source of help to married couples in trouble. Other reputable marriage counselors can be found who do not belong to either of these organizations, such as clinical psychologists and psychiatrists.

Marriage counseling methods and techniques vary widely, which is understandable since marriage counselors represent so many different professions, each with its own kind of training. Some counselors use couple-centered counseling methods; others emphasize behavior modification; some stress childhood personal development; and others concentrate on the present family situation. Some try to help couples find solutions to particular problems, while others aim at improvement of husband-wife communication so the partners can more effectively work toward a solution themselves. Blood and Blood's (1978, 384–388) review of marriage counseling procedures and practices is recommended for those who are interested in more details on this topic.

There are many benefits a couple may gain from professional marriage counseling, including the mediation of disputes. Gurin and associates (1960) found that advice on how to settle a dispute or resolve an issue was the benefit clients most frequently reported. Another benefit is "therapeutic intervention." Here the professional counselor helps the partners gain insights into their emotional difficulties and gradually restore their confidence and love, thus creating conditions for rational decisions and cooperation. As related benefit the counselor can then offer some actual training and practice in rational behavior. Training programs are held in which the couple actually practice making decisions and solving problems under the marriage counselor's supervision. Patterson, Hops, and Weiss (1975) found such training sessions to be effective in increasing the couple's ability to compromise and arrive at positive solutions in an atmosphere of relaxed give-and-take, while at the same time decreasing the amount of disruptive behavior and "put-downs." The net result of such training sessions was generally an increase in marital satisfaction.

KEEPING THE MARRIAGE ALIVE AND WELL

What can a married couple do to help prevent their marriage from becoming devitalized? What may be done to keep their marriage alive and well? There are, fortunately, many things—some large, but many small and seemingly insignificant—which add up to a significant whole. A good-morning kiss, a compliment on his or her appearance, an anecdote brought home from work to be shared at dinner, or flowers bought on a whim. Unexpected things add zest to the day and show thoughtfulness; expected gestures demonstrate affection and reinforce satisfying routines. Such things express the high priority of their marriage.

One important reason many marriages go downhill over the years is that the husband and the wife become involved in their jobs, their children, their friends, and their personal goals and interests, so that they have little energy or time left over for their marriage. From their marriage counseling experience, Blood and Blood (1978, p. 565) observe that most of the couples who come to them for counseling are in trouble because their marriage has dropped to low priority in their lives. The hour or two spent in counseling each week is often the only time the husband and wife have to talk together. This is not enough to revitalize their marriage. A truly vital marriage requires continued effort, a daily renewal

Farmer's wife provides her husband with latest market information by C. B. radio

U.S.D.A. photo by Michelle Bogre

of commitment. As Rogers (1972, p. 201) expresses it, a vital marriage entails a commitment "to working together on the changing process of our present relationship because that relationship is currently enriching our love and our life and we wish it to grow."

A marriage stays vital not only through sharing enjoyable experiences but also through struggling together with problems and frustrations. Crises and difficulties become opportunities for cooperative effort and for fashioning new dimensions of understanding, appreciation, and growth. No matter how long a couple is married, there are always new opportunities for their relationship to grow.

Personal growth is also necessary in a vital and growing marriage. Personal growth of the wife and the husband sparks marital growth. Each is an individual engaged in a life journey, but since they have decided to make the journey together as a married couple, their separate journeys have become "mutually contingent." People change as the years pass, and a marriage cannot remain static. As each partner changes, the couple face the challenge of "matching the husband and wife in phases of development" (Foote, 1956). This matching requires them to carry on a continuing dialog.

New experiences help vitalize a marriage. Separate experiences can contribute when they stimulate the growth of the individual and are shared vicariously through conversation. New experiences that stimulate the mind and feelings can renew one's attractiveness to the marriage partner. Shared new experiences, intellectual as well as social and recreational, help keep a marriage vital and growing. And sharing memories of past shared experiences helps too.

Marriage enrichment programs and workshops are now becoming more available for couples desiring to work at revitalizing their marriages. An increasing number of organizations now offer a variety of experiences to couples, including marriage encounters, marriage retreats, and couple workshops. A national organization, the Association of Couples for Marriage Enrichment (ACME), promotes these opportunities for couples. Blood and Blood (1978, p. 569) think that the greatest value of these marriage enrichment programs lies in their providing a structured setting in which couples can examine their relationship, appreciate what is positive in it, and explore possibilities for making any changes they wish.

C H A P T E R   8

Sex and sexual adjustment
in marriage

This chapter will examine human sexuality in the context of marriage and the part sex plays in marriage. Marital sexuality will be compared to premarital sexuality, male and female differences in sexuality will be discussed, and changing viewpoints toward marital sexuality will be considered. A good deal of attention will be devoted to sexual adjustment in marriage, focusing on problems wives and husbands encounter in sexual interaction and adjustment. The research literature on sexual adjustment and marital adjustment will be reviewed, and various interpretations and assessments presented. Attention will be given to extramarital sexual behavior in the United States today.

MARITAL SEXUALITY

GENERAL OVERVIEW

Few Americans would deny that sex is important to marriage. To some people, sexual satisfaction in marriage may be almost synonymous with marital satisfaction itself. However, most authorities agree that while good sexual adjustment is important for marital satisfaction, it is not the sole determinant of a good marriage. Research shows that good sexual adjustment in marriage will not necessarily produce good overall marital adjustment, nor will poor sexual adjustment necessarily destroy an otherwise good marriage. The importance or salience of sex in marriage varies from individual to individual, from couple to couple, from one period in the marriage cycle to another, from one religious group to another, and from social class to social class (Levinger, 1976, p. 34; Bell, 1979, p. 278).

Much has been said and written about the human sex "drive," or "need," as something innate and universal for the species. It is, however, of a different order than such other basic biological needs as hunger and thirst. Although human sexual functioning is on one level a natural physiological process, it has a unique quality that other physiological processes such as bladder or bowel functioning do not. Sex for human beings can be conditioned along many different tracks; it can be repressed or sublimated; it can be delayed or postponed; it can even be completely denied. As Masters and Johnson (1970, p. 10) put it: *"Sexual responsivity can be delayed indefinitely or functionally denied for a life time.* No other basic physiological process can claim such malleability of physical expression." This unique, malleable quality of sex for human beings helps explain individual differences in sexual behavior, group differences in sexual orientation and expression, and variations in cultural norms and taboos regarding sexual expression in and out of marriage. Some cultures are sexually restrictive while others are permissive; some emphasize male sexuality, as did 19th-century England, while others emphasize female sexuality, as did the Trobriand tribes in the South Pacific (Malinowski, 1929).

In any given society, individuals may vary dramatically in their sex orientations, attitudes, and behavior, according to experience and socialization. One American youth, socialized in an extremely secular, hedonistic, macho-oriented subculture, may become highly active and promiscuous sexually, with his self and group image enhanced each time he "scores" with a different woman. At the opposite extreme, another American youth, socialized in an extremely conservative, traditionally religious family and community, may take vows of lifelong continence as a priest. The lesson here is that we must be well aware of varied and oft-changing historical, cultural, and social contexts as we attempt to describe and understand human sexuality, both in and out of marriage.

We have noted earlier that human beings in every society have a tendency to be ethnocentric about their beliefs and practices. Members of a given society will normally come to believe that their customs and their ways of doing and thinking are truly right and good; that they are the way God intends people to be. We are brought up to accept and believe that *our* political, economic, religious, and family institutions are right and probably superior to those elsewhere. This ethnocentric tendency is especially strong in certain areas of human conduct, including politics and religion as well as sex. The extremely personal and private nature of sexual behavior, and the myths and taboos surrounding human sexuality, have contributed to this ethnocentrism and its accompanying intolerance of variations from the culturally prescribed norms. People in one society are apt to assume, due to their narrowness of experience and knowledge, that their sexual norms and practices are the only right and normal ones, thus finding it difficult to take a detached, unemotional view of the sexual codes and behavior found in other societies or groups. As Gagnon and Greenblat (1978, pp. 282–283) tell us, it is important to keep all this in mind as we study human, and especially marital, sexuality,

> because it is particularly easy to fall into the trap of ethnocentrism (of time as well as place) in the domain of marital sexuality. Unlike premarital sexuality, it is *permitted* everywhere, so the tendency is to assume it is the same everywhere. However, the frequency, the positions, the times, the emotions, and most importantly the meanings given to marital sexuality are highly variable. Thus, marriage may tell us *who* we are to have sex with, but it does not automatically answer the script questions of what? when? where? and why?

Marital sexuality versus premarital sexuality

There are, of course, both continuities and discontinuities between marital and premarital sexuality. One's premarital sexual socialization and experience will normally strongly influence one's sexual attitudes and conduct in marriage, especially in the early years of marriage. The views and expectations one takes into marriage may reflect the influences of parents, friends, lovers, teachers, clergy, and the mass media, including T.V., movies, and assorted literature. As indicated in Chapter 4, an increasing number of young American women and men have now had premarital sexual experience, including intercourse. Just how this premarital sexual experience affects marital sexuality and adjustment is not entirely understood yet, as will be seen later in this chapter.

An important difference between premarital and marital sex is that the former has been traditionally defined as nonlegitimate while the latter has been defined as highly legitimate. While premarital sex is becoming less nonlegitimate in many secular circles today, other traditionally oriented circles still consider it nonlegitimate. It is probably still correct to say that premarital sex is not yet normatively approved in the American population at large (Glenn & Weaver, 1979). For most young people, therefore, premarital sexual experience has been somewhat secretive and clandestine, often occurring under hasty and anxious conditions not always conducive to full sexual satisfaction, especially for the woman. This secretiveness and furtiveness may be conducive to sexual excitement and yield some degree of sexual satisfaction, but for most the whole setting and experience is probably quite different from sex after marriage. Kinsey (1953) found that most women tend to learn how to achieve full sexual satisfaction (orgasm) after marriage, because sex in marriage is socially supported and defined as legitimate.

While marriage provides the socially approved setting for sexual expression, it may also have a dual and somewhat contradictory influence on the sexual behavior of the marriage partners. On the one hand, marriage provides a favorable environment for sex, with social approval, privacy, and freedom from guilt feelings. As the marriage progresses, however, there tends to be some gradual diminution of sexual stimulation and response with the loss of novelty and with the sustained intimate association of husband and wife. The period of high sexual excitement and eroticism during the early or "honeymoon" phase of the marriage is difficult to sustain for most couples, and often comes to be replaced by less high-pitched marital routines. It would seem that although full sexual expression is now legitimate, sexuality declines in importance both emotionally and physically as the marriage progresses. This change is due partly to the intrusion of other demands on the time and energy of the marriage partners as they move on through the various periods of the family cycle. Children, school and community interests, kinship obligations, and occupational demands intrude on the sex lives of married couples. With so many wives now adding occupational roles to all their other marriage and family roles, exhaustion by the end of the day in not uncommon, and fatigue is not conducive to sexual desire.

Unrealistic perceptions and expectations of sex in marriage

Unmarried people may have visions of marriage as a kind of sexual paradise where one's sexuality may be fully expressed and one has immediate and endless access to all the sex one wants. One may envision that each sexual encounter with one's spouse will be sublime, tender, passionate, and mutually satisfying. Such high fulfillment may be experienced by many married couples some of the time, and by a fortunate few a good deal of the time; but for most couples it is probably an unrealistic goal most of the time. The point is that marital sex takes place within the larger context of the whole marital relationship, and marital sexuality reflects the ups and downs of marriage in general, the frustrations and achievements of daily life, its pleasures and pains. While sex before marriage was apt to be a sudden peak expression of intimacy, sex in marriage is only one of a number of ways of expressing and communicating marital intimacy. Full marital intimacy is achieved through the sharing of much more than sex—the whole complex process of living together, of dreaming, planning, striving together, of loving and sharing together, is involved.

Of course the importance of sex in marriage should not be minimized, but neither should it be exaggerated. And the difficulty is that many young people do enter marriage with an exaggerated preconception of what to expect of marital sex. As LeMasters (1957b, pp. 356–362) observes, there are various myths and folklores about sex and marriage in American culture, some of which contribute to unrealistic marital expectations. One such myth is that the honeymoon provides a good test of the newlywed's sexual compatibility. Since sexual behavior for humans is not instinctive but must be learned, to expect full sexual satisfaction and mutuality at once is unrealistic for most and especially for those who have had limited sexual experience prior to marriage. As noted, even those who have had premarital sexual experience find many differences between such experiences and marital sex. Not only does marital sex have to be learned by the couple together, there is also often the need for some *unlearning,* especially for the male. Benedict (1939) points out some of the discontinuities and inconsistencies in the sexual socialization of American youth. The male may learn from his peer group that sex is strictly physical, that females are sex objects, that he should be sexually aggressive, and that his sexual prowess yields status among his male peers. After marriage however, he finds that this male sex code does not always fit his wife's expectations. He finds she probably does not want to be treated as a sex object, and that she sees sex as something more than physical. She associates sex with sentiment and love. For the bride too, some unlearning is apt to be necessary. For those brought up in the tradition of premarital chastity, sexual inhibitions and emotional self-control are expected upon marriage to give way to uninhibited sexual responsiveness and passion. And even for women with more premarital sexual experience, the honeymoon situation is not always conducive to the fuller sexual satisfaction and mutuality which come with time and togetherness.

Another myth is that married people are well informed about sex and human sexuality. A great many people enter marriage woefully uninformed or misinformed about sex, and as marriage counselors attest, even after years of marriage many are still less than well informed. Kinsey (1948; 1953) found that married men and women often have erroneous ideas about the sexual physiology and response of the opposite sex. Until recently, sound and thorough sex education has often been hard to come by for American youth. Many parents have felt inadequate or reluctant to assume this educational responsibility, and many school systems have been reluctant to enter this politically sensitive and often controversial area. Finally, the adequacy and reliability of peer-group sex education leaves much to be desired.

TRADITIONAL CONCEPTIONS OF MARITAL SEXUALITY

While historical evidence is not complete and not always as reliable as social scientists would like, there is some agreement among authorities that in the American past marital sexuality was probably viewed along the following lines.

1. In keeping with prevailing Victorian norms, marital sex was treated

with considerable circumspection by 19th-century husbands and wives. There was little open discussion of attitudes or expectations between husband and wife. Marital sex probably was not part of the regularly weekly married life of most couples (Shorter, 1975, p. 248).

2. The majority of 19th-century women probably had little interest in marital sex. According to Hunt (1974, p. 197) "the majority of middle-class and working-class women found intercourse only tolerable, at best, and a substantial minority regarded it as revolting, messy, vulgar, animalistic, shameful, and degrading." This may be an overstatement, of course. Some historians claim that by the late 19th century more urban, middle-class women were beginning to look more favorably on marital sex.

3. The traditional justification for marital sex was not in its pleasure or personal gratification, but in its potential for reproduction. Any pleasure derived from the sex act was at best a by-product of the more important goal of procreating children. Marriage guides for 19th-century couples propounded this view, along with the idea that women had few, if any, sexual desires. One such guide for married couples offered this counsel:

> As a general rule, a modest woman seldom desires any sexual gratification for herself. She submits to her husband, but only to please him; and, but for the desire of maternity, would far rather be relieved from his affections. The married woman has no wish to be treated on the footing of a mistress. (Hayes, 1869, p. 227).

4. In the past, male and female sexuality were considered to be basically different. As just seen, women were considered to have little in the way of sexual need or desires, while men were seen as being endowed with greater sexual needs. A common complaint of husbands was that their wives were not sexually responsive enough, while wives were apt to complain that their husbands were oversexed.

While the 20th century has brought many changes in ideas and beliefs about male and female sexuality, and about acceptable conduct for marriage partners, some of the earlier views have continued to persist, including the notion that women's sexual needs are weaker than men's. Scully and Bart (1973) found this view set forth in many current (as well as early) gynecology textbooks.

CONTEMPORARY CONCEPTIONS OF MARITAL SEXUALITY

Ideological trends, along with advances in biology and the behavioral sciences, contributed to changing ideas about human sexuality. The rise of feminism, trends toward equality of the sexes, the increasing emphasis on individual rights and freedom, along with the works of such specialists as Freud and Ellis, brought new views and understandings of human sexuality. Women as well as men were acknowledged to have sexual desires and interests, and in intellectual circles at least, these desires were thought to be proper and legitimate.

Scientific studies of sexuality began in the early decades of the 20th century, but it was not until the publication of the Kinsey research in the late 1940s and early 1950s that human sexuality was brought into the public limelight and a factual basis was established for understanding male and female sexuality. These studies showed that sexual activity both in and outside marriage was more extensive and varied than previously thought. The studies also pointed up the fact that most married men and women are uninformed or misinformed about human sex anatomy and functioning. Kinsey (1948; 1953) and his associates helped emancipate American society from much of its earlier tradition-bound sexual orientation, and helped prepare the way for the current, more enlightened and permissive orientations.

Perhaps the foremost change in 20th-century conceptions of marital sexuality has been the trend toward sexual equality in marriage. This has meant an emancipation from the inhibitions and fetters of Victorianism, for women especially, and a recognition of the importance of a mutually satisfying sex life for both wife and husband. Husbands have come to assume a greater responsibility for satisfying their wives sexually, and many wives are more open in conveying their sexual desires to their husbands. There is evidence of both greater frequency and greater enjoyment of sexual intercourse in marriage (Hunt, 1974). There are indications that with the sexual emancipation of women, some wives may not only catch up with but may pass their husbands in sexual desire and interest (Hunt, 1959; Bell, 1979).

Related to the trends toward sexual equalitarianism and sexual satisfaction for women is an increased concern with sexual performance in marriage. It is each partner's responsibility to see that the spouse achieves sexual satisfaction in lovemaking. This responsibility for the other's sexual gratification has in a way shifted the old notion of sex as a duty of the wife to sex as a duty of the husband. To satisfy his wife he must know how to perform properly and thus must learn the right techniques. A conscientious husband may carefully peruse the latest sex manuals to learn the best techniques for bringing his wife to orgasm. While this attention to technique may be helpful, overconcern with sexual performance can defeat the whole purpose. A mechanistic approach to sex can diminish the spontaneity and emotional intimacy so crucial to mutual sexual satisfaction. The husband's overconcern with high performance standards can make marital sexual relations more of a task than a pleasure, as pointed out by Lewis and Brissett (1967) in their article entitled "Sex as Work: A Study in Avocational Counseling." These authors' examination of numerous marriage manuals reveals that marital sex as depicted therein emerges as "an activity permeated with the qualities of work." Husbands and wives are advised to prepare for marital sexual relations the same way they would for a job. There are certain job skills and techniques that must be acquired if the "work goals" of female and male orgasm are to be attained. In fairness, it should be noted that some of the more recent marriage manuals are less technique oriented, recognizing the importance of spontaneity and flexibility in marital sexual relations.

Value conflicts regarding modern marital sexuality

When an area of human activity as fraught with strong sentiments and moralistic beliefs and values as human sexuality is combined with cultural heterogeneity and rapid social change, value conflicts are bound to exist. In some conservative and traditional religious groups, many of the earlier viewpoints and values tend to persist, while in other modern, secular groups change and experimentation are being encouraged and new and different values are being shaped. Also, as new knowledge and theories are developed by behavioral scientists, earlier theories and related values come to be questioned. Gagnon and Greenblat (1978, pp. 290–293) identify some of the resulting value conflicts pertaining to marital sexuality today.

1. A persistent 20th-century view is that women develop sexually later in life than men; for women the peak years are allegedly the late 20s or early 30s, while for men the peak years are allegedly the mid to late teens. This male-female sexual differential is being questioned now by some who point out that the research on which this generalization is based took place in the 1930s and 1940s, when boys and men were encouraged to be sexually active earlier in life and girls and women were discouraged from developing their sexuality until later. Given full equality with males, females may well develop their sexuality as early as males.

2. Differences of opinion exist about the sexual responsiveness of women. The traditional view that women are less capable of sexual response than men gave way in recent decades to the view that women are as capable as men of sexual response but that it takes the woman longer to become sexually aroused. Kinsey (1953) found that women tend to respond less to visual stimuli than men. Some more recent research suggests that as women become more sexually free and experienced, their rate of arousal and response will probably be about the same as men's and they will respond to erotic materials with essentially the same intensity as men (Hunt, 1974; Gagnon, 1977).

3. There are also some conflicting views on the matter of the importance of love and emotionality in female sexual response. A widely held viewpoint is that female sexuality is more emotional than male sexuality and develops more from love than from physical desire (Gordon & Shankweiler, 1971). Here again it is necessary to point out the particular social context in which females have been sexually socialized. Sexual training of young women has generally taken place in a social context where love has been a critical value. Love has legitimized female sexual responsiveness as a precondition to mate selection and marriage. While this is

still probably true for the great majority of women, there are some indications that more women are now willing to have sexual relationships without deep emotional attachments (Gagnon & Greenblat, 1978, p. 291).

4. Is sex for reproduction or for fun? Many different meanings and values may be attached to human sexuality. Traditionally, sex as reproduction has been a culturally encouraged value choice for women. At the opposite pole is the highly secular view of sex as fun only, the Playboy value-orientation. Between these extremes are other values attached to sex, such as sex as the expression of manhood or as the affirmation of womanhood, or sex as the expression of deep emotional feelings and love, or sex as the gratification of physical or mental health needs (Reiss, 1981). The range of value orientations toward human sexuality in America today is considerable, as we saw in Chapter 4 (Rubin, 1965).

MARITAL SEXUAL ADJUSTMENT

As compared to the amount of quality research on premarital sexuality, that devoted to marital sexuality is small. There are still gaps in our knowledge about marital sexual behavior and adjustment, and methodological and substantive questions have been raised about some of the studies that have been made. As Gagnon and Greenblat (1978, p. 296) observe, most of the studies on marital sexual behavior have focused on relatively narrow aspects of sexual activities and have tended to overlook broader aspects of the interrelations between sex and the rest of the married life of the couple. Methodological questions that have been raised about some of the studies include questions about sampling procedures, the kinds of questions asked couples about both sexual and nonsexual aspects of their marriage, and various biases related to studying mostly intact, middle-class marriages.

PROBLEMS IN MARITAL SEXUAL INTERACTION AND ADJUSTMENT

As suggested in our foregoing discussion of marital sexuality, there are many factors bearing on marital sexual interaction, and numerous things that affect the sexual satisfaction or dissatisfaction of the husband and wife. The marriage partners may have different sexual attitudes and needs, stemming from different kinds of experience and socialization. Marital sexual behavior and adjustment may be affected by changing sex codes and values, by changing sex-role definitions related to the women's liberation movement, and by concerns with sexual satisfaction and performance induced by alleged sex experts and popular writers, such as Rubin and Comfort.

Bell (1979, p. 417) correctly observes that problems related to the sexual satisfaction of both individuals and couples in marriage are complex because they are causally related to so many factors, social, psychological, and biological. In their analysis of sexual inadequacy, Masters and Johnson (1970) come to the conclusion that sexual dysfunctions or problems in marriage are virtually always marital problems and seldom only personal problems of the wife or husband. The authors also emphasize the role that anxiety or fear of inadequacy play in sexual problems of married people today. They see the fear of sexual inadequacy as "the greatest known deterrent to effective sexual functioning, simply because it so completely distracts the fearful individual . . . by blocking reception of sexual stimuli either created by or reflected from the sexual partner" (Masters & Johnson, 1970, p. 3). Such fears are often related to a concern with the end product of sexual relations rather than with the total activity or process. A person with this concern seems to be watching his own sexual performance critically, as a kind of spectator or third person. Kaplan (1974, p. 119) sees this "spectatoring," which focuses attention on what one wants to have happen rather than on the enjoyment of what is happening, as a frequent cause of sexual dysfunctioning in marriage. Also, as the years go by, declining energy, boredom, and loss of interest by one or both partners may become problems in the sexual adjustment of married couples. The realization that their sexual enthusiasm and responses are no longer what they once were can be a source of frustration and anxiety.

In his analysis of sexual adjustment in marriage, LeMasters (1957b, pp. 376–384) identified a number of interrelated sex problems of American wives and husbands. While not equally salient for all wives and husbands today—probably least so for the most sexually emancipated—these problem-inducing conditions and factors are probably significant in the lives of a great many average, conventional American men and women today.

Some sexual problems of wives

Sexual socialization of the wife. Reference has been made to differences in the sexual conditioning and experiences of females and males. American girls and young women are apt to be brought up to repress their sexual desires and interests and to look upon sex as part of a larger love relationship. They tend to romanticize sex, or perhaps to degrade it at the point in their growth when they become aware of the male peer-group approach to sex. Young women with this background may enter marriage with mixed feelings about sex, and many experience some problems in adjusting to the sexual attitudes and conduct of a husband socialized along quite different lines.

Difficulty in achieving sexual satisfaction. While this problem may not be as widespread as it once was, there appear to be many wives today who still have difficulty achieving full sexual satisfaction. Terman

(1938) found about one third of the married women in his sample reporting inability to achieve orgasm. Gagnon (1977) found some increase in orgasm achievement among married women in recent years by comparing women who were born in three different decades, 1930–39, 1940–49, and 1950–59. However, even now there are many wives who do not achieve full sexual satisfaction consistently, according to Gagnon. He says the data make it clear that "only four or five of ten women had orgasm between 90 and 100 percent of the time" (Gagnon & Greenblat, 1978, p. 306).

Frigidity represents the extreme situation where a woman is unable to achieve orgasm in sexual relations, and is also unable to be sexually aroused. Severe frigidity can prevent sexual intimacy, both physically and psychologically. There is evidence that the causes of most frigidity are psychological rather than physical. Masters and Johnson (1970) found that most women suffering from this disability had repressed their sexuality due to ignorance, fear, or authoritarianism often associated with a rigid religious background. Kaplan (1974, p. 148) corroborated this position, finding among her sex therapy patients suffering from frigidity many who had experienced a restrictive upbringing accompanied by "an extremely punitive and moralistic attitude in their family during their childhood." Another factor contributing to the wife's frigidity may be her feelings toward her husband. If his approach to sex is antagonistic to her's, if he does not live up to her expectations, sexual or otherwise, if she comes to the point of disliking him or finds him physically repelling, the wife can become sexually nonresponsive (Masters & Johnson, 1970, p. 235).

Professional sex counseling and therapy can help the great majority of sexually frigid women. Masters and Johnson (1970, p. 235) report that 80 percent of the women they treated became sexually responsive and achieved orgasm in intercourse.

Fear of unwanted pregnancy. Another problem affecting the sexual adjustment of some wives is an underlying concern with the possibility of an unwanted pregnancy. Despite wider availability of information and advice on family planning and the greater availability of more reliable contraceptive techniques, unplanned pregnancies continue to occur, as the demands for abortion attest. Human error, lack of husband-wife communication, and the lack of completely safe birth control methods all contribute to this anxiety among married women which can detract from their enjoyment of sexual relations.

Fatigue and child care. Chronic fatigue can interfere with the sex lives of married women, especially in the early periods of childbearing and childrearing (Dyer, 1963). Before the arrival of the first child—in the honeymoon phase of marriage—the young wife normally has plenty of time and energy to devote to her husband and to the development of their intimate lives together. When the baby arrives with its unrelenting demands, the husband and his personal needs will probably take second place, at least for a time. The husband may resent the fact that his wife has much less time and energy for him now, even though he can understand the fact that his new son or daughter needs a mother's attention constantly. And, as we have seen earlier, most married women have other roles at home and in the community, all placing demands on her energies. With all she has to do day in and out it is small wonder that mothers of infants and small children tend to experience periods of chronic fatigue (LeMasters, 1957a, p. 350). And fatigue is not conducive to good sexual relations.

Some sexual problems of the husband

The husband's sexual socialization. As we saw in Chapters 2 and 3, most American boys become aware of sex early in life and begin to develop attitudes and interests toward sexuality, some of which are quite different from those developed by American girls. Much of his sex education is apt to take place within the all-male peer group. He is taught to see sex as mainly physical, and the physical terms used to describe sex may be crude and vulgar. As he becomes a teenager he is conditioned to display his sexual prowess, and seeks to prove his masculinity via "scoring" sexually with a number of female partners. This results in a husband's sex socialization probably being different from that of his wife. Some modification may be needed before marriage or during the early years of marriage.

Some of this modification takes place, of course, during the more serious phases of courtship, from the reactions and cues from young women who are candidates for marriage. Still, this male relearning process might continue into the early years of marriage. He may have to learn to associate sex with deep love and tender sentiments, thus bringing his views more into conformity with those of his wife.

Problems associated with male sexual functioning. For whatever reasons—biological, psychological, or cultural—males in our society seem to become sexually aroused more easily and quickly than females; and once aroused, the male may be brought quite rapidly to climax, often before his female partner has reached that point. This seems to be a problem particularly during the earlier years of marriage, a time when the couple are less experienced and the husband may be overanxious about his performance. Patience and experience together normally reduces this as a problem in marriage.

Another problem affecting some husband's sexual functioning is impotency—the inability of the male to have an erection sufficient for sexual intercourse. Kinsey (1948, p. 213) found that impotency was much less common among men than had been generally believed and that it tends to increase with age. Only about 1 percent of his respondents under age 35 suffered this disability. He found that impotency gradually increases with age, but by age 70 only 27 percent of the males in his sample had become impotent. Factors shown to contribute to impotency include rigid religious background, fear of inadequacy, excessive drinking of alcoholic beverages, using narcotics, and certain illnesses, such as diabetes (Masters & Johnson, 1970, p. 213; Kaplan, 1974, p. 69). Removal of fear and other factors contributing to it can help reduce the problem of impotency for many men. Masters and Johnson (1970) succeeded in aiding about 75 percent of the impotent men under treatment who had previously been potent and more than 50 percent of those who had always been impotent.

Interruptions of marital sex life. In our mobile society, marriage partners may be separated from each other frequently, and in some occupations the business or professional person may be absent from his or her spouse for sustained periods of time fairly regularly. This spousal separation is on the increase as more wives enter the labor force. Also, during periods of the wife's pregnancy and intensive infant care, as well as during periods of illness or exhaustion, the husband may be frustrated by interruptions in normal marital sexual relations. Such intrusions and difficulties may impose hardships on both husband and wife, of course, but may be more acutely felt by the husband. Such interruptions and related frustrations may contribute to the amount of extramarital sexual relations (Kinsey, 1948; 1953; Gagnon & Greenblat, 1978).

It should be kept in mind that not all married couples experience or suffer significantly from many of the above problems or conditions. In fact, the vast majority of married couples seem to have a satisfactory sexual relationship much of the time. Now let us look at the larger picture of sexual adjustment as it interrelates with marital adjustment.

SEXUAL ADJUSTMENT AND MARITAL ADJUSTMENT

What is the connection between sexual adjustment and marital adjustment? Does good sexual adjustment in marriage assure good overall marital adjustment? Does poor sexual adjustment mean that the marriage is doomed? Let us see what research has to offer in the way of enlightenment on these questions.

Studies and interpretations

Several early studies found a positive relationship between sexual adjustment and marital adjustment. Terman (1938) found sexual adjustment to be one of several factors in the marital relationship basic to good marital adjustment. He also found that an otherwise good marriage can tolerate sexual inadequacies of the marriage partners. Locke (1951) found that sexual satisfaction in marriage does much to help sustain a marriage, helping to keep the couple together and close emotionally. Burgess and Wallin (1953) found that the husband's sexual satisfaction is especially important for a good marriage, but that sexual satisfaction per se is not sufficient to sustain a marriage. They also found that "although good sexual adjustment increases the chances of high marital success, poor sexual adjustment by no means precludes it." (Burgess & Wallin, 1953, p. 692). Thomason (1955) found that mutually satisfying sexual relations were related to good marital adjustment. He also found that both sexual adjustment and marital adjustment tended to be better under certain conditions, including (1) if sexual intercourse takes place according to mutual desire of the partners; (2) if the partners are willing and able to have intercourse as often as they wish; and (3) if the marriage partner is perceived by the spouse as being sexually attractive.

Clark and Wallin (1965) found a relationship between the quality of the marriage and the sexual responsiveness of the wife. Wives whose marriages are consistently positive in quality are increasingly likely to be sexually responsive, especially in the early years of marriage. The authors also found that a deterioration of the quality of marriage after the early years may be accompanied by a decrease in the sexual responsiveness of the wife. This negative quality of the overall marriage can have an inhibiting influence on the wife's sexual responsiveness, even though earlier in marriage there had been a pattern of good sexual responsiveness.

Hunt (1974) discovered that marital intercourse was about 50 percent more frequent in marriages that were affectionately close compared to marriages in which the husband and wife were more distant affectionally. He interprets this to mean that marital sexuality is probably more generally satisfying in the affectionally close marriages. He found a correlation between emotional closeness and the sexual satisfaction of the partners, especially for wives. (See Table 8–1.) Gebhard (1966), using Kinsey's data, had also found that in those marriages reported as very happy, the partners are more apt to have greater sexual satisfaction.

Findings of the above studies plus the empirical data on human sexual behavior gathered by Kinsey and his associates, taken together with the sexual theories of Freud and other psychologists, resulted in some overcompensation for earlier Victorian-derived sexual inhibitions in marriage. Many couples now looked upon sexual adjustment as the central factor in marital success or adjustment, rather than as one of a number of important elements. This overemphasis on sex contributed to the anxieties of wives and husbands pertaining to sexual adequacy and performance. Popular media and marriage manuals have contributed to this overemphasis on the importance of sex in marriage.

A persistent problem confronting us in interpreting the relationship between sexual adjustment and marital adjustment is sorting out cause and effect. Sexual satisfaction or sexual adjustment is a difficult concept

Table 8–1

Sexual pleasure by marital closeness (percentages)

| | Marital relationship | | | | | |
| | Very close | | Fairly close | | Not too close, or very distant | |
Marital sex life in past year was:	Males	Females	Males	Females	Males	Females
Very pleasurable	79	70	46	30	12	10
Mostly pleasurable	20	26	50	58	47	28
Neither pleasurable nor nonpleasurable	1	1	2	8	17	45
Mostly or very nonpleasurable	0	3	3	4	24	17

Source: *Sexual Behavior in the 1970s* by M. Hunt. Chicago: Playboy Press, 1974.

to deal with, both intellectually and methodologically (we saw in Chapter 7 how difficult the concept of marital adjustment is to make operational and measure). Also, where relationships are found between these two variables, it is apt to be difficult to determine causality. One must be cautious in inferring that good sexual adjustment causes good marital adjustment or, conversely, that poor sexual adjustment causes poor marital adjustment. It could be equally plausible that poor marital adjustment causes poor sexual adjustment, or that good overall marital adjustment is conducive to good sexual adjustment.

Other research has found little, if any, relationship between sexual adjustment and marital adjustment. Komarovsky (1962) found only a very low relationship between sexual and marital adjustment among working-class couples. She found that many unhappily married women still have satisfying sexual relations with their husbands. Her data also revealed that the positive relationship between sexual adjustment and various aspects of marital adjustment increases with the educational level of the wife. This finding tends to corroborate the hypothesis that sexual satisfaction may be a more sensitive barometer of marital happiness in the middle class than in the working and lower classes. Just how true this is for the middle class is still a matter of some disagreement. The Cuber and Harroff (1965) study of upper-middle-class marriages presents a rather mixed picture of the role marital sex plays in the lives of these highly educated and successful business and professional people. Cuber and Harroff (1965, p. 172) found that in this group of married couples

many remain clearly ascetic where sex is concerned. Others are clearly asexual. For still others, sex is overlaid with such strong hostility that an *anti*sexual orientation is clear. In sum, we found substantial numbers of men and women who in their present circumstances couldn't care less about anything than they do about sex.

There is, however, little question that most Americans believe sex to be important in their lives and marriages. But do we, perhaps, in this modern era of sexual emancipation, tend to exaggerate the salience of sex for marital satisfaction? In a nationwide study of American men, "in their prime years"—between ages 18 and 44—conducted in 1976–77, Harris and associates investigated the attitudes of 1,990 men regarding the importance of sex in their lives and their assessments of their sexual satisfaction. Of the 1,990 men interviewed, 60 percent were married and the remainder were single, separated, divorced, or widowed. Simon and Miller (1979) reported the findings of this study. One surprising finding was that only slightly less than half (49 percent) of all these men in their prime years described sex as being very important to them personally for a happy, satisfied life (Simon & Miller, 1979, p. 13). Fewer than 1 man in 12 (about 8 percent) regarded sex as among the 2 or 3 most important factors contributing to their personal happiness; and 17 percent went so far as to say that sex is among the 2 or 3 *least* important factors to them personally. A breakdown of the sample showed that Innovators (who show a strong enthusiasm for what is new), and Contemporaries (whose preference for the new is tempered by a concern for continuity within the established order), generally attach higher importance to sex than do Conventionals (who prefer the established order and the familiar), and Traditionalists (the staunchest defenders of the past and time-honored values). (See Table 8–2.)

In comparing single men and married men, Simon and Miller (1979, pp. 13–14) found that 50 percent of the latter versus 45 percent of the former stated that their sex life was very important for a happy, satisfied life. When asked how satisfied they felt at the present time with their sex life, 53 percent of all the men said they were very satisfied. Sexual satisfaction was lowest among lower-class men (44 percent) and students (38 percent). Twice as many married men (66 percent) as single men (33 percent) reported being very satisfied with their sex lives. This finding suggests possible difficulties for the sexual adjustment of men who post-

Table 8–2

Sex life very important personally for one's happy satisfied life* (*percentages*)		Tradition- alists	Conven- tionals	Contempo- raries	Innovators	Total
	Single	36	35	52	51	45
	Married	46	47	56	52	50
	Postmarried	41	41	62	73	57

* Number of men (N) = 1,990
Source: *The Playboy Report on American Men* by W. Simon and P. Y. Miller. Chicago: Playboy Enterprises, 1979.

pone marriage and those who are seeking alternatives to conventional marriage.

While Simon and Miller (1979, pp. 13–14) found no significant difference between the sexual satisfaction of middle-class and working-class men (about 60 percent of both groups were very satisfied), only 44 percent of the lower-class men expressed satisfaction with their sex lives. When the sample was divided into the 4 types mentioned above, men classified as Innovators reported the lowest level of sexual satisfaction (45 percent) as compared to 59 percent of the Traditionalists and about 55 percent of the Conventionals and Contemporaries (See Table 8–3). Simon and Miller (1979, pp. 13–14) suggest that the higher levels of sex satisfaction in the latter three groups do not necessarily represent greater sexual fulfillment, but perhaps greater resignation or at least lower sexual expectations than those held by the Innovators, who are seeking new and more varied sexual experiences and are, therefore, probably applying different criteria of sexual satisfaction.

It is worth reiterating that only about one half (49 percent) of all these men in the prime of life felt that sex was very important for their own personal happiness, and that more than half (53 percent) felt very satisfied at the time with their sex lives.

Some conclusions regarding sexual adjustment and marital adjustment

Without doubt, there are important but complex interrelations between sexual adjustment and marital satisfaction or adjustment. Sexual adjustment between husband and wife needs to be seen within the context of the total marriage, and within the larger social context of past, present, and changing attitudes and values regarding marriage and human sexuality. Traditional views and attitudes on differences between male and female sexuality still persist in some circles. In others, the sexual equality and the sexual needs and rights of the wife are being espoused. While many married couples holding these latter views may now experience greater sexual fulfillment, others may set their sexual expectations unreal-

Table 8–3

Very satisfied at present time with one's sex life* (percentages)		Tradition-alists	Conven-tionals	Contempo-raries	Innovators	Total
	All men	59	54	55	45	53
	Singles	35	30	36	30	33
	Married	66	66	71	60	66
	Post-married	35	33	42	50	42

* Number of men (N) = 1,990

Source: *The Playboy Report on American Men* by W. Simon and P. Y. Miller. Chicago: Playboy Enterprises, 1979.

istically high, and the resulting pressures for sexual performance and achievement may be a source of anxiety, negatively affecting both marital sexual satisfaction and marital adjustment. Many American women and some men are still sexually inhibited due to their early family and religious socialization. Others, while intellectually emancipated, still experience some emotional difficulty in living up to the newer sexual emancipation norms of their peers. As Adams (1975, p. 287) says, for many married couples today

> the combination of overtones of guilt, plus over-emphasis on the importance of sex, plus new expectations of mutuality, serves to intensify the problem of sexual adjustment in the contemporary U.S. family, and will continue to do so until the attitudinal and behavioral inconsistencies are reconciled.

Masters and Johnson (1970) suggest that half of all American marriages involve some sexual dysfunction and maladjustment. This high incidence may be partly due to an idealized view of what good marital sexual adjustment is. However, the increasing popularity of sex therapy, sex manuals, and sexual advice columns suggest that many people, married and single, are concerned about trying to improve their sex lives. But to assume that the frequency of intercourse, the attainment of orgasm by the wife, or uninhibited sexual expression in marriage necessarily add up to good sexual adjustment is questionable, and gives us only a part of the picture. Again, it is necessary to keep in mind the close connection between marital sexuality and the total marriage, or the reciprocal relationship between marital sexual adjustment and the larger marital adjustment. Good sexual adjustment may be one of several indicators of good marital adjustment, but good marital sexual adjustment alone will scarcely sustain an otherwise shaky marriage.

EXTRAMARITAL SEXUAL BEHAVIOR

Not all married people restrict their sexual activities to relations with their marital partners. Some seek sexual satisfaction outside marriage, at least occasionally. Anthropologists such as Murdock (1949) have observed that cultural norms found in some societies, including ours, that require marriage partners to be completely sexually faithful to each other are unrealistic. Lifetime marital sexual monogamy is a high cultural standard which many people find difficult to sustain over the years. Then too, while the taboo against extramarital sex has been general in America, it has not always been uniformly applied to both men and women. Males socialized according to the more open sex codes of the male peer groups may have greater difficulty remaining monogamous than women socialized in the more restrictive female subculture (Weis & Slosnerick, 1981). In fact, the long-standing double standard for female-male sexual behavior

Table 8–4

Response to question about wrongness of extramarital sex relations (*percentages*)		Year				
		1973	*1974*	*1976*	*1977*	*1980*
	Always wrong	69.6	74.1	68.7	73.0	65.4
	Almost always wrong	14.8	11.8	15.6	13.6	14.8
	Wrong only sometimes	11.6	11.6	11.5	10.1	9.2
	Not wrong at all	4.1	2.5	4.3	3.2	3.4
	N (Number of men)	1491	1460	1475	1510	1557

Source: "Attitudes Toward Premarital, Extramarital, and Homosexual Relations in the U.S. in the 1970s" by N. D. Glenn and C. N. Weaver, *The Journal of Sex Research*, 1979 *15*, 113.

is reflected in the greater percentage of men than women who engage in extramarital sexual relations (Kinsey, 1948; 1953; Bell et al., 1975). (See Table 8–4.)

As compared to people in some other countries, Americans take a strong stand against extramarital sexual relations—adultery. Christensen (1962, p. 130), in comparing a midwestern American sample and a Danish sample, found that while 41 percent of the Danish men and 36 percent of the Danish women approved of extramarital sex under certain conditions (such as long absence of spouse), this approval was expressed by only 12 percent of American men and 5 percent of American women. Using data from seven independently drawn national survey samples of about 1,500 respondents each during the 1970s, Glenn and Weaver (1979), examined the attitudes of adult Americans toward various kinds of sexual relations. They found that standards concerning extramarital sex remained highly restrictive throughout the 1970s. Young adults, persons with higher education, and persons with no religion were somewhat less restrictive than the population as a whole; while older persons, persons with less education, and Protestants were more restrictive than the general population. Glenn and Weaver conclude that their data provide no bases for predicting a high degree of extramarital permissiveness in the foreseeable future.

Americans, as is true of people in many other societies, oppose adultery on several grounds. It is believed to be a threat to the institutions of marriage and family; it is believed to endanger the mother-child relationship; it is seen as a source of distrust and conflict between the marriage partners, leading to personal disillusionment, unhappiness and broken marriages; it is considered deviant and immoral by many traditionally oriented people. Evidence indicates that adultery is lowest among the most religiously devoted and highest among those most nonreligious (Kinsey, 1953, p. 424). Adultery is still against the law in all 50 states, and is legally punishable, although prosecution is rare. It is one of the most frequently cited legal causes of divorce. Given the strong taboo against extramarital sex, it is usually practiced with deceit and in secrecy.

REASONS FOR EXTRAMARITAL
SEXUAL RELATIONS

Kinsey (1953, pp. 432–435) found a wide variety of reasons, motives, and explanations given by the respondents in his study for their extramarital involvement, including the following.

1. Sexual boredom or monotony in marriage, which created a desire for something new, different, more exciting. In some cases the marriage partner was said not to be meeting one's sexual needs, leading one to seek a more responsive sexual partner.

2. Extramarital sex served as a means of enhancing one's social status via an alliance with a new partner of higher social status.

3. For some, extramarital relations represented an accommodation to a respected friend of the opposite sex. Close friends at times developed their attachment to the point of emotional and sexual involvement.

4. For others, extramarital sex served as a retaliation for one's spouse's extramarital involvement. The motive was one of revenge, to show one's spouse that "if he can do it, so can I."

5. Another motive was rebellion. Extramarital relations were an assertion of one's independence from one's spouse, liberation from conventional restrictive sex codes and from the confinements of monogamy.

6. Other spouses sought new emotional attachments and satisfactions. Some spouses did not feel their personal ego needs were being adequately met in the marital relationship.

7. In some cases the respondent's extramarital relations were actually encouraged by one's marriage partner, who was probably having—or thinking of having—an extramarital affair.

8. The aging factor played a role in some extramarital sexual behavior. Kinsey (1953) found that the highest rates of extramarital sex for women occurs in the age group 36 to 40. Sexual desires and interests were found to be high among women in this age group, due in part to a reduction of many sexual inhibitions that these women had when younger. At the same time, many husbands were experiencing a decrease in sexual drive and interest. Also, wives entering this "middle-age" period may experience concerns about losing their youth and attractiveness, and thus respond to extramarital advances in order to prove they are still desirable.

When is a married woman most vulnerable to the temptations of extramarital relations? In their study, Bell and associates (1975, p. 384) found that the variable most predictive of extramarital sex was the rating of the marriage itself. For married women, the combination of factors most predictive of a high rate of extramarital sex was a combination of a low-rated marriage and attitudes of sexual liberalism, along with a liberal lifestyle. It seems apparent that the trend toward sexual liberalism is contributing to a weakening of traditional monogamous sex codes and their effective control over husbands and wives. The resulting change in increasing extramarital experience of wives is most significant. Philandering husbands have been numerous until recently, though philandering wives have not (Bell, et al., 1975).

Just how extensive is extramarital sexual behavior? Because of its secretive nature, reliable rates are difficult to come by. However, let us see what the existing evidence indicates.

RATES OF EXTRAMARITAL SEXUAL BEHAVIOR

Despite strong traditional disapproval of extramarital sex, there are indications that it is not infrequent and is probably on the increase. The Kinsey studies (1948; 1953) probably still provide the most reliable data on extramarital relations in the United States. Kinsey found that by age 40, 26 percent of the married women and 50 percent of the married men had engaged in extramarital sex at least once. While these percentages surprised many people by being higher than supposed, the actual incidences and number of extramarital partners were low for most men and women. Forty-one percent of the wives had limited their extramarital sex to only one partner, and another 40 percent to two to five partners. Kinsey also found that the rates were higher for the younger women in his sample, suggesting a trend toward increases in extramarital sexual behavior among women. Some more recent studies tend to support this. The *Redbook* study (1975) found that 31 percent of the sample of married women had engaged in extramarital sex, and Bell (1979, p. 425), who conducted the study, estimates that ultimately the rate for those women in the study who were under the age of 30 may rise to about 50 percent. Hunt (1974) found a similar increase in the extramarital sexual behavior of young women, who are closing the gap between female and male rates among young married people. Reiss (1976, p. 288) finds these recent trends comparable to those which occurred earlier in premarital and marital sex. As women become more emancipated from traditional and confining homemaking and mother roles, and as they become more independent and self-reliant, the long-standing restrictions on their extramarital contacts and relations will likely continue to weaken.

More data are needed before it can be said with confidence just what the actual rates of extramarital sex are today. A cautious generalization would be that while we really do not know how many married men and women engage in extramarital sex, the number is probably substantial and increasing. However, evidence suggests that extramarital sex probably accounts for a small proportion of the total sexual expression of American men and women.

C H A P T E R 9

Marriage and occupational roles

The worlds of work and family have been intertwined throughout history. In most preindustrial societies home and family were the centers of economic productivity as well as economic consumption, and women and children as well as men had important productive roles. Whole families often worked together as a team on the land or in the shop to turn out goods for home consumption or for the marketplace.

The industrial revolution brought about a separation of the worlds of work and family, so that in such modern urban-industrial societies as America the family provider normally goes off each day to his or her place of work while other family members remain in the home. Until the last half of the 20th century, when massive numbers of women returned to the labor force, the removal of economic production from the home to factories and business centers had resulted in (1) a separation of work settings for husbands and wives, and (2) the removal of women and children from direct contributions to economic productivity.

With the development of the urban-industrial economic order, occupational roles became more specialized and the division of labor by sex became more pronounced. The man now had the main responsibility for providing for the family's economic support while the wife had the main responsibilities for emotional support of family members and taking care of the home. This division of responsibilities along sex lines became normatively established early in the modern industrial era with the result that most men have felt strongly compelled to seek employment and provide for their families, and most women—until recently at least—have felt a strong commitment to assume and perform satisfactorily their conventional domestic roles. Consequently many wives and mothers who accept employment outside the home today are still apt to look upon their occupational roles as supplemental to their traditional family roles, and some may also experience a degree of guilt about leaving home and family for an outside job.

Let us now turn our attention to some of the interrelations between the world of work and occupational involvement and marriage and family life.

OCCUPATION AND MARRIAGE AND FAMILY

THE WORLD OF WORK AND MARRIAGE AND FAMILY

In their article "Work and Family in Contemporary Society," Rapoport and Rapoport (1965) note that in traditional societies work and family structures tended to be closely linked as parts of an integrated whole. The relationships between work and family life thus were a matter of conformity to dominant and consistent cultural norms. However, in our urban-industrial society the worlds of work and family tend to be separated and the norms of each world are different and not necessarily consistent. The relations between work roles and family roles are not so well structured and can be complicated. Rapoport and Rapoport identify four current issues in work-family interrelations as the focus of their analysis.

1. Family and work have become increasingly differentiated from one another in our society. The major productive processes are outside the home, and work roles have become highly varied and specialized in the economic division of labor. The world of work, with its universalistic norms, bears no necessary relation to the intimate world of the family with its particularistic norms.

2. Work and family roles vary in their relative salience in the lives of people. The importance of work roles varies with the type of work one does. In general, the professions require the strongest commitment and are therefore potentially more competitive with the worker's family roles. An example would be the member of the clergy who considers the profession a "divine calling." The salience of work roles normally declines as one descends the social class hierarchy. In fact, in some lower-class manual occupations where work rewards and satisfactions are low, work may take on a negative significance.

3. Work and family modes of interaction tend to be isomorphic, that is, tend toward a similarity of behavior patterning. How one thinks and

acts at work tends to affect how one thinks and acts at home, and vice versa. As stated by Oeser and Hammond (1954, p. 238), "The breadwinner's pattern of relations in both regions (work and family) is likely to have much the same form because in both cases his behavior will depend upon his beliefs and expectations about his 'self' and others." Studies show that fathers in business or a profession tend to judge their children's behavior at home in terms of the aggressiveness and competitiveness expected in the father's occupational world (Aberle & Naegele, 1952; Miller & Swanson, 1958; Kohn, 1977).

4. Life cycle stages affect relations between work and family life. One goes through various stages in one's family life and work career, and these will intersect and interrelate in various ways. Critical role transitions may occur at the same time in both areas, as when a young couple graduate from college, get married, and one or both start out in work careers. Their family and work situations are different at this juncture than they will be at later stages when children arrive and the husband-father becomes firmly established in and absorbed by his career; and they will be different even later when the children are grown up and gone and the man is facing retirement from his job and must reapportion his interests and involvements in family and other nonwork interests.

Keep these four issues in mind as we move on to a closer look at occupational involvement of one or both marriage partners.

Occupational involvement and marriage

Except for independently wealthy couples, occupational involvement is compulsory for at least one of the marriage partners. Since such occupational involvement is both necessary and legitimate, it can become an insidious threat to marriage. A husband preoccupied with his career can argue that he is working hard only to support his wife and children and thus can counter criticisms that he is not spending enough time at home.

Let us look now at some of the effects on marriage of the separation of the worker from his family, of different kinds of occupations, and of occupational success.

Separation of worker from marriage partner.
As noted above, employment today generally takes the worker away from home and spouse. The length of time on the job, the work schedule, and the regularity of the hours and days of work, all have effects on the relations between the worker and the spouse. Mott et al. (1965) found that the marriages of working-class men on the day shift in the factory were consistently better than marriages of workers on the evening or night shifts. For workers living in suburbs, both the hours of work and the added commuting time extend the length of time a worker is separated from home and spouse. Gans (1967) found that in Levittown the commuting husband-

Male occupational involvement starts early in the life-cycle

David Bell

father generally arrived home from work so late he saw very little of his young children on working days, and was too exhausted to help his wife much when he got home. These time and separation problems are greater in some jobs than others, of course.

Occupational differences and marital relations.

In general, the greater the satisfaction a worker derives from his or her occupation, the less the strain on the marriage (LeMasters, 1957b; Harrell & Ridley, 1975). Situations in which the job imposes continuous strain or frustrations often produce negative side effects on the marriage. The exhausted or dissatisfied worker may take out his frustrations on family members. One of the individual-serving functions of marriage is to provide affection and ego need-satisfaction, and emotional therapy when needed. After taking hard knocks and tensions all day, which are associated with some jobs, the worker may come home at night in need of "psychological first aid." If the marital relationship is good in other areas it may be able to carry this emotional overload created by the occupational experience; if not, the marriage may falter under the strain.

Some types of occupations put greater strains on the marriage than others. In comparing the broken marriage rates of different professional workers, Rosow and Rose (1972) found that authors and social scientists have higher divorce rates than editors, accountants, and physical scientists. The former occupations often seem to have a combination of more financial uncertainties, less regular work schedules, and greater contacts with people resulting in more opportunities for extramarital interests, while the latter occupations tend to have more routine work schedules, regular incomes, and are more conservative socially.

Some occupations may exact heavy demands on the worker's time and energies. In a study of Protestant clergymen, Scanzoni (1965) found the ministers' wives reporting that the demands of the church on their husband's time regularly interfered with their family life, leaving little time for companionship with their husbands. The church tended to take priority over home and family for these clergymen.

In a widely publicized study entitled *The Organization Man,* Whyte (1957) found that big corporations may interfere in the marriages of their employees in numerous ways, some subtle and some not so subtle. The wife of a promising executive may be put through a series of "tests" to see if she has the requisite qualities and skills needed to help advance her husband's career in the organization. She must display the proper social skills at social gatherings and when acting as a hostess. She must conform to the corporation's expectations and above all show that she realizes her husband belongs first to the organization, then to her. A defiant or overly independent wife could jeopardize her husband's career and find her marriage in serious trouble.

Some possible effects of occupational success on marriage.   As suggested above, some of the effects on marriage of career-striving and occupational achievement are not necessarily beneficial. While the rewards of higher income and enhanced prestige per se may benefit the couple, there may also be some dysfunctional consequences of career-striving and success. In a study of social mobility and marriage in Sweden, the author (Dyer, 1970) found that upward occupational mobility was negatively correlated with marital adjustment when one marriage partner was more ambitious that the other, when the husband's occupational success was rapid, and when the husband's career advancement had carried the couple from the lower class to the middle class. Under these conditions the marriage partners often held different value orientations, communication between them was more difficult, and the husband's occupational success tended to introduce strains in their relationships.

In a study of 400 middle-class married couples, Dizard (1968) found that the marital happiness of both partners decreased with the husband's early to mid-career occupational success. The more effort the men expended in their career advancement—changing jobs, seeking salary raises, and so on—the less happy their marriages were either for themselves or for their wives. The men who had more stable occupations and incomes—even lower incomes—had happier marriages.

Scanzoni (1968) compared a sample of recently divorced middle-class women with a sample of middle-class married women and found a great difference in the satisfaction these women felt toward their husband's or ex-husband's jobs. Eighty-seven percent of the married women expressed satisfaction with their husband's occupation, as against only 37 percent of the divorced women. Nearly two thirds of the divorced women (63 percent) had been dissatisfied with their husband's jobs due to the husbands' overinvolvement in their occupations. The divorced husbands seldom complained about their jobs, however, so a picture emerges of broken marriages in which the husband was preoccupied and satisfied with his work while his wife felt neglected and unhappy.

From this brief look at some of the possible effects of occupational involvement on the marriage let us move to a more specific consideration of the occupational role of the husband, its importance to the family, and the interrelations between the man's occupational role and his other marriage and family roles.

OCCUPATIONAL ROLE OF THE HUSBAND

Traditionally the most important adult status-role of the American male has been that of his occupation, while the most important status-role of the adult female has been that of wife-mother. While this traditional pattern is undergoing change today, especially for females, the normative expectations are still strong for the male to support himself and his family. The work ethic, stemming from Old World traditions, is still powerful. It emphasizes the value of work, both for economic well being and for the personal and spiritual needs of the male (Weber, 1930). From this viewpoint a man is not only expected to work, but to commit himself to some honorable occupation and strive conscientiously to succeed in it.

IMPORTANCE OF THE HUSBAND'S OCCUPATIONAL ROLE TO THE FAMILY

For most families the husband's occupation has been the main source of economic support, and the main basis for the family's social standing in the community as well. The income the man's job provides determines in large part the lifestyle the couple and their children will be able to maintain for most conventional families where the wife-mother still remains at home.

Studies show that, for the American middle-class family at least, the occupational role of the man is considered to be his primary role, more important than his other family roles including "husbanding and child-rearing" (Benson, 1968; Lopata, 1975). Thus it appears that the most important role of the man is performed outside the family circle. For most men, and especially for middle-class men, this occupational role is the principal source of self-esteem and success. In general, a man's wife and children view his occupational role the same way. His occupational success reflects on them; and a successful man is apt to be more firmly established as the head of his household than is a less successful man. In a study of the effects of the Great Depression on family life, Elder (1974) found that as men lost their jobs and income, they sometimes also lost their sense of purpose, self-esteem, and family leadership. Their wives assumed most of the responsibility for the children and the household. In some cases the wife became the principal breadwinner. She gained power as her husband became increasingly estranged and peripheral in family life.

The income for the man's occupation is obviously important to the family. The size and steadiness of his income and the prospects he has for increasing his income in the future, are all basic to the family's standard of living, the kind of home they can afford, and their plans for their children's education. The likelihood of a man's wife having to work outside the home is correlated with the adequacy of his income. Also, unstable incomes are associated with unstable marriages (Becker et al., 1977; Ross & Sawhill, 1975; Huber & Spitze, 1980).

In addition to providing the principal financial resources for the family, the husband's occupation is generally the main basis for the social position or class placement of the family in the community. In this context the social evaluation or ranking of the husband's occupation may be more important than the actual amount of income it provides (Tumin, 1967; Kohn, 1977). White-collar occupations, such as clergyman or educator, which have modest remuneration, are generally more prestigious than some higher-paying occupations, such as truckdriver or automobile mechanic. The husband's occupation will thus be a principal determinant of the social class identity of the family, and this social standing will affect whom family members will associate with, their acceptance in various social groups and clubs, and the social as well as economic prospects of their children.

Socialization for male occupational roles

Socialization for occupational roles starts early in life for most American males. The typical preteen boy learns that he will work at some regular job when he grows up. While some will have mixed feelings about this prospect few will question its inevitability. That he is going to spend his adult years working is perhaps more certain than that he will ever get married and have a family. He may anticipate his future occupational role with enthusiasm, seeing it as a source of personal satisfaction and perhaps fame and fortune, or he may be less than enthusiastic, envisioning his future work at best as a necessary source of income or at worst as a drag and a necessary evil in order to survive.

In contrast to earlier times when a boy was apt to be taught his future occupational role by his father or other male kinsman, in modern industrial societies such as America the father has much less direct influence in preparing his son for future participation in the world of work, including his choice of an occupation (Benson, 1968). The father may still represent a work-role model for his son to some degree. For middle-class sons especially both parents will probably be active in socializing their son to accept the work ethic with its implied ambition and career-success goals.

The educational experience of the growing boy and young man provides an important background for his adult attitudes toward work and the occupation he will choose. Whether he ends his formal education with high school—or even earlier—or whether he goes on to college, will be a crucial factor in his occupational future. By stopping at the high school level or earlier, he will likely be excluded from the more prestigious and higher paying white-collar business and professional occupations. While career or occupational counseling is more available now to college youth it is still less available to high school youth. Since the choice of an occupation is one of the most important decisions a young man or woman makes in a lifetime it is unfortunate that so many make it while poorly informed and ill-prepared. As DeFleur and DeFleur (1967, p. 777) point out: "They formulate their occupational preferences and make their choices on the basis of information supplied for the most part by unsystematic sources of unknown validity about which we know relatively little."

Repairing heavy farm machinery is still generally considered man's work

U.S.D.A. photo by Michelle Bogre

The growing boy or girl will likely have some work experience in part-time jobs after school and during summer vacations, which will help him or her learn some things about the world of work but which may bear little relationship to the final occupational choice. One generally learns about different kinds of occupations informally, and this may result in idealized or stereotyped notions about many occupations. Studies show that the impressions children get of occupations from the media, especially TV, are apt to be superficial and sometimes misleading (DeFleur & De-Fleur, 1967). Many youth in the working class seem to drift into their adult occupations. For those who go to college—middle-class or working class—the choice of occupation may be more rational and systematic.

CONFLICT POTENTIAL BETWEEN HUSBAND'S OCCUPATIONAL ROLE AND HIS FAMILY ROLES

An issue in many American marriages is the relative commitments of the husband to his occupational role versus his marriage and family roles. American men, especially in the middle class, have been socialized to have a strong personal commitment to their careers. A man's ego and self-esteem are tied to his occupational achievement. Loss of a job, or even a demotion, can have a detrimental effect on a man's self-esteem, and if his unemployment persists it can undermine his status in his family (Cavan, 1959).

To the career-oriented American man who has accepted the work ethic, his occupation may in a sense come first, and his other family roles second. This career emphasis varies, of course, from person to person and according to the nature of the job. As explained by Aldous (1969, p. 708), "The relative salience of the job in comparison with family roles is important in this connection. If the occupation is of intrinsic interest to the man, it often competes with or even supplants the family as his major concern." A man may be expected by society to put his family ahead of his occupation if it comes down to making an actual choice; but if it becomes necessary for him to sacrifice his family roles in the pursuit of an occupational role which benefits his family, he will probably be applauded for his devotion to his work. A "workaholic" may thus rationalize his behavior to his family and the community. A man who enjoys his work may find his relations with his fellow workers more satisfying than at least some of his relations with family members. He may spend long hours at the office to avoid family demands and tensions. Conversely, a man who is unhappy or unsuccessful in his work may use his family roles as an escape or rationalization for staying away from the office, or for seeking a change of jobs. He may discover that his family is expecting him to be home more often, and few people will fault him for his attention to his wife and children (Aldous, 1969).

Viewpoint of the wife

Since the typical wife has traditionally staked her economic and social well being in large part on her husband's occupational success, she has a large investment in his occupational choice and role performance. She is well aware, as are their growing children, that the whole family stands to gain or lose by the husband-father's success of failure in his occupational role. Middle-class wives may help nuture and support their husband's careers in many ways: by being a good homemaker, by being a sounding board for his work-related problems, by being a sympathetic therapist after he's had a difficult day at work, and by being the family social secretary and hostess with an eye to developing the social contacts important to his job advancement.

But what if the wife and husband do not agree on the importance of his occupational role? If they differ considerably in attitudes as to the importance or primacy of his career, then his occupational role can become a point of stress and conflict. Most wives like to see their husbands do well in their jobs and are willing to support their efforts, but many wives may also resent the amount of time and energy their husbands devote to their work. Thus even a highly supportive middle-class wife may on occasion feel neglected by her highly successful husband. Such feelings of neglect or resentment are not restricted to middle-class wives, of course. In his study of working class marriages in Wisconsin, LeMasters (1975) found the wives of construction workers expressing strong resentment toward their husbands because of the large amount of time they spent with their fellow-workers both on and off the job. These wives voiced the opinion that their husbands placed the job first, the male peer group second, and home and family third.

There seems to be a kind of inevitable competition between the man's occupational role and his family roles. He has only so much time and energy, and occupational success seems to demand a large portion of these finite resources. The wife and children also have legitimate demands on his time and attention. He is caught between the legitimate demands of job and family, and if his wife doesn't understand this—if she puts excessive pressure on him to pay more attention to home and family at the expense of his career—the stage is set for marital conflict.

Differences in compatibility of jobs and family roles

Some occupations seem to be more compatible with or to synchronize better with marriage and family roles than do others. Some jobs require the man to be away from home and family for long or irregular hours or even days at a time. Production workers on the night shift, doctors on constant call, military personnel, and traveling salesmen will likely find their occupational roles less compatible with the roles of husband and father than most 9 to 5 workers. Periods of separation and odd or irregular working hours tend to undermine normal husband-wife relations, and at the same time may create opportunities for other personal involvements, especially for the worker who is away from the normal constraints and social controls of his home and community for lengthy periods of time.

In an analysis of occupational characteristics and role performance of the man in his family, Aldous (1969) concluded that those occupations requiring night work or irregular hours, and those which take the worker away from his family for days at a time, tend to limit his participation in other marriage and family roles. Such jobs tend to inhibit the communication skills important in marital interaction, limit the man's opportunities to assist with family decisions and tasks, and interfere with his relation with his children.

OCCUPATIONAL ROLE OF THE WIFE

INCREASED EMPLOYMENT OF MARRIED WOMEN

In recent decades American women have been surging into the labor force at an unprecedented rate. In 1976, among women aged 20 to 65, more than 56 percent were employed (U.S. Department of Labor, 1976a). The number of American women employed had doubled in about 25 years, from 19 million in 1951 to nearly 39 million in 1976. Between 1970 and 1978 the annual average labor force participation rate for women increased from 43 to 50 percent (U.S. Bureau of the Census, 1980a). The U.S. Department of Labor has called this increase in the number of women who work outside the home one of the most spectacular changes in the American economy in the 20th century. Others have called it "the single most outstanding phenomenon of our century"(Stencel, 1977, p. 23).

It is not only single women who are swelling the labor force; wives and mothers are joining the ranks at a great rate too. The 1970 U.S. Census showed that 41 percent of married women with husbands present were in the labor force. Fifty-eight percent had children under age 18 and 30 percent had children under age 6 (U.S. Bureau of Labor Statistics, 1970). Increases in employed wives and mothers have been greatest since World War II. By 1975 there were more than 21 million married women in the labor force and over half of them had children under 18 years. From 1960 to 1976 the number of families in which both the husband and wife were employed has jumped from 29 percent to 42 percent (U.S. Department of Labor, 1975; 1976a). (See Table 9–1.) The increase in employment has been fastest among married women with preschool age children. In 1960 only 19 percent of these mothers were in the labor

214

Women join men in operating a cotton gin

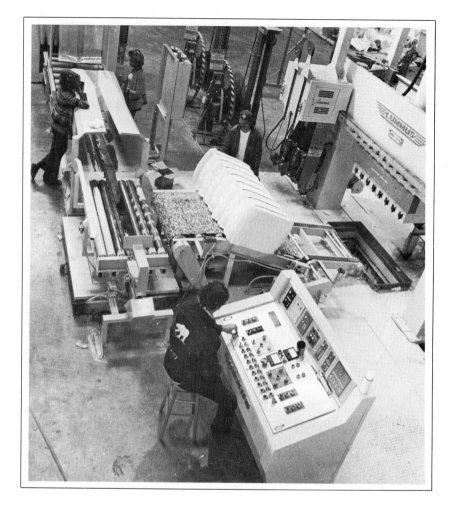

U.S.D.A. photo by David Warren

force; by 1979 the number had grown to 43 percent (U.S. Bureau of the Census, 1980a). Why this big increase in the employment of wives and mothers? This is a question deserving attention.

Factors contributing to increased employment of married women

Economic needs and desires, an expanding economy with greater job opportunities for women, inflation, rising social and economic expectations, and upward social mobility strivings, all are important factors in the sharp rise of women (including married women) in the labor force. Economic needs and pressures are clearly among the foremost. Of the more than 21 million married women in the labor force in 1975, nearly 26 percent were married to men earning less than $10,000 a year. And

Table 9–1

Women in the labor force, 1947–1978	Year	Number (in thousands)	Percentage*
	1947	16,683	31.8
	1951	19,054	34.7
	1956	21,495	36.9
	1961	23,838	38.1
	1966	27,333	40.3
	----	------	----
	1971	32,132	43.4
	1972	33,320	43.9
* Percent of female population	1973	34,561	44.7
aged 16 and over.	1974	35,892	45.7
Sources: "Women Workers	1975	37,087	46.4
Today," U.S. Department of	1976	38,520	47.4
Labor, October, 1976; *Statistical*	1978	41,000	50.0
Abstract of the United States, 1979.			

nearly three million married women workers had husbands who were unable to work or were unemployed for other reasons (U.S. Department of Labor, 1976a). In the middle socioeconomic group, with high inflation and expanded family needs, more families have come to depend on the second income provided by the wife-mother to maintain or improve their standard of living. Without her employment the family could not now afford to buy their house or send their children to college. Economists estimated that in the mid-1970s it cost between $70,000 and $100,00 to raise a child for the first 18 years of his or her life (Association of American Colleges, 1976). More recent estimates run even higher, due largely to escalating inflation. Espenshade (1980) estimates that when the mother's loss of income due to staying home with the child is added to the direct maintenance costs (including a college education), the total cost of having and raising a child in 1980 ranges from about $100,000 in a low-income level family to nearly $140,000 in a middle-income family.

Another economic-related factor contributing to the increased employment of married women is the high divorce rate, with the increasing probability that a marriage will end in divorce. So it is becoming increasingly risky today for women to rely solely on their marriages for economic security and social status. Many a young woman who would prefer to be a full-time housewife will not do so—if she is rational—because to do so is to run the risk of ending up divorced without any marketable skills with which to support herself. That is, the "housewife only" married woman today runs a considerable risk of becoming an economically insecure "displaced homemaker" when divorced.

Economic needs and motives are not the only explanation by any means for the great increase in the employment of women. These needs and pressures have been present before and were often just as great as they are today. Some of the noneconomic factors contributing to the rising employment of women include (1) the increasing number of college educated women; (2) the greater life-expectancy of women; (3) more efficient birth control methods and the trend toward fewer children per family; (4) more labor-saving devices in the home; (5) expanded job opportunities for women; and (6) legal action reducing job discrimination based on sex (Stencel, 1977, pp. 24–26).

Probably as important as anything else in the rising employment rates of women in recent decades is the dramatic change in attitudes toward the employment of women outside the home. This change in public opinion is related to a number of social trends and movements, including feminism and the women's liberation movement, and a belated recognition by men that women also have the capacities to develop the skills and knowledge required in the whole range of white-collar jobs and most blue-collar jobs. Related attitude changes include more widespread approval for married women to expand their interests beyond traditional wife and mother roles if they so desire. The extent to which attitudes have changed here may be seen by comparing two public opinion polls, one taken in 1936 and the other in 1976. A Roper poll of American opinion in 1936 showed that only 15 percent of the population believed that married women should have a full-time job outside the home. Forty years later a Gallop poll found the 68 percent of those interviewed approved of wives working outside the home (Stencel, 1977, p. 26).

The increasing employment of women needs to be understood in the larger context of social and ideological changes. Feminism, equalitarianism, freedom of choice, individualism, and the recent emphasis on self-enhancement provide the social setting within which more and more women

Young woman handles tractor and plow with ease

U.S.D.A. photo by Don Breneman

become motivated to expand their horizons beyond conventional home and family roles. As more women go to college they not only get the training necessary to compete for jobs; they also become socialized to want or need to break out of the traditional mold. Margaret Mead once said that the more education a woman has the more dissatisfied she is being just a housewife. Many educated women today tend to assess their self-worth and their value in the eyes of the community more in terms of occupational achievement than in terms of home-based role performance.

SOME CONSEQUENCES OF THE WIFE'S EMPLOYMENT ON THE MARRIAGE

How does the wife's occupational role affect her relations with her husband? Does it have any effects, positive or negative, on their marital adjustment? The few early studies touching on these questions were inconclusive. Burgess and Cottrell (1939) found that in nonstress situations the employment of the wife was associated with good marital adjustment. Locke and Mackeprang (1949) found no significant difference between the marital adjustment of working couples and couples where the wife was not working. Nye (1959) found increasing marital conflict and decreasing marital happiness among working mothers who had children in grade school. Blood and Wolfe (1960) found a differential pattern of marital adjustment associated with the employment of the wife and the income of the husband. Employed wives of husbands in lower-income groups indicated greater marital satisfaction than did working wives whose husbands were earning more money. Gianopulos and Mitchell (1957) found poorer marital adjustment among working couples when the husband disapproved of his wife's employment.

In a study of middle-class working couples in Wisconsin in the mid-1950s the author found marital happiness to be related to various family role and authority patterns and expectations of the husband and wife (Dyer, 1959). Marital happiness was greater for couples who shared more in their family roles and who were equalitarian in authority patterns, that is, when the husband and wife had become partners in other areas of family life as well as in family providing, and when each had an equal voice in making family decisions, determining family policies, and settling differences. Also, marital happiness was greater for those working couples who held partnership or equalitarian family role and authority expectations, that is, for those who had achieved an essential emancipation from traditional views of "man's place" and "woman's place" in the family. In addition, marital happiness was greater when the husband and wife were in close agreement as to the ways family roles should be played and family authority allocated and exercised.

Axelson (1963) compared the marital adjustment of a sample of husbands of working wives with a sample of husbands of nonworking wives in a small western town in 1961. He found a definite pattern of poorer marital adjustment in the working-wife couples, especially when the wife was working full time. In this population the working wife appears to be seen as a real threat by the male. These men believed that the children would suffer if their mother were employed, and they feared her increased independence would threaten the man's traditional dominance, especially if she enjoyed greater economic success. Axelson concluded that when a husband holds such views the movement of the wife into the labor market will not be made without some cost in satisfactory marital adjustment.

In their study, "Working Wives and Marital Happiness," Orden and Bradburn (1969) found that if the wife felt she *had* to work, then her employment is most likely to cause marital dissatisfaction. Wives who said they would not continue working if their families did not need the money were those most likely to report marital dissatisfaction. But if the wife chose to work, both wife and husband reported fewer marital tensions and greater satisfaction in their marriage. Marriages in which the wife worked part time were the ones in which both partners reported greatest satisfaction with their roles; and marriages in which both husband and wife were highly educated are most likely to be associated with high marital satisfaction.

In a comparison of a sample of marriages in which the wife was employed with a sample in which she was not employed, Burke and Weir (1976) found in general that working wives were more satisfied than were nonworking wives. The latter group reported having more worries than did the working wives, including worries about being "in a rut," about sickness in the family, and about difficulties in demonstrating their affection to their husbands. The principal worry of the employed wives was "not having enough time to spend with my family or for relaxation." Working wives were happier in their marriages and reported greater agreement with their husbands on most matters. However, the authors found that the husbands of working wives were less satisfied that the husbands of nonworking wives. Husbands of working wives were less happy with their marriages, and were more concerned than the other husbands about money problems, housing problems, and communicating with and showing affection for their wives. Burke and Weir suggest that the adjustment to a dual-career marriage is more stressful to the husband than to the wife. Such marriages seem to result in more identity problems for the man than for the woman. Though the wife's employment may raise her self-esteem, at the same time it may threaten the husband's self-esteem and status.

The two studies reported above plus some earlier ones suggest that the employment of the wife may be a source of stress for the husband. In an attempt to further test this hypothesis, Booth (1977) interviewed members of 560 households in Toronto, using more sophisticated research methods than those used in the Burke and Weir study, which he was attempting to replicate. Booth found that employed women evidenced greater stress than full-time housewives, particularly at the time they just entered their jobs and just after leaving a job. But, contrary to earlier findings, husbands of employed wives showed no more stress than husbands of nonworking wives. He concluded that husbands and wives today are more readily adaptable to the wife's participation in the labor force, and that couples generally experience more benefits than disadvantages from the wife's employment. Otherwise there was little difference between wives who had been working full time and housewives who had never been in the labor force. Husbands whose wives were employed enjoyed as happy or happier marriages and showed less stress than those married to housewives.

The Booth study should be reassuring to those who are concerned about the possible negative affects of the wife's employment on her husband and on their marital adjustment. Another recent study sought the effects the wife's occupational superiority would have on husband-wife relationships. That is, do marital troubles result when the wife has a more prestigious occupation than her husband? Richardson (1979), using data from the National Opinion Research Center's 1972–1977 General Social Surveys, found no significant relationship between the occupational prestige level of the wife and the marital happiness of the partners. He concluded that the data offer no support for the hypothesis that marital troubles arise in dual-career families where the wives are higher in occupational prestige than their husbands. It may be true that equalitarian attitudes are further advanced in the population than was thought. Richardson's findings should also be reassuring to those concerned about the possible negative effects of the middle-class wife's career on marital adjustment.

In a somewhat different vein, Wright (1978) examined the question of whether or not working married women are really more satisfied than nonworking married women. The purpose of this study was to gather the most recent and generalizable evidence on the long-standing question of whether housewives or working women have the more enriching and satisfying lives. Wright's data were collected between 1971 and 1976 from six large national surveys conducted by the University of Michigan and the National Opinion Research Center in Chicago. He compared patterns of marital and personal satisfaction among white, married women who were either in the labor force or were housewives. His subjects came from both the working class and the middle class.

Wright (1978) found no consistent, substantial, or statistically significant differences in the reported personal happiness between working wives and housewives in either the working or the middle class. The data provided only weak support for the hypothesis that outside work is more satisfying than housework to married women; and this finding pertained largely to middle-class working women. An interesting finding was that, apart from the money their outside employment brings, a higher percentage of working wives of both social classes said that their housework was more important to them personally than outside work for which they were paid. In marital satisfaction there was no consistent pattern of differences. Among middle-class wives there was no difference in the marital satisfaction between housewives and working wives. Among working-class wives there was some evidence that employed wives are very happy in their marriages, but not significantly happier than the housewives.

Wright concludes that the national survey data do not support earlier findings by Ferree (1976a; 1976b) that married women who work outside the home are happier and more satisfied with their lives and marriages than are women who are solely housewives. Wright (1978, p. 312) interprets his findings thus:

> We do not mean to imply through this research that fulltime housewifery is the "best of all worlds" for the modern American woman, and least of all do we wish to promulgate the "myth of the happy homemaker." What we do wish to emphasize, however, is that in the aggregate "homemakers" are just as happy as are women who work and that little purpose is served in denying it. The imagery of confusion, isolation, loneliness, and alienation among American housewives, we suggest, is just as mythical as the opposite number it is meant to replace. Neither of these myths is especially well-suited to a full understanding of the situation of women in contemporary American society.

It is sensible to warn against exaggerating the benefits for the wife derived from working outside the home. For one thing, the personal benefits and satisfaction experienced by a highly educated woman pursuing a successful career in the business or professional world are quite different from those of an uneducated woman running a punch press eight hours a day or a typist in a big impersonal bureaucracy. Evidence shows that both occupational roles and homemaking roles have their advantages and disadvantages, their costs and benefits. While the social trends of the day—women's liberation, equalitarianism, individual growth—tend to underline the many satisfactions available to women who work outside the home, the Wright study and others indicate that there are still many satisfactions experienced by wives who remain in the home as housewives or homemakers.

There are, of course, many adjustments required of dual-career couples. One problem is finding suitable employment for both spouses in the same locality. Another is resolving conflicts which arise when one spouse needs to move to further his or her career, while the other needs or wants to stay in the present location. One possible solution is a commuter marriage, with the husband, for example, moving to Dallas while the wife continues working in Houston. Such commuter marriages obviously entail serious problems, such as separation during the workweek, maintaining two households, and the time and expense of traveling back and forth weekends for one of the spouses.

In addition to various marital and personal adjustments, partners in dual career marriages will likely face certain career adjustments. For example, what effect may the employment of one spouse have on the career development of the other spouse? In a study of "Husbands, Wives, and Careers," Ferber and Huber (1979) found that for a career woman holding a Ph.D., marriage to a man holding a Ph.D. does negatively affect her career. Her husband's need or desire for geographic mobility to advance his career acts as a constraint on the wife's career advancement. Also, marriage to a highly educated woman affects the husband's career in certain ways. While having a Ph.D. wife had no direct effect on his salary, it did reduce his professional activities, including his scholarly productivity and the number of offices held in professional associations.

Is the employment of the wife outside the home conducive to divorce? Increases in divorce rates have accompanied increases in the employment of married women, and some authorities see a connection between the two (O'Neil, 1967; Cherlin, 1979; Scanzoni, 1979). In traditionally oriented marriages, if the wife goes to work the husband may feel threatened by her independent resources; at the same time, she is better able to support herself and thus may be less willing to put up with a poor marriage. This could also be true in marriages where the wife with a high education and readily marketable skills is well able to support herself and is thus more apt to seek a divorce if the marriage is not to her liking.

The push for equal partnership in marriage means that educated women are not only expecting marriage to be satisfying in terms of affection and companionship; they are also expecting marriage to provide opportunities for them to continue growing as persons, including sharing the provider role and having equal power in decision making. When these expectations are not met, more women may now be willing to end their present marriages. Women who marry for the first time after the age of 30, who presumably have had time to become economically self-sufficient, are now more likely to divorce than women in their 20s. And among women with graduate school education, a higher percentage have been divorced than is true of women at any other educational level (Glick & Norton, 1977, pp. 15–17).

While more study is needed on the relationship between divorce and the employment of the wife, there is much that suggests that the wife's working does increase the probability of divorce. A cyclical relationship may be operating here: more women are working because they perceive marriage to be less secure than earlier, and then their employment increases the possibility of divorce.

SOME POSSIBLE CONSEQUENCES OF THE MOTHER'S EMPLOYMENT ON THE CHILDREN

The large increase of married women in the ranks of the employed has meant that more mothers today are spending many hours each work day away from their children. As noted earlier, a majority (58 percent) of employed married women had minor children living at home, according to the 1970 census. Department of Labor figures for 1975 show that more than 11.4 million employed married women had children at home under 18 years of age (Stencel, 1977, p. 37). Thus the questions and issues being raised about mother-child relations in families where the mother is employed outside the home are timely and salient.

Does maternal employment mean maternal deprivation for children? Are there widespread negative effects on children that can be attributed to the employment of the mother? Results of early studies seeking answers to such questions have generally been inconsistent and inconclusive. Some findings suggested that maternal employment did not necessarily result in maternal deprivation, and that the effects of maternal employment on children were quite complex and entangled with other factors, such as the mother's attitude toward her employment, the kinds of child care available, and the social class position of the family (Spitz, 1945; Bowlby, 1951). Hoffman (1961) found that the children of employed mothers who disliked their employment were more aggressive and rebellious than chil-

Some women still prefer to stay home and be full-time mothers

Julie Heifitz

dren of mothers who liked their jobs. Hoffman (1963, p. 204) concluded that "when the mother's employment is gratifying to her, the mother-child relationship is a warm one. . . . When the mother's employment is not satisfying, the mother-child relationship is almost the opposite." Harrell and Ridley (1975) corroborated this position in a study of Pennsylvania families in which the mother was employed. They found a significant positive relationship between maternal work satisfaction and the quality of the mother-child interaction. They interpreted this finding to mean that when a working mother finds her job satisfying she is happier in general and in a better frame of mind, which in turn enables her to be more enthusiastic and effective in her domestic and mother roles, especially enhancing the quality of her relations with her children.

Rossi (1964) found no evidence of negative consequences of the mother's employment on the welfare of the child that could be directly traceable to the employment of the mother. Rossi emphasizes the importance of the child's being properly and lovingly cared for while the mother is away at work. If the child shares the love of the mother with a warm and caring parent-surrogate in a stable enviroment, "it is probable that he will prosper at least as well as and potentially much better than the child reared more exclusively by his mother" (Rossi, 1964, p. 273). Harrell and Ridley (1975) investigated further the relationship between substitute child care and the quality of the mother-child relationship by interviewing working mothers whose children were enrolled in child-care centers. They found that mothers who were satisfied with the substitute child care provided by the day-care centers were more apt to be satisfied with their own work situation. Those mothers who were assured that their children were being well cared for in the centers were more relaxed and enjoyed their jobs more. In turn, the mother's work satisfaction was positively related to the quality of the mother-child interaction.

It is apparent from the above study and others that the availability and quality of good parent surrogates in child-care centers or elsewhere is very important to the well being of working mothers and their children. But how available is such child care today? There is certainly a big gap between the supply of good private and publically supported child-care centers and the increasing need for them as millions of mothers enter the labor force. This issue will be raised again in later chapters dealing with childrearing and parent-child relations.

CHAPTER 10

Marital dissolution and remarriage

The current high and climbing divorce rates in the United States are a cause of concern to many Americans. Is marriage as we have known it on the way out? Do the increasing divorce rates threaten the very existence of the family as a social institution? Since Americans have long believed that marriage should be permanent—" 'til death do us part"—and that the strength of our society depends on the permanence and stability of our marriage and family systems, it is understandable that many people are alarmed by the current trends in marital dissolution. The media publicizes divorce rates in newspapers and on T.V.; the clergy decries the trends from the pulpit, and legislators recommend remedial laws. Some writers critical of traditional marriage itself cite the climbing separation and divorce figures as evidence that the conventional institution of marriage has outlived its usefulness in our modern society, and argue that we need to seek new, more appropriate alternatives to marriage.

MARITAL FAILURE, OR BREAKING UP

PERSPECTIVE ON MARITAL FAILURE

As we shall see shortly, there are different kinds of divorce rates and ratios, some of which may be misleading. For example, one widely cited figure is the ratio of divorces to marriages contracted in a given year. In 1978 there were 1,122,000 divorces and 2,243,000 marriages in the United States (*Statistical Abstract of the United States,* 1979d). This is a ratio of about one divorce for every two marriages, which some people erroneously interpret to mean that one out of every two marriages will end in divorce. The fallacy in this interpretation is that the two figures used in the ratio have different population bases and therefore should not be used together. The 2,243,000 marriages are for the one year (1978) only, while the 1,122,000 divorces, although obtained in 1978, are from a much larger population of marriages, not only those contracted in 1978, but also including marriages contracted in 1977, 1976, 1975—way back to 1940, or even earlier.

The media, and various political and religious leaders, are prone to use this misleading ratio as evidence that marriage and family are breaking down in America. The figure of one divorce for every two weddings in 1978 has led to the alarmed assertion that young people entering marriage today have only a 50–50 chance of a lasting marriage. There are, however, more accurate and less alarming ways of figuring divorce rates. Let us see what they are.

One standard measurement used by demographers is called the *crude divorce rate.* This is the number of divorces per 1,000 persons in the population. (See Figure 10–1.) This rate has the advantage of being easy to figure, but it has the limitation of using *all* persons as a base upon which

Figure 10–1

Fluctuations in United States divorce rates, 20th Century

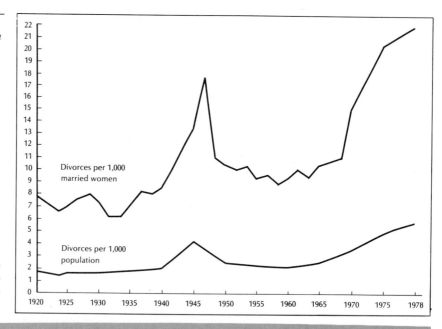

Divorces per 1,000 married women

Divorces per 1,000 population

Sources: Various vital statistic reports of the U.S. Department of Health and Human Services and National Center for Health Statistics.

to calculate divorces. This presents a problem because many persons in this total population base, such as children and unmarried adults, are not "at risk" when it comes to divorce. The crude divorce rate in the United States for 1979 was 5.3 divorces per 1,000 population.

Another way of calculating divorce rates which does not have the limitation of the crude divorce rate is to include only married women in the population base. This is called the *refined divorce rate*. Refined rates are more precise because they focus on the logical group from which the divorces come. Demographers Norton and Glick (1979) figure that in the 1975–1977 period there were on the average 37 divorces taking place annually for every 1,000 married women.

Some media coverage may lead to the belief that American marriages today are of short duration compared to earlier times. On the contrary: A couple marrying today can expect about 35 years of married life before the marriage ends either by divorce or death. They will enter marriage earlier and remain together longer than did their grandparents. It should be noted that increased longevity accounts for a good deal of this longer duration of marriage.

Although we do not wish to minimize the significance of marriage failure in America today, looking briefly at marital failure in the larger world situation should help us better understand the current American picture.

Cross-cultural perspective on marital failure

America is not the only society to have high marital failure rates. Other nations have had as high or higher. In a cross-cultural comparison of 40 different past and present societies, Murdock (1950) found that all but one (the Incas) had provisions for dissolving marriages. While in some of these societies divorce was rare, in about half the marital dissolution rates were found to substantially exceed the rate in the United States at that time (1949). Murdock (1950, p. 198) found that among the Crow Indians divorce was exceedingly frequent, and a man might be ridiculed if he lived too long with one woman. In one Eskimo tribe, women may be married and divorced two or more times a year. In some polygynous Moslem societies, divorce rates have been very high; a man could divorce one of his wives simply by saying three times before witnesses, "I divorce thee."

Grounds for divorce vary widely from one society to another, and often change over periods of time in any given society. They range from relatively trivial things, such as quarrelsomeness and nagging, to serious reasons, such as repeated adultery, sterility, and cruelty.

Anthropologists find that a certain amount of marital failure and dissolution is virtually universal. Why should this be so? LeMasters (1957b, pp. 564–566) offers some insightful suggestions:

1. It is somewhat naive and unrealistic to assume that all marriages

will succeed, human nature being what it is. The demands and responsibilities of marriage are many and heavy, and some individuals are not mature enough, or are otherwise incapable of performing the roles of husband or wife. In many societies, including ours, individuals enter marriage with idealistically high expectations, which increase the probability of disappointments.

2. The nature of the American courtship system is such that a certain proportion of marriages are likely to be mismatches. Our open marriage market allows, even encourages, immature young people who fall in love to go ahead and get married even though they may not actually be well suited to each other or ready for marriage.

3. Even when the courtship system functions well in sorting out males and females into compatible married couples, a certain number of these marriages would still founder due to external societal strains and problems. Economic depressions, wars, social revolutions, and other crises take their toll in broken marriages, as 20th-century America well attests.

4. It may be argued that human nature itself is not fully compatible with the expectation of a lifelong marital union. Lifelong sexual monogamy is a high standard, and although in many societies extramarital sex is not very likely to result in marital dissolution, it is true that marital infidelity is one of the most frequently named causes for divorce in many modern societies.

Historical background of marital dissolution in America

While divorce appears to be prevalent throughout the world, and probably constitutes a problem to some extent wherever it exists, the degree to which it is considered a problem certainly varies a great deal from one place to another. Divorce would be seen as a greater problem in a traditional, sacred society as compared to a modern, secular society, for example. In our own society, the range of attitudes toward divorce varies considerably, as we shall see.

In the pre-Christian era, the Hebrew husband had almost unlimited power to divorce his wife, although she had almost no right to divorce him. Mosaic laws allowed the husband to hand his wife a bill of divorcement stating, "Be thou divorced from me" (Deuteronomy 24:1–2). However, religious beliefs and public opinion, as well as the Hebrew emphasis on the importance of marriage, tended to prevent abuse of divorce privileges by Hebrew husbands. Gradually the wife gained some rights of divorce too. The divorce situation in ancient Greece was somewhat similar. In early periods, the Greek husband had broad powers of divorce; it was not until the later periods of urbanization that the Greek wife also gained limited rights of divorce. During the period of the ancient Roman republic, one of the strongest patriarchal family systems in history existed, and as would be expected, the husband had greater rights than his wife in all matters, including the right of divorce. A man could divorce his wife for adultery, preparation of poisons, or for wine drinking (Leslie, 1979, p. 161). However, during these early centuries divorce was discouraged and was quite uncommon. It was not until later, in the days of the dissolute Roman Empire, that divorce became more common.

Under Christianity the sentiments against divorce became increasingly strong, due in no small part to the reactions of early Christians to the marital instability among Romans of the time. By A.D. 140 the Christian Church permitted divorce only on the grounds of adultery, apostasy, covertness, and fornication. Church policy became increasingly strict until finally, in A.D. 407 the Council of Carthage abolished divorce per se (Leslie, 1979, p. 167). Marriage was a religious sacrament not to be broken.

Following the Protestant Reformation, responsibility for marriage was gradually transferred from church to state, which led to the recognition of absolute divorce in many Christian nations. Protestant leaders rejected the idea of divorce by mutual consent, holding that divorce should be granted only on very serious grounds, such as adultery, desertion, or cruelty, which must be provable in court. Divorce was to be granted the innocent party as redress for gross wrongdoing by the spouse. In most Western nations, divorce became a legal adversary process with the court determining the outcome of a suit brought by the aggrieved spouse against the accused spouse.

The American divorce system has generally reflected this recent historical background. Most state legislatures came to adopt divorce laws based on two traditional principles: (1) Divorce should be granted only for grave and serious reasons; and (2) one party, and only one party, is guilty or at fault (Kephart, 1977, p. 444). Among the serious or sufficiently grave grounds for divorce found in most states are cruelty, adultery, neglect, desertion, criminality, and insanity.

Recently, the concept of "guilt and innocence," whereby one marriage partner is legally defined as "at fault" while the other is "innocent," has been challenged to the point that many states have now instituted the no-fault divorce, in which the requirement of legally proved fault or guilt of one partner is eliminated. This no-fault system of divorce, which originated in California in 1970, will be discussed in some detail below.

The ending of marriage: Types of marital dissolution

Divorce is not the only way marriages may be terminated, of course. Marriages may also be dissolved by death, desertion, legal separation, and annulment. Before continuing with our analysis of divorce in America, let us briefly compare the various ways a marriage may end.

Death. Sooner or later all marriages not dissolved some other way will end with the death of one of the partners. In recent years bereavement has accounted for the ending of about two thirds of all first marriages in America. Actually, bereavement has accounted for about twice as many endings of marriage as divorce. The surviving spouse assumes a new social and legal role of widow or widower. Bereavement differs from the other kinds of marital dissolution in that it is involuntary and normally occurs in the later years of life.

Desertion. Sometimes referred to as "the poor man's divorce," desertion is an informal means for ending or altering marriage. When one marriage partner deserts, the marriage ends socially but not legally, although desertion may become a legal ground for a subsequent divorce. While either partner may desert, the husband, at least until recently, has been more apt to desert his wife and children. As women become more economically independent, desertion among wives is becoming more frequent. Estimates of the amount of desertion in the United States are not reliable since so many desertions are not ever recorded. Some estimates run to about 100,000 per year (Kephart, 1979, p. 530). For the remaining spouse, desertion may be more traumatic than divorce because it is unannounced and will likely take the surviving spouse (and children) by surprise.

Legal separation. A marriage may be terminated by a court action which legally separates the marriage partners "for cause," forbidding them to cohabit thereafter. This amounts to a limited divorce. Certain basic obligations of the marriage still continue, however, such as the obligations of the husband to continue supporting his wife and children. Legally separated spouses are not allowed to find other marriage partners. In a legal sense the marriage is really altered rather than ended, but socially the marriage generally ends with legal separation. Such legal separation may be resorted to when there are strong reasons for not getting a divorce; or it may be a way of assuring economic support for an estranged wife. Estimates are that legal separations account for between 1 and 2 percent of the total marital dissolutions in the United States (Bell, 1979, p. 531).

Annulment. This is a legal process by which a marriage is cancelled, and the man and woman are restored to their single statuses again just as if they had never been married. In fact, a decree of annulment means that legally no marriage had ever taken place. For an annulment to be granted a legal reason invalidating the marriage ceremony must be established. Annulment is based on the position that the couple were not legally eligible to marry, for reasons such as one or both being below marriageable age, under duress, insane or a bigamist. One partner may have fraudulently misrepresented himself or herself to the other before the wedding. Such a case would exist where a man already married led a woman to believe he was single.

The concept of annulment has its roots in the canon law of the Catholic

Church, which has long held that a marriage is indissoluable except by death. The Catholic Church has permitted annulment, however, which is a declaration that, because of premarital impediments the marriage has been null and void from its inception. This concept has long since become incorporated into civil law. Since a devout Catholic cannot get a divorce and remarry and remain in the Church some Catholics seek a religious annulment, which then enables them to do so.

Legally, annulment is quite different from divorce. In the former the parties were never legally married, while in the latter a legal marriage has been terminated. However, even though an annulled marriage never really existed legally, it probably did socially. While some annulments are obtained shortly after an invalid marriage ceremony, other annulments may take place after the couple have been living together as husband and wife for months or even years. Estimates are that annulments account for about 3.5 percent of the total marital dissolution in America.

Absolute divorce. This is a legal process that terminates a legally contracted marriage. Next to bereavement, divorce accounts for the large majority of marital dissolution in the United States. The issues and problems pertaining to divorce are serious and complex, and their ramifications for marriage and family life constitutes the subject matter of most of the remainder of the present chapter. We shall look at the extent and trends in divorce in America. The legal nature of divorce will be reviewed, with attention to the new no-fault system of divorce. This will be followed by an effort to identify some of the causes and conditions of the increasing amount of divorce. Next will follow a discussion of some of the consequences of divorce for the marriage partners and for children with divorced parents. Finally, attention will be directed to postdivorce adjustment and remarriage.

DIVORCE IN AMERICA

EXTENT AND TRENDS OF DIVORCE

In colonial America divorce was rare, and it continued to be so infrequent up to mid-19th century that no one bothered to keep national figures on the number of divorces per year before the Civil War. Divorce laws were liberalized somewhat in the post–Civil War period so that divorce became more frequent, and pressure was exerted to gather figures on divorce throughout the nation. The first figures published by the U. S. Bureau of the Census showed a total of 9,937 divorces for the year 1867, or 0.3 per 1,000 population (Jacobson, 1969). By 1900 the number of divorces had risen to 55,751, or 0.7 divorces per 1,000 population. (See Table 10–1.) By 1979 there were 1,170,000 divorces, or 5.3

Table 10–1

United States divorce rates, 20th century	Year	Number of divorces	Divorces per 1,000 population
	1900	55,751	0.7
	1910	83,045	0.9
	1920	170,505	1.6
	1930	195,961	1.6
	1940	264,000	2.0
	1950	385,144	2.6
	1960	393,000	2.2
	1970	715,000	3.5
	1975	1,026,000	4.8
Sources: Various vital statistic reports of the U.S. Department of Health and Human Services and National Center for Health Statistics.	1976	1,077,000	5.0
	1977	1,091,000	5.1
	1978	1,122,000	5.1
	1979	1,170,000	5.3

divorces per 1,000 population. Not only have the numbers of divorces increased greatly in the 20th century, but also the rates of divorce. From 1950 to 1979 the divorce rate had risen from 2.6 per 1,000 population to 5.3 per 1000 population, doubling in 29 years (U.S. Bureau of the Census, 1972; 1980b).

While there is little hope that the long-range trend toward high divorce rates will soon be reversed, there are some signs that it may be losing some momentum. Glick (1979, p. 2) notes that over a nearly 2-year period, from April 1976 through January 1978, the divorce rate remained almost unchanged, at about 5.0 per 1,000 population, and then fell off to 4.4 per 1,000 population in January 1979. Glick (1979b, p. 2) thinks that certain demographic trends point to some decline in the divorce rate in the years just ahead. First, since the divorce rate is logically related to the marriage rate, the declining marriage rate of the late 1970s can be expected to depress the divorce rate, as about half of all divorces after first marriage occur in the first seven years of marriage. Another factor is the increasing age at first marriage. From 1970 to 1977 the average age at first marriage rose for women from 20.8 to 21.6 years and for men from 23.2 to 24 years. This means that proportionally fewer very young people are getting married, and this age group is the most divorce prone. Also, Glick (1979b, p. 2) points out that a part of the explanation for the big jump in divorce between 1968 and 1975 lies in the disproportionate number of young people in the early years of marriage when most divorces generally occur. These are the post–World War II baby-boom youth who are now entering this stage of their life cycle. Once this population wave has moved past the high divorce risk years, it will have less effect on the overall divorce rate. Of course, there may be other factors and trends that will override trends which reduce divorce.

The increasing independence of women, the expectations of high individual satisfaction in marriage, and further softening of community barriers to divorce could outweigh the effects of the demographic changes reviewed above. Only time will tell.

Divorce rates fluctuate and vary with changing social and economic conditions, from region to region, from rural to urban areas, and by social class, race, and religion. Let us briefly examine some of these variations.

The Great Depression of the 1930s was influencial in temporarily lowering the divorce rates. The divorce rate fell from 7.9 per 1,000 married women in 1929 to 6.1 in 1933. From then on through World War II the divorce rate climbed steadily, and jumped to a peak of almost 18 per 1000 married women in 1946 (Jacobson, 1969). (See Figure 10–2.) Part of the explanation for the lower divorce rates during the depression is economic. Many people who would have divorced were unable to do so because divorce was so costly. The increase in divorce following World War II was due in part to a backlog of postponed divorces accumulated during the war, when it was not practical to get divorced and was considered unpatriotic to divorce a serviceman. Once this postwar peak was past, the divorce rate dropped back almost to prewar levels, where it hovered until the mid-1960s, when it began to rise significantly again.

Divorce rates vary by region. Divorce is lowest in the Northeast, followed by the North Central region, then the South, and finally the West, where divorce is most frequent. While a full explanation of these regional

Figure 10–2

Probability of divorced and single women marrying, by age

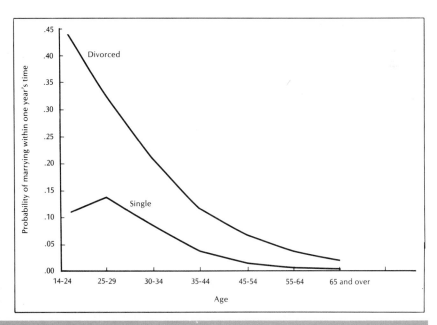

Source: *Marriage and Divorce: A Social and Economic Study* by Hugh Carter and Paul C. Glick, 1976.

differences is lacking, among the contributing factors appear to be the greater percentage of young and other divorce-prone people in the West, while in the East and North there are larger proportions of religious and ethnic groups more strongly opposed to divorce, especially Catholics (Glick, 1963). In general, divorce rates are higher in urban than in rural populations. The conditions of life in large, urban centers with mobile, secular, individual-oriented populations, are more conducive to divorce than are the more traditional conditions of marriage and family life found in rural America.

There appear to be some differences in divorce rates between racial groups in the United States. Census figures show that in 1977 there were 161 divorced black Americans per 1,000 married blacks, as compared to 77 divorced white Americans per 1,000 married white (U.S. Bureau of the Census, 1978a, p. 4). However, although blacks had higher divorce rates in 1977, it should be noted that the proportional increases in divorce rates for blacks and whites were about the same from 1960 to 1977. And it should be noted that the above "prevalence rates" (the number of divorced blacks compared to the number of divorced whites) not only reflects the greater propensity of blacks to divorce, but also the lesser likelihood that divorced blacks will remarry within a short period of time.

Studies show an inverse correlation between socioeconomic status and divorce, with higher rates at the bottom of the social class structure and a steady decline in divorce as one moves upward. Goode (1956), Kephart (1955), and Monahan (1955), all found that the upper occupational categories contributed less than their proportional share of divorces, while such middle categories as clerical and salespeople contributed almost exactly their share, and such lower categories as semiskilled and unskilled laborers contributed from two to four times their share of divorces. These variations reflect social class differences in values and norms pertaining to marital permanence, but they also reflect a more important variable: The different conditions of life within the classes, with the lower socioeconomic groups suffering more stress and having more personal and financial problems contributing to marital instability.

THE LEGAL NATURE OF DIVORCE

Divorce laws—and all other domestic relation laws—fall under the jurisdiction of the states, since the United States Constitution does not grant the federal government power to enact such legislation. Thus there are 51 separate sets of divorce laws in America, one for each state and one for the District of Columbia. This makes for some confusion, since divorce laws often vary from state to state. For example, the grounds for divorce have varied considerably, and courts in one state may interpret the grounds differently from courts in other states. Some states have many legal grounds for divorce, such as Kentucky with 20. New York, which until 1966 granted divorce for adultery only, now has five grounds—adultery, cruelty, desertion, imprisonment, and living apart for two years after a legal separation. The great majority of divorces throughout the states have been granted on grounds of either cruelty or desertion. Until quite recently, the legal divorce process throughout the states was an adversary process, based on the fault system of divorce.

The fault system of divorce

Under this long-standing procedure, one of the marriage partners must bring legal charges against the other partner, suing for divorce on one or more of the legal grounds allowed in that state. Furthermore, the plaintiff must not be guilty of any offense that is a ground for divorce. Thus, the fault system requires one party to be innocent and the other guilty. This system is based on an old legal concept of guilt and innocence and the adversary concept that justice can best be determined by a contest between two parties, each of whom presents, or has presented, one side of the case in court. Occasionally, such a divorce suit is a genuine legal contest with both spouses and their attorneys appearing in court; most times it is not. Usually the husband and wife have agreed to get divorced, and have more or less decided which of them will be the plaintiff, what the grounds will be, and that the defendant will not contest the suit. The two attorneys then work out the details of the settlement, and present a recommendation to the judge, who normally approves it without much modification. The defendant spouse usually does not even appear in court, and is assumed guilty by reason of default. About 85 percent of these divorces in the United States are uncontested (Leslie, 1979, p. 545).

In recent years the fault system of divorce has drawn a great deal of criticism. The clergy, politicians, the legal profession, and social scientists have decried the unfairness and irrationality of the guilty and innocent concept as applied to broken marriages, and the hypocrisy the process engenders. These shortcomings of the traditional fault system finally led to a new legal approach to divorce that has come to be called the no-fault system. In 1970, California enacted the first of the no-fault laws, and since then most of the other states have adopted at least limited no-fault systems.

The no-fault system of divorce

The purpose of no-fault divorce laws was to do away with the old adversary system and along with it the hypocrisy and legal make-believe which had characterized so many divorce cases. The 1970 California law even abolished the word *divorce*, substituting for it the new term, *dissolution of marriage*. It also eliminated all fault-related grounds for marital dissolution, such as adultery, cruelty, and desertion, substituting the no-fault criterion of "irreconcilable differences which have caused the irremediable breakdown of the marriage" (Wheeler, 1974, p. 20). Thus if the marriage bond was really irremediably broken in the eyes of the spouses, the court was obliged to declare the marriage dissolved. It would no longer be necessary for one spouse to accuse the other of some legal wrongdoing.

One of the main difficulties with the no-fault method lies in interpreting the terms *irreconcilable differences* and *irremediable breakdown*. If both husband and wife agree that such differences exist and the breakdown has occurred, there is little problem; but what if they do not agree and only one spouse wants the divorce? In California the courts have generally taken the word of just one party that the marriage has broken down irremediably, and has granted the divorce (Wheeler, 1974, p. 22). Critics of the no-fault system also say that some divorce is too easily obtained, often for trivial reasons, and that the best interests of children are often disregarded. For these and other reasons, many states that have enacted some kind of no-fault system are also holding onto their older fault system so a person can still sue for divorce where necessary on the traditional grounds of cruelty, desertion, and so forth. In such cases, the plaintiff may be able to obtain a better settlement from the ex-spouse, such as alimony or child support.

CAUSES AND CONDITIONS OF INCREASING DIVORCE

There are many dimensions to the question of causality in divorce. What are the personal difficulties and relationship problems of the divorcing couple? What are the motives of one or both in seeking divorce? What are the social and cultural conditions conducive to divorce in a given community or population, to which a couple may succumb? What social changes are contributing to increasing divorce probabilities?

Sociocultural factors contributing to increasing divorce

According to Goode (1963, p. 93) one of the most important social changes contributing to the 20th-century rise in divorce rates is the lessening stigma of divorce itself. Half a century ago almost anyone who got divorced lost esteem in his or her social circle. Today the stigma has so diminished that in most circles a divorced person is not considered deviant, or even unfortunate. Most divorced persons who wish to do so can remarry; in fact, most do. Also, a divorced woman today has a greater likelihood of being self-supporting than earlier. The diminishing of disapproval of divorce has been the result of various changes, including the ascendency of individualism and personal criteria of marital success, some questioning of the traditional viewpoint of what marriage itself means, and greater tolerance of the unconventional.

In fact, an important factor contributing to increased divorce is a kind of redefinition of marriage that is going on in secular America. The old, traditional concept of marriage as a religiously based institution ordained by God and therefore inviolable, has given way in some circles to a concept of marriage as a practical arrangement between a woman and a man for their mutual gratification. Martial happiness—actually the individual happiness of each partner in the marriage—becomes the measure of marital success, and a diminution of personal happiness can become a sufficient reason for divorce. For those who have this view of marriage, divorce becomes an acceptable solution for marital difficulties or conflict. Since so many people see marriage as the most important source of personal satisfaction in life, they may feel they owe it to themselves to seek another partner when their high expectations are not met by their present partner. In this regard Farber (1964) has advanced a "permanent availability" theory of marriage which assumes that people now define marriage as temporary rather than permanent, and that even when already married a man or woman is still on the lookout for a better marriage partner. Such persons are permanently available to be approached by other prospective and potentially more suitable partners. As Farber (1964, p. 109) expresses it: "Each adult individual, regardless of his current marital status, is available as a potential mate to any other cross-sex individual at any time." The proportion of American adults who have become this "liberated" and secular is really not known.

Kephart (1977, pp. 478–480) sees a number of interrelated social changes contributing to the increasing divorce rate.

Changing family functions. The loss or reduction over the years of many traditional family functions, such as economic productivity and religious, educational, and recreational functions, has reduced the family as a functional unit and therefore removed some of the traditional reasons for keeping marriage intact.

More casual marriages. Hasty marriages as well as marriages among the immature are some of the most divorce prone.

More jobs for women. With the entrance of increasing numbers of women into the labor force, a long-standing economic barrier to divorce has been lowered. Many women are no longer dependent on their husbands for economic support.

Decline in moral and religious sanctions. Most Protestant denominations now recognize divorce, and although the Catholic Church still does not recognize or condone divorce, its hold over its members may be weakening. The general trend away from the old, sacred value orientation toward a modern, secular orientation is weakening the religiously based sanctions against divorce.

The philosophy of personal happiness. As noted earlier, modern couples regard happiness as the principal goal of matrimony. If happiness fails to materialize in a given marriage, divorce may well be considered.

More liberal divorce laws. Down through the 19th century, divorce was rare and was presumed to be granted only for "grave and serious reasons." During the 20th century, most states greatly expanded the grounds for divorce, and since 1970 some form of no-fault divorce has been adopted by most states, making it easier to obtain divorce.

Personal factors in divorce today

When considering various personal or individual factors which may lead to divorce, it should be kept in mind that many of these same factors could have been present in earlier periods too, but did not result in divorce due to the pressure of prevailing opinion and norms opposing divorce.

In a study of divorced women in Detroit, Goode (1956) inquired as to the causes of their divorce. Among the most frequently mentioned factors of a personal nature were "consumption problems, nonsupport" (21 percent), "drinking, gambling, helling around" on the part of the husband (12 percent), "authority problems" (12 percent), and "personality clashes" (11 percent). Some other personal problems often thought to be important in contributing to divorce were found to be quite unimportant, including the "triangle" or other woman (6 percent), desertion (3 percent), and sexual problems (1 percent).

In a study of 600 couples who were applying for divorce, Levinger (1970) found that the complaints cited by wives against husbands exceeded those of husbands against wives by a ratio of about two to one. Among the main complaints of wives were physical and verbal abuse by the husband, inadequate financial support, the husband's drinking habits, his neglect of home and children, his lack of love, and mental cruelty. Complaints by husbands exceeded those of the wives on only two items: sexual incompatibility and in-law troubles. When the respondents were separated according to social class, Levinger (1979, p. 132) found that middle-class spouses were more concerned with emotional and psychological relationships, lower-class partners were more concerned with financial problems, and lower-class wives with "the unsubtle physical actions of their partners."

THE SOCIAL PROCESS OF MARITAL FAILURE AND DIVORCE

Divorce may be perceived as one of the end results of marital failure. However, not all marital failure results in divorce. There have always been marriages which have in effect failed at some point and died, but which for religious or other reasons have continued on in name only. Some of these name-only marriages have been aptly called "holy deadlock" marriages by LeMasters (1957b).

What are the dynamics of marital failure and eventual divorce? What are the internal processes in a marriage that signal its failure and which may result in the ending of the marriage? Let us see what some studies show.

In a study of 200 divorced couples in Indiana, Locke (1951) concluded that marriages seldom "crack up" suddenly, although a couple may be able to cover up their failing marriage so their friends and even relatives may not know it until the couple set about getting a divorce. Rather, marriages which fail are more apt to deteriorate over a period of time, during which the husband and wife become increasingly alienated from each other. In Locke's (1951, p. 358) words:

> The alienation process is generally a slow cumulation of conflicts and disagreements, accompanied by the psychological withdrawal of one or both spouses. If the course of the alienation process is far advanced, the spouses tend to express derogatory attitudes toward each other, tend to have many complaints about the mate and the marriage, and tend to exaggerate the deficiencies of the mate and the marriage.

This gradual alienation and deterioration process had been observed in one of the earliest studies of divorce by Waller, reported in his *The Old Love and the New* (1930). Waller's discussion of the alienation process is so compelling that we will review it carefully. First, his description of the alienation process (Waller & Hill, 1951, p. 513):

> Alienation is a process which moves in a cyclic fashion to its dénouement in divorce and readjustment to life without the marriage partner. It rests upon crises after each of which the relationship is redefined upon a level of greater alienation and greater instability; these crises are interlarded, usually, with periodic reconciliations and periods in which the couple make a determined attempt to adjust to life with one another. Alienation is a summatory social process; like mating, it is a process in which each response leads to the next in line and the motive for each new step is furnished by the experiences of the process up to that point; it is characteristic of such processes that they cannot easily be arrested. Paralleling the developments of the social process of alienation are certain changes of personality which (*a*) bring the process into being, (*b*) are furthered by it, and (*c*) contribute to its further progress.

Waller then identifies some of the typical marital crises upon which the alienation process rests (Waller & Hill, 1951, p. 514).

1. Rather early in the alienation process there is usually "some disturbance in the affectional-sexual life of the pair." This disturbance in sexual relations may arise with loss of rapport between the partners and a withholding of affectional response.

2. As crises keep occurring, the recovery level keeps dropping and

the relationship gradually deteriorates until the moment arrives when one partner "mentions the possibility of divorce."

3. At some point "the appearance of solidarity is broken." The couple may have been able to keep their troubles to themselves up to that point, but now it is out in the open. They have lost face, and each is apt to blame the other to some extent. The fiction of marital solidarity has now been destroyed; and once destroyed, it is very difficult to rebuild.

4. Next comes "the decision to divorce." While in some cases the actual decision may be made in anger, perhaps precipitated by something one partner does or says, it is more often the result of long discussion.

5. Next comes the "crisis of separation," which is apt to be traumatic. Breaking up a household is hard enough, but when there is also the severance of an intimate, emotional relationship, the emotional impact can be severe, sometimes approximating the grief experienced during bereavement.

6. The divorce is the final severance of the marital relationship.

7. Following divorce there is still a "period of mental conflict" and readjustment of personality, as the divorced person confronts the actual work of reconstructing his or her life.

Most marriages do not break easily. Among the crises which represent different landmarks en route to divorce are typically a number of "crises of reconciliation," in which the couple struggle to resolve their problems. To some extent, they may succeed. Marriage exerts a strong pullback upon all but the most discordant marriage partners. If after each period of reconciliation the accumulated hostilities break out again, perhaps even more seriously than before, the level of recovery keeps dropping until the final break and separation takes place.

CONSEQUENCES OF DIVORCE

Few people take divorce lightly. While many newly divorced people initially feel a sense of relief from what had become an intolerable marital relationship, most also experience a complexity of psychological, social, and economic effects. Waller's position that divorce is a traumatic experience has been widely corroborated by subsequent studies (Krantzler, 1973; Weiss, 1975; Spanier & Castro, 1979).

Some consequences of divorce for the marriage partners

Waller (1930) found that divorce generally resulted in a profound disruption of the individual's life; it affects one's emotional and sex life, one's self-image, one's living arrangements and standards, one's circle of friends, one's recreational patterns, and not least of all one's financial affairs.

The ambiguous role of the divorced person. The status-role of the divorced individual is not well defined in American society. Friends and associates may feel uncertain as to how to relate to a newly divorced man or woman. Does one offer a divorced person condolences or congratulations? Neither of those responses may be appropriate, considering the probable trauma the person has entailed and the mixed feelings he or she probably has toward this new, unsettled, single status. The newly divorced person is probably feeling a keen sense of failure as a spouse and will likely suffer some loss of self-esteem. This feeling may be partly assuaged by putting the blame for the marriage failure on the divorced mate.

While there is a more tolerant public attitude toward divorce today, there also tends to persist a viewpoint that in any divorce there is one innocent party and one guilty party. A coolness or aloofness on the part of some friends of the couple may be interpreted by a divorced person as their receiving the blame. It is often difficult for a divorced person to continue the same kind of relationship with former friends of the couple. (Goode, 1956) found most divorced individuals in his study reporting that the changed attitudes of former friends and associates often left them feeling confused, disoriented, and rejected.

Emotional impact of divorce. In addition to feelings of failure, self-doubt, and wounded pride, separation and divorce can bring on a strong sense of personal loss and loneliness. The loss of love and sexual response is keenly felt by most, although most also experience these deprivations prior to divorce. Emotional loss and disorientation may induce depression and even health problems. Goode (1956) found that for the divorced women he studied, loneliness was one of the most universal and poignant problems; it was generally much more difficult to cope with than they had anticipated. At the time Goode interviewed them, which was six months to two years after their divorces, the majority of the divorcees were still seeking ways out of their loneliness.

Divorced men and women today are likely to have more resources and experiences to draw from to aid their personal adjustment to divorce, as compared to earlier generations of divorcees, including those studied by Goode and Waller. Women today, for example, are more likely to be employed and have wider opportunities and more freedom to aid their economic and social adjustment. The more liberal climate, plus the large number of other divorced people around them, helps ease their adjustment.

The large majority of divorced persons do eventually recover from the trauma and loneliness, which are most acute in the early stages of separation and divorce. The whole experience can make the person wiser, more mature, and ready for a better marriage later. Levinger (1976) points out that, despite the distress associated with divorce, it can also have positive effects. A divorced person is free of the demands and stresses of a deteriorating marriage, free to reorganize life on his or her own terms. Renne (1971) found that many people who were unhappily married and stayed married had more health problems than those who were unhappily married and had divorced. In her sample, the unhappily married were the most depressed, followed by the separated and then the divorced. Least depressed of all were those who were happily married.

Some economic consequences of divorce.

When a conventional family—in which the husband-father is the sole family provider—is split by divorce, his one income now has to stretch to cover two households, although seldom equally. When both husband and wife are employed, the economic consequences of divorce may not be so bad, but again, two households must be supported where only one was before. Some reduction in living standards usually follows.

In a study of the economic and financial consequences of divorce, Espenshade (1979a) sought answers to two basic questions: What economic hardships does divorce create for family members? How is the economic burden of divorce distributed among husbands, wives, and children? The sample consisted of 2,400 men and women in Michigan who were married in 1968 and had been kept track of until 1974, including those who had divorced. When comparing those who were continuously married from 1968 to 1974 with those who were separated or divorced in 1974, Espenshade (1979a, p. 617) found that the real income of the continuously married couples had increased 21.7 percent, while the incomes of the divorced men had decreased by 19.2 percent and that of the divorced women by 29.3 percent over the same period of time. Women divorced or separated by 1974 had incomes of about half that of married women and their families. That divorce is apt to be economically harder on women than men was demonstrated by the fact that divorced women had suffered a reduction of 6.7 percent in living standards while divorced men had experienced a 16.5 percent gain over the 1968–1974 period. During this time the still-married couples had enjoyed a 20.8 percent increase in living standards.

Even with the help of alimony (and only a minority of divorced women receive alimony), and with Aid to Families with Dependent Children (AFDC) for divorced mothers, more divorced women than married women have to go to work to help support themselves. Using 1970 census data, Waldman and Gover (1972) found many more separated and divorced mothers than married mothers in the labor force. A breakdown of the percentages of working women with preschool children showed 30 percent married mothers, 41 percent separated mothers, and 62 percent divorced mothers. The employment rates for all married women versus all divorced women were 41 percent for the former and 70 percent for the latter.

While these and other studies show that divorced women especially may suffer economically from divorce, it should be kept in mind that divorce may be an effect as well as a cause of low income or poverty.

Table 10–2

Estimated number of children involved in divorces and annulments, 1954–1977	Year	Estimated number of children	Average number of children per decree	Rate per 1,000 children under 18 years of age
	1977	1,095,000	1.00	17.0
	1975	1,123,000	1.08	16.9
	1972	1,021,000	1.20	14.8
	1969	840,000	1.31	11.9
	1966	669,000	1.34	9.5
Source: "Final Divorce Statistics, 1977," U.S.	1963	562,000	1.31	8.2
Department of Health and	1960	463,000	1.18	7.2
Human Services; *Monthly Vital*	1957	379,000	0.99	6.4
Statistics Report, 1979, 28, (2), 5.	1954	341,000	0.90	6.4

As noted earlier, divorce rates are higher among the poor. And reduced incomes are not the only negative economic effects of divorce on women. Banks, department stores, and other credit-granting agencies may refuse credit to a divorced woman or, adding insult to injury, grant her credit only in her ex-husband's name (Brandwein et al., 1974, p. 353)!

Some consequences of divorce for children

The number of children involved in divorce is increasing, and the concern for their welfare is a pressing issue. In 1977, fully 55 percent of all divorces involved children. In the same year, 17 children out of every 1,000 experienced parental divorce, as compared to 10 in 1967 and 6 in 1956 (U.S. Department of Health and Human Services, 1979). (See Table 10–2.) The actual number of children under age 18 involved in divorce has exceeded 1 million consistently since 1972. It has been estimated that as many as 40 percent of all children born in the 1970s will be involved in marital disruption before reaching the age of 18, with divorce accounting for between one half to two thirds of the total (Bane, 1976b; Bumpass & Rindfuss, 1978).

Since the large majority of these children live with their mothers rather than their fathers, the effects of divorce on female-headed families is especially salient. The economic consequences alone are impressive and disheartening. Espenshade (1979a, p. 616) found that in 1977 50 percent of all related children under age 18 in female-headed families were living below the poverty level, as compared to 8.5 percent of children in families with a male head. Since divorce rates are highest in low-income families, one of the immediate effects of divorce in this population, when children are present, is to create female-headed families without adequate financial support, which then become candidates for AFDC.

There is evidence that children who live with their divorced fathers are generally better off economically than are those who live with their divorced mothers. In a study of the economic well being of children of divorce aged 10 and under, Duncan and Morgan (1976) found that families

244

of children who remained with their mothers experienced a decline in family income of 13.8 percent from 1968 to 1974, while families of children who lived with their fathers had an increase in income of 49.4 percent over the same time span.

Divorced women with children to support usually find that employment is a more acceptable alternative than welfare, if they can manage a job and take care of their children and their home at the same time. Hoffman (1977) found that in Michigan in 1973 more than 10 times as many white divorced mothers and 4 times as many nonwhite divorced mothers took jobs as those who went on welfare. Eighty percent of white divorced mothers were employed while 7 percent received welfare; about 70 percent of nonwhite mothers were employed and 17 percent were receiving welfare.

Contrary to some views many people hold, child-support payments from divorced fathers to their ex-wives tend to be meager or nonexistent. Hoffman (1977) found that in Michigan in the mid-1970s, fewer than half of the separated and divorced mothers who had custody of the children were receiving any alimony or child support from the children's fathers, and for those mothers who did, the average yearly payment was $2,351 for white and $1,554 for black mothers. Jones et al. (1976) estimate that child support payments average about $2,000 per family per year. There are many complaints from divorced mothers that their ex-husbands often do not keep up their child-support payments, and that many courts are lax in enforcing child-support obligations of divorced fathers (Brandwein et al., 1974, p. 501).

The psychological or emotional effects of divorce on children are less easy to demonstrate than the economic or financial consequences. Many people believe that children of divorce are apt to be more emotionally unstable or maladjusted than children brought up in intact marriages; they are wont to argue that parents who are unhappily married should stay together for the sake of their children. The evidence supporting this viewpoint is not very convincing, however. Nye (1957) compared the personal adjustment and behavior of children from broken homes with that of children from unbroken but *unhappy* homes. He found that children from broken homes (whether the homes were broken by divorce or bereavement) fared better and were better adjusted than the children from unhappy, unbroken homes. The children from the broken homes had fewer emotional problems, showed less delinquent behavior, and were better adjusted to their parent or parents than were the children from the intact but unhappy homes. Burchinal (1964) studied the effects of divorce on the school relationships and adjustments of adolescent children. He found no evidence to support the hypothesis that divorce has detrimental psychological effects on children. Some other studies (Locke, 1951; Duncan & Duncan, 1969; Hetherington, 1972) have found evidence that growing up in a divorced family can induce aggressive behavior and may be associated with difficulties in relating to members of the opposite sex—including greater divorce proneness when one gets married—and possibly with less career success for the male in later life.

In conclusion, while it is likely that most children growing up in a two-parent family in which the husband and wife are reasonably happily married are better adjusted than many children living with a single divorced parent, there is also evidence that children in a happy one-parent family are no worse off—and may be better off—than children in an unhappy two-parent family.

AFTER DIVORCE

What happens to divorced men and women? How do they adjust to being single again? In this section, we will examine the reactions of divorced men and women to being single again, and look at their relations with members of the opposite sex. Then, since most divorced persons do remarry, we will conclude with an examination of subsequent marriages of divorced persons and what the studies tell us about the probable success of these remarriages.

SINGLE AGAIN

Even though divorce may bring relief from the tensions and hassles of marital conflict, and a new sense of freedom, it also brings feelings

Father and sons alone

of loss and apprehension about the future. One's life has to be reorganized along different lines now that one is single again. The transition is difficult enough for those who have been married only a few years; for those who have been married 20 years or more, the transition can be extremely difficult and traumatic.

The divorced person generally has some new roles to learn, since the division of labor between marriage partners no longer exists. The divorced man may have to learn to cook and do other housework generally done by the wife, while the divorced woman may have to learn car maintenance, how to do home repairs, and so forth. One of the side benefits of modern equalitarian marriage is that both partners are apt to share more roles, and are thus better prepared to cope with additional role requirements should their marriage end in divorce. Also, divorced wives who have been employed during marriage are generally better prepared to support themselves after divorce than are traditional housewives who have never been employed. A great many divorced mothers today find that even with child support from their former husbands, they still need the additional income of their own employment to make ends meet. The divorced parent who has custody of the children must now raise the children single-handedly. Since about 80 percent of the children of divorce live with their mothers (Espenshade, 1979a, p. 621), it seems she now generally has to be both mother and father.

Relations of the divorced with members of the opposite sex

Being single again, even after a stormy marriage, brings loneliness. Even for a divorced mother who still has her children, there is an emptiness left by the departure of an adult of the opposite sex. The trauma of divorce and disenchantment with one's marriage partner may bring withdrawal from association with members of the opposite sex for a while. But when the divorced person feels the need for companionship again enough to risk reentering mixed company, there will probably be candidates of the opposite sex in the same situation.

Hunt (1966) observed that divorced men and women were apt to find that dating formerly married persons was more satisfying than dating never-married or widowed persons. Previously married people share a common experience and a sense of sympathetic identity with each other, and often find it easy and rewarding to strike up a companionship. However, many divorced persons may feel they have lost their "dating skills" during their years of marriage, and also are reluctant to start all over again in the "dating game" which now seems immature and even distasteful to them as experienced adults. They prefer to move more quickly into a meaningful relationship; at the same time they are wary of making any new commitment. Relatives, friends, and, if necessary, personal therapy, can help the vulnerable divorced person move into new relationships and learn to trust members of the opposite sex once more. Many divorced women and men may limit themselves to superficial relationships at first until they gradually feel secure enough to rish deeper involvements. As Hunt (1966, p. 174) observes, "It may be only through loving partially that the Formerly Married can become capable of loving completely."

Even in cases where the sexual aspect of marriage had diminished or even disappeared before the divorce, formerly married men and women often feel sharply the loss of marital sex, and after divorce face a period of sexual deprivation. However, there is some evidence that many divorced men and women begin postmarital sexual relations within a year of their divorce. Gebhard (1971) found this a common practice among divorced women. Hunt (1974) found that over 80 percent of the divorced persons in his sample became sexually active again within the first year of separation from their spouses. He also found that once they started, divorced men and women have sex as frequently or more frequently than married men and women. Furthermore, they usually have several sexual partners. The typical divorced man in Hunt's sample had eight different partners while the typical woman had four different partners in the first year. Hunt believes that postmarital sexual relations are used by many divorced persons to help redefine themselves, to rediscover their manhood or womanhood, to learn to love again, and to move toward remarriage. On the other hand, one shortcoming of postmarital sex, according to Blood and Blood (1978, p. 596), is in the instability of many of these relationships, in their superficiality as compared to the fuller sexual relations associated with marriage. Such superficial sex could result from casual encounters in a singles bar, or from pressure to engage in sex by a dating partner.

Sooner or later, the great majority of divorced women and men reestablish new and meaningful relationships with members of the opposite sex and eventually remarry.

REMARRIAGE

Most divorced people appear to be more disappointed with their own prior marriage than with marriage per se. They have given up on a particular marriage partner, but are willing and often eager to find another and try again.

According to 1970 census data, over 80 percent of all divorced men and over 70 percent of all divorced women in the United States eventually remarry (Carter & Glick, 1970). In any age group, proportionately more divorced people than single people get married. (See Figure 10–2.) This is especially apparent in the 20 to 35 age group. For a woman particularly, the younger a divorced person is, the higher the probability of remarriage. Not only do most divorced persons remarry, they also generally do so soon after getting divorced. About one half remarry within three years of their divorces. Glick and Norton (1971, p. 313) found that one fourth of divorced men and women remarry within one year, one half within three years, and three fourths within nine years of their divorce. Women tend to wait a little longer to get remarried than men. Both divorced men and women remarry sooner than the widowed, who would be expected to observe a longer period of mourning over the loss of a loved spouse. The divorced person often feels a great urge to rectify an unsatisfactory marriage by promptly entering a second better marriage.

As we noted earlier, one of the problems confronting divorced persons is the lack of established or institutionalized means for coping with the divorce experience. According to Cherlin (1978) the same thing is true for remarriage. He says, "The difficulties of couples in remarriages after divorce stem from a lack of institutionalized guidelines for solving many common problems of their remarried life" (Cherlin, 1978, p. 642). This lack of institutionalization and its concommitant problems is apparent in the legal system, in language, and in certain customs. Remarried people do not even have an accepted terminology for new parent or child, and misunderstandings arise concerning who calls whom what. Other practices, such as discipline of children, are lacking in customary guidelines. Legally our society is not always clear on property, financial, sexual, and other responsibilities and prohibitions for people in remarriages.

Some other authorities agree with Cherlin. Bohannon (1970b, p. 137) argues that remarriage today "approaches chaos, with each individual set of families having to work out its own destiny without any realistic guidelines." Others are more sanguine, such as Duberman (1975), who sees reconstituted families becoming increasingly institutionalized and stable in the future. As a matter of fact, remarriages today are not dramatically less stable than first marriages, as we shall see next.

Remarriage success

Compared to their first marriages, most remarriages of divorced persons are successful. Between one half and two thirds of those who remarry will remain married to their new partner (Glick, 1977, p. 12). However, when compared to the overall success rates of first marriages, remarriages tend to show a lower rate of success. Such comparison may not be fair, however, since the length of the remarriage is generally shorter (because the divorced person is older at remarriage) and the divorced person who remarries belongs to a select group of the total first-married population (those who have shown they will turn to divorce if not satisfied with marriage). Accordingly there is evidence that the more marriages one has, the greater the likelihood that each successive marriage will end in divorce (Monahan, 1952). There is also evidence that remarried persons who are dissatisfied with their new marriages tend to split up sooner than persons in first marriages (Carter & Pratt, 1970). They may, having failed once, become more easily discouraged with the next attempt; and their previous experience with divorce makes it somewhat easier to go through the divorce process again.

To keep perspective on the issue of remarriage success or failure, let it be clear that the majority of second marriages do endure, and may be more successful in other ways. Goode (1956) found that of the divorced women he studied in Detroit who had remarried, 87 percent rated their new marriage as "much better" than their first. They were delighted with the improvement over their first marriage. Weiss (1975) found also that a remarriage is especially likely to be successful when it has the approval of the divorced person's children as well as that of other kin and friends.

There is some evidence that those who remarry after divorce are about as happy in their subsequent marriages as people in first marriages. Glenn and Weaver (1977), in a comparison of the reported marital happiness of ever-divorced and never-divorced white married respondents in three large U.S. national surveys, found significantly greater marital happiness for the never-divorced women but not for the never-divorced men. Remarried men were equally as happily married as were never-divorced married men. But even between the never-divorced and the divorced and remarried women, the difference in percentage between those who said their marriages were "very happy" was less than 10 points. The authors conclude that remarriages of divorced men and women are about as happy or successful as are intact first marriages (Glenn & Weaver, 1977, p. 331).

Those concerned about the future prospects of marriage and its effectiveness in meeting the needs of the marriage partners may take some comfort in the above findings. As Glenn and Weaver (1977, p. 332) point out, the effectiveness of marriage in meeting individual needs is best judged by the number of people who enter into satisfactory marriages eventually, rather than by the number whose first marriages are successful. The data suggest that the increased divorce rate in recent years has not been accompanied by any significant decline in the marital happiness of remarried persons compared to that of married persons who have never been divorced. Since the remarriage rate is high, remarriage apparently continues to be a satisfactory solution to an unsatisfactory prior marriage for the large majority of divorced men and women. In sum, for divorced persons the prospects of remarriage are high, and the prospects for a good marriage seem fairly high for those who do remarry. What does this portend for the future of marriage? Glenn and Weaver (1977, p. 336) sound a cautiously optimistic note:

> [Our] findings, considered in conjunction with recent data which show that married persons, as a whole, report substantially greater global happiness than any category of unmarried persons (Glenn, 1975b), are convincing evidence that marriage in American society is not yet obsolete and ineffective in meeting individual needs. If the divorce rate continues to rise, marriage may lose its effectiveness in meeting individual needs, since the psychological functions of marriage must surely depend on feeling that the relationship is reasonably secure. So far, however, divorce and remarriage seem to have been rather effective mechanisms for replacing poor marriages with good ones and for keeping the mean level of marital happiness fairly high.

CHAPTER 11

Alternatives to conventional marriage

Not all American men and women have conventional monogamous marriages. In recent years increasing numbers are trying one or more temporary alternative lifestyles before settling down into conventional marriage, while some others are seeking more permanent alternatives. Why is this happening? Does the recent wave of experimentation in alternative male-female relationships mean that American people are on the whole disillusioned with traditional marriage? Are most American men and women ready to turn to other kinds of intimate association in the hope of satisfying their personal needs for love, sex, companionship, and growth? Does American society, increasingly urban, mobile, and secular, require basic changes in conventional marriage? Or are entirely new forms of intimate male-female association perhaps needed? These are some of the issues and questions which will be addressed in the pages ahead.

This chapter presents a review and analysis of present-day experiments in male-female relationships and lifestyles which differ from conventional marriage patterns. However, since experiments in alternatives to marriage are not new in America, we need to give at least passing recognition to the historical antecedents of some of the current forms.

HISTORICAL BACKGROUND TO CONTEMPORARY ALTERNATIVES TO MARRIAGE

Suggestions for revising marriage and family or for substituting new forms of male-female relationships for old ones crop up here and there throughout history. For example, in *The Republic* Plato proposed a reorganized society in which conventional marriage and family would be eliminated. In Plato's ideal republic, there would be communal or group marriage in which selected groups of men and women would have sexual access to each other, and all would share parental responsibilities for children born to the women of the group.

In American history, religious and political freedom attracted people who sought change in these areas. The general atmosphere of freedom and laissez faire also encouraged those who wished to experiment in other areas of life, such as marriage and family. Thus it is understandable that in early American society there were many interesting experiments in alternatives to traditional marriage and family. Most of these early American efforts to restructure marriage and family life were parts of larger religious and/or political-economic utopian efforts to reorganize society, starting at the community level. Goals included the elimination of exploitation, discrimination, selfishness, jealousy, and other "vices" associated with traditional social institutions such as marriage and family. During the 19th century there were more than 100 such experimental communities in America, most of them short lived, such as Robert Owen's idealistic experiment New Harmony, Indiana, which lasted about three years (Lockwood, 1905). A few, however, lasted longer, including the Oneida community in New York State, which endured from 1848 to 1879.

ONEIDA: AN EXPERIMENT IN GROUP MARRIAGE

The Oneida community was founded by and operated under the leadership of an unorthodox religious leader, John Humphrey Noyes (Robertson, 1970; Carden, 1969). Basing his appeal on his religious doctrine of "perfectionism," Noyes attracted a following, first in Vermont in the early 1840s, then in central New York State, where he established a new community on the banks of Oneida Creek in 1848. The Oneida community flourished under his guidance for approximately 30 years. At its peak it numbered about 300 members. The community was organized along the lines of "Bible communism," which meant the elimination of private property and a sharing of all possessions and wealth.

Noyes had become critical of monogamous marriage because he saw it as encouraging exclusivity, selfishness, and jealousy. He argued that monogamous marriage should be replaced by a form of communal or group marriage, which he called "complex marriage." This meant that in principle all adult men and women in the community were married to each other. However, their marital relations were strictly defined and circumscribed by a set of norms worked out by Noyes and his fellow leaders in the community. A man had the right to seek sexual relations with any woman; she then had the right to accept or reject his overture. It was customary for sexual proposals to be conveyed from a man to a woman via a go-between (often a member of the central committee). This method made it easier for the woman to respond; and easier on the man too, should his overtures be rejected.

According to the Oneidan principle of perfectionism, older people were believed to be more spiritually advanced than younger people (Carden, 1969, p. 16). Thus relationships between the young and the old were encouraged on the basis of a doctrine of "ascending fellowship," which resulted in considerable sexual contact between younger women and older men and young men and older women. Sexual exclusivity was strongly discouraged, and partners were changed frequently. Sex was defined as good and an important part of love. Sex was, in fact, "love in its most natural and beautiful form" (Carden, 1969, p. 54).

While all adults were entitled to the privileges of complex marriage, only certain selected men and women were believed qualified to become parents. A kind of eugenics program was implemented, with a select committee deciding which men and women possessed the requisite spiritual and physical qualities to make them worthy parents. This planned-parenthood program seemed to work remarkably well, as only 13 of the

John Humphrey Noyes and the Oneida Community, mid-19th century

Oneida Community Historical Committee

58 children born at Oneida between 1869 and 1879 were not "planned" children (Gordon, 1978, p. 265). The success of the planned-parenthood system and the complex-marriage system was due in no small part to the birth control technique of "coitus reservatus," or "male continence," by which sexual intercourse stops short of orgasm for the male.

The Oneidans were, it must be remembered, a very devout and disciplined religious group, and their sexual and other personal relations were an integral part of their religious system. Along with their emotional and sexual freedom went a very real sense of personal responsibility to each other, to the community, and to their religion. The Oneida community began to break up not long after its founder and charismatic leader, John Humphrey Noyes, resigned in 1877. Of the many community experiments in 19th-century America, Oneida was in many ways the most successful during its lifetime.

The short-term success of the Oneida experiment was due largely to the remarkable John Humphrey Noyes, who was not only a strong, charismatic leader, but an innovator and highly able administrator, as well. Then, too, the experiment was sustained and justified by strong religious beliefs. Women were accorded higher status and more rights and freedom than most women outside the community. Both children and adults found the life stimulating and romantic. Esprit de corps was high and, at least until its final years, the community closed ranks in resistance to outside criticisms and pressures to change.

The ultimate failure of the Oneida experiment may be understood in terms of the weakening of many of the above supports, and a massive buildup of outside pressures and criticisms which finally resulted in forcing the Oneidans to give up their practice of complex marriage, and brought about Noyes's resignation. No other leader arose to take his place, and internal dissention soon brought an end to the experiment. The history of Oneida nicely illustrates Goode's (1964) contention that for a revolutionary or utopian experiment in family to succeed, favorable conditions, a high degree of ideological fervor, and strong leadership are required. Once these things diminish, the tendency is to revert to more conventional marriage and family patterns.

Let us now return to the present and examine some of the 20th-century experiments and alternatives to conventional marriage, and the social conditions contributing to their development.

PRESENT-DAY ALTERNATIVES TO CONVENTIONAL MARRIAGE

FACTORS CONTRIBUTING TO THE RISE OF ALTERNATIVE LIFESTYLES

As seen above, experimentation in lifestyles is not new in America. However, although present-day experiments bear some resemblance to those of earlier times, many have distinctive flavors of their own, reflecting social, cultural, and demographic characteristics of mid to late 20th century. Thus the social context within which the current experimental and variant forms have developed deserves some attention.

There are numerous social forces and changing conditions that have contributed to the new waves of alternative lifestyles of the 1960s and 1970s. Whitehurst (1975) sees much of the current search for alternatives arising from shortcomings and failures of conventional marriage and family created largely by a rapidly changing and unstable society. These social changes have made some new forms of marriage and family both possible and, from some points of view, desirable. From this position, certain alternatives can be perceived less as threats to the institutions of marriage and family than as means for reconstituting marriage and family in improved and somewhat new forms.

Let us now identify some of the current social processes, changing conditions, and demographic factors which taken together have led to the recent rise in alternatives to conventional marriage, especially from the 1960s onward.

Increasing criticism of conventional marriage and family

A good deal of the current criticism of conventional marriage had been directed toward the kind of marriage associated with the urban nuclear family of our times. Critics "see the nuclear family as inadequate, restrictive, and counter-productive in meeting individual goals, aspirations, and desired lifestyles" (Cogswell, 1975, p. 392). Such a viewpoint carries the argument that the conventional nuclear family is based on the idealized notion that one man and one woman should marry and in so doing make a contract to satisfy all of each other's personal, emotional, and physical needs for the rest of their lives. Critics see this idealized model of marriage as placing heavy demands on a single male-female relationship and furthermore imposing many restrictions on personal freedom, such as the requirement of sexual exclusiveness.

Critics cite the rising divorce rates, rising illegitimacy, and increasing numbers of unmarried adults, especially women, as further evidence of the inadequacy or failure of conventional marriage (Dyer, 1979, pp. 397–399).

Social unrest and the youth contraculture

The 1960s and early 1970s were years of political and social turbulance and change which left their imprint on many American institutions. The civil rights movement swept over the nation, the women's liberation movement became strong and militant, and the Vietnam war divided America. Many American youth decided to drop out of the "straight," or conventional, life and turn to various alternative lifestyles, many of which were associated with what came to be known as the contraculture or the counter-culture (Yinger, 1960).

While the counter-culture recruited youth from many different backgrounds, most of its leaders and strongest adherents came from the educated middle class. Alienated from traditional, middle-class values and norms, these generally well-educated young men and women became vocal critics of conventional American social institutions, including marriage and family. Many of them became active advocates of social and moral reform, seeking new values, norms, and interests as bases for human relationships, which they believed would be better than those persisting in the straight world (Whitehurst, 1972; Loomis & Dyer, 1976, pp. 55–56).

Recent demographic trends

Not only were numerous American youth becoming disenchanted with many aspects of traditional American society in the 1960s; there were also more of them than usual in this period. This was the period when the post–World War II baby-boom youth were coming of age. From 1960 to 1970, about 13.8 million young people were added to the 14- to 24-year age group, representing an increase of 52 percent in one decade (Leslie, 1976, p. 385). This sheer quantity of young people would be expected to make itself felt at any time, but coming as it did at a period of turbulance and change, its impact was indeed considerable. Enough of these young people joined the counter-culture movement to shake up the political and educational establishments, and, to some extent, the marriage and family establishment also.

For a significant minority of American youths, this was a period of experimentation in the use of drugs, in premarital and extramartial permissiveness, in cohabitation, and in communal living. When the demographic center of gravity moved from this late teen and early 20s age group to the mid and late 20s age group in the late 1970s, there was a sharp decline in counter-culture type of activities. Most of yesterday's rebellious youth were becoming today's respectable husbands, wives, and parents. This demographic change helps explain the recent leveling off or decline in interest in certain alternative lifestyles in the late 1970s. However, there still seems to be a sufficient continuing interest in a number of alternatives to conventional marriage, such as cohabitation and staying single, to warrant our attention.

Other reasons for experimentation

Other reasons for more experimentation in alternative lifestyles in recent years include the high personal expectations for love and intimacy people have today, and the greater freedom and expanded means for seeking these goals (Whitehurst, 1975). In the independent nuclear family, these expectations put a heavy emotional burden on the husband-wife relationship. This is especially true for couples living in large, impersonal, urban environments, where they are removed from close relatives. Where kin ties are weak or lost and there is little sense of community, marriage and conjugal relations may be expected to carry the full weight of meeting an individual's intimate, emotional needs. In addition to these higher expectations for emotional need-satisfaction, there are certain social changes which can induce women and men to seek such gratification outside of conventional marriage if they see marriage as failing to live up to their expectations. Such changes include (1) the lifting or weakening of many traditional religious, legal, and community controls which until recently discouraged many alternatives by defining them as immoral, illegal, or otherwise deviant; and (2) the greater freedom and expanded opportunity for men and women today to meet other people and to seek out like-minded individuals with whom new relationships may be established, whether at work, at school, or in singles bars. As Whitehurst (1975, p. 168) explains:

> The rise in alternative forms can be seen in part as a response to conventional family failure to satisfy many of the needs that have been developed recently in a freer kind of society. In contemporary life, custom, religion, and community have come to mean less. The needs for family and marriage, however, have come to mean more. . . . We have expected more intimacy from relationships today, and we have provided more means of searching for it than in former times.

Whitehurst (1975) sees the current search for alternatives as a logical, probably necessary development; less a threat to conventional marriage than a needed effort to modify marriage in keeping with changing conditions and needs. Furthermore, it need not be feared that masses of people will be "dropping out" of their marriages and joining "swinging" clubs or group marriages. Traditional institutional norms and forces will continue to exert sufficient control and strength to prevent mass defections from conventional marriage. Only a minority of people comprising those who are emancipated and highly secular can be expected to join the ranks of experimenters in alternative forms. According to U.S. census data for 1978, only about 1 percent of Americans were living in unmarried households or living arrangements, while most of the remainder were living in essentially conventional households (Glick, 1979b, p. 3). (See Figure 11–1.)

VARIOUS TYPES OF ALTERNATIVES TO CONVENTIONAL MARRIAGE

Staying single

There is evidence that today a larger proportion of American adults are remaining single—for a time at least—than ever before. In 1971, there

Figure 11–1

Living arrangements of American people, 1978

Source: "Future American Families," by Paul C. Glick, *Coalition of Family Organizations Memo*, 1979, 2 (3), 3.

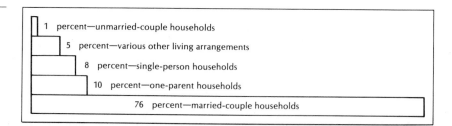

1 percent—unmarried-couple households
5 percent—various other living arrangements
8 percent—single-person households
10 percent—one-parent households
76 percent—married-couple households

were nearly 41 million single adults in the United States, including 15.5 million men and 12.5 million women who had never been married, and 3.5 million divorced men and women (Moran, 1972, p. 338). It has been estimated that there were more than 50 million unmarried adults in the United States in 1976, including those widowed and divorced (Kephart, 1977, p. 489). While most authorities agree that the great majority of singles will sooner or later get married, there is an increasing likelihood that more of them will, intentionally or unintentionally, continue their single status year after year to the point where the probability of marriage falls off sharply. Moran (1972) found that while most of the singles she studied seemed to be in a kind of temporary "way-station," either waiting to get married or remarried, or not quite yet ready to marry and settle down, others found such satisfaction and freedom in singlehood that they were content to remain single year after year.

Various social, economic, and demographic factors help explain the increase in the number of single young men and women. Demographically, the increasing delay in first marriage is due in part to an unbalanced sex ratio resulting in what has been called the "marriage squeeze." According to Glick, (1979b, p. 2):

> During recent years the number of women in the United States who were in the age range when most of their first marriages occur (18 to 24 years) has been 11 percent higher than the number of men in the age range when most of their marriages occur (20 to 26 years). This imbalance or squeeze is a consequence of past fluctuations in the birth rate. For example, many women born in 1957 at the peak of the baby boom, were ready to marry at the age of 21; but the pool of men three years older—the men most likely to include a prospective husband for them—were born in 1954 when the birth rate was somewhat lower.

Glick (1979b, p. 3) sees a probable reversal of this marriage squeeze by the mid-1980s, when there will be more young men than young women in the age range when most people enter their first marriage. This reversal will be due to the declining birthrates during the 1960s, and should enable more young women who wish to do so to get married in their early 20s.

Other reasons for the increasing number of single women in recent

Single life has its compensations

U.S.D.A. photo

years include sharp rises in the number of women with a college education, expanding job opportunities for women (which enable more of them to be self-supporting), the recent women's liberation movement, and the fact that more couples are living together outside of marriage (Spreitzer & Riley, 1974). Another contributing factor is the virtual disappearance of the old stigma that was for so long attached to the never-married adult, especially for the "old maid." Today, except in certain traditionally oriented circles, a young woman who prefers a career to marriage, or who prefers to hold her independence in order to travel or do other things instead of marrying and settling down, is not only not stigmatized but is apt to be admired for her spunk and independence (Kephart, 1977, p. 488).

Some young women and men intentionally remain single, despite cultural and psychological pressures to get married (Stein, 1975). The satisfactions and rewards of singleness enable them to resist these pressures, for a while at least. Rewards which validate their single lifestyle include increased opportunities for friendships, greater personal growth, and a sense of independence. As one young woman expressed it (Stein, 1975, p. 489):

> Well, today I think I'll stay single forever. It's a hell of a lot more freedom than it would be either in marriage or an exclusive relationship. . . . This affords the opportunity of getting to know well and be friends with a lot of different people. No restrictions except the restrictions I happen to choose.

The independence and freedom of singleness perhaps best suits the better-educated, economically successful middle-class young adult. Working-class and lower-class young men and women would likely have more problems supporting a life of singleness in an apartment or a house of their own. As Jacoby (1974) observes, without enough money it is difficult to translate the theoretical freedom afforded by the single life into a reality. Successful middle-class women who are self-supporting, and who have the education and self-assurance to be on their own, are in a better situation to realize the potential benefits and rewards, as well as to manage the hazards and disappointments, of single life.

Postmarital singlehood as well as premarital singlehood is on the increase, as noted in Chapter 10. In view of current high divorce rates and the uncertainties of remarriage, and given today's less censorious social climate, it seems likely that more divorced men and women, as well as more of those widowed, will opt for longer periods of singlehood in the future. This option will be encouraged by the greater ability of single people to satisfy more of their needs outside of marriage, and (while they last) by certain tax advantages of living together as singles.

In conclusion, it is not only in avant-garde circles that the single life style is found today. While remaining single indefinitely is still somewhat contrary to American social expectations, an atmosphere of greater tolerance is developing, making it easier for young women and men to postpone first marriage, and for those who are divorced or widowed to postpone remarriage.

To keep the singles picture in proper balance, however, we must reiterate that, so far, the evidence indicates that for most adults singleness is not a permanent condition, and that most will eventually marry. Census figures show that by the age of 30 almost all adults marry. The author agrees with Whitehurst (1975) that for some time to come singles in America will constitute a small proportion of the adult population. Most Americans still think that marriage is by far the best way to live, and many who never marry would like to do so.

Cohabitation

Although a certain amount of living together without benefit of clergy, or cohabitation, has existed historically in American society, especially in lower-class groups, the recent rapid increase in this lifestyle has made it more conspicuous. The extent to which cohabitation constitutes a serious alternative to marriage itself rather than a preliminary step toward marriage is a much-debated question. Some authorities, such as Whitehurst (1975), Bowman and Spanier (1978), and New comb (1979), think that cohabitation cannot yet be considered seriously as a permanent alternative; they see it as a preliminary step to marriage for most participants. Others do see cohabitation as an emerging alternative for marriage for at least some of the never-married and for some divorced and widowed people (Lyness, 1978).

Cohabitation has been defined as a nonmarital heterosexual living arrangement (Macklin, 1972); or a "semi-permanent or permanent heterosexual relationship initiated without benefit of clergy" (Clayton & Voss, 1977, p. 273). Newcomb (1979, p. 598), elaborating on these definitions for operational purposes, identifies cohabiting couples as those "living together at least five days a week for at least three months, not legally or religiously married, yet sexually intimate, with or without the goal of marriage in the future." This enables us to distinguish cohabitation from more conventional courtship and dating, and from common-law marriage in which couples live together as husband and wife and so represent themselves to others.

While accurate figures on cohabitation are hard to come by, there is no doubt that it is on the increase. Glick and Norton (1977) judge that the number of persons cohabiting about doubled from 1970 to 1977, when the total was about 2 million persons. These cohabitators represented 3.6 percent of all unmarried adults in 1977 and 4.2 percent of all couple households.

Does this jump in the extent of cohabitation mean that it has become or will soon become a true or permanent alternative to marriage? As noted above, most authorities doubt this, but some others see signs that it may become a short-term alternative to marriage for some previously married people and for some of the elderly (Newcomb, 1979). For example, some divorced men and women—especially those divorced more than once—may prefer cohabitation rather than running the risk of another marital failure (Clayton & Voss, 1977). With continuing high divorce rates and with cohabitation gaining acceptance as a lifestyle, it seems likely that cohabitation will continue to increase in the divorced population.

There are also indications that cohabitation is on the increase among the elderly. While there has been little research on cohabitation in this population, Norton and Glick (1977) found 85,000 men over the age of 65 cohabitating, which represented 1.3 percent of the men in that age group. Yilo (1978), on the basis of a national sample, found that cohabitating was three times as prevalent among those over 60 years old as in the 51 to 60 age group (0.9 percent for the former versus 0.3 percent for the latter). She attributed this increase in the older group to the fact that the social security system tends to encourage those over 60 years of age to cohabit by reducing benefits of elderly women who remarry. Cavan (1974) sees potential advantages in cohabitating for the elderly, including financial gain, companionship, sexual gratification, and reinstatement of the role of spouse. She sees as a potential negative consequence of cohabitation the risk of disapproval in the community and from relatives.

There are a number of disadvantages and potential problems associated with cohabitation as a permanent alternative to marriage. Bowman and Spanier (1978, pp. 43–44) see potential legal problems, especially if the cohabitating couple have children, or if the relationship is terminated. Since a cohabitating couple does not have a common-law marriage, the partners are not normally under the protection of laws which define and regulate common-law relationships. The legal status and rights and obligations of cohabitators are not yet well defined, so that dissolution of the relationship creates numerous legal problems concerning the disposition of jointly accumulated property, money, and debts. Also, the child of an unmarried cohabitating couple will normally be considered the illegitimate child of the woman. The rights of the cohabitating father may be in doubt in many states. He may need to file a statement with the court claiming his paternity. In fact, lawyers have said that cohabitating couples could avoid many of the potential legal problems by drawing up a legal contract to protect the rights of each one as a cohabitating partner, but so far such written contracts appear to be rare.

On this point of the advisability of drawing up a legal contract, two young cohabitators who both are lawyers offer the following advice (Ihara & Warner, 1979). They contend that while drafting a legal contract may not seem romantic to a young couple in love, it really is the thing to do. The process of drawing up such a contract forces the partners to clarify their situation and to find out if they have the same or different assumptions. Studies show that cohabitating partners often have different expectations and definitions of the situation (Newcomb, 1979). For example, who is going to support whom? If both work, are their incomes going to be pooled and shared or kept separate? The lawyers advise keeping incomes separate and maintaining separate bank accounts too, which will make it simpler all around if they break up. If the couple buys a house, they will want the contract to specify who will be named as owner or if it is to be owned jointly, and who gets it or how it will be disposed if they break up. And what about children? There can be serious legal difficulties for a cohabitating couple who have a child out of wedlock. The paternity of the child must be made absolutely clear because this is so important for the child's inheritance, insurance benefits, and social security benefits. These lawyer-cohabitators strongly advise both father and mother to sign a statement acknowledging their parenthood. Each partner should keep a copy and a third copy should be put in safekeeping for the child. (Many cohabitators avoid these problems by getting married before the child is born.)

These lawyers also advise cohabitators to draw up wills specifying what property each wishes to leave the surviving partner. Without such a will, the property of the deceased will go to his or her closest blood relative. They point out that the Lee Marvin case and other recent cases involving money and property disputes between cohabitators have made written contracts more important than ever. California courts have said they will now enforce such written contracts between cohabitators.

Cohabitation is unlikely to become a permanent alternative to conventional marriage for several reasons. For cohabitation to become a major alternative, it would have to demonstrate clear and compelling advantages over a conventional marriage. To live together instead of marrying in order to avoid the difficulties later of a possible marital break-up is not so important now with no-fault divorce. And for those who have had a lengthy cohabitation relationship, the emotional effects as well as many of the social consequences of a break-up probably will be as difficult as in a break-up of a legal marriage. Furthermore, the often-cited advantage of cohabitation over conventional marriage—that the former allows freedom whereas the latter is too confining—may be diminishing today. Modern marriage is becoming more open and flexible, and more couples are finding that they can define their own marriages in ways that enable them to meet their personal and conjugal needs with few of the traditional restrictions.

In his review of the empirical research on cohabitation in America, Newcomb (1979) attempts to assess the various consequences of this lifestyle. He sees the most significant positive consequences for cohabitants as companionship, sexual gratification, and economic gain. Since these are among the most important things conventional marriage has to offer, such "advantages" for cohabitators would seem to apply mainly to temporary cohabitators who are not yet ready for marriage or remarriage. The most significant negative consequences for cohabitators according to Newcomb (1979, p. 601) are "the resolution of conflict concerning property rights upon termination of the relationship and the increased risk for female cohabitants due to their differing expectations as opposed to males with regard to marriage and sexual exclusivity in these relationships." He also sees negative consequences for children in the lack of legal protection with regard to child custody decisions and child support in the event of the termination of the cohabitating relationship. Further study is needed on the matter of consequences of cohabitation for children born to cohabitants.

The author agrees with Bowman and Spanier (1978) and Newcomb (1979) that while cohabitation has risen dramatically in the 1970s and will likely continue into the forseeable future, most cohabitors see it as a temporary rather than a permanent arrangement. Thus cohabitation will probably not become a substitute for marriage for the great majority of Americans.

Open marriage

The idea of "open marriage" or "open-ended marriage" has attracted considerable interest in recent years, due in part to a book by Nena and

George O'Neill entitled, *Open Marriage,* published in 1972. As an alternative to, or more accurately a modification of, conventional marriage, open marriage necessitates major redefinition of the husband-wife relationship. The stress is on each partner's retaining his and her personal identity, and it emphasizes the personal growth and development of each partner via mutual support and encouragement, but without most of the restrictions to individual action associated with traditional marriage. As the O'Neills (1972, pp. 39–40) see it:

> Open marriage means an honest and open relationship between two people, based on equal freedom and identity of both partners. It involves a verbal, intellectual, and emotional commitment to the right of each to grow as an individual within the marriage. . . . Open marriage is a relationship of peers in which there is no need for dominance nor submission . . . , or stifling possessiveness. . . . Being individuals, both the woman and the man are free to develop and expand into the outside world. Each has the opportunity for growth and new experiences outside the marriage.

Open marriages are highlighted by a movement away from traditional sex-role stereotypes and by a mutual respect for personal autonomy. This new open marriage contract would be characterized by individual freedom, flexible roles, open and honest communication, mutual trust, equality, and living spontaneously. The O'Neills (1972) see this as a needed improvement over the old conventional marriage contract, which they feel provides little respect for individual autonomy while demanding absolute fidelity, total exclusivity, and virtual ownership of the mate.

The O'Neills (1972) concede that most married couples are not yet ready to achieve completely open marriages; but many can use open marriage as an ideal or model as they seek to improve their own marriages. While open marriage is not proposed as a panacea for all marital problems, its proponents argue that such individual-oriented marriages would help reduce many of the problems associated with the more confining and rigid traditional marriage.

An issue often raised about open marriage is that of open sexuality in such marriages. While the O'Neills (1972) did not recommend extramarital sex, neither did they advise open-marriage practitioners to avoid it. They took the position that extramarital sex may be included in such a marriage if the married couple has sufficient trust and open communication. How have such marriages fared? Among the few studies of sexually open marriages are those of Whitehurst (1977), Knapp and Whitehurst, (1977), and Ramey (1975).

In their study of 35 couples (23 of which were legally married and 12 not), all of whom defined their relationships as sexually open, Knapp and Whitehurst (1977) found that most couples were enthusiastic about their sexually open relationships, which they believed yielded new experiences, provided more zest to life, and enhanced the self-esteem of both partners. However, few couples seemed able to achieve total success and stability in their primary or marital relationship along with satisfactory outside sexual relationships. Among problems reported were jealousies involving fear of personal loss, feelings of possessiveness or desire to control the mate. Although they worked toward equality, conflict could arise between husband and wife when they discovered that each had a different commitment to or involvement in a sexually open relationship. Whitehurst concluded that sexually open marriages were not advisable for people who are not emotionally equipped to handle freedom, complex interrelationships, or "the inevitable struggle of possessiveness versus autonomy."

Findings of the Knapp study (Knapp & Whitehurst, (1977) and the Ramey (1975) study were similar to those of the Whitehurst (1977) study. Benefits or advantages of sexually open marriage included greater fulfillment of personal needs; the stimulation and excitement of new experiences, both sexual and social; increased enjoyment of marital sex; and greater opportunity to be fully oneself. Problems and disadvantages reported by those involved in sexually open marriage included resentment of the outside partner by one's spouse; jealousy; time-sharing problems and scheduling difficulties; pressures on the marital relationship, and concern over possible exposure or discovery by significant others holding more conventional values.

In her more recent book, *The Marriage Premise* (1977), Nena O'Neill modifies her earlier position regarding sexually open marriage. She cites evidence of the potential destructiveness of open sex on the marriage. She believes that most marriage partners are now expecting marital fidelity even in an otherwise open marriage.

Group marriage

Group marriage represents the most radical departure from conventional monogamous marriage. Whereas open marriage is generally a modification in varying degrees of legal monogamous marriage, and other extramarital relationships such as spouse-swapping and having affairs are practiced by certain still-married people, group marriage is a different kind of "marriage relationship" per se. Group marriage has been defined as a multilateral arrangement "in which three or more individuals (in any distribution of sex) function as a family unit, sharing in a community of sexual and interpersonal intimacy" (Constantine & Constantine, 1970, p. 44).

Group marriages also differ from communes, in that in communes the individual member has a greater or lesser commitment to the commune itself and its purposes and ideology, while in a group marriage the individual is committed to a total and intimate relationship with specific other *individuals* rather than to an organization (Constantine & Constantine, 1972, p. 211). Group marriages are not recognized as legal in any state.

Probably the best known research on group marriage has been undertaken by Larry and Joan Constantine (1971; 1972; 1973). Due to their transience and secret or semisecret nature, group marriages are hard to locate. Out of 101 such marriages identified, the Constantines were able to find and study only 26. Most of these group marriages had four people, two women and two men; some were triads; and the largest group marriage consisted of six partners. Most of the participants were legally married couples who later entered a multilateral relationship as a couple. Most members of these group marriages came from middle-class backgrounds and were college educated. While sexual variety was certainly one of the motives for entering such a multilateral relationship, emphasis on personal growth and fulfillment, plus some disillusionment with conventional marriage, were also important motives.

The Constantines (1972) found that life in a typical group marriage tends to be complicated. Much time and energy is expended on matters ranging from division of labor between the sexes and within the household, to what system of rotating sleeping arrangements will be followed, to how and by whom the children will be disciplined. While jealousy was a frequently mentioned problem, it was not listed as a major problem in any of the group marriages studied. Although most of these group marriages did not last very long, with only 49 percent surviving the first year and 7 percent enduring for 5 years or more, while they did last there was evidence of high emotional involvement and group cohesion in those studied.

Ellis (1973) tries to assess the advantages and disadvantages of group marriage as an alternative to conventional marriage. He finds that multilateral marriage offers greater opportunities than conventional monogamous marriage for personal growth, and enhances the love relationship by enabling participants to live with and relate intimately to more than one adult member of the opposite sex. Group marriages offer a greater variety of sexual experience; they also provide economic and social advantages in the group's sharing a common residence and in multiple financial support. Disadvantages include difficulty of finding a group of three or more adults of both sexes who can live together in harmony in such intimacy; the high probability of sex, love, and jealousy problems arising; and the need to be at least semisecret about their lives since there is still strong, widespread community disapproval of this "deviant" lifestyle. Concern with discovery, public censure, and possible loss of jobs all add to the difficulties of sustaining such group marriages.

Most authorities who have looked into group marriage (Constantine & Constantine, 1972; Ellis, 1973; Houriet, 1971; Whitehurst, 1975) agree that the complexities and problems of four or more people being married to each other are so large that this alternative form is impractical for most people.

Now that we have reviewed some of the principal types of alternatives to conventional marriage, it should be a matter of interest to see what young people in America think about such alternatives vis-à-vis conventional marriage. How interested are young men and women in trying something different, in experimenting in some alternative way of living instead of getting married as their parents did? Let us see what the current research indicates.

ATTITUDES OF AMERICAN YOUTH TOWARD ALTERNATIVES TO CONVENTIONAL MARRIAGE

Several studies have probed the attitudes and viewpoints of American youth—mostly college students—on alternatives to conventional marriage. How attractive do young people find the various alternatives? Are they interested in experimenting?

White and Wells (1973), using a random sample of 651 students at Washington State University, inquired as to their level of interest in different alternative marital and family forms, and found that while few expressed any strong interest, a large proportion expressed at least "some interest" in a few of them. The two alternative forms which evoked the most interest were "ad hoc marriage" and "contract marriage," with 81 percent and 71 percent expressing "some interest" in these respective alternatives. The authors define *ad hoc marriage* as "an arrangement of two people living together for the advantages of traditional monogamy without being formally married (including common-law marriages)." They define *contract marriage* as a "legalized monogamous arrangement for a limited period of time (e.g., five years) at the end of which the couple has the option to renew the contract" (White & Wells, 1973, p. 281).

In another study, Whitehurst (1977) asked 300 first-year Canadian college students what they thought was wrong with their parents' marriages, and found that the most frequent response was that "nothing is wrong." About 12 percent said that marriage in the generation of their parents was too tradition-bound, and 7 percent said it was too dull. Other less frequent responses were that conventional marriage is too materialistic, females are subordinated, and there is too little communication between husband and wife (Whitehurst, 1977, p. 295). When asked what they would like to do to make their own marriages better and to avoid the pitfalls of their parent's generation, a large majority of the students (73 percent) said they would stay single longer. As for other things to do to improve their marriages, only a small minority (7 percent or less) mentioned such things as working out a more open marriage, practicing better family planning, and not worrying so much about the future. A large majority (96 percent) felt confident they could make a good marriage. About half of the sample said they would modify their marital and sexual lifestyles somewhat from those of their parents (Whitehurst, 1977, pp. 297–300). The author concludes that, on the basis of his data, it is not possible to project any potential for rapid or revolutionary change in conventional marriage.

Another study focused on the willingness of students to actually participate in various alternative forms of marriage and family. Strong (1978) got information from a random sample of 354 single undergraduate college students at the University of Connecticut as to the degree of their willingness to participate in 12 alternative marriage and family forms. Respondents were asked to express their views by using a 6-point scale ranging from "very willing to participate" to "very unwilling to participate" on the following 12 alternatives:

1. Remain single.
2. Long-term cohabitation.
3. Traditional sex-role-segregated marriage.
4. Egalitarian marriage.
5. Role-reversal marriage.
6. Child-free marriage.
7. Consensual extramarital sex.
8. Spouse swapping.
9. Five-year evaluation and renewal of marriage.
10. Serial monogamy.
11. Group marriage.
12. Rural commune with shared sex among consenting adults.

The much preferred choice for both women and men was "egalitarian marriage." For women, the next three preferences—all three a long distance behind their first choice—were "five-year evaluation and renewal of marriage," "long-term cohabitation," and "traditional sex-role-segregated marriage." To say that these were the second, third, and fourth choices of the women is, however, somewhat misleading, since only a minority expressed any willingness, while a majority of the women expressed an unwillingness to participate in all three alternatives (Strong, 1978, p. 495). For the men, the first choice was egalitarian marriage, the next three preferences were long-term cohabitation, traditional sex-role-segregated marriage and five-year evaluation and renewal of marriage. Here also it needs to be pointed out that these "next three" choices of the men were considerably behind their first choice of "egalitarian marriage," with the whole sample of men split about 50-50 between willingness to participate and unwillingness to participate in these three alternatives.

Majority opinion expressed by both men and women toward all the other alteratives was that of disapproval, or an unwillingness to participate. Women expressed greater unwillingness to participate in group marriage, spouse swapping, serial monogamy, and consensual extramarital sex. For men, the greater unwillingness to participate was directed toward role-reversal marriage, serial monogamy, and group marriage (Strong, 1978, p. 495). Strong concludes that there is a basic agreement among the men and women making up his sample that an equalitarian and sexually monogamous marriage is the form in which they are most willing to participate.

ASSESSING THE IMPACT OF ALTERNATIVE FORMS ON CONVENTIONAL MARRIAGE

Is it possible now to make at least some educated guesses as to the future direction of American marriage in light of the expansion of experimental and variant forms in recent years? Will marriage as we have known it be basically altered due to these alternatives? Or will conventional marriage only be modified to some extent? Are most of the alternative forms merely passing fads? Or are some of them probably going to endure and attract greater following in the future? While it is certainly too soon to try to answer these questions with much confidence, some marriage and family specialists are now addressing these and related questions as to the possible lasting impact of the alternative lifestyle movement on conventional marriage. Let us see what some of them have to say.

In a thoughtful article entitled "Variant Family Forms and Life Styles: Rejection of the Traditional Nuclear Family," Cogswell (1975) makes some general comparisons between conventional marriage and a wide range of experimental alternative forms. Her purpose is to seek out the advantages and disadvantages for the individual and for society of the new alternative forms as compared to conventional marriage and family. What are the pros and cons of the new forms versus the old form of marriage? Cogswell's main comparisons will serve as points of departure for the following discussion.

1. One of the general contrasts between conventional marriage and the alternative forms is that in the former the husband-wife relationships are more restricted while in the latter they are more diffused. Traditional marriage has been expected to satisfy virtually all the personal needs of the marriage partners, thereby reducing intimate relations with outsiders. Any extramarital relations are defined as infidelities or at least disloyalties. Cogswell (1975, p. 402) argues that such restrictions have a "caging" effect on the marriage partners. It is to escape this caging effect that the O'Neills (1972) have advocated an open marriage, which would allow each partner to seek meaningful relations with outsiders in various sectors of life, such as at work and at leisure. Such diffuse and sectorized relations would offer the advantages of greater variety and flexibility in personal relationships. On the other hand, it can be argued that conventional marriage would normally offer more depth in intimate relationships and a greater security and predictability.

2. Another contrast is that the alternative forms offer multiple primary relations versus the single primary relationship of monogamous marriage. The alternative forms encourage and expect multiple intimate relations,

concurrently and serially, which may develop to the point of sexual intimacy. From the point of view of traditional marriage, these extramarital relations would be viewed as illicit and deviant. Advantages of the alternative forms are the variety they offer in primary relations, and the openness and frank communication between husband and wife about these relations which is encouraged. Supporters of conventional marriage, however, see disadvantages in the transience and possible superficiality of such multiple, changing relations, as compared to the opportunity offered in conventional marriage for a deeper, lifelong intimate relationship.

3. Still another contrast is that the alternative forms are supposed to emphasize and encourage spontaneous and open person-to-person relations as alternatives to the role-defined relationship of the wife and the husband in traditional marriage. Much of the interaction in conventional marriage tends to be prescribed and proscribed by the traditional marital statuses and roles of wife and husband. Many subscribers of alternative life styles see such "role behavior" as anathema because it "stereotypes" persons by sex or age and thus discourages or prohibits "natural" and spontaneous person-to-person relations. Such open and role-free relations would allow a broader range of experiences and acceptable behavior than would be possible where traditional marriage statuses and roles prevailed. It could also be easier to break off a relationship that proved unsatisfying.

But those who support conventional marriage and its culturally defined status and role structure, argue that there is nothing built into the conventional statuses and roles of husband and wife that preclude openness and honesty, self-revelations and real intimacy—the very things so valued by the advocates of the alternative forms of relationships. On the contrary, one may argue that conventional marital statuses and roles embrace these things and more. The "more" would include long-term reciprocal commitments and responsibilities between husband and wife to love, support, and stick with each other (Dyer, 1979, p. 414). Such traditional marital role-expectations and norms are conducive to greater personal security and well being, as well as probably yielding greater efficiency and predictability in relationships.

4. One of the significant differences between traditional marriage and family structure and the alternative types is that the latter are generally defined as temporary while the former are defined as permanent. As Cogswell (1975, p. 401) says: "Individuals enter a legal marriage with the expectation that the relationship is permanent. On the other hand, almost all who enter variant [forms] do so with the expectation that relationships will continue only so long as they serve the mutual benefits of the members." In the alternative forms, the emphasis is on immediate personal fulfillment instead of on the long-term obligations and unqualified commitments of traditional marriage. Further obligations of one person to another are apt to be lacking or of a low priority in the alternative arrangements. This emphasis on immediate personal gratification and lack of long-term commitment can of course lead to a quicker dissolution of a

relationship that is no longer viewed as mutually beneficial. In contrast, traditional marriage carries responsibilities and commitments that are expected to last a lifetime.

The minimizing of obligations and the limitation of commitment in the alternative forms lead Cogswell (1975, p. 401) to raise an important sociological question about these alternative life styles: "Are the goals held by those entering [alternative forms] adequate or sufficiently inclusive to sustain individuals over a life-span?" Her response to this question is: "Although there are insufficient data to arrive at an informed opinion, it seems likely that the [alternative form] goals are most appropriate in short-term, fair-weather contexts" (Cogswell, 1975, p. 401). It may be that certain alternative forms could handle some kinds of short-term difficulties better than conventional marriage and family can, such as identity problems, divorce adjustment, or the changing of jobs. But what about long-term individual needs and problems which require substantial effort and heavy commitments of time, money, and other resources? For example, can the alternative forms provide the long-term intensive daily care needed by a member who becomes seriously ill or disabled? Would a cohabitating partner or even the members of a commune be willing to contribute the large sums of money needed for medical services in such an event, or for the legal fees one in serious trouble with the law might need to pay? Within conventional marriage and the nuclear family, it is expected that all such personal needs will be met to the fullest extent of the family's financial and human resources. Although there is really not enough information yet to know from actual experience if or to what extent the various alternative forms would make these long-term efforts and sacrifices, Cogswell (1975, p. 401) offers her considered opinion: "On the basis of current information, I would be inclined to think that experimental families would default on heavy responsibilities for the care of other members."

More research and analysis are needed on the alternative lifestyles so that better comparisons may be made between them and conventional marriage. At present and in general, the alternative forms appear to offer greater freedom and opportunities with fewer obligations, constraints, and less security, while conventional marriage offers more security with greater obligations and constraints—but at the expense of wider opportunities and greater freedom.

Cogswell (1975, p. 397) sees the lack of constraints and obligations as one of the more serious shortcomings of the alternative forms.

> People entering [these] forms, in their determined attempt to escape the restrictions of the . . . nuclear family, forget that some restraints are necessary if partners as well as they themselves are to achieve "the good life." Thus, . . . a disregard of constraints is one of the potential deficits of most experimental . . . forms. Without some obligations by members of a family to each other, the relationship would tend to be unstable and individuals could be left without support in times of need.

It is apparent that there are some inherently contradictory needs that we bring into marriage, and that we have to give up maximal satisfaction of one set of needs or another. One cannot expect to have maximal freedom and maximal security at the same time; most of us probably seek a compromise in order to have some degree of both in marriage.

Ideally, marriage relationships of the future would combine the advantages of conventional marriage and the new alternative forms, while seeking to avoid the disadvantages of both. It may be argued that what is needed is a better balance between constraints and opportunities, between responsibilities and freedom. Toward this end, Rapoport and Rapoport (1975) recommend that men and women work toward "equity" in their relationships, in marriage and out. By *equity* they mean a fair allocation of both opportunities and constraints, taking into account gender differences while at the same time destereotyping traditional sex roles. Equity, they say, is different from equality:

> It is comparable to the distinction sometimes made between equality of conditions vs. equality of opportunity. We mean by equity the presence of equal opportunity *plus* the feeling of fairness if there is inequality of conditions. Thus, fairness in the allocation of constraints is an essential feature of the equity concept (Rapoport & Rapoport, 1975, p. 421).

The pursuit of equity in marriage requires the partners to be continuously revising and adjusting their lives, separately and in relation to each other, in various areas including husband-wife relations, parent-child relations, and their occupational roles. This pursuit takes constant thought and adjustment to accommodate changing conditions and new knowledge and, in fact, to determine what is equitable.

Insofar as the spate of experiments and alternative forms have served to point out shortcomings and problems of conventional marriage, often highlighting such needed changes as more freedom, opportunities, and equity, the effects may be seen as potentially beneficial for the institution of marriage. The more extreme experimental alternatives, where constraints are minimal and the relations are short lived, are less likely to have lasting effects on marriage than are the more moderate alternative forms, such as the open marriage idea, which can be incorporated into and thus modify conventional marriage. In addition to these modifications of marriage itself, it can be expected that the trend toward more premarital, postmarital, and extramarital alternatives such as staying single and cohabitation will continue as long as American society continues to stress the individual's needs and wants (Adams, 1975, p. 386).

PART FOUR

Family and kinship relations

CHAPTER 12

Transition to parenthood: Pregnancy and childbearing

The large majority of married couples (about 90 percent) in America will have one or more children during their span of reproductive years. Young couples today are confronted with the question of how many children to plan for and when to have them, or whether to have any at all. The development and availability of reliable techniques of birth control make such family planning increasingly effective, providing there is adequate knowledge and communication and cooperation between the marriage partners. In this chapter we shall examine the current social context within which couples develop their attitudes toward parenthood and then make decisions about having or not having children. Those couples who go on to become parents, either by design or by accident, find themselves confronted with many new and challenging experiences.

The transition from married couple to parents entails changes as great or even greater than those found in the transition from being single to being married. The new roles and responsibilities of mother and father are quite different from those of husband and wife, and are thrust upon the couple in an abrupt and demanding way. This transition is one of the main themes of the chapter. What is the impact of the first child upon the marriage partners? Does the arrival of the child constitute a crisis for the young couple? What kinds of adjustments are necessary now that a third number has joined the family?

ANTICIPATING PARENTHOOD: THE CURRENT SOCIAL CONTEXT

THE MYSTIQUE OF PARENTHOOD

Many people seem to hold somewhat romanticized or idealized notions of parenthood. Over the years, a body of folklore about parenthood has built up, somewhat like the romanticized mystique of marriage. LeMasters (1974) notes that in some ways the romantic complex surrounding parenthood in America is even deeper and more unrealistic than that surrounding marriage.

While affectional ties between parents and children were certainly not unknown in earlier times and in other societies, in the past parental love generally did not receive the emphasis it now does in contemporary Western societies, including America. Modern American parents are expected to love their children, and sons and daughters are expected to return this strong affection.

This parenthood mystique, with its idealization of childbearing and rearing, has been perpetuated by both the popular culture and the behavioral sciences. It has been an inducement for couples to have children, and has also contributed to both the joys and frustrations of being parents. Although there is a trend in recent years to look upon parenthood in less idyllic terms than a generation or so ago, parenthood is still envisioned by many couples as a time of unmitigated happiness and fulfillment. Some psychological theory defines parenthood as a stage of normal personality development, especially for the woman, whose motherhood represents the crowning achievement of her life and the main justification of her existence (Skolnick, 1978, p. 292). For males, fatherhood has traditionally been viewed as proof of manhood.

American folklore about parenthood

America, like many other societies, has a body of folklore, or folk beliefs, about parenthood, which accounts for its mystique. (A folk belief is one that is widely shared but not always supported by facts.)

In his *Parents in Modern America* LeMasters (1974) identifies a number of folk beliefs about parenthood that pervade American culture. Some of these (LeMasters, 1974, pp. 19–30) are:

1. Childrearing is fun. While childrearing may be challenging, interesting, or even exciting, few parents would agree that it is really fun. "The truth is—as every parent knows—that rearing children is probably the hardest, and most thankless, job in the world" (LeMasters, 1974, p. 19).

2. Children will turn out well if they have "good" parents. While

the children of dedicated parents who have skill and ability are probably more apt to turn out well, even superparents do not always "bat one thousand." Juvenile delinquents and ne'er-do-wells appear in many families despite the best efforts of parents.

3. Childrearing today is easier because of such things as modern medicine, modern appliances, and child psychology. While automatic dishwashers and clothes dryers can reduce some of their physical labor, in many respects "mothers today are in much more of a rat race than their grandmothers ever dreamed of" (LeMasters, 1974, p. 23). They are poorly paid cab drivers for their children, they help run the P.T.A., they are buddies to their husbands, and many hold down a job, too. While modern medicine and child psychology have much to contribute to child care and rearing, these sciences have also made many parents more anxious about "all the terrible things that can happen to children," against which the parents are expected to take preventive action.

4. Love is enough to sustain good parental performance. While no amount of scientific knowledge about child development will do much good unless it is mixed with love for the child, it can be argued that the opposite is also true. The most loving parent also needs sound knowledge, insight, and self-discipline.

5. All married couples should have children. The idea that a marriage is really incomplete until the couple become parents is a time-honored one. While group pressures on young, childless couples are not as strong today as even a generation ago, they still exist. Rationally speaking, a certain percentage of married people are not well suited temperamentally, and others are not well situated economically, to assume the arduous tasks and responsibilities of parenthood. Childless couples are not necessarily frustrated and unhappy. In fact, some studies show that for many couples marital happiness declines during the childbearing and childrearing years (Rollins & Feldman, 1970).

6. Children improve a marriage. While there is some evidence that children help stabilize marriages (Winch, 1971, p. 254), it is questionable that many marriages are improved by children. Many authorities on marriage and parenthood agree that children are apt to put stress and strains on the marital relationship, reducing marital happiness, seldom improving or enhancing the couple's ability to handle marital problems (Feldman, 1971; Benson, 1968).

In sum, modern parenthood is still so surrounded by folklore and myth that most couples do not really know what they are getting into until they actually become mother and father (LeMasters, 1974, p. 32). This situation can create many problems in the transitions to parenthood when the new mother and father find their parental roles and responsibilities more demanding and frustrating than they had expected. This topic will be pursued more fully as we look at adjustments to new parental roles, and the impact of children on the marital partners.

FERTILITY TRENDS IN AMERICA

Even though most married couples will sooner or later have children, they will, on average, have less than earlier generations of parents had. In fact, except for the period immediately following World War II—the baby-boom years—the birth rates in the United States have followed a generally downward direction for more than one hundred years. The average family in the early years on the 20th century had four children, whereas it had only three children during the 1930s. During the 1950s, family size increased to about four children per family, but declined again during the 1960s and 1970s to a low of just under two children per family in 1976 (U.S. Department of Health and Human Services, 1977). (See Figure 12–1.)

More married women are now delaying having their first child. For couples who got married in the 1975–77 period, the median interval from first marriage to first birth was 2 years, which was about 10 months longer than for those who got married in the 1960–64 period (U.S. Bureau of the Census, 1979a, p. 1). Furthermore, the number of children a married couple can expect to have is still declining. Between 1967 and 1970 the average number of children expected by wives in the 18–34 year age group dropped from 3.1 to 2.3 births per wife (U.S. Bureau of the Census, 1979a, p. 5). Actually, the youngest wives, aged 18–24, could expect to have an average of 2.14 children in their life span. Also, the number of couples who expect to remain childless has increased, up to about 11 percent for all women in the 18–24 age group, and as high as 14 percent for women with one or more years of college (U.S. Bureau of the Census, 1979a, p. 1). However, while it is too soon to tell what the future holds, birth rates did rise moderately in the late 1970s, from 14.8 per 1,000

Figure 12–1

Birth rates in the United States, 1940 to 1980 (births per 1,000 women, age 15–44).

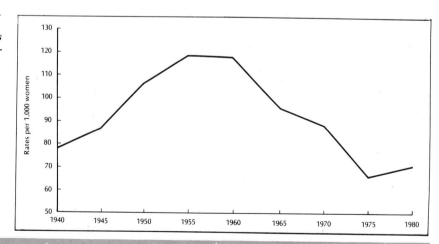

Source: *Statistical Abstracts of the United States,* 1973; 1980.

Table 12–1

Childless marriage trends in the United States, 1967 to 1976	*Wives expecting to remain childless, by percent*	
Age group	*1967*	*1976*
20–21	0.04	4.0
22–24	1.7	5.3

Source: U.S. Bureau of the Census, *Current Population Reports*, 1975; 1976.

population in 1975 to 15.3 per 1,000 population in 1978 (U.S. Bureau of the Census, 1980a).

Why the big decline in the number of children per family and the increase in childless couples in recent years? Have Americans become disenchanted with parenthood? Let us look next at various factors which may now be affecting the attitudes of married couples having children.

ATTITUDES TOWARD PARENTHOOD

Factors influencing attitudes toward parenthood

Throughout its history American society has placed high value on childbearing and childrearing. Not only were large families practical during our long frontier and rural periods, they also have been revered and encouraged by religious, economic, and political leaders (Calhoun, Vol. 1, 1945). In fact most major social institutions have promoted large families. Our expanding economy has generally encouraged parents to bear an ample new generation of workers; schools and churches have encouraged parents to produce children for them to educate and train in the faith. The early American tradition of large families was reinforced during the 19th century and well into the 20th century by the huge influx of immigrants whose native cultures almost invariably placed high value on large families (Dyer, 1979).

Declining birth rates and reduction in family size in America has generally been associated with our historical change from a rural, agricultural-oriented society to an urban-industrial society. The majority of American population was rural until about 1920, but by 1980 nearly 80 percent of us had become urban dwellers. Urban conditions of life are generally not as conductive to childrearing and large families as is a rural environment, and the rural to urban change transformed children from eco-asset to eco-liability. In addition, various social and ideological developments in recent years have influenced people's views regarding having children, including the women's liberation movement, the increased employment of married women, marital instability, and concern about overpopulation.

LeMasters (1974) sees a current trend toward higher standards for parents today, imposed by professionals and community, as well as by parents themselves. This raising of standards for child care and rearing tends to reduce the number of children in families espousing these high standards, most evident in the more educated middle-class families. Women's liberation has brought on expanded opportunities and interests outside the family for wives and mothers, which have contributed to reductions in family size for those affected, such as the two-career couples.

The very high cost of bearing and rearing children is also contributing to the reduction in family size. Espenshade (1979b) has attempted to compute the various monetary costs involved in having children. It's very expensive! While this is hardly news, the spiraling costs of parenthood today are enough to make many potential parents reduce the number of children they plan to have, and to make some couples postpone having children perhaps indefinitely. Espenshade (1979b) estimated that having and bringing up a child in 1977 could cost a couple about $100,000. Since then, spiraling inflation has increased the estimate. In an updated estimate, Espenshade (1980) puts the total cost in 1980 at about $100,000 in a low-income family, and nearly $140,000 in a middle-income family. These figures include direct maintenance costs and a college education, plus the loss of the mother's earnings due to staying home with the

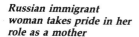

Russian immigrant woman takes pride in her role as a mother

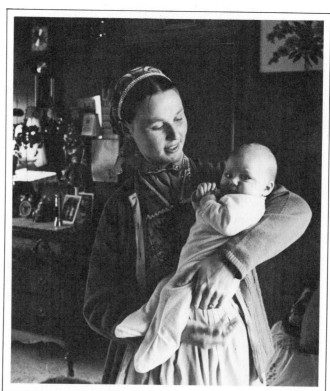

U.S.D.A. photo by Charles O'Rear

child. And it is quite likely that costs will increase with continuing inflation.

Such costs need to be balanced against the rewards and values of having a child, of course. In his article "The Value of Children," Berleson (1979) attempts to identify the various reasons why people may desire to have children—a question simple enough to ask, but far from simple to answer today. The question can be raised in a nonrhetorical way now in light of current issues of overpopulation, widespread practices of birth control, and the woman's revolution in which raising a child is no longer viewed as the only, or even the primary, role of women.

Are there in the human species any residues of biologically based maternal or parental instincts which would help explain why so many people have children, often in spite of what would appear to be adverse personal, social, or economic conditions which rationally would seem to discourage or even prevent them from having children? Most social scientists would question the role of parental "instincts" in humans, while conceding that the instinct to reproduce is very real for other species. Some authorities believe, however, that while personal and social motivation account for most human reproduction, this does not necessarily mean that all biological factors are completely obliterated for the human species (Berleson, 1979; Rossi, 1977; Hess, 1970).

Childbearing is everywhere strongly influenced by social and cultural factors. Cultural values and norms surrounding fertility and childbearing are universal, and while such values and norms differ from society to society and frequently differ within a given society, their existence generally induces a certain conformity to approved childbearing patterns. People have children because it is the thing to do; it is socially approved, encouraged, and supported by the institutional order. Having children is widely rationalized as natural, good and in accord with the will of God. Historically in America children have been looked upon as economic assets, and thus were wanted to help on the farm or in the shop, contributing to the support of the family (Dyer, 1979, p. 30). Such economic motives for having children have diminished in modern urban-industrial America, however. Most city children have little if any economically productive roles in the family; in fact, children today may come to be viewed by urban dwellers as economic luxuries or liabilities.

From a cross-cultural, as well as an historical perspective, children have been desired for familistic reasons; to keep the family name alive, to extend the family line. Old Testament parents were told to "be fruitful and multiply," and to bear sons "that your name be not lost to Israel." In some societies the failure of a wife to bear children is considered a sufficient cause for divorce (Berleson, 1979, p. 245). Throughout history, parenthood has generally conferred prestige on the mother and father. In traditional Chinese society a woman's status depended on her childbearing ability, especially on the bearing of sons. And to be the father of many children has been one of the few almost universal means of achieving honor for a man throughout history. In many societies an adult is considered to have become a real or complete man or woman only after having become a parent (Berleson, 1979, p. 246).

There are, of course, many personal reasons for wanting children: to demonstrate personal competence, to display male virility and female fecundity for the woman, to participate in the miracle of reproduction and birth of a new human being, to experience the ecstasy and agony of having, loving, and watching the growth of your own flesh and blood. Parenthood is a unique human experience that sets apart those who experience it from those who do not.

While American historical and cultural background has favored parenthood, and the vast majority of American couples do sooner or later become parents, they are having fewer children per couple now, and an increasing number of couples are opting to have no children at all (Glick, 1979a). Are there significant changes today in the attitudes of married couples toward having children? Let us examine this question next.

To have or not to have children

During the 1960s and early 1970s, the media as well as social scientists began to raise questions about birth rates and the number of children people should have in view of population pressures and the troubled turbulent times. Some said couples should have no more children than it took to replace the parents; a few suggested rejecting the ideal of parenthood (Bernard, 1972). The nationwide Organization for Non-Parents (since changed to National Association for Optional Parenthood) formed to promote childlessness as a superior way of life, and to lend support to couples who agree that parenthood should be optional. Has the idea of childless marriages caught on to any significant extent? Among the few studies of deliberate childlessness are those of Ory (1978) and Blake (1979).

In recent years the fertility decline which followed the earlier baby boom has been accompanied by a sharp increase in childlessness among young married women. Marriage cohorts of the late 1960s showed marked increases in childlessness as long as five years after marriage. To illustrate, those women in the 1965–1969 marriage cohort still numbered 23 percent childless after 5 years of marriage as compared to 13.6 percent childless after 5 years of marriage in the 1960–1965 cohort (Blake, 1979, p. 245).

In an effort to find factors associated with the decision of whether or not to become parents, Ory (1978) compared the attitudes toward parenthood of two samples of middle-class married couples, one made up of voluntary parents and the other of voluntary childless couples. She found a high agreement in both samples about the general desirability of having children, but for the childless couples, the desire to have children themselves fell off sharply at marriage or shortly thereafter. This was in contrast to the parent-couples whose desire to have children continued onward throughout their marriages. Most of the childless couples were well aware that their preference to remain childless was viewed as somewhat deviant by others and they expected unfavorable reactions from other people. Pressures to conform to the norm of having children came from family members, friends, and coworkers. Both nonparents and parents in the study saw the prevailing attitude in the community toward childlessness as negative. Couples who did not have children were seen as "selfish," "immature," "of a questionable state of mind," and "missing out" (Ory, 1978, p. 535). The nonparent couples tended to define their own childlessness in more positive terms, and sought to insulate themselves from the negative views of others by minimizing contacts with couples who had children and other proparent friends, and by joining organizations supportive of their decision to remain childless, such as the National Association for Optional Parenthood.

Although the proportions of couples expecting or preferring to be permanently childless appear to be still quite small, they have been increasing in the past decade, according to the U.S. Bureau of the Census. Whereas in 1967 only 0.04 percent of wives aged 20–21 and 1.7 percent of wives aged 22–24 expected to remain childless, in 1976 these figures had increased to 4 percent and 5.3 percent respectively (U.S. Bureau of the Census, 1976a, p. 5; 1977, p. 25). (See Table 12–1.) These figures led Blake (1979) to conduct a study of American attitudes toward childlessness in the 1970s. She queried a random sample of 1,600 adult men and women in 1977 as to their views on its advantages and disadvantages. She found that most men and women explicitly deny that children are an "economic investment," nor are they viewed as "consumption goods." There was considerable agreement that children represent an important "social investment" to their parents, specifically as hedges against loneliness in old age; that they give greater meaning to the lives of the parents, and that they help cement marriages and provide fulfillment for women. For the less-educated respondents especially, children are seen as valuable in providing women with an important social status. A major finding of the study was that men from all social strata are significantly more likely than women to regard childlessness as disadvantageous (Blake, 1979, p. 255).

What are the implications of these findings for the future? Is there likely to be a large increase in childlessness which will contribute to extremely low fertility rates in the United States? Judging by the findings of her study, Blake says no. In sum (Blake, 1979, p. 255):

> There is a high level of consensus that non-parenthood is not an advantaged status and, although offspring are not regarded as economic investments, they are viewed as being socially instrumental—not solely as consumption goods. A desire for children, thus, is not as vulnerable to cost factors as one might think on the basis of a consumer model of reproductive motiva-

tion. Indeed, our results suggest that the application of consumer theory to reproductive behavior is inappropriate since children are important social investments.

In conclusion, the emerging evidence suggests that the great majority of married couples still want at least one child. The goal of many young married people today seems to be to have fewer children rather than no children.

It should be noted that not all of the anticipated rewards of parenthood are necessarily borne out. For example, are children hedges against loneliness in old age, as Blake's (1979) sample of parents hope? Not necessarily, according to a study by Glenn and McLanahan (1982) of the effects of offspring on the psychological well being of older adults. They found that while relations between some aging parents and their adult offspring may be rewarding, for others such relationships are neither pleasant nor rewarding.

PREGNANCY AND REPRODUCTION

FAMILY PLANNING

For thousands of years, the arrival of children to married couples was taken as a matter of course, as the natural and inevitable consequence of the marital partners' sexual relations. Today, childbearing has become for increasing numbers a planned event, a matter of deliberate decision on the part of the couple. Modern contraceptive knowledge and techniques now make it possible for couples to consciously plan whether to remain childless or to have children, and if they choose parenthood, how many children to have and when to have them. The availability and widespread use of contraceptives today does not necessarily mean, however, that all married couples using birth control techniques are completely successful either in having children when they want them or not having children when they do not want them. A nationwide survey of contraceptive users in 1970 found that over a one-year period 14 percent of the couples wanting no more children had an unwanted pregnancy, and 24 percent of those couples wishing to delay any further pregnancies had an unexpected one (Leslie, 1979, p. 478).

While there are still differences of opinion in the United States as to what methods of birth control are acceptable, the vast majority of people now approve of family planning via some kind of prevention of conception. A survey conducted in the early 1970s showed 91 percent of American adults approving some method of contraception, and of the opinion that children should definitely be planned (*Better Homes and Gardens,* 1972, p. 82). Although there is not yet available a perfect contraceptive—that is, one that is 100 percent effective, safe, easy to use, and inexpensive—

progress in this direction is being made every year. At present, millions of American couples are using oral contraceptives (the Pill), intrauterine devices (IUDs), and a variety of other methods of controlling conception including the rhythm method, which is still the only one approved by the Catholic Church.

The effectiveness of family planning and contraception does not depend simply on the method used nor the efficiency of the technique. Human and social factors play a part too. Rainwater (1965) found that family planning success varies from one social class to another, and that success is definitely related to the quality of the sexual interaction and communication between husband and wife. In general, sexual satisfaction, good husband-wife communication, and success in family planning seem to be better at middle-class levels than at working- and lower-class levels. (Komarovsky, 1962; LeMasters, 1975).

Implications for marital and parent-child relations

With the excellent birth control techniques available today most married couples have it within their power to prevent unwanted conception without interfering with sexual relations. While less-educated couples still have more difficulty in controlling the number and timing of their offspring as compared to couples with more education, and couples of certain religious persuasion, such as Catholics, have less freedom in choice of birth control methods, in general the trend is now toward greater control in family planning for virtually all groups.

Is it possible that rational planning of parenthood will bring about changes in the meaning and quality of parenthood and parent-child relations, and perhaps of the marriage itself? Throughout most of human history parenthood has been viewed as a gift of fate; children "just happen" to a married couple, they arrive as a natural, "blessed event." There was no need to justify any decision to have children. Now, however, with reproduction subject to rational control, parenthood enters the arena of marital decision making, with wide personal, social, and economic ramifications, for the future of the marriage and the family unit. Before they are conceived, children are envisioned as fitting into the couple's overall plan for the development of their marriage and for the self-enhancement of each marriage partner. Such a rational view of parenthood seems bound to affect parent-child relations. "Planned" parents may have a heightened ego-involvement with each child, and an acute sense of responsibility, since the child arrived due to their deliberate decision to have it. A planned child may have greater advantages and receive more individual attention from the parents. Parents may take great pride in watching the development of their planned child, or feel great disappointment or perhaps guilt if their son or daughter does not live up to "planned" expectations. There is now more potential for people to have regrets about their decision to have children. When having children was not generally a result of a rational decision, people had less reason to regret having them.

PREGNANCY AND CHILDBEARING

Readiness for childbearing

Not many married couples are really ready to become parents in the first year of marriage. Adjusting to each other as husband and wife, and learning marital roles and responsibilities, are big enough jobs without the additional heavy responsibilities of parenthood. No matter how mature they are, newlyweds need a period of time without children in order to provide a gradual transition from premarital to marital life. If children come too soon, young parents may feel trapped, to the detriment of their marriage. Christensen (1962) found that the longer the time from marriage to the arrival of the first child the lower the divorce rate. He attributed this to a greater readiness for parenthood and a lower proportion of unwanted pregnancies among those who delayed having their first child. There is evidence that the arrival of the first child constitutes a crisis for many married couples (LeMasters, 1957a; Dyer, 1963; Feldman, 1971). The more mature and better adjusted the couple have become as marriage partners the more resources they have to draw from in overcoming the various crises associated with pregnancy and the arrival of their first child.

Marriage counselors, such as Blood and Blood (1978, 414), recommend that a young couple wait at least two years after marriage before having their first child. This will increase the likelihood that they have become experienced enough in their marital roles and relations; and they are also more likely to be emotionally ready for parenthood. One sign of such readiness is an expressed desire to have children. This is true for husband and wife both. That is, the expressed readiness for fatherhood on the part of the husband is equally as important as the readiness of the wife for motherhood. If either husband or wife really do not want children, it would be advisable to avoid having them (Blood & Blood, 1978, p. 415).

Given the high divorce rates, and the high likelihood that if divorce occurs it will do so in the early years of marriage, it may be advisable for couples to wait at least four years before having children. If all recently married couples had done this, nearly half of the more that one million children affected by the divorce of their parents in recent years would not have been thus affected, and the divorces would have been easier on the couples.

Readiness for parenthood involves more than personal and emotional maturity, as important as these things are. Economic or financial readiness is no small matter in these days of spiraling costs. While the costs of having a baby will vary by type of community, by social class, and with individual family circumstances, the actual costs of having one in 1975 and raising it through its first year was estimated to be about $2,300 (Williams, 1976). In a study of how well prepared couples were for the arrival of their child Westoff et al. (1961) found that 41 percent of the new parents reported being financially unprepared, while 26 percent wished that they had waited to have their child in order to have had more time to enjoy doing other things together. Nineteen percent said they really had not had time enough to get adjusted to each other as husband and wife before their child arrived. The most enthusiastic parents were those who had waited two or three years before having their first child.

Pregnancy

The "expectant couple" have about eight months to prepare for the arrival of their child, since they are generally not aware of the wife's pregnancy for several weeks following conception. During these months the expectant mother will experience significant physiological changes, and both she and her husband will normally undergo some psychological and social adjustments (Heinstein, 1967; Chertok, 1972). The woman's

Expectant couple

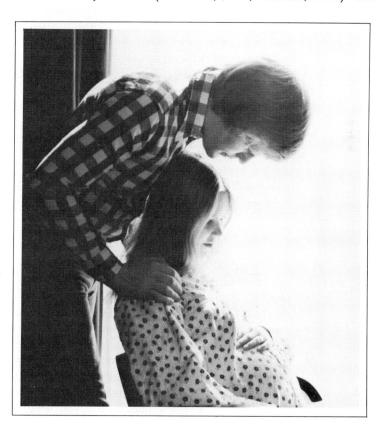

The photography of H. Armstrong Roberts

body chemistry is transformed in order to nurture the growing embryo within her. While pregnancy brings some physical problems to many women, most experience no significant change in their general health, and many feel that pregnancy has beneficial effects on it (Landis et al., 1950). Women who are unhappy or insecure are more apt to react to pregnancy as if it were an illness (Rosengren, 1961). However, when the wife wants the child, and is secure in the knowledge that her husband shares this desire and will share with her in this new adventure of creating and supporting a family, the first pregnancy can produce an emotional euphoria not unlike that of falling in love.

The wife's reaction to her pregnancy depends in no small part on her husband's reaction to it. If he is happy, enthusiastic, and supportive, and lets her know he loves her, her adjustments are easier and her morale is reinforced. In a study of obstetrical patients Stott (1952) found that a majority of the expectant couples said their love had become deeper and the prospective baby had drawn them closer together as marriage partners. Rausch and associates (1974) found that while pregnant wives often became more demanding, their husbands in turn became more responsive and conciliatory during the pregnancy period. Landis and associates (1950) found that among young expectant mothers there was a widespread fear of the approaching experience of childbirth, and that the supportive role and nurturance of the husband then was crucial for the well being of the mother-to-be.

Pregnancy brings on sexual changes in the wife which require adjustments in the sexual relations of the couple. Masters and Johnson (1966) found that among women in their first pregnancy, three quarters experienced some loss of interest in sex during the first three months. This changed during the second trimester, when many women became more sexually responsive than usual. Then in the last trimester both wife and husband generally lost interest in sex as the fetus became larger. During the last six weeks most couples refrain from sex relations for fear of harming the fetus. Most doctors prescribe this abstinence.

The childbearing stage of family life

The arrival of the first child marks the entry of the married couple into the second stage of the family life cycle, the childbearing stage. The first stage—the honeymoon stage—is over. As Duvall (1977, p. 213) points out, during this second period of the family cycle life the participants undergo considerable change, preceeding at a rapid pace through a series of overlapping phases. A new, third member joins the family circle; the husband and wife abruptly have thrust upon them the full responsibility for care and upbringing of this newcomer; they must learn and perform adequately their new roles of mother and father; they must see to the child's developmental progress; and they must reorganize their

Mother and baby

The photography of H. Armstrong Roberts

individual and marital interests and activities in keeping with the pervasive needs and relentless demands of their new son or daughter.

The first phase of the childbearing stage is usually a matter of rejoicing. Experiencing the miracle of birth, seeing and holding one's own flesh-and-blood, is like no other human experience. The happy mother and proud father experience a sense of accomplishment and euphoria amidst the congratulations of family and friends. This emotional "high" may be sustained until the mother and baby come home from the hospital and mother and father are faced with the realization that they alone are now responsible for the round-the-clock job of taking care of their new baby. A feeding schedule has to be worked out. Now, the new mother can get some help from father with this task. For thousands of years, only mother could satisfy baby's demands for food in the dead of night. Today, bottles and formulas enable the father to take his turn

Fathers now share the birth experience more frequently

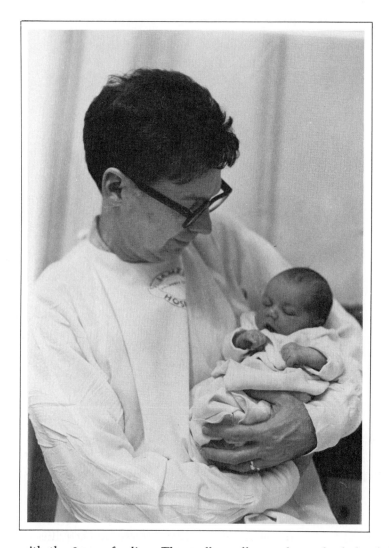

Reynolds Photography

with the 2 A.M. feeding. The endless effort to keep the baby fed, clean, and dry, on top of her many other wifely and home-care responsibilities, often leads the new mother to experience periods of exhaustion and discouragement, often referred to as the "postpartum blues." The new father's sympathy and help are crucial during this period of transition to parenthood (Dyer, 1963).

As mentioned above, there is a good deal of evidence that the arrival of the first child constitutes a crisis for the married couple. Life must now be reorganized, new roles taken on, new needs met, new priorities set. The old, comfortable couple-oriented patterns of the prechild honeymoon will not suffice any longer. The remainder of the chapter will be devoted to an analysis of the impact of children on the married couple, and how they adjust.

TRANSITION TO PARENTHOOD: IMPACT OF CHILDREN ON MARRIAGE PARTNERS

PARENTHOOD AS CRISIS

Over the years, a good deal of attention has been paid to the effects of parents on the development, socialization, and personality of the child. Only recently has much attention been directed toward the impact of the child on the parent. This has become a focal research issue only since LeMasters (1957a) published his research findings in an article entitled "Parenthood as Crisis." It is generally agreed that the birth of the first child is a maturing experience for the new parents. Is it also, as LeMasters (1957a) suggests, apt to be one of the main crises in their lives?

Prior to the arrival of the first child, the typical husband and wife are able to give full attention to each other and to their conjugal and individual interests. When the child arrives, the exclusivity and reciprocity of the dyad is destroyed. The family is now a triad, with the new third member demanding full attention without regard for the feelings or wishes of the other two. Henceforth each adult must compete with the child for attention from the other adult, and the child is generally the winner. Both parents are also confronted with many new responsibilities and tasks and with reordering their marital and personal lives. To what extent does all this constitute a crisis for them? Let us see what the research reveals.

In a study of 43 young, middle-class married couples living in an urban community in Wisconsin, LeMasters (1957a) found 83 percent reporting extensive or severe crisis following the birth of their first child, even though they had planned for and desired their children. (LeMasters (1957a, p. 353) defined *crisis* as any sharp or decisive change for which old patterns are inadequate, a situation in which the usual behavior patterns are found to be unsatisfactory and new ones are called for immediately.) LeMasters noted that these were normal, generally well-adjusted couples. Why did the arrival of their child hit them so hard? First, they held unrealistic and often romanticized ideas of what it was going to be like to be a parent. Second, most had very little, if any, effective preparation for parenthood. Third, new mothers who had been employed and who gave up their jobs for motherhood were experiencing considerable trauma.

The author did a replication of the LeMasters research in 1963 in Texas, with a sample of young, married, middle-class urban couples who had had their first child within two years of the time studied (Dyer, 1963). Fifty-three percent of the couples reported extensive or severe crisis; the remaining 47 percent experienced only moderate or slight crisis. How was the crisis manifested? Reactions of the new mothers to the arrival of the child were, in descending order of frequency mentioned: feelings of tiredness and exhaustion, loss of sleep, feelings of neglecting husband, feeling of inadequacy in being able to fulfill the mother role, inability to keep up with the housework, and difficulty in adjusting to being tied down at home.

Reactions of the new fathers to the arrival of the child were generally in the same vein as those of the new mothers, with some additional complaints, including difficulty in adjusting to new responsibilities and routines, upset daily schedules, ignorance of the great amount of time and work the baby would require, and financial worries and adjustments necessitated by added expenses of the child, and by loss of wife's income (in 62 percent of the couples, the wife had been employed prior to the birth of the child).

The experience of becoming parents was less crisis-fraught for couples who reported having excellent marital adjustment, for those who had taken preparation for marriage courses in high school or college, had planned their child, or had been married three or more years before having their child. The large majority of couples recovered from the crisis, although this often followed a difficult period of several months duration.

Some subsequent studies of new parenthood using broader samples, including working- and lower-class couples (Hobbs, 1965, 1968; Russell, 1974), have reported less crisis, which suggests that working- and lower-class couples may view the arrival of their first child somewhat differently than do middle-class couples. Some studies that have addressed this issue

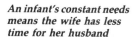

An infant's constant needs means the wife has less time for her husband

U.S.D.A. photo by Michelle Bogre

will be reviewed shortly. But first let us look at the broader picture of why the transition to parenthood may be difficult for American couples in general.

Rossi (1968) sees a number of social and cultural factors existing in contemporary America which tend to make the transition to parenthood more difficult than many other important role-transitions (such as transitions from single to marital roles or occupational role changes). Transition to parenthood needs to be understood in the following terms.

1. The need of the newborn child for the mother is absolute. The child's need is greater than the need of the mother for the child. The mother must accept this burden immediately after the birth of the child.

2. There is a lack of preparation for parenthood among American couples today. Neither formal education nor informal preparation for parenthood is available to most young married couples. Few new mothers, and fewer fathers, have experienced more than occasional care of a younger sibling or limited baby-sitting as a teenager. Some have had a course in child psychology. The learning opportunities for either prospective parent during the wife's pregnancy are generally limited. The transition to parenthood is abrupt rather than gradual.

3. Cultural pressure to assume the role of parent is still strong enough that a married couple may feel compelled to have a child in spite of latent desires not to do so. The woman especially may believe motherhood is necessary to the fulfillment of her womanhood. This is the cultural equivalent of the pressure on the male to assume a productive occupational role.

4. Conceptions still occur in spite of efforts to prevent them. While such conceptions can be terminated by abortion, this is still not generally socially approved. Pregnancy, unlike engagement, is not easily terminated. There must be many more unwanted pregnancies than unwanted marriages.

5. Unlike most other role-transitions, such as marriage or occupational roles, parenthood is irrevocable. Once a child is born, the new roles of mother and father are thrust upon the husband and wife whether they like it or not. There is little possibility of undoing the commitment, except in rare instances of placing the child for adoption. Parents do not generally have the option of resigning their roles of mother and father, or of renegotiating the contract.

6. In spite of advances made in behavioral sciences, there is still a lack of generally agreed-upon guidelines for successful parenthood. There are disagreements among the various authorities as to the best way to bring up children. Educated middle-class parents may be more confused than helped by the often changing "party line" of the specialists.

These, then, are some of the general aspects of the transition to parenthood which make it different from other role-transitions and contribute to the difficulty many couples experience as they become new parents.

Social class differences

We mentioned above that there is evidence that this transition process may be viewed and experienced somewhat differently from one social class to another. Let us look briefly at the literature on this question.

In a study of married women in Chicago, Lopata (1971) found significant differences between the way lower- and working-class couples confronted the arrival of children and the way middle-class couples did. She found that for lower- and working-class wives and their husbands, "parenthood roles add an important and meaningful bond to a limited relation, bringing the husband and wife 'closer together' through the creation of a common interest" (Lopata, 1971, p. 199). She also found that these women frequently expressed the idea that children introduce a common interest otherwise missing in this sex-segregated, blue-collar world. On the other hand, middle-class college-educated wives expressed mixed emotions about the change they experienced in their relations with their husbands in the process of becoming mothers. They see the change as a decrease in the time and attention previously shared with their husbands, an inability to continue companionate interests and activities enjoyed up to that time. These middle-class wives were more apt to express concern over increasing social distance between themselves and their husbands engendered by the arrival of children.

For the more traditional-oriented lower- and working-class women, the transition to parenthood seemed more normal, with fewer disruptions than for middle-class women. The former have lived in a more sex-segregated world of women and children; and they also generally have had more experience with infants and children before their own begin to arrive. On the other hand, equalitarian-oriented middle-class women with wider extrafamily interests tend to see the transition to parenthood as not only reducing their shared activities with their husbands, but also resulting in a loss of enjoyable activities and relations in the community. Lopata (1971, p. 200) found that many middle-class wives kept reminding her that they would again have more time to devote to their husbands and outside activities "as soon as the children grow up." From her study Lopata (1971, pp. 200–201) concludes that

> the event causing the greatest discontinuity of personality in American middle-class women is the birth of the first child, particularly if it is not immediately followed by a return to full-time involvement outside of the home. It is not just a "crisis" which is resolved by a return to previous roles and relations, but an event marking a complete change in life approach.

Jacoby (1969) addressed the question of why middle-class parents may find the transition to parenthood so difficult in contemporary America. After reviewing the various "parenthood as crisis" studies, he arrived at these conclusions.

1. Middle-class standards of child care and rearing may be higher than

those of the working and lower classes. There is evidence that duties and responsibilities of parenthood are defined differently in these classes (Duvall, 1946; Kohn, 1963). Middle-class parents tend to regard childrearing as more problematic; they tend to be more anxious about doing the right thing for their child, and have more doubts about their ability to cope and be a good parent.

2. The working-class woman places greater intrinsic valuation on having children than the middle-class woman does. The working-class girl grows up expecting to get married and have children. This is her main route to adulthood and womanhood. In contrast, the middle-class woman may be able to validate her adulthood and womanhood through other achievements in the educational and occupational structures. Meyerowitz (1964) found that working-class couples rated the importance of having children much higher than did professional middle-class couples.

3. The principal sources of gratification for the lower- or working-class wife are located within the family circle, whereas the middle-class wife, with her wider opportunities and sense of independence, may find many extrafamilial sources of gratification. Gavron (1966) found a large difference between the number of friends outside the family circle working-class wives and middle-class wives had. Most of the middle-class wives went out with their husbands frequently or occasionally, while over half of the working-class wives never did this.

4. Parenthood is far more likely to interfere with the career aspirations of middle-class mothers than working-class mothers. The former more often complain that pregnancy, childbearing, and childrearing interrupt their educational and vocational plans. The child-career conflict experienced by middle-class mothers has been observed by many researchers (Gavron, 1966; Newson & Newson, 1963; Rossi, 1968).

5. Middle-class mothers are apt to be less experienced in the care of infants and children than working-class mothers. Since so many middle-class wives come from small, middle-class families themselves, they are apt to have had less experience in handling babies and caring for children than working-class wives from larger families where older sisters routinely help with younger siblings. Gavron (1966) found that 81 percent of his middle-class respondents had had absolutely no prior experience in caring for infants before the arrival of their first child.

6. The middle-class husband-wife relationship is apt to be more strongly established as affectively positive than is the working-class husband-wife relationship in the prechild stage of marriage. When this is the case the first child is more apt to be perceived as a threat to the conjugal relationship by middle-class couples. The arrival of the child represents less of a threat to the husband-wife relationships in working- and lower-class marriages which have often been characterized by sex segregation and separate male and female interests (Komarovsky, 1962; Rainwater et al., 1959; LeMasters, 1975). On the other hand, the more affectively and companionship-oriented middle-class couple may feel an

acute sense of loss of their prior monopoly on each other when their first child appears (LeMasters, 1957a; Dyer, 1963; Ryder, 1973).

In sum, the transition of parenthood seems to pose a number of difficulties of a personal and social nature for contemporary middle-class couples. A combination of limited experience with children and high standards of parenting, plus various strains and incompatibilities between the new parental roles and other roles and interests—conjugal, occupational, and community—make the arrival of the first child somewhat problematic for many middle-class couples.

PARENTHOOD AND MARITAL SATISFACTION

How does the arrival of the first child affect the marital adjustments or satisfaction of the husband and wife? In a study of 799 middle-class couples, Rollins and Feldman (1970) found that general marital satisfaction fell off sharply for wives, and significantly but not quite so sharply for husbands, with the arrival of the first child. As the couple entered the childbearing stage both wife and husband reported that things were not going as well between them as before their child arrived. During the childbearing stage the wives, but not the husbands, reported increases in negative feelings resulting from interaction with their spouses, such as feelings of resentment and not being understood by their husbands. Both wives and husbands reported sharp declines in companionship experiences as they moved into the childbearing stage. Rollins and Feldman (1970, p. 27) conclude that their data suggest that the experiences of childbearing and childrearing have a profound, negative effect on the marital satisfaction of middle-class wives, and on middle-class husbands also to a lesser degree. The husband's occupational and other outside roles and activities tend to soften the loss of his wife's companionship when the children begin to come.

From subsequent studies Feldman (1971) reported corroborating evidence that the marital satisfaction of couples with children is generally lower than that of childless couples, and that couples with good marital satisfaction before the birth of their child frequently experience decreasing marital satisfaction after their child arrives. However, not all couples experience this decline in marital satisfaction after having a child. Feldman and Feldman (1977) found one group of new parents which experienced improved marital satisfaction following the arrival of this child. How did these parents differ from those whose marriages worsened following childbirth? Five factors distinguished those to whom parenthood brought improved marital satisfaction: (1) These marital partners were less companionship-oriented before their child was born. (2) They had a longer period of aquaintance before getting married. (3) They held more traditional sex roles definitions, with the woman as homemaker and mother and the man as family provider. (4) The wife had more pronounced "maternal attitudes." (5) The husband and wife generally agreed in their views on childrearing. These findings fall in line with those of other studies reported above that compare the adjustment of working-class and middle-class couples to the parenthood experience. Couples that conform more to the traditional family model seem better prepared to derive satisfaction from the parenthood experience than couples who have moved further toward the secular equalitarian model.

In a study of children and marital happiness, Glenn and McLanahan (1982) analyzed data from six U.S. national surveys conducted from 1973 through 1978 to estimate the effects on parents' marital happiness of the presence of a child in the home. Their findings corroborated a large body of accumulating evidence which indicates that on the average children adversely affect marital quality (LeMasters, 1957a; Dyer, 1963; Rollins & Feldman, 1970; Glenn & Weaver, 1978; Campbell, Converse & Rodgers, 1976; Spanier & Lewis, 1980).

The negative effects of children on marital happiness or satisfaction of the parents were found to be quite pervasive, apparently outweighing positive effects among spouses of both sexes and of all races, major religious group, educational levels, and employment statuses. Glenn and McLanahan (1982) believe that the negative effects of children on marriages are likely explained largely by the failure of many married couples to control the number and spacing of their children, and that the effects are generally more positive when the births of children are planned and desired.

GRATIFICATIONS OF PARENTHOOD

The above discussion may well leave the impression that the transition to parenthood is mostly problem-fraught and that new parents are beset by many difficulties in assuming their new roles of mother and father, and in their ongoing relations as husband and wife. Most studies also show that the large majority of couples who experience crisis upon becoming parents do make a successful recovery fairly soon (LeMasters, 1957a; Dyer, 1963; Russell, 1974). The most difficult time for many new parents seems to be in the months immediately following the birth of the child. Once new family routines are established the couple will generally be in a better position to enjoy their child and experience the gratifications of parenthood.

Among the many gratifications or rewards of becoming parents are: (1) Experiencing the miracle of birth. While no father can really know what the mother actually experiences at childbirth, he can share in a small way by being present during her labor and delivery. (2) The joy and pride of reproducing your own flesh-and-blood. (3) Sharing with one's marriage partner in the caring for and raising of your child, with its alternating phases of joy, frustration, and pride. (4) Experiencing personal growth and maturity as parents. It has been said that parenthood rather than marriage marks the final transition to personal maturity. Parenthood is conducive to greater tolerance, unselfishness, and certainly humility.

In a study of problems and gratifications associated with the transition to parenthood, Russell (1974) found that urban couples who had babies aged from 6 to 56 weeks were able to identify many specific gratifications associated with the arrival of their first child. Among them were pride in the baby's development, fewer periods of boredom, increased appreciation for family and religious traditions, more things to talk about with one's spouse, enjoying the baby, feelings of personal fulfillment, and a purpose for living. Russell's sample included both middle-class and lower-class parents, and her findings showed that middle-class parents may experience fewer gratifications from the initial period of parenthood than lower-class parents do (Russell, 1974, p. 301).

Belsky (1979) studied a sample of conventional two-parent middle-class families with infants 15 months of age. He found that while the roles of spouse and parent may not always be compatible, they are potentially compatible in that the child provides a basis for pleasurable interaction between the husband and the wife. Families in which both mother and father were actively involved in parenting rated high in sharing pleasure in their child and in spousal harmony. It is probably safe to assume

Parenthood has many rewards

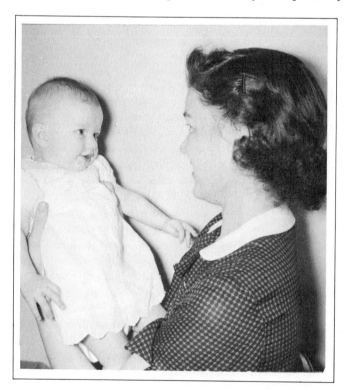

E. D. Dyer

that most middle-class parents, as well as other parents in America, derive a good deal of pleasure and satisfaction from their children, along with the frustrations and disappointments. They enjoy being with their children, playing with them, going places with them, and teaching them things. The frustrations of childrearing and the various deprivations experienced by parents are probably more than offset for most by the gratifications of parenthood. Glenn and McLanahan (1982) think that there are enough people in the United States who do or could derive from parenthood a favorable balance of psychological rewards over penalties to sustain any desired population level.

SUGGESTIONS FOR POTENTIAL PARENTS

Is it possible to prevent or at least minimize the "crisis effect" of the arrival of the first child? How may potential parents be better prepared for the changes and disruptions that the new third member will bring into their lives? The following suggestions have been gleaned from the marriage and family literature. While we do not as yet have sufficient empirical evidence as to their effectiveness, it is believed these suggestions can be of value to those who are contemplating parenthood.

1. Wait until the marriage has stabilized and matured before having children. It seems advisable to postpone the first child until the early phases of marital adjustment have taken place, and the partners are secure in their roles of husband and wife (Dyer, 1963). The crisis of first parenthood is apt to be more acute for those who are emotionally and personally immature (Freedman & Coombs, 1966).

2. Some married couples should probably avoid having children. There are those who are so strongly conjugally oriented, who give such primacy to their marital relationship, that there is really no place in their lives for children. There are couples whose many outside interests and commitments, such as career couples, are such that the price of becoming parents may be too high. And finally there are some who are just not tempermentally suited for the rigors of parenthood (Blood & Wolfe, 1960; LeMasters, 1974).

3. It is very important that the new parents continue to "work at" their marriage. Amidst the incessant demands of the infant on their time and energies, the couple must create time for purely husband-wife activities. The demands of parenthood should not be allowed to engulf the marriage completely. The "institution" of the baby-sitter is part of the middle-class answer to this need to get away from the young child even for a few hours. Working- and lower-class parents often exchange baby-sitting stints with relatives or close friends. Couples who are able to plan some time together away from their child or children generally find that this adds zest to their marriage, and may make them more appreciative of their children (Udry, 1974, p. 300).

4. Pay more attention to the role of the father. The literature reveals a diminishing role for the father in postpatriarchal modern families (LeMasters, 1971; Benson, 1968; Feldman, 1971). If the husband feels neglected because his wife is devoting so much time to their new infant, his increased participation in infant care and childrearing can help fill the gap and furthermore be a source of sharing with his wife that can bring them closer together. The father's help with diaper changing, early morning feeding, and so on not only serves to relieve the pressure on his wife but also boosts the father's feeling of being a partner in their new undertaking. They are both active parents, cooperating in a difficult but rewarding joint enterprise in a way that should prove beneficial to their marriage as well as to their child.

5. Proper planning and preparation by the couple are necessary. New parents interviewed by the author (Dyer, 1963) repeatedly recommended to others who might be contemplating parenthood: "Be prepared!" As seen earlier in this chapter, childless couples often hold idealized and naive ideas about pregnancy, childbearing, and childrearing. Authorities (Feldman, 1971; LeMasters, 1974) recommend better preparation for parenthood through family life education courses and programs. Some go so far as to say that "since parenthood is such a demanding and important task, it probably should not be entrusted to amateurs. Those who become parents should have some training for the task" (Feldman & Feldman, 1977, p. 7). Educational programs for expectant parents can help in many ways, not only by providing practical knowledge and skills in infant and child care, but also by revealing differences of opinion the husband and wife may have about such matters. Couples are well advised to explore their attitudes about having and rearing children before they have any. Differences between husband and wife in attitudes toward childrearing can have a marked effect on marital happiness (Feldman, 1971).

6. Expectant parents will do well to line up their family and other social support systems. The expectant mother's own mother is usually the single most valuable person just before and after the arrival of the child. Other relatives and close friends can be very helpful too.

In sum, there are many things a married couple can do ahead of time to help prepare themselves for the arrival of their child, thereby reducing the crisis effect and easing the transition to parenthood. Knowing ahead of time what you are in for is half the battle.

CHAPTER 13

Parenthood: Childrearing and parent-child relations

By mid-20th century, America had become a child-centered society. Private, public, and professional interest in children, childrearing, child welfare, and children's problems continues at a high level today. There is a general belief that childhood experiences are among the most important determinants of adult personality and adjustment. Thus what happens during childhood sets the stage for the following periods of the individual's life cycle.

Here we will look first at changing views of children and childrearing practices in America from early times to the present. We will review some crucial modern theories of child development, as well as the kinds of professional advice that have been offered to parents on how to care for and raise their children. Since childrearing practices and parent-child relations still differ significantly from one social class to another, some comparisons will be made betweem the upper, middle, working, and lower classes. Next we shall treat some of the salient current issues in parenthood in America, such as child care and parent-child relations in families where both parents are employed, or where there is only one parent to care for and rear the children. Finally, we will try to assess the future of parenthood in America.

CHILDREN AND CHILDREARING IN AMERICA

EARLY AMERICAN VIEWS OF CHILDREN AND CHILDREARING

In colonial America, preceptions of children and how to rear them tended to be rigid and strict. Children were believed to be naturally willful, and according to some religious viewpoints, to be naturally wicked, and thus in need of strict discipline and correction. Good parents should "not spare the rod and spoil the child." John Eliot, writing in 1678, advised parents: "Withhold not correction from the child . . . , thou shall beat him with the rod and deliver his soul from hell" (Illick, 1975, p. 329). Children needed discipline and correction both to control their natural antisocial tendencies and also to help them achieve religious salvation.

It is difficult for people today to realize that throughout most of Western history childhood was not generally considered a very important period in life. During the Middle Ages, for example, the concept of childhood as we know it was generally lacking. Children were seen as miniature adults. According to Aries (1962, p. 411):

> In the Middle Ages, children were mixed with adults as soon as they were considered capable of doing without their mothers; in other words, at about the age of seven. They immediately went into the great community of men, sharing in the work and play of their companions, young and old alike.

This medieval view of children as small adults had changed considerably by the 17th century, however, superceded by a developing view of children as different from adults, as preadults in need of guidance and training in preparation for future adulthood. Child training was thus oriented toward obedience, industriousness, and dependability. Discipline was strict, and, as noted above, punishment could be severe. Filial piety was stressed in the patriarchal colonial family, and children were admonished to "honor thy father and mother." Not that colonial parents lacked affection for their children; rather, the prevailing norms apparently discouraged open demonstrations of affection. The emphasis in parent-child relations seemed to be on imparting needed skills, industriousness, rules of conduct, morals, and a belief in God (Calhoun, Vol. 1, 1945). Such childrearing values fitted the rural, familistic type of society prevalent during the colonial and early frontier periods of American history.

With the coming of urbanism and secularism—especially in the 20th century—the traditional-patriarchal nature of the American family began to change. It was inevitable that practices of childrearing and views of parent-child relations should change too. Families became smaller, formal education increased, traditional patriarchal grounds for strict child discipline was increasingly challenged, and new views of the needs and rights of children emerged. New views of child development and childrearing were well established by mid-20th century, as educators and behavioral scientists paid increasing attention to the child in the family setting.

Let us now briefly review some of the leading theories or explanations of childhood and child development. These theories have helped shape the views of the professional experts in child care and training, and have directly or indirectly influenced millions of American parents in their attempts to be scientific in bringing up their children.

MODERN THEORIES OF CHILD DEVELOPMENT

Freud: A psychosexual theory

Freudian theory stresses the great importance of infancy and childhood as determinants of adult personality. This theory focuses on the emotional and sexual development of the individual from infancy onward. When first propounded in the early 20th century, Freud's theories were revolutionary, shocking laypersons and many scientists too, who found it hard to accept the idea that infants and young children had a sexual nature. According to Freud (1956), the individual moves through a series of stages of psychosexual development, starting in infancy when the infant derives sexual pleasure from exploration of its erogenous zones (oral, anal, and genital). During this early stage of infancy the child also derives pleasure from being nursed by the mother, and this physical relationship normally leads to a strong love attachment on the part of the child for the mother.

At about the age of five or six there begins an "oedipal" phase when the child develops a strong attachment to the parent of the opposite sex, and the child sees the parent of the same sex as a rival. Next is a "latency" phase during which the child's sexual urges are at a minimum, with the child preferring to associate with members of the same sex. With the arrival of puberty, where physical sexual development matures, there begins a "genital" stage. In this phase, mature genital sexual activity can be expected and heterosexuality is normally established.

Childrearing, according to Freudian theory, requires a delicate balance of parental tolerance in allowing the child some gratification of its unconscious needs for pleasure (the id), and of discipline in helping train the child's conscience (the super-ego) so the child will act in ways acceptable to society.

Implicit in Freudian theory is a concern about overstrictness in childrearing. Too much punishment can have traumatic results which may be felt throughout the rest of one's life. Freud emphasized that parental love was a vital element in the personality development of the child. Growing up is a matter of living through and leaving behind these successive phases of life. Understanding and tolerance as well as discipline are needed on the part of the parents in order to see the child through these stages successfully.

Erikson: A psychosocial theory

Like Freud, Erikson (1963; 1968) sees the child moving through a natural sequence of stages, each of which must be properly adjusted to and assimilated. Erikson also attributes certain personality problems in later life to an unsatisfactory working out of or adjustment to an earlier stage of development.

Erikson identifies eight overlapping stages of life as being critical in human psychosocial development. The first five stages, similar to Freud's, carry one from infancy through adolescence, and thus are most relevant for our consideration here. Each stage involves a "crisis" which must be resolved successfully if the next stage is to be reached and its crisis resolved. In each stage there is a struggle between existing negatives and positives which must be resolved adequately, if not completely. Here are Erikson's first five stages of life.

Infancy: Trust versus mistrust.   The first "task" of the infant is to develop a basic sense of trust in himself and in his environment, a confidence that the world is a safe place in which to live. This basic sense of trust derives from proper parental care of a quality that transmits a sense of trustworthiness and goodness. There is a danger, especially in the second half of the first year of life, that discontinuities in care may lead the infant to develop a sense of mistrust. This mistrust could last throughout life. Thus the first year of life is crucial to later personality development.

Early childhood: Autonomy versus shame and doubt.   As the child commences to mature physically it begins to experiment with "holding on and letting go," with looking around and reaching, which are important in developing a sense of being an autonomous or distinct person. Bowel and bladder control at this period are important in the child's developing feelings of autonomy. There is a danger in this period that the child may acquire a sense of shame and doubt if deprived of the opportunity to develop an autonomous will while learning responsibility from his or her bigger, stronger parents.

Play age: Initiative and imagination versus guilt.   This stage begins about the time the child commences to walk freely and communicate. It is a period of high activity, avid curiosity, and fantasies. The parents have new responsibilities in dealing with the child's more complex behavior and endless questions. The child begins to develop a sense of conscience, which can lead to feelings of guilt and anxiety if the child feels unable to live up to parental expectations. This crisis must be successfully resolved so the child will not develop a deep conviction that he or she is essentially bad, and also have its initiative and imagination stifled.

School age: Industry versus inferiority.

This period corresponds to the Freudian period of sexual latency just before puberty. The child wants to learn how to make things and do things with others. One learns how to accept instruction and develops the capacity to work. The child seeks approval and recognition by producing things and doing good work. A danger in this period is that the child may develop a sense of inadequacy or inferiority if he or she does not receive recognition and approval for these efforts. This can result in laziness and indifference.

Adolescence: Identity versus identity diffusion.

In early adolescence comes the crisis of identity. The adolescent undergoes a "physiological revolution" at puberty, which forces the youth to redefine who he or she is. The difficult task here is to integrate earlier childhood identifications with the basic biological drives, one's native endowments, and the opportunities offered by social roles in one's groups. Erikson believes that the young person must develop a clear sense of what one is, where one belongs, and with whom. This is not always easy in a period of physical and psychological upheaval. The danger of an unclear sense of identity is that identity diffusion may result in a permanent inability to "take hold" of some clear conception of what one is in life. Many delinquents, dropouts, and runaways are apt to be confused about or dissatisfied with their identities, according to Erikson. The nonresolution of this identity crisis can be of great concern to the parents of an adolescent.

Erikson believes that a successful passage through these five early stages of life will facilitate movement into and through the remaining stages of adulthood.

Piaget: A cognitive development theory

Piaget (1926; 1969) has been especially interested in how the growing child develops the ability to know and to think. He postulates a number of successive stages of cognitive development for the child, allowing for variations in the length of each stage.

The sensorimotor stage.

This first stage in the cognitive development of the child starts at birth and lasts until about the age of two. The emphasis here is on the biological basis of knowing. It is sensorimotor in that the learning is purely in terms of sensory and physical contact with things in the child's environment. Lacking language, the child cannot "think" about his world yet in any meaningful way. The child responds to various stimuli and learns to modify its behavior to fit the circumstances. As the child gains increasing knowledge of the language in the latter part of this stage its cognitive development will speed up considerably.

The preoperational stage. In this stage, which covers roughly age two to seven, the young child begins to accumulate images and forms intuitions about things and people. The youngster begins to learn symbolic thinking. The word "ball," for example, is first learned as being the round object the child plays with, then later as standing for any such round object. With their increased command of the language, children at this stage become capable of thinking about objects in general, whether or not a specific object is actually present.

The concrete operational stage. From about age 7 to 12 the thinking of most children is still largely tied to the concrete world; for example, they learn to count and classify objects by size, length, and weight. The child can now perform various kinds of operations related to the size, weight, quantity, and speed of concrete objects in the physical world.

The formal operational stage. By about age 11 or 12 the child develops the ability to think and reason in increasingly abstract terms. It is now possible to understand and think in terms of various theories, abstract concepts, and generalizations not tied to the immediate environment. The intellectual development in this stage enables the youth to reason logically from premises to conclusions, and to use general rules to solve various classes of problems. Individuals differ in the degree in which they develop in this stage; some never progress much beyond the concrete operational stage and thus have great difficulty in understanding abstract ideas. This can be true of those children who have had little exposure to formal thinking or intellectual stimulation in their social environment, such as may be the case in some lower class families.

In sum, behavioral and social scientists in the 20th century have paid ever-increasing attention to the child, its development, upbringing, and welfare. How have the theories of these behavioral scientists been translated into recommendations for parents in rearing their children? Let us next review briefly the development of professional advice on child care and rearing in contemporary America.

PROFESSIONAL ADVICE ON CHILDREARING: VIEWS OF THE EXPERTS

How may parents best guide their children through their various stages of development? There now exists a plethora of literature on the subject of infant care and childrearing. Professional advice to parents abounds in newspapers, magazines, books, and other media, based on various theories, old and new. In middle-class circles especially a kind of cult of "scientific" childrearing has grown up in recent decades. Parent education has become a big thing. Highly educated American parents, eager to do what is right and best for their children, are now apt to place more trust in the scientific experts than in the traditional but nonscientifically based methods of their parents or grandparents.

However, the experts do not always agree as to what is right or best in childrearing; and as theories change, the practices recommended by the experts are apt to change too, sometimes in a cyclical fashion. For example, the United States government publication *Infant Care*, first brought out in 1914, has gone through numerous revisions since, some of which represent remarkable changes in advice to parents (Gordon, 1968). In a way these changes suggest the swinging of a pendulum from one position to its opposite (Kephart, 1977, p. 423). To illustrate: In the 1920s and 1930s, thumb-sucking by an infant was considered a dangerous impulse which parents had to curb; in the 1940s, parents were advised that such thumb-sucking was really harmless. In the 1950s, parents were cautioned by experts that too much coddling or pampering of a young child could result in the child becoming a "tyrant" (Wolfenstein, 1953); in the 1960s, the pendulum swung the other way with *Infant Care* now taking a permissive position on such things as pampering, toilet training, and weaning (Gordon, 1968).

One reason that childrearing advice varies so much is that a comprehensive and agreed-upon body of scientifically based knowledge about children and childrearing has yet to materialize (Kephart, 1977, p. 424; LeMasters, 1974, pp. 33–39). This doesn't necessarily mean that the advice of the experts is without value. It certainly can be argued that the overall effects of parent education are quite beneficial. There is little doubt that parents are now better informed than before in matters of child health ranging from nutrition to polio immunization to proper dental care. Parents have become more aware of the specific problems involved with child behavior, and what the leading scholars are saying about controversial matters. Parents may thus gain new insights not otherwise attainable which can be helpful in handling their particular child.

Permissive approach versus restrictive approach to childrearing

Much of early vacillation in professional advice to parents was due to different and often competing philosophies on childrearing. Two such philosophies, known as the "restrictive school" and the "permissive school" represented two opposite viewpoints on one of the most important issues in childrearing: how much freedom should be accorded the growing child?

The restrictive school, based on the more traditional position that the child must be firmly controlled for its own good and the good of society, advocated parental strictness and authoritarian parent-child relations (Mogey, 1957). This viewpoint held that the child's personality development depends more on character building and respect for others than on freedom of expression. It was also believed that during infancy such practices as extensive fondling and caressing of the child tended to result in a spoiled child. Permissiveness was seen as encouraging a lack of self-control and lack of respect for the rights of others. While advocates of the restrictive approach did not reject parental affection, they held that descipline and respect were paramount. Restrictive-oriented parents would be more apt to show their love for their children through inculcating them with the values of responsibility, respect, and order, rather than catering to their immediate whims or impulses.

The permissive school came to the fore about mid-20th century. Advocates of this philosophy generally share the viewpoint that the early years of the child's life (birth to age five) are crucial to its personality development and will thus have lasting consequences throughout the rest of life. Most adult personality and behavioral problems are seen as caused by an unhappy childhood, especially by unhappy relations between the child and its parents. While advocates of this permissive school do not reject child discipline altogether, they emphasize the importance of love, understanding, greater freedom, and the satisfaction of the growing child's needs. There is far more reliance on "psychological" methods of discipline than on physical punishment or threats (Bronfenbrenner, 1961). It is held that if the child develops without frustrations in a loving relationship with its parents, he or she will normally become a conforming, affectionate, and productive person.

Since the 1940s the general trend in America has been away from the older restrictive approach toward the newer, more flexible permissive approach. While middle-class parents were generally first to adopt the permissive philosophy, there is some evidence that its influence has also been felt in working-class families too (Bronfenbrenner, 1958).

Which of these approaches is better? Scientifically, it is impossible to say. There have been studies that challenged certain assertions made by the permissive school advocates to the effect that specific infant training practices, such as early toilet training and weaning, will determine later personality development of the individual (Sewell, 1952; Lindesmith & Strauss, 1950). This does not mean that other kinds of early childhood experiences may not have significant effects on personality development, of course. Many child-care experts now seem to be seeking a middle way, trying to combine the best of both the restrictive and the permissive approaches. In his well-known *Baby and Child Care,* Spock (1957) advised parents to take a relaxed but still firm approach toward the raising of their children. He emphasized that a loving attitude, coupled with a solid understanding of the physical aspects of child care, are more important than strict parental adherence to any program of specific childrearing techniques. "Good-hearted parents who aren't afraid to be firm when necessary can get good results with either moderate strictness or moderate permissiveness" (Spock, 1957, p. 46).

Other experts, such as Salk and Kramer, stress the personal needs of both the parents and the child, and the value of emotional and physical contact in parent-child relations. The real job of the parents is seen as stimulating the child's development in ways conducive to maximizing the capacity to deal effectively with the environment in which the child lives, "to grow up able to love, to learn, to work, and eventually to be a good parent himself" (Salk & Kramer, 1969).

HOW CHILDREN LEARN FROM PARENTS

What are some of the ways and means parents have at their disposal for guiding their children toward maturity and independence in later life? As Blood and Blood (1978, p. 455) note, while parental love lays the foundation for the child's social development, if parents did no more than provide love, their children would probably never grow up, remaining dependent and immature. So, what else can parents do beyond giving their children plenty of love?

For one thing, parents can present themselves as models for their children. The examples parents set by their everyday behavior have a powerful effect on the growing child. Bandura (1964) found that parental modeling was more important than reinforcement in enabling children to learn new behavior. Daily parental behavior gives the child a picture of what it is expected to learn, of how it is expected to act.

Parents also may set standards for their children. In addition to learning from the examples the parents present, children also learn from what their parents tell them about what is right and wrong, what is appropriate and inappropriate behavior. As noted above, excessive permissiveness on the part of parents may deprive the child of needed standards and norms, while high standards, kindly but firmly set by the parents, provide the child with a favorable climate for personal and social development. Baumrind (1966) found that kind but firm parental discipline helped to prevent children from becoming delinquent, while too much laxity or too much strictness were associated with higher rates of delinquency.

Consistency on the part of the parents helps the growing child to understand and accept the standards; confusion may arise if parents vacillate from one day to the next, if the father and the mother present contradictory norms and expectations, or if one parent is strict and the other is permissive. Peck (1958) found that children whose parents were consistent in their control had stronger egos, stronger consciences, and showed a greater willingness to conform to social norms.

Parents can also help their children learn and develop favorably by reasoning with them, by taking a rational rather than an authoritarian approach to childrearing. When a child asks a parent why he or she

Farmer's son learns from watching his father

U.S.D.A. photo by Jonathan Wright

Son helps mother haul sacks of cranberries

U.S.D.A. photo by Earl Otis

must do something, the busy parent may take the easy way out and respond, "Because I say so." This response may or may not resolve the immediate issue, but there is evidence that taking the time to reason with and explain to the child pays off in the long run. Sears et al. (1957) found that parental reasoning promoted the development of conscience in kindergarten children. Nye (1958) found that parents of nondelinquent teenagers more often explained to them the reasons for any behavior required and for any punishment administered than did parents of delinquent teenagers. Coopersmith (1967) found that grade-school boys were more apt to hold themselves in high esteem if their mothers granted the boys the right to question the thinking of the parent and the right to express their own opinion on family issues and decisions. An atmosphere of mutual respect between parents and children helps create children who have self-respect. By the time they are adolescents, children seem to need a considerable amount of autonomy if they are to mature into self-reliant adults (Rehberg et al., 1970). This all suggests that families with a democratic rather than an authoritarian orientation probably provide the more favorable atmosphere for the child development.

It is obvious that there are many different kinds of parents with many different views of how to bring up children. Some of these different views are due to individual and personality factors; others reflect the various social and cultural backgrounds of the parents. As noted earlier, significant differences in definitions of parenthood may be found among various ethnic, religious, and social class groups. Let us look briefly at some of these differences in parenthood and parent-child relations in the various social classes in America.

PARENTHOOD AND SOCIAL CLASS

The differences between social class family patterns in America are not as great or as distinct as in many other, older societies. Class differences in parenthood from one social class to another are not clear-cut, and the trend is probably toward greater similarities. However, there is some evidence of differences in childrearing practices and parental values.

Most of the research on childrearing and parent-child relations has dealt with middle-class, working-class, and lower-class families. However, some evidence exists that aristocratic families share certain views about children and their upbringing that are distinctive.

UPPER-CLASS CHILDREARING AND PARENT-CHILD RELATIONS

It should be pointed out that by "upper class" we mean essentially the "old aristocrats" rather than the "new rich." The former have a more tradition-oriented, distinctive lifestyle which is reflected in their conceptions of parenthood, while the latter still tend to define parenthood along middle-class lines (Dyer, 1979, p. 210).

Children are very important to upper-class families, representing the next generation to carry on the illustrious family name and traditions. Sons, accordingly, are especially desired. The proper upbringing of children is thus a matter of great concern to upper-class families. The values and traditions of the upper class itself, as well as those of the particular family, are impressed on the growing sons and daughters in daily living through family rituals and customs (Amory, 1947).

Parental surrogates are given much of the responsibility of the actual daily care and rearing of aristocratic children. There are nurses and governesses in early childhood, tutors and counselors later. Adolescents, especially sons, may spend a good deal of time away from home in boarding schools, camps, and preparatory schools, before going on to an Ivy League university. Franklin D. Roosevelt, for example, was sent off to Groton preparatory school after having had a series of nurses, governesses and tutors during his boyhood at Hyde Park (Gunter, 1950). As these adult intermediaries intrude between parents and children, some children may come to develop not only great affection but also strong emotional dependence upon a favorite nurse or governess. This can weaken the bond between the child and its parents (Cavan, 1969, p. 94). The many business, political, and social responsibilities of upper-class parents seem to make it necessary for them to have such help in rearing their children (Wakeford, 1967).

LeMasters (1974, pp. 83–84) points out that in spite of their many economic and social advantages, upper-class parents in America are prone to have certain problems in their relations with their children.

1. The "shadow of the ancestor" may haunt the children of illustrious forebears. Children and also grandchildren of famous people, realizing they cannot match the famed one's achievements, may have problems of trying to achieve some sort of self-identity other than being the son or grandson of the great man or woman. Some of Winston Churchill's children had this problem, as did those of Eleanor and Franklin Roosevelt (Lash, 1971).

2. Parents of great prominence and wealth generally have a problem of not spoiling their children, of keeping them level-headed. There also may be a related problem of motivating sons and daughters to "do something" in the world, which is not easy for children who already have more than most other people will achieve in their lifetime.

3. Upper-class parents and their children often face problems of constant exposure to the public limelight, of the glare of publicity in their daily lives. This can make normal parent-child relations difficult. Such people as Jacqueline Kennedy Onassis have been known to complain bitterly about being constantly hounded by reporters and photographers.

MIDDLE-CLASS CHILDREARING AND PARENT-CHILD RELATIONS

The middle class in America is a large, complex grouping with some internal variations in childrearing practices; however, numerous norms and practices tend to be rather widespread throughout the middle class in general. For example, there is evidence that middle-class parents tend to be both more supportive and regulative, that they are more likely to train their children by using reason and appealing to guilt, and are less likely to use physical punishment than working- and lower-class parents (Walters & Stinnett, 1971, p. 95). Middle-class parents pay more attention to the advice of experts on child care and training; they tend to see childrearing as more problematic than do most working-class parents (LeMasters, 1975). Middle-class parents regard it of prime importance for the growing child to learn to decide for itself how to behave, and that the child have personal resources upon which to base its decisions (Kohn & Carroll, 1960). Middle-class parents try to convey to their children norms and values leading to receptive conformity toward adults and individual autonomy toward other children (Emmerich & Smoller, 1964).

Middle-class children are more likely than working-class or lower-class children to see their parents as successful, smart, ambitious, and secure (Rosen, 1964). Middle-class parents normally expect their children to acquire adequate social skills, to be self-reliant and ambitious, to defer gratification, and to be respectable (Cavan, 1969, p. 122).

As noted earlier, in recent decades there has been a general trend toward permissiveness in America which has generally been led by middle-class parents (Bronfenbrenner, 1958). A study by Miller and Swanson (1958) showed the connection between this permissive trend and various middle-class attitudes. They observed that the way in which the family is integrated into the social class system has a major influence on the childrearing philosophy of the parents. Especially important is how the values and interests of the parents are molded by the economic structure in which the father works. The traits and behavior which are valued and rewarded at work are carried over into the home and are emphasized in childrearing. The parents then evaluate their children the same way they judge themselves, in keeping with the values and expectations derived from their world of work. Miller and Swanson (1958) see American society as moving from an earlier, middle-class orientation of an "individualistic-entrepreneurial" nature, in which excessive competition and risk taking was emphasized, toward a new, middle-class "welfare-bureaucratic" orientation in which cooperativeness and fitting into the organization are emphasized. As more and more middle-class fathers—and mothers now too—have such employment experiences, they tend to convey to

314

Old-world patterns of childrearing are still the custom in some families

their children the values of cooperativeness and of getting along with other people. These attitudes and values tend to encourage permissiveness in childrearing.

Kohn (1977) found that middle-class parental values tended to differ from those of the working-class. Middle-class mothers, for example, valued self-control, considerateness, and happiness in their children, while working-class mothers were more likely to value neatness, cleanliness, and obedience. Furthermore, middle-class parents stress the development of internal standards of conduct in their children, and are thus likely to discipline a child on the basis of the parent's interpretation of the child's motive for a particular act. This perception differs from that of the working-class parent, who is more likely to react and discipline on the basis of the perceived consequences of the child's behavior. That is, working-class parents are more apt to punish the child when its behavior is seen as annoying, disobedient, or destructive. For example, if a child spills his milk at the table the working-class parent would be more apt to react to this as wasteful, and possibly as destructive to the furniture, while a middle-class parent would try to find out whether it was merely an accident or perhaps a willful act to get back at the parent. Gecas and Nye (1974) found evidence to corroborate Kohn's findings. They found middle-class parents reacting differently toward a child who "intentionally disobeyed" as compared to a child who "accidently breaks something." This distinction was not generally made by working-class parents.

Why these social class differences in childrearing? Kohn (1977) finds the answer in differences in parental values which are rooted in the different types of occupations of the parents. Middle-class white-collar occupations are characterized by an emphasis on self-direction, individual initiative, and facility in working with ideas; whereas working-class occupations are characterized by obedience, manipulating things rather than working with ideas, and group orientation. These occupational conditions, in turn, foster conformity in the working class as opposed to the self-direction of the middle class. The value of self-direction helps create the ideal image of the child who is curious, self-controlled, and thinks for himself; the value of conformity creates an image of a child who is obedient, neat, and cooperative. In stressing these different values, parents in each class are essentially preparing their children to cope with the world as the parents see it. White-collar parents, accordingly, stress the development of internal controls, while blue-collar parents try to develop external standards in their children. Other studies have tended to support Kohn's thesis (Franklin & Scott, 1970; Wright & Wright, 1976).

As indicated earlier, some differences may be found within the middle class itself in definitions of parenthood. This should not be surprising, since the middle class is so large and encompasses a wide range of white-collar occupational groups. It is a long way from a drugstore clerk to a surgeon, yet both of these occupations are apt to be found in the middle class. The former would probably be in the lower middle class; the latter would have upper-middle-class status.

Bronfenbrenner (1961) found that lower-middle-class boys get more punishment from parents than do girls, who get more attention and warmth. These differences tend to be reduced in upper-middle-class families where direct discipline of boys drops off and indulgence and protectiveness of girls decreases. Upper-middle-class boys run risks of being "over-socialized," thus losing some of their capacity for independent accomplishment. Girls in the upper middle class tend to excel boys in such things as responsibility and social acceptance. In the lower middle class, boys tend to surpass girls on such traits as competitiveness, levels of aspirations, and leadership (Walters & Stinnitt, 1971).

Lower-middle-class parents tend to be ambitious for their children, pushing them toward college even though the parents themselves may not be college graduates. If the children succeed in moving up the social class ladder the family may suffer from "differential social mobility" (LeMasters, 1954; Dyer, 1972). That is, as the upwardly mobile become socialized into their new social class, they may leave their less successful siblings and their parents behind. This can produce strains among kinfolk.

While parents at the bottom of the middle class may suffer certain economic and social disadvantages, those at the top occupy one of the most comfortable positions in the American class system. Most are highly educated professional or business executives with comfortable or even affluent incomes. Parents can give their children many advantages, homes in the best neighborhoods, choices of good colleges, and in general help prepare them for life in our competitive society. The parents cannot, however, assure their children a position in the upper middle class. While their sons and daughters have a head start over lower-middle-class youth, upper-middle-class sons and daughters must as adults study and work to achieve this position themselves, just as their parents did before them.

WORKING-CLASS AND LOWER-CLASS CHILDREARING AND PARENT-CHILD RELATIONS

We have already noted some of the differences between working-class and middle-class practices in childrearing and parent-child relations. Middle-class parents tend to be more permissive, emphasize internal standards of conducts, and use verbal reprimands, while working-class parents tend to stress conformity, cleanliness, and are more apt to use physical punishment (Kohn, 1977; Gecas & Nye, 1974). While such differences have been found, it should be pointed out that in recent decades there is evidence that working-class parents are tending to become more permissive, thus moving in the same direction as the middle class, though more slowly and unevenly (Bronfenbrenner, 1958; Gecas & Nye, 1974).

Certain differences in views of parenthood and childrearing practices have been observed between working-class families (where the father has a well-paying skilled manual job) and families at the very bottom of the class hierarchy, variously called lower class, or lower-lower class, or those living below the poverty line (Warner, 1960; Harrington, 1963). These parents face great disadvantages in trying to bring up their children. Low-paying, unskilled jobs, high rates of unemployment, poor housing, and greater health problems all add up to chronic stress which make normal parent-child relations difficult (Rainwater, 1960; LeMasters, 1974). Parents face almost insuperable problems in rearing their children properly, regardless of their strong devotion to them. With their generally low education, meager job skills, and low incomes, it is hard for parents, especially fathers, to keep the respect of their growing children. Discipline tends to be more authoritarian and harsh than in working-class and middle-class families. In spite of their overwhelming disadvantages, many lower-class parents do manage to bring their children up successfully, sacrificing for them, and encurging them to study and work hard to improve their lot in life (Rodman, 1964: Hill, 1971).

Working-class parents, with better incomes from more stable, skilled jobs (for instance, in construction, plumbing, and manufacturing), are

Parental encouragement has helped Heidi win first prize at the State Fair

U.S.D.A. photo by Gordon Baer

generally in a better economic and social position to bring up their children successfully. The families are able to live in better neighborhoods and the children go to better schools. However, in spite of these real advantages over lower-class parents, working-class mothers and fathers may face certain problems in raising their children. For one thing, the proportion of mothers employed outside the home tends to be high, which creates the problem of providing adequate care for the young children—and adolescents too—after school when both parents are still at work. For another thing, the generation gap problem may be greater here than in middle-class families. Working-class parents are apt to be holding onto older, more traditional values and norms while their children, with more education, are caught up in recent changes as they look toward jobs and life in the middle class (LeMasters, 1974, pp. 76–78).

There is evidence that working-class mothers and fathers differ in their views of how to bring up their children, and in their aspirations for their sons and daughters. The mother, in lower-middle-class occupation's such as sales clerk or hairdresser, has more daily exposure to middle-class people and values, while the father, perhaps a construction worker or truck driver, lives a more isolated daily life in the male blue-collar world of work. As LeMasters (1975, p. 111) found in his study of construction workers, the father wants to bring his son up to be like him, to live by the traditional "male code" which emphasizes physical strength, "guts," and "the ability to handle women." The mothers, however, who read magazine articles on childrearing and who watch middle-class soap operas on TV, want something different for their sons, such as a higher education and a white-collar career. They want their sons to become good husbands and fathers, to spend more time with their families than their fathers do. LeMasters (1975, p. 114) found that working-class fathers and mothers disagree less on the proper way to bring up their daughters. The fathers believe the girls need less education than the boys (the mothers may disagree with them on this point). The men think that most of what a girl needs to know can be learned at home from her mother, who is best able to prepare the daughter for her future roles of wife and mother. The mothers want their daughters to be "nice girls" who will grow up to be good wives and mothers. Mothers believe that their daughters need a good education, or at least training in some practical

Poor parents are often at a disadvantage in rearing their children

E. D. Dyer

skill such as typing or nursing, so they will not be completely dependent on their husbands for their livelihood.

LeMasters (1975, pp. 115–116) concludes that some of the views of parenthood and practices in childrearing adhered to by these working-class fathers were in marked contrast to those of middle-class parents. (1) These fathers expect strict obedience from their children. (2) They rely on traditional methods in rearing their children. They believe that love and firm discipline will produce a "good kid." (3) They have little respect for the professional experts on childrearing. (4) These men do not want the husband-wife relationship to be sacrificed to the child-mother relationship. If there is a conflict between the woman's role of wife and her role of mother, the wife role should come first.

It can be argued that these working-class men represent an anachronism in late 20th-century America, holdouts of 19th-century male-centered, patriarchal views of parenthood who are doing their best to resist modern, middle-class changes. They are probably fighting a losing battle. It is likely that despite the efforts of their fathers, most of these sons and daughters will move toward the prevailing middle-class orientation, desired by their mothers.

CURRENT ISSUES IN PARENTHOOD

Viewpoints and practices in childrearing and parent-child relations in America are influenced by the historical and cultural diversity of American people and by the forces of social, economic, and ideological change. Many of the problems confronting parents today—such as the rapid increase in the employment of mothers and the related problem of adequate child care while both parents are away at work—relate directly to these forces of change. Increasing divorce rates have brought on more single-parent families. The reduction of the stigma toward birth out of wedlock has accentuated the issue of the unmarried parent and his or her child. Let us now turn our attention to some of these present-day issues in parenthood.

EMPLOYED MOTHERS AND THEIR CHILDREN

In our earlier discussion of marriage and occupational roles it was noted that the recent increases in married women in the labor force is resulting in more mothers being separated from their children during the workday. (See Table 13–1.) U.S. government figures for 1978 showed that more than 12.5 million employed married women had children under age 18 living at home (U.S. Bureau of the Census, 1979a). And 53.7 percent of the working mothers in intact marriages had children ranging from age 6 to 17, while 37.4 percent had children under the age of 6 (U.S.

Table 13–1

Employment status of married women by age of youngest child, 1978

Age of youngest child	Women employed outside the home (percent)*
Less than 1 year	29.0
1 Year	33.7
2 Years	41.0
3 Years	44.4
4 Years	42.0
5 Years	49.8
6 or more Years	56.9
Total	50.9

* Percent of all married women, aged 18–34, husband present.
Source: "Fertility of American Women," U.S. Bureau of the Census, *Population Characteristics,* June, 1978.

Department of Labor, 1976a, p. 22). With so many mothers now spending a large part of each workday away from home, questions inevitably arise as to the care and rearing of their children. Does the employment of the mother result in maternal deprivation for her children? Are the children of working mothers less well developed and less well adjusted than children of nonemployed mothers? In spite of considerable interest in these questions there has not yet been much empirical research on them, especially in the effects of maternal employment on very young children (Cohen, 1978). Somewhat more attention has been paid to the possible effects on older children.

Most of the earlier studies (prior to 1960) focused on the concept of "maternal deprivation" (Spitz, 1945; Bowlby, 1951). Did maternal employment result in maternal deprivation? The results of these early studies were inconsistent and unclear. They did seem to indicate that maternal employment was not a clear case of maternal deprivation; that the effects of the mother's employment on her children were not simple and direct but rather complex and entangled with numerous other factors. This led subsequent researchers to try to locate and control for some of these other factors. Hoffman (1961) suggested that the effects of maternal employment on children would differ from one social class to another, and also vary according to the mother's attitude toward her employment, and furthermore would differ according to the adequacy and quality of the substitute care the child received while the mother is at work. Hoffman's research (1963) showed that children aged 8 to 11 of employed mothers who liked their jobs were less rebellious and aggressive toward other children than were children of mothers who did not like their jobs. She concluded that a positive attitude toward her work role was a significant factor in sustaining a warm and satisfying mother-child relationship. More recent studies have supported Hoffman's conclusions. Harrell and Ridley (1975) found a positive correlation between maternal work satisfaction and the quality of the mother-child interaction. They conclude that when an employed mother finds her outside job personally satisfying she tends to be happier in general, which in turn helps her to be a more enthusiastic and effective mother.

In a comparison of infants of employed and unemployed mothers, Hock (1976) found that during the first year of life there was no difference between the two groups in the quality of the mother-child interaction. Cohen (1978) also compared mother-child interaction in two comparable groups, one where the mother was employed and another where she was not. The subjects were observed in a semilaboratory situation. All the children were in their 21st month of life. She found no difference between the two groups of mothers in positive or negative attentiveness toward the child. There was some difference between the two groups in the child's responses to the mother, and in the child's cognitive functioning, with the children of the employed mothers responding less adequately. More study is needed, however, before it can be stated with confidence just what the effects of maternal employment are on very young children and their development.

Gold and Andres (1978) found that the child's cognitive performance and its sex-role concepts are related to maternal employment, but more so for preteenage than for teenage children. Based on earlier studies (Douvan, 1963; McCord, McCord & Thurber, 1963), which had shown that delinquency of youth was greater in families where the mother was employed than where the mother was not employed, Gold and Andres (1978) compared two groups of teenaged children (aged 14 to 16), one whose mothers had jobs and the other whose mothers did not. Their hypothesis was that the children of employed mothers would have more academic problems and personal adjustment problems. Their findings, on the contrary, showed that both sons and daughters of employed mothers were better adjusted. The researchers believe that this was probably due to less restrictive childrearing attitudes in the families of employed mothers, greater paternal activity, and the greater satisfaction with the mother role reported by mothers who were employed. They conclude that maternal employment is probably a much less salient factor in the development and adjustment of adolescent children than in that of younger children.

Substitute parents: Day care

As suggested above, the manner in which children of employed mothers are cared for while the parents are at work can be important in the development and adjustment of the children, especially the very young. Rossi (1964) stressed the importance of the young child's being lovingly cared for by a parent surrogate while the mother is at work. Harrell and Ridley (1975) found that when working mothers are satisfied with the quality of the substitute child care provided by good day-care centers, they were both more relaxed and satisfied in their jobs, and this was beneficial to the quality of their interactions with their children.

There has been a good deal of public interest in recent years in the availability and quality of substitute child care. What are the effects of day care on the child, and on mother-child relations? Here again, the existing research does not provide clear and consistent answers. Although studies have increased in recent years, most investigations have been conducted in high-quality day-care centers, which are not really representative of the great variety of facilities and personnel found throughout America (Belsky & Steinberg, 1978). Most studies have been limited to the direct effects of the day-care experience on the child, with little or no attention to the broader issues of the impact of day care on the parents or the family.

From a careful review of more than 40 studies on day care, Belsky and Steinberg (1978) summarize the main findings of the effects of day care on the child.

1. With regard to the child's intellectual development, in general, day care has neither beneficial nor deleterious effects. For children from economically disadvantaged backgrounds, however, day-care experiences tend to reduce the declines in IQ frequently found in youngsters from this background.

2. With regard to the child's emotional development, the evidence indicates that day care is not disruptive to the emotional bond with the mother, even when day care is started in the first years of life. Also, there is no indication that day-care experiences decrease the child's preference for its real mother in comparison with mother-substitutes at the day-care center.

3. With respect to the child's social development, studies indicate that, when compared to other age-mates reared at home, day-care-reared children do interact more with their peers in both positive and negative ways. Some evidence suggests that children enrolled in day-care centers for extended periods show increased aggression toward their peers and toward adults.

Belsky and Steinberg (1978, p. 946) conclude that the present state of our knowledge regarding day care is "grossly inadequate in assessing the overall impact . . . upon the child, his parents, and the society in which he lives." More and better studies are needed on the differential consequences of center-based day care, of family day care, of care by relatives in the child's home, and of care at home by nonrelatives.

SINGLE PARENTS

Even though the number of people living in the one-parent families represents a relatively small proportion of the total population, this number still is large and increasing. Glick (1979a) reports that in 1978 about 19 percent of the 63 million children 18 years old and under were living with only one parent. The comparable figure for 1960 was only 9 percent. A breakdown of the 1978 figure of 19 percent showed 17 percent of the children living with their mothers and the remaining 2 percent living with their fathers. Two thirds of these children were living with a divorced or separated parent and one third with a widowed or never-married parent. Since 1960, the number of children aged 18 and under living with a separated parent had doubled, those living with a divorced parent had tripled, and those living with a never-married parent had increased sevenfold. The number living with a widowed parent had declined by 20 percent. Three times as many black children as white children were living with a single parent. (See Figure 13–1.)

It should be emphasized that most of these one-parent families are only temporary arrangements, as indicated by the high remarriage rates and the fact that most never-married parents with children at home will get married sooner or later. Thus most children who are living with one parent only are in a transition period between two successive two-parent families.

A number of recent social and economic changes have contributed to the great increase in one-parent families. Expanding educational and employment opportunities for women and the removal of many traditional restrictions on freedom of action for women, along with rising divorce, desertion, and illegitimacy rates, have swelled the ranks of one-parent families. More unwed mothers are now opting to keep and raise their

Figure 13–1

Children aged 18 and under living in single-parent households, 1960 and 1978

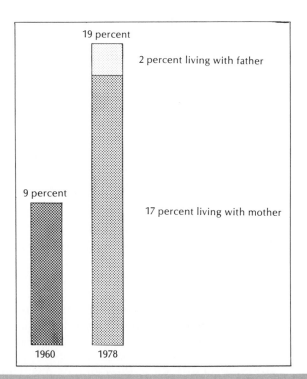

19 percent

2 percent living with father

9 percent

17 percent living with mother

1960   1978

Source: "Future American Families," by P. C. Glick, *Coalition of Family Organizations Memo,* Summer/Fall, 1979.

children themselves rather than put them up for adoption. And liberalized adoption laws now make it easier for single and divorced women and men to adopt children and establish a home for them without the presence of a marriage partner (Schorr & Moen, 1979).

The single-parent family has long been viewed by the general public as something of a social problem (Burgess, 1970). These families have been variously labeled "broken homes," "unstable," and "disorganized." While the problems and demands confronting the single parent are many and real enough—such as being both mother and father, being sole family provider, and being the homemaker, all at the same time—these families still often face a society which looks upon the single parent as somewhat different from other parents, and tends to isolate these families "from the mainstream of their former socio-economic way of life" (Burgess, 1970, p. 140). The assumption that single-parent families breed pathological conditions which have harmful effects on children has been widely challenged (Savage et al., 1978; English, 1974; Hill, 1971; LeMasters, 1974). Many authorities now agree that the alleged negative aspects of the one-parent family have been exaggerated, and that one good parent can probably do a better job at childrearing than two parents with serious marital conflicts (Burgess, 1970; LeMasters, 1974).

Mothers without fathers

Since, as noted above, the great majority of single parents are mothers, let us first examine parenthood and parent-child relations from the point of view of the single mother.

LeMasters (1974, pp. 141–144) identifies a number of general characteristics of mothers without marriage partners.

Reduced financial circumstances. They tend to be poorer than two-parent families, and experience more financial stress (Goode, 1956; Bernard, 1964). Divorced, deserted, and widowed mothers are likely to experience a considerable drop in income. These reduced financial resources almost invariably affect the personal well being of these women and their children.

Role-conflicts and overloads. Since mothers without partners have to add the father role to their mother role, they face the problem of being overloaded, or in conflict over their various role commitments. And since many of these mothers are employed outside the home, their work hours may conflict with those of the school system; they may have to remain at work several hours after their children are out of school in the afternoon. Being a mother, father, homemaker, family provider, and head of the household adds up to a heavy load of responsibilities.

Role-shifts and adjustments. As mentioned earlier, most single-parent family situations are temporary. Between 80 and 90 percent of

Mother and daughter alone

U.S.D.A. photo by Betsey Frampton

mothers without partners will remarry sometime. Thus they face not only the difficult task of taking on for a while the additional roles of father and head of the household, but also later having to relinquish these roles. For some this will be a relief, but for others such role shifting is not easy (Hill, 1949). Another difficult role shift is that of relinquishing the wife role upon divorce or death of the husband, then sooner or later assuming a new courtship role in anticipation of remarriage.

Ambivalent public attitudes.   Although such attitudes have softened somewhat in recent years, many American people still tend to regard mothers without partners as somewhat different, as somehow deviant. (The exception to this would be widows.) While partnerless mothers may receive sympathy and some help, they are also often viewed with ambivalence because they were unable to sustain their marriage, and thus are believed to be at least partly responsible that their children no longer have a father.

Social isolation and loneliness.   Smith (1980) has observed that loneliness and lack of social support are among the most serious social consequences of the single-parent status. This is apt to be especially true for single mothers. The spouse, the love-partner, has been taken away, and whether by divorce or death, the personal and emotional impact is essentially the same. Former friends, particularly those with intact marriages, tend to withdraw from the surviving partner. The early months and years are generally the most lonely and difficult. In England a national association of one-parent families called Gingerbread has recently been organized to assist single parents in reducing the loneliness and social isolation during the transition period (Smith, 1980, p. 76). Parents Without Partners in the United States offers similar assistance.

Fathers without mothers

Although there are far fewer of these families than mother-without-father families (see Figure 13–1), fathers trying to care for and rear children alone are also confronted with many problems and adjustments (Gasser & Taylor, 1976; Mendes, 1976; Orthner et al., 1976). These men must try to be both mother and father to their children, at the same time they are working in a full-time job to earn the family living. The award-winning movie *Kramer versus Kramer* dramatized the difficulty of trying to fill all these roles at once. When the father put his son's health and school needs first, thereby getting behind in his job, he was fired. While studies of father-only families are few, it seems likely that these fathers do experience many of the same role-conflict and overload problems single mothers do, plus some others. Unlike most single mothers, many fathers who have lost their wives will have to learn the role of home-manager, and learn how to perform many housekeeping tasks, how to prepare meals, and how to meet the daily physical and emotional needs of young children (Gasser & Taylor, 1976).

Men who have lost their mates suffer personal problems similar to those experienced by women who are without partners: loneliness, sorrow, a sense of failure among those who are divorced, some degree of social isolation, and changes in their style of life (Hetherington, et al., 1976). Again, the period is only temporary (although perhaps several years long), since most single fathers will eventually remarry.

The preceding discussion of problems and role adjustments of single parents may leave the impression that such families may be deficient if not pathological, and that negative consequences for children may result. We need to reiterate our initial statement that a good deal of evidence challenges this view. Bell (1979, pp. 419–420) reviews several studies that question the assumption that two parents are necessarily better than one. Kadushin (1968) reviewed a large number of studies in an attempt to determine whether the one-parent family was inherently pathological or dysfunctional. He concluded that "the association between single-parent familyhood and psychosocial pathology is neither strong nor invariable" (Kadushin, 1968, p. 40). Feldman and Feldman (1975b) found no significant difference in the adjustment of adolescents in father-absent families as compared to father-present families. Burgess (1970) concludes that good evidence indicates that children are better off with a single caring parent than with two parents who are unhappy or in serious conflict.

THE FUTURE OF PARENTHOOD

Urban-industrial developments over the past century have contributed to social and ideological changes which have materially affected parenthood and parent-child relations in America. In the expanding middle class especially, nuclear families have reduced their ties with their parental families, thus assuming virtually full responsibility for the care and rearing of their own children. At the same time, the man in the nuclear family, enwrapped in his career, has assumed less and less responsibility for the daily care and training of the children. This resulted in the mother's assuming most of the parental responsibilities, and the mother's role of chief parent gained ascendency (Parsons, 1959; LeMasters, 1971). Some authorities go so far as to say that the two most significant changes in the upbringing of American children in 100 years are the increasing role of the mother and the declining role of the father (Fullerton, 1972, p. 158).

The conventional division of roles in the American family has been pretty well taken for granted, at least until recently. It seemed logical for the wife and mother to care for and bring up the children while the father was away at work earning the family living. Now, however, under the influence of equalitarianism and women's liberation, and with the accelerated employment of mothers outside the home, and with concerns about revitalizing the role of the father, questions are being raised about the future of parenthood in America. What directions will it take? Given the prevailing secular, rational social trend in America, it seems likely that increasing numbers of parents will be amenable to suggestions for improving and enhancing their parental roles.

PROSPECTS FOR IMPROVING PARENTING

Suggestions from many sources are being made for improving the quality and efficacy of parental roles and parent-child relations. Most suggestions focus on the needs and welfare of the child, but some include improving the family itself via creating a more equitable division of responsibilities between the mother and the father. Let us now look at some of the proposals and programs being suggested.

Licensing parenthood

Some social scientists say it is time to consider licensing parenthood, just as we now license marriage. Feldman and Feldman (1977) have concluded that parenthood is too important and too difficult to be left randomly in the hands of rank amateurs. Mead (1966) advocated a two-stage marriage, each with a separate license. The first would license the couple to live together as husband and wife while the second, after some years of successful marriage, would license the now mature couple to have children. A married couple applying for a license for parenthood would be required to show themselves to be qualified to be parents, biologically, economically, and emotionally.

It is obvious that given our present American sentiments and norms regarding individual rights and freedom of choice that there is little likelihood in the near future that any state legislature will pass such restrictive legislation. Perhaps sometime in the distant future marriage partners will have to demonstrate their fitness to become parents, but certainly not in the immediate future.

More planned parenthood

Increasing emphasis on planned parenthood seems more feasible for the immediate future, even among the less educated and in religious groups which have traditionally been opposed to most birth control methods. Techniques of birth control are becoming more effective and convenient, and will continue to be more widely disseminated throughout the population. This trend, along with more abortions, means that there will be fewer unwanted children. When parents have only those children they plan for and are ready for, their chances of being good parents and for healthier and happier parent-child relations should increase (Duberman, 1977, p. 160; Bernard, 1964, p. 333).

Collective child care

Having some group or agency help with the care of children is widely practiced in many lands, and to some extent in the United States. With the increasing employment of mothers this trend will continue in America, though probably not to the extent found elsewhere. In the Soviet Union, for example, children's collectives were created in the 1950s to shift a major part of infant and child care from the parents to day nurseries (Meers & Marans, 1968). These centers care for children from the age of three months to seven years.

In Israel, collective communities called kibbutzim have for generations practiced collective infant and childcare and training, using trained nurses and teachers. The parents have little responsibility for the rearing of their children. The children actually live with other children and the adults operating the child centers, rather than living with their parents. Children spend some time in the evenings with their parents after working hours. The idea is to leave the more difficult problems of child care and discipline to the professionally trained and experienced nurses and teachers, while the parents, freed of such problems, can develop affectively close relations with their children. How have children raised this way turned out? Studies show that the consequences are generally positive. Rabkin and Rabkin

(1969) found that the intellectual and social development of children raised in kibbutzim to be superior to other Israeli children and to American children raised in conventional families.

In America there have been some experiments in collective or communal childrearing, such as the Oneida community in the 19th Century, and such current experiments as Harrad West in California. However, given our predominant value system, which emphasizes the right and responsibility of parents to care for and rear their own children, it seems unlikely that more than a small minority of American children will be exposed to such collective or communal care, at least in the near future.

More help for mothers

A number of practical and viable suggestions for improving parenting focus on providing more help and support for the often overloaded mother. Duberman (1977, p. 162) sees significant changes in this direction resulting from two major social trends: (1) the trend away from traditional sex-role diffentiation toward equality between men and women, and (2) the expanding role of public and private agencies in child care and rearing. More and more women are demanding liberation from the traditional roles of wife and mother and are seeking their identities in the labor market as men do. They want men, in turn, to share more in the responsibilities of parenting and homemaking.

As more women reject the maternal role in whole or in part, it becomes necessary to find adjuncts or substitutes to serve this maternal function. Such additional aids include a facility such as a day-care center, or a privately employed parent surrogate, a cooperative relative, or a father. A number of authorities are now emphasizing the importance of reintegrating the father into the modern American family (Benson, 1968; Duberman, 1977). In most cases the father is not expected to reverse roles completely with his wife (unless that is what they both want). Instead, he would assume a larger share of the child care and training responsibilities. It is argued that where fathers and mothers play more nearly equal roles in raising their children, all should benefit. Advocates of these views expect or hope that mothers will be relieved of full-time routines of parenting and be able to pursue other interests in the community. Fathers will be encouraged to play a more nurturant and expressive role in their relations with their sons and daughters. Children will benefit because they will have deeper relations with both parents (Farrell, 1975). Few would disagree that fathers should play active parental roles. Realistically, however, there is a price to pay, because transferring more parental responsibilities to fathers can, for most men, come only at the cost of some diminished commitment to their careers.

As for other possible mother substitutes or adjuncts, female relatives have served such a purpose for many years in the working and lower classes; and to some extent in the middle classes, in situations, for example, where the mother is employed and leaves her child with its grandmother during working hours. Toffler (1970), among others, has advocated the development of a group of specially trained "professional parents" in American communities to aid the biological parents in the care of their children during the day when both are at work. Such professional parents would have a certified degree in parenting. Their role would be to train, socialize, love, and help care for the children.

Day-care centers as parent surrogates have already been discussed. Some other countries, such as France and Sweden, have gone much further than the United States in providing day care for working parents. In the United States there has been considerable controversy surrounding the day-care movement, especially on the questions of public subsidies of day-care centers and on what the consequences of a more comprehensive day-care system would be (Angrist & Lave, 1973). Advocates believe that these expanded day-care facilities not only would ease the burden for employed mothers who now have the problem of obtaining adequate care for their children during working hours, but also would enhance the child's development. Critics fear that such parent-surrogate systems can undermine parental authority, diminish parental involvement with

Fathers as well as mothers have important roles in childrearing

Luis Medina Photo

their children, and be extremely costly to taxpayers (Bruce-Briggs, 1977). As seen in our earlier review of the effects of day-care experiences, studies show few ill effects on the child or on the parent-child relationship (Belsky & Steinberg, 1978). While more and better day-care centers would be a valuable aid for many working mothers, someone has to pay the price. Recent U.S. census figures showed that only about 4 percent of the children aged three to six of employed mothers to be enrolled in a day-care center (U.S. Bureau of the Census, 1978a). It is still much more common for working mothers to have their young children cared for during working hours by relatives or friends. In view of the high costs of quality day-care facilities and personnel, and due also to current political opposition, it is unlikely that the immediate future will witness a great expansion of publicly supported day-care programs (Angrist & Lave, 1973).

In sum, it seems likely that families in the future will be more carefully planned than they are today, and parenthood will become increasingly professionalized as more parents obtain higher education and seek the advice of experts in child care and childrearing. While the expanding middle class is in the forefront of these trends, other social classes are moving in the same direction.

Parents in the future will likely have a greater number of options open to them. While many mothers and fathers will continue to prefer the traditional ways of bringing up their children themselves, other parents may seek the help of "professional parent substitutes." Some parents will probably turn to nurseries and day-care centers, while others continue to look to grandparents, siblings, and friends for help during hours of employment. Overall, it seems likely that parent-child relations will become more flexible, informal, and relaxed (Dyer, 1979, p. 444).

CHAPTER 14

Kinship relations:
Relatives and in-laws

Marriage joins together a man and a woman who up to that point in their lives have normally been closely tied to their respective parental families. In America, despite pressures to be independent and self-reliant, most married partners will continue to be closely tied to and influenced by their respective families of orientation, especially by parents, who have cared for them and brought them up. In America today, even though conjugal ties are often emphasized over kin ties, most young adults do not terminate their relationships with their parents and siblings at marriage. It is those continuing ties and relations with relatives and in-laws that we are concerned with in this chapter.

How important are relatives and in-laws to American nuclear families? Is the nuclear family here considered a part of a larger extended family, as is the case in many other societies? What kinds of contacts and relations do the husband and wife and their children have with the couple's parents, siblings, and assorted grandparents, aunts, uncles, and cousins? How do Americans tend to look upon and relate to their inlaws? We shall explore these and other such questions in the present chapter. But first, in order to provide a background for an understanding of kinship in America, it is necessary to devote a little space to kinship in cross-cultural perspective.

KIN TIES AND RELATIONS

KINSHIP IN CROSS-CULTURAL PERSPECTIVE

In a great many preindustrial and nonindustrial societies, most human activities and relationships have been predicated upon kinship ties of one kind or another. As Adams (1980, p. 318) points out, both the personnel and the institutions of these traditional societies are embedded within the larger kinship unit. In traditional Confucian China, for example, the larger kin unit, called the Tsu, claimed the first loyalty of the individual, while obligations and loyalties to one's spouse were of secondary importance (Levy, 1949). This is in contrast to many modern urban-industrial societies where spousal ties and obligations come first and obligations to most kin may be minimal, as may be the case in many American middle-class families.

Cross-culturally, kin groups have performed a number of important societal functions, including (1) property holding and inheritance, (2) housing, (3) aid to members in times of need, and (4) the provision of affectional, emotional ties (Adams, 1980, p. 55). The first function, property holding and inheritance, is clearly a kinship function in societies where the productive land or other income-producing property is tied to the kinship lineage. This is in contrast to such societies as the American where an individual or a married couple would own and control their own property, and decide who will inherit how much of it and when.

The housing sharing and maintaining function may assume a number of different forms. In the Ibans tribes in Borneo, members of an extended kin group may all occupy a longhouse in which the men live apart from the women and children. In India, a joint family made up of adult brothers and their wives and children may share a dwelling. Among the Amish of Pennsylvania the aged parents live with one of their married sons or daughters and their children. In some societies the nuclear families composing the larger kin group live in separate residences adjacent to each other, or as close together as possible. The Amish have a tradition that relatives shall live no farther apart than a distance at which they can see the smoke from each other's chimneys (Loomis & Dyer, 1976, p. 15). While separate residence is generally the norm for contemporary American nuclear families, kin may share housing temporarily (Haller, 1961).

The aiding function is based on the normative expectation that kin are obliged to help each other in times of need. Such an obligation varies greatly from society to society and also within societies. In strongly familistic societies, one's kin obligations may be to parents and grandparents, to siblings, and even to aunts and uncles. The strongest sense of kin obligations in contemporary America appears to be between aging parents and their adult offspring (Adams, 1980, p. 320). Kin obligations in the United States vary from one social class to another, and are probably weakest in the middle class and strongest in the working and lower classes (Farber, 1971, p. 114).

The affectional or emotional function among kin members also varies considerably among societies. The focus and strength of affectional ties among kin may differ greatly. In societies where one kin line has close authority and control over the individual, his or her closest emotional ties may be with members of the other kin line. For example, in some patriarchal societies one's closest affectional ties are often with members of the mother's kin line (Goode, 1963). In America today, close affectional ties often continue between an adult and his or her aging parents, and to some extent between adult siblings, but less so among secondary kin.

Now let us look in more detail at kinship ties and relations in America.

KINSHIP IN AMERICA

Kinship in contemporary America generally plays a less important role than it did in our preindustrial past, when the family was the main economic productive unit. Under those conditions, the kin group was more important economically, and the individual and married couples came under more direct influence of relatives. Industrialization removed the productive function from the family, liberating the individual from economic dependence on the kinship group. Kin ties and relations thus have become more voluntary than compulsory. The significance of kin ties for Americans today has been said to reside "in visiting, in recreation, in exchanging of news and advice, in attendance on ceremonial occasions and at the crisis of life" (Queen & Habenstein, 1974, p. 341). True, the significance of kin ties and relationships today still varies a good deal from rural to urban communities, from one class to another, and among ethnic groups. The maintenance of close kin ties is very pronounced in some ethnic groups, such as Mexican-Americans, who tend to sustain their traditional familistic orientation.

Kinship terms

Each human society has a system of kinship terms which identify the statuses and roles composing the kinship system, and help define and regulate relations among kin folk (Murdock, 1949). The terms used in the American kinship system, derived largely from European cultural origins, manifest both the bilateral nature of kinship ties (normatively equal ties with both the wife's and the husband's kin), and the special importance attached to the nuclear family. Specifically: mother, father, son, daughter, brother, and sister (Fox, 1967). One of the interesting characteristics of the American kinship terminology is the wide variations of alternative terms used for the same individual, according to Schneider and Homans (1955, p. 1195). For instance, mother may be called "mother," "mama," "mom," "ma," "mummy," or by her first name, a diminutive, or a nickname. Father may be called "father," "papa," "pa," "pop," "dad," "daddy," or by his first name or a diminutive, or "old man." Schneider and Homans (1955) found that use of the more formal terms *mother* and *father* generally symbolized a more formal and less close relationship between the child and the parent. It was also found that females used a wider variety of terms for parents than did males; males are more likely than females to address aunts and uncles by their first names alone.

Farber (1971) found differences in kin term usage among the social classes. In the upper classes the more formal terms *mother* and *father* are used, while in lower classes first names are more apt to be used, to show that they are friends and not just kin. This difference applies to those related by marriage as well as by blood.

Kin terms in America do not always carry clear-cut role-expectations. In fact, the actual relations among kinfolk often have to be worked out by trial and error to some extent. This ambiguity is related to the American emphasis on the individual and status achievement rather than on status ascription. As Adams (1980, p. 324) puts it:

> It is very likely that the fuzziness of kinship designations in the United States, and the flexibility with which kin ties are interpreted by specific people, are related to the great emphasis that is placed on personal achievement rather than on ascription. This emphasis is related both to the restricted terminological system . . . and to the great variability in the actual relations between people holding the same structural positions within the kinship system, such as mother-son or uncle-niece.

Kin ties in America

The flexibility and variability of kin ties in America was examined by Schneider (1968) in his work *American Kinship: A Cultural Account.* He found variations in kin closeness and distance, and that kinship distance may mean at least three different things in America. (1) *Genealogical distance,* which is the relative closeness or distance of people who have blood ties. Thus a second cousin is more distant than a first cousin, genealogically. (2) *Socio-emotional distance,* which designates the closeness or distance in affectivity between kinfolk, not necessarily corresponding to genealogical closeness or distance. Some studies have found that grandparents are affectively closer to a person than one's aunts and uncles, and that on the average maternal relatives are closer to one than paternal relatives (Robins & Tomanec, 1962). (3) *Physical or residential distance,* which carries the idea that while intense ties and relations normally require physical proximity, such geographical closeness does not guarantee intimacy among kinfolk, nor does physical distance preclude intimacy among kin. One may maintain intimate ties with one's parents even though they live thousands of miles away, while aunts, uncles, and cousins living in the same neighborhood are seldom seen.

Parsons (1943) has commented on some of the peculiarities of the American kinship system. First, compared to many other societies, American kinship is less important functionally. In the general institutional framework of American society the kin network has fewer functions and plays only a small role in meeting societal and individual needs. Second, the normal household unit in America is the nuclear, conjugal family, living in "a home segregated from those of both pairs of parents (if living) and . . . economically independent of both. In a very large proportion of cases the geographical separation is considerable" (Parsons, 1943, p. 27). Third, the relatively isolated, open, and bilateral kinship system with nuclear family households is most functional for and best suited to the American occupational system in our urban-industrial society. It makes residential mobility in pursuit of jobs much easier than would be the case if the individual worker were tied more strongly to and restricted in his movements by the larger kinship group. The nuclear family is free to go where occupational opportunities beckon in an expanding industrial economy.

Some of Parson's views have been challenged by other family sociologists. Although Parsons was writing about middle-class family and kinship mostly, subsequent research has generally shown that middle-class nuclear families do not generally become separated from their kin to the extent that Parsons indicated (Sussman, 1959; Reiss, 1962). Also, research shows that the American kin network in the middle class as well as in other

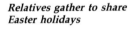

Relatives gather to share Easter holidays

James R. Holland/Stock, Boston

classes does "function" in various ways, providing help to members when needed, as well as maintaining affectional ties, and even providing support and encouragement for social and residential mobility of ambitious kin members (Litwak, 1960a; 1960b).

Kin ties vary from one social class to another, and often change throughout the individual's life cycle. Some lower-class individuals and couples may be isolated from their kin, and some highly mobile middle-class couples may have little to do with their less mobile or successful relatives (Stuckert, 1963b; Dyer, 1972). Also, younger married couples are apt to be more mobile, thereby reducing kin propinquity, while later in life they may close the residential distance with their kin again (Osborn & Williams, 1976). Farber (1971) found that working-class people tend to cluster with their kinfolk, and that upper-class people (the old aristocracies) are greatly concerned with kinship identity and ties, past and present, and attempt to preserve their "symbolic family estate."

In sum, Parsons's critics seem to be saying that although Parsons has claimed that kinship in America is relatively unimportant, and that this unimportance frees the nuclear family to pursue interests consistent with the needs of our economic-industrial order, evidence shows that kin networks still exist and do function, and that their functioning is not inconsistent with the economic-industrial structure in America. In fairness we should allow Parsons, who acknowledged the findings of his critics, a response. From a comparative perspective, Parsons sees his views and those of his critics on the isolated nuclear family as complementary rather than contradictory (Parsons, 1965, p. 35):

> The concept of isolation applies in the first instance to kinship structure as seen in the perspective of anthropological studies in that field. In this context our system represents an extreme type, which is well described by that term. It does not, however, follow that all relations to kin outside the nuclear family are broken. Indeed, the very psychological importance for the individual of the nuclear family in which he was born and brought up would make any such conception impossible.

In conclusion, it may be said that compared to many other societies and compared to our own past history, kinship ties in America today are less binding and serve fewer needs. This does not mean that kin networks perform no significant functions today, or that kinfolk are necessarily isolated from one another; nor does it mean that existing kin ties are inconsistent with the goals of American workers or the needs of employers. We need to be cautious in making generalizations about kin ties and relations in America. A crucial difference between kin ties in our society and in most other societies is that, with the exception of parent-offspring relations, the kin ties in our society are voluntary rather than obligatory. Rather than trying to look at "the kinship network" in general, it may be more fruitful to look at existing relations between specific kinds of kin, such as parents and their adult offspring, or between adult siblings. This is what we shall do next.

KINSHIP RELATIONS IN AMERICA

In general, it appears that kin relations in America are extremely flexible, and thus open to a variety of situational and interpersonal influences. As Sweetser (1968, p. 407) notes, kin relations in America today may exhibit certain regularities, but not the normatively enforced regularities found in so many other societies or in our own preindustrial past. Considering the lack of consistent norms and the fluidity in kin relationships now, the existence of even modest similarities in relations between the nuclear family and its relatives is rather remarkable.

Relations between parents and adult offspring

Mutual aid. Studies in the 1950s showed a middle-class pattern of parents giving moderate aid and services to their married adult children (Sussman & Burchinal, 1962). This aid pattern included direct financial assistance for such larger expenditures as the purchase of a home, or gifts of money, or such less direct financial assistance as gifts of furniture or household equipment, and providing services, such as baby care or provisions for vacations. Few married children received monetary gifts regularly, however. After an initial financial gift at marriage, most parents limited their financial contributions to birthdays and anniversaries, or for their grandchildren, or for emergencies.

Financial aid from adult children to their parents was found to be a different matter. Sussman (1953b) found that 96 percent of the middle-class parents in his New Haven study said they "would never accept financial aid from their children." This may represent an idealized notion that upon reaching maturity American couples are expected to be financially independent. However, Sussman and others found that a sense of filial responsibility exists in America. In his Cleveland study Sussman (1959) found that in a sample which included both working-class and middle-class families, 56 percent of the respondents gave varying kinds of aid to their parents.

In reviewing the different studies on parental aid to married children, Sussman and Burchinal (1962, pp. 331–332) conclude that financial aid exchanged between parents and their married children constitute one of the activities that bind nuclear families with their kin along generational lines, especially among middle-class people. During the earlier years of the child's marriage the aid generally flows from parents to their children; then, as the married children become middle aged, the stream of aid may become reversed and they will now provide help for their aging parents. For the most part, aid by parents is offered voluntarily on the

Adult daughter takes time from her secretarial job to help her father on the farm

U.S.D.A. photo by Don Breneman

basis of sentiment and affection. Such aid is intended to assist rather than to influence the recipients, and is generally given with no strings attached.

Subsequent studies have confirmed these findings regarding the mutual aid pattern between parents and their adult offspring. (See Table 14–1.) Adams (1970) and Osborn and Williams (1976) found strong continuing ties between parents and their adult children, which may be characterized

Table 14–1

Aid received by married children and parents*

Type of aid	Received by married children from parents	Received by parents from married children
Economic	49%	17%
Household management	25	23
Child care	78	n.a.
Illness	18	21
Emotional gratification	21	37

* 321 Families in Minneapolis–St. Paul. Parents mostly aged 46–55; married children in their 20s.
n.a. = not available.
Source: *Family Development in Three Generations: A Longitudinal Study of Changing Family Patterns of Planning and Achievement* by R. Hill et al., Cambridge, Mass.: Schenkman, 1970.

as a continuing "positive concern." One of the significant ways this positive concern is expressed is through providing substantial mutual aid. Immediately after marriage of the son or daughter, the aid generally flows from the parents to the young married couple, in the form of cash, loans, household equipment or furniture, and if the parents live fairly close by, such services as baby-sitting and help with the housework when grandchildren begin to arrive.

Visiting and communication. The positive and active concern for one another felt between parents and their adult children is widely manifested in the frequency of contacts between them. If they live far apart there is contact via letters and phone calls. When they live closer there is a good deal of visiting back and forth. Adams (1970) found that in such cases weekly or even more frequent interaction is the rule. Even when separated by a considerable distance, communication by mail or phone tends to be at least monthly. Even when many hundreds of miles separate them, visits are planned and made by car, train, or plane, especially for such holidays as Thanksgiving or Christmas.

As long as the aging parents live, their adult children generally continue to keep in touch with them via letters, phone calls and visits, thus expressing their affection and positive concern.

Relations among adult siblings

Mutual aid. Mutual aid among siblings appears to be far less frequent than between parents and their adult offspring. While many brothers and sisters are quite close during childhood and adolescence, once they grow up and go their separate ways the closeness tends to wane (Adams, 1968; Allan, 1977). This diminution of sibling ties is probably greater in the urban middle class than in the other social classes, but it also exists in the working, lower, and upper classes to some degree. Relations between adult siblings also may vary from one period of the life cycle to another. According to Cumming and Schneider (1961) adult sibling ties may become stronger again in the latter stages of the life cycle, after their own children have grown up and departed. Allan (1977) believes that in America relationships among adult siblings tend to be quite selective, reflecting the element of personal choice permitted in our mobile, achievement-oriented society. He found that the most important factor in determining adult sibling interaction was "the sibling compatibility and liking for one another," rather than the fact of blood relation (Allan, 1977, p. 181).

Adams (1980, p. 330) thinks that the terms that seem to sum up the ties and relations between adult siblings in America are *interest* and *comparison/identification*. Interest refers to a general feeling that one should keep in touch with one's brothers and sisters and be interested in their lives

Adult siblings and their spouses enjoy frequent visits

Ellis Herwig/Stock, Boston

and activities, but that there is little need for the frequent contacts one maintains with one's parents. Giving or receiving material or other aid is infrequent, generally restricted to crisis or emergencies. Except for the occasional exchange of baby-sitting by adult sisters who live in the same area, giving or receiving services, money, or material things among adult siblings may create tensions and problems. Adams (1980, p. 330) notes that "the sharing of financial or other forms of aid between siblings is likely to become a bone of contention or even a basis of alienation" between them. Also, when siblings grow up and leave home there is apt to be some continuation of sibling rivalry, which becomes transformed into comparison and identification. In our individualistic and competitive society "brothers and sisters are the comparative reference group par excellence." (Adams, 1980, p. 330). How well one is doing can be answered by comparing one's achievements and progress with that of one's siblings. Alienation between siblings can result from differential social mobility and divergence in career success among brothers and sisters (LeMasters, 1954; Stuckert, 1963; Dyer, 1972). Sometimes such success or prestige divergence between adult siblings can result in a one-way, unreciprocated identification, in which the less successful sibling takes pride in the more fortunate sibling, who does not reciprocate this feeling. (Turner, 1970, p. 477; Adams, 1980, p. 330).

In sum, while adult siblings generally continue to be interested in each other's activities and progress, this interest generally does not extend to sharing or exchanging financial or other forms of aid, except in unusual circumstances.

Visiting and communication among adult siblings. Allan (1977) found that among adult siblings the main focus of the relationship is to maintain a "diffuse, limited involvement." There is a considerable range of actual contact and communication. Some brothers and sisters may send each other Christmas cards or birthday greetings but rarely see each other over the years. Others keep in touch regularly by letters and phone calls and may visit each other quite often. There seems to be a cultural normative pressure to sustain sibling contact even though some adult siblings seem to have little in common as the years pass (Schneider, 1968). It is normatively more permissible to quietly forget a neighbor or a former close associate than to completely "drop" a brother or sister.

The range of activities that the majority of adult siblings engage in together tends to be quite limited and modest. For most siblings Allan (1977) found the activities limited to visits in each other's homes, or perhaps meeting in the home of their parents (for younger adult siblings). These visits may involve nothing more than sitting and discussing matters of mutual interest over a drink or at dinner. Chatting and being sociable seemed sufficient to maintain sibling solidarity, for most. No elaborate planned activities or entertainment is expected. For siblings who come from afar for a visit of several days or more, the host brother or sister may plan some external activities, such as eating out or sightseeing in the local area.

Relations among secondary kin

Adult Americans generally have weaker ties and less frequent contacts with secondary kin, such as cousins, aunts and uncles, than with their parents and siblings. Again, these secondary-kin ties vary among classes and ethnic groups. Adams (1980, p. 331) designates relations between secondary kin by the terms *circumstantial* and *incidental.*

In a study of kin relations in Kansas City, Coult and Habenstein (1972) found that most of their respondents consider no more than two or three secondary kin to be important enough or close enough to them to be mentioned. In fact, secondary-kin relations in America seldom involve frequent contact, common interests, mutual aid, obligatory concern, or strong affectional ties. The incidental nature of secondary-kin contacts is seen in instances in which one may drop in on a cousin or an aunt or uncle while on a trip back home to see one's parents or siblings. Also, secondary kin are sometimes brought together by special circumstances involving the larger kin network, such as at the marriage or death of one of the kin group. Schneider (1968, p. 70) speaks of "wakes and weddings" as special occasions where secondary kin get together.

Cousins enjoy a Sunday visit

Jean-Claude Lejeune/Stock, Boston

There are, of course, some exceptions to this infrequent and circumstantial contact pattern among secondary kin. One exception would be relations between young adults and their aging grandparents. This three-generational kin involvement, however, generally does not last very long. Other exceptions to the circumstantial pattern of secondary kin contacts would be in some racial and ethnic groups, such as blacks and Jews, where the mutual concern for welfare and survival involve extended kinship networks (Leichter & Mitchell, 1967), and in the old upper classes, where the social circle may be restricted to people of similar high status, including secondary kin who share the revered family name and ancestry (Amory, 1947).

Class and ethnic differences in kin relations

There is general agreement that certain relationships among kinfolk are to be found in all social classes, and in all racial and ethnic groups in the United States (Sussman & Burchinal, 1962; Farber, 1971). However, as suggested above, the interests, norms, and conditions affecting kin ties and relations may vary a good deal from one group to another. Upper-class people may be quite actively concerned with kinship links, past and present, often devoting much attention to their genealogies or family trees, and to maintaining close contacts with both primary and secondary kin, all of whom bear the illustrious family identity. Not only do the old aristocratic kin members have frequent and close interaction, they are also prone to intermarry more often than in the other social classes (Amory, 1947; Cavan, 1969, p. 93). Such upper-class kinship endogamy functions to help keep the prominant family blood lines "pure," and help keep the family property intact and in the family circle. Farber (1971, p. 6) observes that in the upper classes such close kinship ties function to sustain social differentiation in society. From the viewpoint of the kin who make up the present generation of the illustrious family, such as the Adams family of Boston, it is only natural that they should cooperate to preserve the "symbolic family estate" (Gordon & Noll, 1975, p. 240). The kinship group here is more of a reference group than a mutual aid or friendship group, as is apt to be the case in the other classes.

Within the large middle class, kin ties and relations may vary from lower-middle to upper-middle class and from one ethnic group to another, with the stronger ties in groups still sustaining traditional familistic patterns, as a rule. As compared to other classes, middle-class people are apt to be oriented more toward the "ascending generations" in their kin contacts—that is, toward parents rather than siblings, and where secondary kin are involved, toward aunts and uncles rather than toward cousins (Adams, 1970, p. 586). This differs from the working class in which people tend to be same-generation oriented. Lower-middle-class people may retain closer ties with same-generation kin (siblings and cousins) than do the more highly mobile upper-middle-class people (Osborn & Williams, 1976, p. 205).

In general, working-class people express a stronger kin orientation, live closer to kinfolk, and interact on a more regular basis with kin than do middle-class people (Adams, 1970; Farber, 1971). Working-class kin are also more likely to feel certain obligations to each other than are

Kinship ties are generally strong among the Chinese

Julie Heifitz

middle-class kin. Komarovsky (1962) found that relatives in the working class often provided the most important source of interaction. In her study, "one-third of the couples either never spent any leisure time with another couple (apart from relatives) or do so only a few times a year; were it not for the circle of relatives they would be completely isolated." (Komarovsky, 1962, p. 238). Women especially play an important role in maintaining contact with kin in the working class (Gordon & Noll, 1975, p. 244).

In his study of sibling relations, Allan (1977) found that in the working class most individuals maintain a very close relationship with one or more adult siblings. This tie went way beyond a general interest in each other's welfare. "Without exception, these siblings were recognized by the respondents as being the most important people in their social network, and were frequently described as their 'best friends.' " (Allan, 1977, p. 181). Such close relations normally occur between siblings of the same sex, and are most pervasive between sisters. Lower-class people also tend to depend on kin for much of their social life, with female relatives clustering together while the men join each other for traditional male activities (Gans, 1962).

Americans of fairly recent ethnic origins, especially those from societies stressing strong familistic traditions, such as Italian-Americans and Mexican-Americans, tend to emphasize kin ties and relations more than most Anglo-Americans. Gans (1962) found that among Italian-Americans in Boston social life centered in "the family circle," consisting of a group of relatives. They view the outside world from this insulated circle; their whole way of life is based on intimate relations among these relatives.

In a comparison of kin ties and contacts between black and white Americans, Hayes and Mindel (1973) found that blacks tend to differ from whites even when such variables as social class, marital status, and family size are controlled. Black men and women interact with their kin more frequently and perceive kinfolk as more important in their lives than do whites. Blacks interact with more of their kin in all categories than do whites, except with parents. Black families receive more help from kin in child care than white families do. Kin networks are more tightly knit for blacks than for whites. Hayes and Mindel (1973, p. 55) conclude that their study tends to support the hypothesis that the black extended family is a very supportive structure which serves as a source of help and comfort in what is often a hostile social environment.

Social mobility and kin relations

There has been some disagreement among sociologists as to the effects of social mobility on kin ties and relations. One point of view holds that social mobility is really detrimental to the continuation of ties and relations with relatives. Parsons (1959) saw occupational mobility as essentially antithetical to extended family ties, and suggested that there is a kind of disharmony between modern urban-industrial society with

Table 14–2

Sibling contacts of married men with nearest age brother, by social mobility status*	Type of contact	Social mobility status	
		Stable	Upwardly mobile
	Joint social activities outside the home	31	18
	Communication by mail or telephone	70	55
	Home visits	65	59

* Percent of married men in Greensboro, N.C., claiming three or more contacts per year.
Source: *Kinship in an Urban Setting*, by B. N. Adams. Chicago: Markham, 1968.

its emphasis on upward mobility and the long-standing tradition of maintaining ties with kinfolk.

A more recent viewpoint challenges Parsons, holding that extended-family ties may not only be compatible with upward mobility, but also may be functional in that relatives may support and encourage able members of the kin group in their mobility efforts. Litwak (1969a), in a study in Detroit, found that extended family members often provided aid to younger members who were in the early stages of occupational mobility. He found that upwardly mobile couples visited their relatives just as much as did the nonmobile couples. In study of occupational mobility and family ties in Wisconsin, Stuckert (1963b) found an inverse relation between upward mobility and extended ties and relations. The more successful couples tended to reduce their contacts with their parents and less successful siblings. His conclusion, opposite to that of Litwak, was that upward social mobility was detrimental to the continuation of extended family ties and relations. Adams (1968) found that upwardly mobile men reduced their contacts with their brothers. (See Table 14–2.)

In a study conducted in Uppsala, Sweden (Dyer, 1972) the author found evidence that upward social mobility was somewhat detrimental to extended kin ties in middle-class families. But other evidence was found that tended to support Litwak's position that upward mobility is not necessarily detrimental to sustaining kin ties in a modern, urban-industrial society. More studies are needed, both in the United States and elsewhere, to seek the various conditions under which social mobility may or may not weaken kin ties and relations (Dyer, 1979, pp. 228–230).

SPECIAL TYPES OF KINSHIP RELATIONS

Divorce and kinship relations

The impact of divorce on kin ties and relations becomes an issue of increasing significance as divorce rates go up. There is very little research on this problem as yet. Earlier studies of divorce and its effects, such as that of Goode (1956), note that divorce generally breaks the ties that had previously united two family lines, but most studies do not deal with the specifics of relations among kin after divorce. Bohannon (1970a) discussed the ways in which divorce will alter kin interaction. The relationship between one parent and the children ceases to be any business of the other parent. Neither divorced parent can control what the ex-spouse does with the children.

Spicer and Hampe (1975) suggest that the first step in trying to understand postdivorce kinship relations is to determine which, if any, of the patterns of predivorce contact continue to exist for both "consanguines" (blood relatives) and "affines" (those related by marriage). It would be expected that there would be less interaction between a divorced person and his or her former affines because the connecting link, the marriage bond, is now broken. The linkage with one's consanguines is not affected in the same way by the broken marriage bond, of course, and some increase in interaction with blood relatives might be expected to help fill the void left by severed ties with affines. In their study of divorced men and women, Spicer and Hampe (1975) found, however, that actual contact with blood relatives remained about the same for the majority of the respondents, but did increase for about one fifth of them following divorce. Also, as expected, there was a higher rate of interaction with consanguines than with affines. Divorced women interacted more with both consanguines and affines than did divorced men, especially when children were present. This greater kin contact by divorced females was due in part to their receiving aid both from their parents and from their parents-in-law. These basic patterns prevailed regardless of differences in age, length of marriage, education, social class, and geographic distance from relatives.

Anspach (1976) continued the research on kinship and divorce by studying the patterns of kin interaction and aid provided by kin (both consanguines and affines) to a sample of divorced women and their children. The great majority (about 80 percent) of these divorcees had less contact with their ex-husband's relatives following divorce, and most reported an increase in contacts with their own kin after their divorce. This suggests that for the divorced women the elimination of relationships with the former spouse's kin may be compensated for by increased relationships with one's own kin. Divorcees who remarried not only increased their contacts with their own kin but also established regular contacts with their new husbands' kin, while eliminating or greatly reducing contacts with their former husbands' kin. Findings in this study also showed that patterns of aid from kinfolk generally followed the pattern of contact and interaction. More women had both interaction with and aid from their own relatives, more than their former husband's relatives, or their present husbands' relatives (for those who had remarried). The data show clearly that, on the average, a divorced woman's own relatives are her most important kin group. Her former spouse's relatives are simply eliminated from the kinship network; and for divorced women who remarry the present husbands' kin are not as important for interaction or aid as one's own kin (Anspach, 1976, p. 327).

What about kin ties and relations of the children of divorced women, and of those who had remarried? Do children of divorce whose fathers are absent have patterns of kin contacts similar to those of their mother, so that they seldom if ever see their paternal relatives? Anspach (1976, p. 328) found that paternal grandparents are seen less often than maternal grandparents by about 69 percent of the children of unremarried divorced women and by 81 percent of the children of the remarried divorced mothers. Thus the children of divorced women tend to follow the pattern of kin relations displayed by their mothers, who no longer see the kin of their former husbands. This in effect denies the child one half of his consanguine kin, which is quite a different matter from the denial to the mother of contacts with some affinal kin. The child grows up in a kinship environment that is one sided. Socioemotional support as well as other resources and supports from the child's paternal kin are lost or greatly reduced. Children of remarried divorcees do see the kin of their stepfather to some extent, but not as much as they see their mother's kin.

Widows and kinship relations

Not much research has been done on the relationships between widows and their kin. Implicit in much of the literature on the modified extended family in America is the notion that aging parents, or a surviving widowed parent, will be looked after to the extent needed, either by adult children, siblings, or perhaps some other relatives. A widow or widower is not supposed to be left to fend alone as the final survivor of a nuclear family unit. At least one study of elderly people (Gibson, 1972) found that the widowed, along with the divorced, tend to be more integrated into the extended kin network than the still married. Kin ties and contacts tend to be more important for the former than the latter. Gibson (1972, p. 13) concludes that for those elderly people who are still married, the nuclear family is more important, while for the nonmarried the extended-kin network becomes more important. The widowed and divorced receive help and support from a higher proportion of kinfolk than do those still married.

Another study found definite limitations to the active, functioning, modified extended-family network of widows. Lopata (1978), in a study of the contributions of extended family kin to the support of widows in the Chicago area, found that apart from the support the widows received from their adult children—and in the case of young widows from their parents—other kin, including siblings, are infrequent contributors to the economic, service, or emotional support of widows. Lopata (1978, p. 356)

Table 14–3

Help received by widowed parent from adult children*

Type of help received	Received by widows	Received by widowers
Companionship	81%	46%
Gifts	78	34
Transportation	54	20
Help with work	23	23
Advice	25	16
Money	20	14
Place to live	23	14

*Parents aged 65 years or older with at least one living child.
Source: *Social Adaptation to Widowhood Among a Rural-Urban Aged Population,* by F. M. Berardo. Pullman, Washington: Washington Agricultural Experiment Station Bulletin No. 689, 1967.

found that most of the widows were getting support from their children. Over 90 percent of these widows had at least one child available for support and the average frequency of contact with such children was "several times a month." Only 14 percent of the widows had mothers still living, and fewer still, 8 percent, had fathers still living. In these instances the widows were apt to see the parent or parents quite frequently. These findings tend to support the thesis that the elderly in America are not really being neglected by their close kin (Shanas & Streib, 1965). However, as indicated above, most of the attention these widows received was from children or parents. While 81 percent reported having at least one sibling alive, the average frequency of contact with a brother or a sister was just over "several times a year." And only one third of the widows reported seeing their late husband's relatives frequently if at all, and other secondary kin were seen rarely. Lopata (1978, p. 362) concludes that her data do not support the thesis of significant contributions from siblings and other external kin to the support of widows. As far as these widows are concerned, the hypothesis of an "active modified extended family network functioning in American metropolitan centers, with exchanges of supports from separate households, is not supported for any relatives other than children" (Lopata, 1978, p. 362).

In sum, the evidence suggests that while those who are widowed may receive more aid and support from their kinfolk than those who are still married, most of this support comes from the adult children of the widowed. (See Table 14–3.)

KINSHIP SUBSTITUTES: SOME SUGGESTED ALTERNATIVES

As we have seen, there has been a good deal of interest recently in the issue of the extent to which the conventional nuclear family has become removed from its extended kinfolk in urban industrial America. Sussman (1965) and Litwak (1960a) found that even mobile middle-class nuclear families are not isolated from their kin. Others, such as Gibson (1972) and Straus (1969), have found that, while many American nuclear families retain some ties with kin, ties other than parent-child relations may not be extensive or important. At any rate, since we seem to be living in an era when kinship ties are more difficult to sustain than before, various suggestions for supplementing kin or perhaps substituting new "kin" for old have been advanced.

Actually, a number of modern alternatives to traditional kin networks have arisen in modern American society. Kempler (1976) examines three such alternative kin networks and evaluates each with respect to its potential value as a substitute for traditional kin relationships and functions. The three are (1) communes, (2) family networks, and (3) affiliated families.

The commune as a substitute for kin

Among the various motives that induce people to join communes is a need to expand their network of intimate relationships, to join a kind of substitute extended family (Berger, et al., 1971). The operation of many communes requires a considerable degree of intimate and interdependent interaction among members in economic, social, and emotional spheres of life. According to Ramey (1972) the most important reason many people have for joining a commune is the opportunity afforded them for expanded intimacy and personal support beyond what they find available in conventional marriage and the small nuclear family.

Among the advantages offered by communes is their form of organization, which facilitates the sharing of goods and services among members in ways that allow them to use their economic, intellectual, and emotional resources in order to cope collectively with problems of living. Also, the opportunity for intimate relationships between family groups in the commune is a meaningful way to solve problems common to nuclear families, which many find better than solving them alone.

There are disadvantages to communes as kin-group substitutes, however (Kempler, 1976, p. 146). (1) Intimate relations among commune members may lead to "swinging" or group marriages, which are potentially divisive and still contrary to prevailing sex norms in the society. (2) The high mobility and turnover of commune members, and the short duration of most communes, means that any kin-type relations are apt to be transitory and temporary, as compared to real kin ties. How would such temporary ties and commitments among commune adults affect children, for example? Would these transitory relations serve as a "model for noncommitment" in personal relationships for children raised in communes? (3) Another shortcoming of many communes as substitutes for extended-kin groups is the absence of an aged generation. Most communes have only two generations (Kempler, 1976, p. 146); thus, the benefits of emotional ties and contact between grandparents and grandchildren in real extended families are not often available in communes. Again, how would this lack of elderly members affect children? Will they be more tolerant or less tolerant of older people? Will they reject three-generational contacts in their adult years as a result of being denied them in their childhood?

On balance, it appears that there are more cons than pros in assessing the commune as a viable substitute for a real extended kin group.

The family network as a substitute for kin

A second proposed alternative, somewhat similar to the commune has been called the "family network" (Stoller, 1970). A family network would consist of two or more nuclear families from the same neighborhood that join together regularly and frequently to exchange services, share problems, and enjoy leisure activities. Although each nuclear family should normally maintain its separate residence, it would join with the others for the above-stated purposes. The family network concept emerged from the experiences of Stoller (1970), Clark and Kempler (1973), and others with family workshops in which groups of nuclear families met together to share problems, assess their family functioning, and work out creative ways for family living. A similar idea has been proposed by Otto (1971) and Pringle (1974), who suggest that many urban residents who do not have enough emotional support from kin, friends, or neighbors might join together into artificial extended families or "family clusters." Such family clusters could include a dozen or more adults of various ages and marital statuses, plus their children. They would meet together regularly to share knowledge and skills, have fun together, and provide one another with "mutual support in joy and sorrow."

Among the merits or advantages of the family network or family cluster set-up would be (1) Isolation for many nuclear families which have minimal contacts with their kin would be reduced. (2) Each nuclear family can profit from the experiences of the others, and have the benefit of feedback about their family functioning as seen by the other families. (3) The family network or cluster can serve as a resource to all members in broadening their options for identification, value choices, and intimate relationships (Kempler, 1976, p. 146).

Many of the previously mentioned disadvantages of communes also apply to the family network. (1) Most such family networks or clusters would be temporary and transitory. Mobility and job relocations would contribute to high turnover rates. (2) Such intimate networks are apt to be both difficult to create and to sustain over any length of time. It takes much time and effort to work out the nuclear family differences and overcome the personal anxieties connected with such networks. And it is not easy to find a half-dozen adults who can be close to each other over a long period of time, to say nothing of a dozen or more. (3) As envisioned by Stoller (1970) the family network had no provision for contact with elderly people. Thus, as with most communes, the family network would provide only a limited, two-generational experience.

In sum, while the family network or family cluster idea is theoretically sound because of its potential for meeting certain unmet needs associated with the isolated or semiisolated nuclear family, many practical problems associated with its organization and operation make it unlikely that such family networks will become viable substitutes for actual kin ties and relationships for very many nuclear families.

The affiliated family as a substitute for kin

Introduced as a concept by Clavan and Vatter (1972a; 1972b), the "affiliated family" is supposed to have the advantage over communes and family networks of providing a three-generational structure. The affiliated family consists of "any combination of husband/father, wife/mother, and their children, plus one or more older persons, recognized as part of the kin network and called by a designated kin term . . . , [who] may or may not be part of the residential household" (Clavan & Vatter, 1972a, p. 499). The basic bond between these people is a "voluntary commitment to responsibility for one another within the unit."

Among the benefits or advantages offered by the three-generational affiliated family are the following. (1) It helps meet the needs of two significant female groups often in need of help today, widows aged 65 and over, and young employed mothers. (2) It establishes a three-generational, extended, family-like network. The adoption of elderly people benefits not only them but also offers the young husband and wife and their children the benefits of extended family relations. (3) It can facilitate role-modeling by the older generation for the younger. (4) It can provide supportive emotional relations between the "adopted grandparents" and their "grandchildren." (5) It can result in greater availability of mothers in the labor market. For those employed mothers who find nurseries and day-care facilities less than satisfactory for their young children, the affiliated family can provide a more satisfactory alternative.

Here also a number of problems and disadvantages must be noted. (1) The degree of intimacy needed for such an affiliated family to function would require considerable time and effort to cultivate. An actual extended family would, in effect, have to be created and established as a going concern. (2) Commitment between affiliated family members, since it is entirely voluntary, would depend on a finely balanced mutuality of needs and interests which could be difficult to sustain. In this respect, the affiliated family commitment is somewhat similar to that of a cohabiting couple. Both arrangements are sustainable only as long as they meet certain needs of the individuals involved. (3) There are many practical and possibly some legal issues concerning the organization of these affiliated families and the rights and responsibilities of the adopted grandparents vis-à-vis the nuclear family members.

All told, while the affiliated family, like the commune and the family network, holds promise of providing emotional, social, and economic needs to those deprived of real kin ties and relatives, the many practical and personal difficulties entailed in setting up and maintaining such adopted kin groups make them a rather unrealistic alternative for most people at present (Kempler, 1976, p. 148). However, this does not mean that kinship substitutes will not continue to appeal to some people who feel deprived of real extended family ties and relations in modern urban society.

IN-LAWS AND IN-LAW RELATIONS IN AMERICA

Each marriage joins together not only a man and a woman, but two previously unrelated families as well. As we have seen, the husband and wife do not normally sever their ties with their respective parental families. Thus each marriage partner has to adjust to the other partner's continuing ties and interaction with his or her relatives. In a sense it can also be said that each marriage partner joins the family of the other partner as a new recruit, as a daughter-in-law or a son-in-law. Thus, following their marriage, the wife and husband each participate in two kin networks. Problems and adjustments in relationships with in-laws have to be worked out by the partners as they create and develop their new family of procreation.

SOCIO-CULTURAL FACTORS AFFECTING IN-LAW RELATIONSHIPS

In-law folklore

The sociology of in-laws is a fascinating topic. In-laws appear rather suddenly at marriage, and we are not quite sure just what they are or how to relate to them. In fact, we may have some difficulty addressing them, even though we had no such problems before we married their son or daughter. Each couple—each married partner really—has to work out, more or less by trial and error, a mutually acceptable term or name to use in addressing one's mother-in-law and father-in-law. Is she still Mrs. Peters as she was while I was going with her daughter? Now that we're married dare I call her Gladys? Or should I call her "mother" or "mom" as my wife does? Some married people never seem to find a happy solution and may try to avoid any terms of address, perhaps solving the problem of addressing a mother-in-law as one long-married man did by "just looking at her and talking."

The ambiguity of in-law statuses and roles in our society contributes to the mixed and uncertain feelings people may have about their in-

In-laws come to dinner

Barbara Alper/Stock, Boston

laws. Prejudice toward in-laws is frequently conveyed through anecdotes and stereotypes that are part of the folklore of a society. LeMasters (1957b) has attempted to identify some of these folk beliefs about in-laws that have existed in American society.

1. In-laws are difficult to get along with. Some tend to regard their in-laws as potential enemies rather than potential friends. We fear they may meddle in our marriage, and interfere in the way we raise our children. Yet, as much of the research shows (Duvall, 1954; Blood & Blood, 1978), in-laws are often the best friends and supports newlyweds have.

2. In-laws are of little importance to a married couple. One hears such expressions as "I'm marrying her, not her family." In certain respects this is a false assumption, as most married people learn. The person we marry has been socialized and shaped by his or her family, and normally will continue quite close ties with them after marriage, as noted earlier.

3. One can simply ignore one's in-laws. Some people get married with the idea that they can preclude any difficulties in getting along with their in-laws by simply moving away from them, perhaps pretending they do not exist. It is unrealistic to expect one's spouse to sever family ties of long duration upon getting married.

The mother-in-law stereotype

Part of the American folklore about in-laws revolves around the stereotyped conception of the mother-in-law, perpetuated in anecdotes and mother-in-law jokes. Duvall (1954) found ample evidence of the existence of a "mother-in-law complex" in American society, with the mother-in-laws perceived as a meddlesome and difficult-to-get-along-with person. This rather pervasive stereotype contributes to negative attitudes toward mothers-in-laws in general, which in turn has tended to prejudice newlyweds against their mothers-in-law. In her early study of in-laws Duvall (1954) concluded that this old mother-in-law stereotype needed to be revised if we are to approach in-law relations rationally and constructively. She and others more recently (Deutscher, 1962; Adams, 1980, p. 335) find a definite trend today toward rejection of the old mother-in-law stereotype, especially among younger, well educated couples.

Some reasons for in-law problems

Marriage joins together a man and a woman whose lives up to that point have been deeply tied to their families of orientation. As the couple go about creating a new family of procreation they may experience transitional problems, boundary problems, allocational problems, or problems of culture conflict (Blood & Blood, 1978, p. 332).

Transitional problems. Waller and Hill (1951) observed that one of the most difficult problems of many American parents is that of letting their children go. Many parents dread to see their children grow up and leave home. Thus too much parental possessiveness can create problems for young married people, making it difficult for a young couple to establish their independence. Also, overly possessive parents can result in overly dependent children, who in turn may have difficulty in becoming emancipated at marriage. This is most apt to be true of daughters and their mothers (LeMasters, 1957, p. 316; Blood & Wolfe, 1960).

Boundary problems. This is related to the transitional problem; it is essentially the problem a married couple may have establishing their autonomy as a family and having both sets of in-laws accept and respect this autonomy. Blood and Wolfe (1960) found that excessive contact with either set of in-laws threatened the autonomy of the nuclear family and tended to weaken marital solidarity. Relatives are a positive and supportive resource in moderation.

Allocational problems. Married couples may experience problems in working out an equitable distribution of the time and attention they will devote to both sets of kin. Both families may keenly want the couple to visit them this Christmas, or on little Susie's first birthday. At times it is hard, if not impossible, to find a solution that does not disappoint one set of in-laws.

Problems of culture conflict. As with most other potential problem situations, the problem of cultural differences between the families of the husband and the wife is a matter of degree. When a young man from an aristocratic family marries a coal miner's daughter the differences in their values and lifestyles may be so great that each partner will probably have difficulty in adjusting to his or her in-laws, and vice versa. Significant differences still exist in America among social classes and religious, ethnic, and racial groups, so that mixed marriages entail potential cultural conflict both between the marriage partners and between each partner and his and her in-laws.

In the ensuing review of research findings on in-law relations, these potential problem areas will help provide direction for our discussion. Lest we leave the impression that most in-law relationships are problem-fraught and difficult, it should be pointed out that, despite the various sources of difficulty just reviewed, the average married couple need not expect much (if any) trouble in getting along with their in-laws. Blood and Wolfe (1960), in their Detroit study, found that more than 70 percent of the wives and almost 80 percent of the husbands experienced no real friction with their in-laws. Most individuals who get along well with their marriage partner also get along quite well with their in-laws.

IN-LAW RELATIONSHIPS

A review of the literature reveals that among the variables found to be related to in-law relationships are (1) gender, (2) parental possessiveness, (3) age, (4) length of the marriage, (5) proximity of residence, (6) presence of grandchildren, and (7) culture conflict. Let us see what selected studies show as to how these variables may influence relations among in-laws.

Gender and in-law relations

A number of studies show that in-law problems and conflicts are more apt to involve women than men (Duvall, 1954; Wallin, 1954; Sweetser, 1968). (See Table 14–4.) In a nationwide study Duvall (1954) found that

Table 14–4

Types of in-laws with whom wives and husbands experienced friction*	In-law	Wives experiencing friction	Husbands experiencing friction
	Mother-in-law	14.7%	9.0%
	Sister-in-law	3.8	3.4
	Father-in-law	3.2	3.2
	Brother-in-law	1.8	0.6
	Two or more of the above	5.9	5.1

* 544 couples in the early years of marriage.
Source: *Building a Successful Marriage,* by J. T. Landis and M. G. Landis, Englewood Cliffs, N.J.: Prentice-Hall, 1958: 406.

women were involved in in-law problems six times as frequently as men; and the person most often complained about was the mother-in-law. Moreover, 9 out of every 10 complaints come from the daughter-in-law. Next to the mother-in-law, the sister-in-law was the most frequent target of complaint. The father-in-law and the brother-in-law were rarely objects of complaint. In fairness it should also be pointed out that Duvall (1954) also found a significant proportion of her respondents making no complaints at all; many of these couples tended to regard their in-laws as allies rather than as meddlers.

In a review of studies of in-laws made in America and abroad, Sweetser (1968) found that the most common and troublesome in-law conflicts are between the mother-in-law and daughter-in-law. In Japan Dore (1963) found that the *mother-in-law daughter-in-law problem* is a commonly used term, and that until recently this "problem" was considered a part of the natural order of things, like typhoons and earthquakes. Wallin (1954) found that the mother-in-law problem was the most acute of all in-law related problems, and that more wives than husbands disliked their mothers-in-law. Rogers and Leichter (1962) found that among Jewish families in New York City the mother-centered emphasis is conducive to strains between the husband's mother and his wife, and that this strain can in turn contribute to marital discord.

Why are the difficulties in relations between in-laws so female centered? The explanation appears to be due in part to traditional sex-role differentiation. Traditionally men have had more freedom and power than women. This is reflected in marriage and family relations, including in-law relations. Since traditionally the principal adult roles of women have been those of wife and mother (until recently), while men's principal role has been extrafamilial (his occupation), women are more apt to approach marriage with fears about their adequacy as wives than men are about their adequacy as husbands. The newlywedded woman is thrown into competition with her husband's mother and is judged in terms of her ability as a cook, a housekeeper, and by how well she satisfies her husband's needs—the very things his mother has been doing for him for 20 years or longer. And the young wife is competing with a woman of greater experience who is apt to be quite critical (Leslie, 1979, p. 246).

The husband, on the other hand, is more apt to be judged on the basis of his performance in his occupation than in terms of his performance as a husband within the family circle. The traditional power and freedom of the husband also means he probably has more options in his contacts and relations with his in-laws than does his wife. For example, he has often had the power, economic and legal, to move his wife and children to another location if he so desires. Today, greater employment opportunities and more legal rights are opening up more options for women, belatedly.

Another reason why women seem to be central to in-law problems is that the marriage of an offspring is apt to be more threatening to the mother than to the father. The mother role is more organized around the child than is the father role. When children grow up and get married, many mothers seem to experience this as a direct personal loss, feeling themselves rendered useless. While the father continues in his occupation, which is his primary source of status and self-esteem, the mother may be tempted to "keep her hand in" by offering advice, help, and so on to her married sons and their wives. The young bride especially may resent this "interference" in her family life.

Parental possessiveness and in-law relations

As suggested, many parents—especially mothers—have difficulty letting their married sons and daughters go. While the emancipation problem exists for both sons and daughters it may be greater for daughters than for sons. Komarovsky (1956) found that young wives in America tend to be less emancipated from their parents than young husbands. She sees the problem as rooted in differential socialization received by girls and boys, with girls being more confined and protected by parents than boys. Then at marriage both the parents and the daughter have more difficulty letting go of each other. These findings were supported by other studies (Wallin, 1954; Stryker, 1955).

The structure of the American family contributes to the problem of parental possessiveness. During childhood the physical and emotional dependence of the daughter or son upon the parents is very heavy in the nuclear family. During adolescence, the youth may try to free himself or herself from this child-like dependence. In fact, for some an early marriage may be a part of this effort to gain independence. The newly gained independence of many young married men and women may be rather precarious (Leslie, 1979, p. 245). Thus they react strongly to any real or presumed threats to their autonomy. And the parents, after having their son or daughter dependent on them for so long, do not find it easy to relinquish their active parental roles. It may take some time for the emotional dependence to recede and be replaced by a more appropriate adult-to-adult relationship involving affection without dependence. While such adult-to-adult relations between parents and their adult children are difficult to achieve for many people today, increasing equalitarianism in the American family may be making this easier for many. As Rossi (1965) notes, relations between many equalitarian-oriented couples and their in-laws "may take on some of the quality of relations with a friendly peer."

Age, length of marriage, and in-law relations

The age at which one marries is related to the problem of independence. Obviously some time and personal maturity are necessary for a son or daughter to become emotionally independent of their parents, and although other factors are important too, age is one index of how far youth have traveled along the road to adult maturity and independence. Duvall (1954) found that older wives have less in-law trouble than younger wives. Blood and Wolfe (1960) found that the younger the bride, the greater the probability of in-law disagreements. For the very young bride—and groom too—the process of transferring emotional priorities and loyalties from parents to spouse is often accompanied by some stress, which shows up in the concentration of in-law problems in the early stages of marriage.

In sum, those who marry very young have to complete their striving for emotional independence after marriage, while those who marry later are more likely to have already achieved a considerable degree of maturity and independence, thereby reducing the possibility of serious in-law problems.

The relationship between the length of time married and in-law problems may be similarly explained. Young age, continuing emotional dependence on parents, and the newness of marriage go together. Many studies show that in-law problems are most acute during the early stages of marriage (Duvall, 1954; Stryker, 1955; Blood & Wolfe, 1960; Landis & Landis, 1963). Given enough time, most married couples gain the independence and confidence necessary for good in-law relationships. Both marital conflict *about* in-laws and a married couple's conflict *with* their in-laws tend to decrease with length of marriage (Adams, 1980, p. 334).

Proximity of residence and in-law relations

Among the least disrupted marriages in terms of in-law contact and relations are those "in which the couple live at least four or five hours away from the two sets of close kin and manifest little emotional dependence upon kin, so that their attention is focused on their own family . . . rather than on their . . . relatives." (Adams, 1980, pp. 334–335). This seems to say that one of the conditions conducive to in-law troubles is geographic proximity. Duvall (1954) found a strong belief among Americans that "the way to get along with in-laws is to keep as far away as possible." Sussman (1954) concluded that, when in-law relations become tense and difficult, an improvement can probably be made by the married couple moving far enough away to preclude regular visits with their parents. Blood and Wolfe (1960) found that for many couples "excessive contact" with in-laws threatened the autonomy of the nuclear family. Relatives who keep dropping in unannounced or uninvited invade the couple's privacy and reduce their marital solidarity. Note that the crucial factor is *excessive* contact with in-laws. Blood and Wolfe (1960) found that contact with kin is consistent with marital satisfaction up to a point. In their sample this point was reached when married couples saw their relatives more than once a week. Such frequent visits normally presume close residential proximity. Blood and Wolfe (1960) conclude that in-laws are a supportive resource for the couple if taken in moderate doses; but the couple—the nuclear family—requires some privacy and autonomy to avoid being overwhelmed by relatives.

Grandchildren and in-law relations

Adams (1980, p. 335) observes that among the least disrupted marriages in terms of in-law relations are those in which there are children. Stryker (1955) found that the presence of offspring in the home is likely to improve in-law relations, especially between the two mothers. Duvall (1954) observed that the arrival of children brings about significant changes in family statuses and roles which tend to improve relationships between the married couple and their in-laws. "Mother-in-law" now becomes "grandmother," and "father-in-law" becomes "grandfather." Duvall (1954), commenting on this situation, points out that theoretically we might expect to find a "grandmother complex" in our society since grandmothers are really only mothers-in-law in disguise. But we find few if any grandmother jokes. In fact, we generally find a quite positive image of "grandma."

In his analysis of the mother-in-law complex, LeMasters (1957b, p. 312) offers an explanation of how the "meddling mother-in-law" becomes the kindly grandmother.

> By some magical means . . . the birth of the first child to the young married couple transforms that old ogre, the mother-in-law, into a kind and loving grandmother, beloved by all of us. . . . This magical transformation is certainly one of the unexplained miracles of reproduction in our society.

Miraculous or not, this role transition is a significant factor in the changing perceptions family members have of each other following the birth of a child. The young bride becomes a mother, which gives her new stature and added respect. The mother-in-law becomes a grandmother, and while many people have mixed feelings and uncertainties regarding the status-role of mother-in-law, everyone not only knows what a grandmother is, but also generally has a quite favorable attitude toward her (Waller & Hill, 1951). While a young husband or wife may not know what to call their mother-in-law, when the first child arrives everyone can relax and call her grandma. Behavior that might have been viewed as mother-in-law interference before now becomes understandable and acceptable as the loving attention of a grandparent. Of course, in certain cases the arrival of the child can precipitate conflict between mother and daughter-in-law if they differ greatly in their views of infant and child care, as we shall see next.

Culture conflict and in-law relations

The potential for culture conflict in in-law relations increases with increasing intermarriage across religious, class, ethnic and racial lines. This conflict potential may be partially offset by other trends, such as equalitarianism and a reduction in sex role differentiation. However, as we saw in Chapter 7, problems of marital adjustment are generally greater in mixed marriages. Background differences in culture are among the most potent reasons for parents-in-laws to intervene in the family life of a young couple. If, for example, the groom's mother believes that her new daughter-in-law is not a good housekeeper, or is not providing her son with the right diet, or worse, is subverting him away from the "true" religion in which he was reared, she will have difficulty not interfering. Leichter and Mitchell (1967) found that in Jewish families in New York City the husband's mother caused a good deal of conflict between the husband and wife by excessively interferring in their daily lives. This interference included regular criticism of the daughter-in-law for not keeping house properly and for not raising the children in the traditional ways.

Cultural diversity tends to put a strain on in-law relations as much or more than it does on marital relations. In-law relationships are apt to suffer when a marriage links two kin networks which are very different culturally.

Suggestions for getting along with in-laws

LeMasters (1957b, pp. 321–324) offers a number of practical suggestions for young couples starting out in marriage which should help them understand and get along with their in-laws. Drawing from LeMasters and other authorities, here are a few guidelines.

1. Get to know your in-laws-to-be before your marriage. As it is generally true that good marital adjustment begins before marriage, so it is also true that good in-law adjustment probably begins before marriage. Try to see them in different situations in order to broaden your understanding of them. LeMasters (1957b, p. 222) suggests it may be revealing to drop in unannounced (but not too often).

2. Approach your marriage with a positive attitude toward your prospective in-laws. Try not to enter marriage with prejudice toward your in-laws based on folklore and mother-in-law stereotypes. Make an effort not only to get to know them but also to like them. Many married people come to love their parents-in-law as deeply as they do their own parents. Deutscher (1962) found that many mothers-in-law make a great effort to overcome the old mother-in-law image in their relations with their sons- and daughters-in-law.

3. Do not try to separate or alienate your spouse from his or her family. Husband and wife should both recognize and appreciate the fact that the parents of one's spouse are still going to be deeply concerned about the welfare of their child after marriage. It is natural for parents to be avidly interested in their child's marriage, and to be concerned that things go well. One should remember that these parents devoted a great deal

of their lives to rearing the person one has married. Some tolerance is needed on the part of both husband and wife as each tends quite naturally to be emotionally involved with his or her parents.

4. Keep in mind that you will likely need some assistance from your in-laws. As seen earlier in the chapter, married couples in all walks of life receive help from their parents, including money, household goods, and child-care services. In the present context this means that for each marriage partner such aid is as likely to come from one's in-laws as from one's own parents. Evidence shows that in times of crisis or need married couples are more likely to turn to kin for help rather than to friends or agencies. In his study of Minnesota families, Hill et al. (1970) found that married children received the majority of their economic, household management, and child-care aid from their parents and grandparents. In times of crisis, relatives and in-laws may virtually be lifesavers to their married children.

CHAPTER 15

Middle and later years
of family life

This chapter deals with the last three periods of the family life cycle: (1) the period of contracting family membership, when the family is "launching" its children out into the world as they become young adults; (2) the post-parental period, or "empty-nest stage," when all the children have departed and the husband and wife are now alone for the first time since their children were born; and (3) the period of the aging family, often identified as those years from retirement to the death of the last surviving spouse.

Many of the changes in family roles and relations that take place during these middle and late years of marriage and family life require special adjustment. The launching period may be difficult for many parents, who see their maturing children leave home for college, jobs, and marriage, never again to return as young children. Parents have to break the patterns and habits of about two decades as they let their children go. Their primary parental roles are now behind them, although most will continue an affectionate and "parent-emeritus" relationship with their adult offspring, as we saw in Chapter 14. The empty-nest period generally frees the middle-aged couple to do things they may not have had time or money to do before, but it may also be a period of difficult adjustment for some parents—especially mothers—who may suffer from the "empty-nest syndrome." There is evidence, however, that many married couples evaluate this postparental phase of the family cycle as being as good or better than the preceding phases (Deutscher, 1964; Rollins & Feldman, 1970); and that the effects on the couple are usually slight and tend to disappear two years following the departure of the last child (Harkins, 1978).

In the period of the aging family, numerous issues and adjustments confront the couple, including the man's retirement from his occupation (and, increasingly, the woman's from hers), the onset of financial and health problems, disengagement from various community roles and activities, changing relationships with younger family members, and widowhood. Finally, there is the death of the surviving spouse.

The chapter begins with a brief overview of demographic and social characteristics and changes which distinguish the middle and later years of family life. Next, the two periods comprising the middle years are treated in sequence: (1) the launching period, and (2) the empty-nest period. Attention is directed to the developmental tasks and adjustments required, including marital adjustment. Then the final period of the aging family is treated, focusing on developmental tasks, preparation for aging, disengagement, kinship relations, marriage and family satisfactions, and widowhood or widowerhood. Finally, some suggestions are offered for coping with old age in the family context, followed by a brief consideration of what the future may hold for aging family members.

DEMOGRAPHIC AND SOCIAL CHARACTERISTICS OF FAMILIES IN THE MIDDLE AND LATER YEARS

AGE PERIODS IN MIDDLE AND LATE FAMILY LIFE

The middle and later years of the family can span three or four decades—or even more if the last child leaves home when the couple is in their early or mid-40s. Accordingly, it is helpful to subdivide this span of years into age-groups. Thompson and Streib (1961) suggest four such age-groups: (1) the family of late maturity (husband and wife in the 45-54-year age span); (2) the family of preretirement (husband and wife ages 55–64); (3) the family of early retirement (husband and wife ages 65–74); and (4) the family of late retirement (husband and wife ages 75 and over). It should be pointed out that these age ranges do not necessarily correspond to the three stages of the family life cycle already mentioned above; nor is it true that all persons in each age range are necessarily in the same stage of the family cycle. Now let us see briefly what characterizes family life in those age-groups.

The family of late maturity (age span: 45–54)

More than 90 percent of all men and women in this age range have been married at least once. The great majority of couples live in their own home, and more than 50 percent have at least one child under the age of 18 still living at home. This period encompasses the "launching stage" when the parents watch their children departing to make their own lives as young adults. The 1970 U.S. census showed that more than 45 percent of the wives in this age-group were employed, and the percentage is undoubtedly greater today considering increases in employed married women since the 1970s (Troll, 1971, p. 272).

The family of preretirement (age span: 55–64)

The majority in this age-group are still living at home as married couples, but sex differences in survival are becoming apparent, resulting in a disproportion of widows. In 1975, 85 percent of the men in this age-group were still married, while only 69 percent of the women still had a husband. 20 percent of the women were widowed versus 4 percent of the men (Bureau of the Census, 1976b, p. 46). Fewer of the still-married women are employed than in the previous age-group. The couples are now in the postparental period of their lives. Their relationship with their young adult children has changed from the earlier periods of full responsibility to release and acceptance of their independence. The couple is alone again for the first time since the honeymoon period. They have more freedom to do things together as well as more resources. The husband is generally at the peak of his career.

The family of early retirement (age span: 65–74)

The gap between the number of surviving husbands and wives widens during this period. In 1975, 84 percent of the men in this age group still had a spouse, but only 49 percent of the women still had a husband living (Bureau of the Census, 1976b, p. 46). Forty-two percent were widows as compared to only 8.8 percent widowers. Very few of the wives are still employed by now. Retirement can bring greater freedom for those who have enough money and still enjoy good health; but for others retirement means a reduced standard of living, boredom, and even loss of self-respect.

The family of late retirement (age span: 75 and over)

The number of men and women with a surviving spouse drops sharply now, especially so for wives. In 1975, 70 percent of the men in this age-group had wives still living, while only 23.4 percent of the women had husbands still living. Sixty-nine percent of the women in this age-group were without living spouses as compared to 23 percent of the men (Bureau of the Census, 1976b, p. 46). These differences reflect the fact that women live longer than men and that most men marry women somewhat younger than they are. Family members in this period tend to have moved out of many of their earlier family and community roles (Troll, 1971, p. 272). Old age and deteriorating health make this a period of reduced activity and increasing dependence on others.

While the above age-groupings or periods are helpful in setting the stage for analyzing marriage and family life in the middle and later years—such as in predicting the change from active parenthood to postparenthood or the survival of a spouse—it should be noted that age per se is not a reliable indicator of actual marriage and family relationships. Some people may feel and act "old" before they are 60, while others retain a youthful outlook and are vigorously active well into their 80s.

THE FAMILY LIFE CYCLE

A more fruitful way of examining family life in the middle and later years is to identify where the married couples are in the overall family life cycle. Much in the same manner as an individual grows, matures, and ages through successive changes and readjustments, so each family moves through its life cycle, following a general sequence of growth and development. Duvall (1977, p. 141), a pioneer in the study of family development, describes it this way:

> The family life cycle, used as a frame of reference, affords a longitudinal view of family life. It is based on the recognition of successive phases and patterns as they occur within the continuity of family living over the years. It opens the way for study of the particular problems and potentials, rewards and hazards, vulnerabilities and strengths of each phase of family experience from beginning to end.

Families begin with a married couple and expand and mature as children arrive and grow up; the family then contracts as the children become young adults and leave home to establish their own homes and families. The busy, hectic years when children are growing up give way to the slower-moving years of the empty nest when the middle-aged and later aging couple adjust to the latter half of their married life as a dyad. As it moves through this life cycle, each family expresses its individuality and adjusts to each stage in its own unique way.

Duvall (1977, p. 144) identifies eight successive stages or periods of the family life cycle: (1) newly married couples (without children); (2) childbearing families (from birth of oldest child to age 30 months); (3) families with preschool children (oldest child 2.5 to 6 years); (4) families with school children (oldest child 6 to 13 years); (5) families with teenagers (oldest child 13 to 20); (6) families launching young adults (first child's departure to last child's departure); (7) middle-aged parents (empty nest to retirement); and (8) aging family members (retirement to death of both spouses).

Earlier chapters dealing with marriage and parenthood have focused on Duvall's first five stages of the family cycle. The present chapter is mainly concerned with the last three stages, which cover more than half of the life span for most people today (Duvall, 1977, p. 140). We will use stage six, families launching young adults, and stage seven, middle-aged parents or the empty-nest period, as points of departure in the following discussion of the middle years of family life, and then stage eight, aging family members, in the final section of the chapter.

THE MIDDLE YEARS OF FAMILY LIFE

THE LAUNCHING PERIOD: CONTRACTING FAMILIES

The period of preparing and releasing young adult children for independence is often a difficult one for many parents, as we saw in Chapter 13. Father and mother see their children leaving home for education, jobs, and marriage, generally with mixed feelings of anxiety, pride, hope, and loss. This period may be short or quite long, depending on the number of children to be launched. On the average it would last six or seven years today.

Developmental tasks of families launching young adults

Developmental tasks are role-expectations or responsibilities that arise at or near a certain time in the life of an individual or a family. Successful achievement of such tasks leads to satisfaction and also to success with later tasks, while failure leads to dissatisfaction, disapproval by others, and difficulty with later tasks (Havighurst, 1972, p. 2). Duvall (1977, pp. 341–350) identifies a number of developmental tasks confronting families at this launching stage.

Reallocation of family resources and facilities. The considerable expenses of college, the expenses of clothing, supplies, and transportation for sons and daughters starting out in jobs, the costs of graduations and weddings, all can put a strain on family resources. Families at this stage are apt to be carrying their peak load of family expenses, and the more children the greater the expense. Fortunately, in many middle-class and working-class families, the father is apt to be near the height of his earning power. And today the mother is likely to be employed too.

Reallocating responsibilities among growing and grown children in the family. Older teenagers and young adults normally desire to assume increasing responsibilities for their own affairs, thus relieving

their parents. The success of this task of transferring responsibilities depends on the flexibility of the parents and the developing abilities and maturity of the daughters and sons.

Rediscovering themselves as husband and wife.

Parents are apt to live vicariously through the joys and woes of their growing daughters and sons, and at the same time may be going through the personal "crisis of the middle years." Being middle aged today seems to be more difficult and complex than in earlier times. A middle-aged woman today, thanks to more freedom and opportunities, is far from ready to retire to her knitting. She is still vigorous and has "a head of steam up," both physiologically and emotionally. What is she to do now that her most active period of motherhood is nearing its end? The father too may face certain crises in the middle years. The multitude of hardworking men who never reach the top in their careers must accept and adjust to this reality. In a society that values masculinity, many middle-aged men must adjust to diminishing masculine vigor. It is important at this middle-life period that each marriage partner understand what the other is feeling and experiencing. We will discuss these matters further when dealing with marital adjustment in the middle years.

Maintaining communication within the family, and reconciling differences in value-orientations.

In addition to adequate communication between wife and husband, it is also necessary that the parents and their young adult children be able to get through to one another. The young adult son and daughter are now working through some of the most important and complex tasks of their lives, and those who can freely bring questions and problems to their parents as counselors or sounding boards are very fortunate. At the same time, parents need to face the fact that their sons and daughters belong to a new generation, and will quite likely question their parents' views on many things that affect them both. The younger generation is more apt to hold liberal attitudes about premarital sex, abortion, or smoking marijuana. This generation-gap in attitudes and values is, of course, a matter of degree, and is probably less pronounced in middle-class families who make considerable effort to keep lines of communication open.

Parents in this launching stage of the family cycle are likely to ask "How well have we done by our children?" The haunting fear may linger that, somehow, someway, they should have done more for their children, done a better job of preparing them for life in a difficult world. Parents are also apt to be aware that the family at the launching stage is being judged on its success through its young adult children as family products. Parents who stand by, offering encouragement and help as needed, can provide a stable home base for the successful launching of their sons and daughters.

THE EMPTY-NEST PERIOD:
POSTPARENTAL FAMILIES

The empty-nest stage of the family cycle starts when the last child leaves home and continues until the retirement of the husband, or the death of one of the spouses. With today's longevity, the married couple has an average of 16 to 18 years remaining from the departure of their last child until the death of one spouse (Duvall, 1977, p. 356).

As seen above, middle-aged parents may enter this phase of life with mixed feelings. The mother especially is likely to feel the loss of her primary mother role, while the father continues a primary occupational role until the time of his retirement. However, many mothers today also have careers and will continue to work after their children have departed. For other mothers, this new freedom presents opportunities to continue their higher education or to become more involved in other out-of-home activities. And she still has her wife role, with more time to devote to it than when the children were growing up.

Research suggests that the majority of families probably face this post-parental period with more relief than gloom (Lowenthal & Chiriboga, 1972; Deutscher, 1962). The couple's childrearing responsibilities are behind them, their income is apt to be highest, their leisure time more plentiful. Deutscher (1962) found that many couples in this empty-nest period defined life as better than during the earlier periods. They saw life as better now primarily due to the greater freedoms—freedom from financial concern, freedom from so much housework, freedom to travel, and freedom "to be oneself for the first time since the children came along." Couples who have prepared themselves ahead of time for this postparental period generally adjust very well. Some anticipatory socialization has taken place when parents send their children to summer camps, to visit relatives, and away to college.

Developmental tasks of postparental families

Duvall (1977, pp. 364–383) identifies a number of developmental tasks for families facing the empty-nest stage. Some represent continuations of tasks of the previous launching period, while others are new.

Revising the home and daily life for comfortable and healthy well-being. With the children gone the wife and husband are free to remodel their home for their own comfort and convenience. They may sooner or later decide to sell their old house and move into a smaller domicile requiring less up-keep and expense. Each spouse needs to help monitor the physical and mental well being of the other. More daily attention has to be given to proper diet, getting regular exercise, relaxation, and other health concerns.

Allocating family resources for both present and future needs. At this stage many couples have fewer debts and more income than before. They can relax and enjoy their resources for a time before retirement and the costs of later years are upon them. This calls for (1) learning to spend money for personal gratification after years of putting the needs of their children first, and (2) planning ahead for a financially secure old age. Retirement means a considerable drop in income for most couples. Also, since most wives outlive their husbands, the couple needs to plan now for her security during the probable years of her widowhood.

Assuring marital satisfaction. For the first time since the honeymoon stage the husband and wife are alone together. Many couples in the middle years find this a new opportunity—in fact for some a necessary task—to "find each other again as husband and wife." Sustaining a good, satisfying marriage is of increasing importance as the years go by, and postparental couples tend to turn to each other and seek to recultivate their marital relationship once their children are grown up and gone (Peterson, 1968; Petranek, 1971). Companionship and shared leisure activities contribute to marital satisfaction in the middle years (Hayes & Stinnett, 1971), as does empathy and high communication (Lowenthal & Chiriboga, 1972). Middle-aged wives may experience renewed interest in sexuality, and many couples do enjoy satisfying sexual relations during their middle years and beyond (Masters & Johnson, 1968; Neugarten, 1970). Additional discussion of marital adjustment in the postparental family appears below.

Enlarging the family circle. There is a good deal of continued contact and interaction between most parents and their adult children, as we found in Chapter 14. Thus, the empty-nest period probably isn't all that empty for most middle-aged parents. The family circle is expanded now as new and generally rewarding relations are established with the families of sons-in-law and daughters-in-law. And when grandchildren begin to appear another new dimension, which many couples find gratifying, is added to the family circle. As the couple go through the middle years of family life, they often have more time as well as a renewed interest in "cementing relationships," with both kinfolk and old friends.

Participating in community life. Longevity has increased to the point that many couples arriving at the postparental stage will have about one half of their lives together still ahead of them. The men still have their careers, and with their mother role completed, increasing numbers of women turn to outside interests and activities. Many return to college to continue degree work interrupted earlier by marriage and motherhood. Many now enter the labor force. Many of those "mothers emerita" see this period as a new opportunity for self-expression and self-enhancement, a time to develop latent talents. Studies show that middle-aged couples in the postparental period generally increase their shared activities both outside and inside the home, and that this sharing is conducive to life satisfaction for both men and women (Rose, 1955; Hayes & Stinnett, 1971).

MARITAL ADJUSTMENT IN THE MIDDLE YEARS

Once their children are married and gone, does the fact that the husband and wife no longer have children present, or childrearing responsibilities to divert them from each other, lead to increased marital satisfaction? Or do the empty-nest syndrome and mid-life crises intrude to the point of reducing marital satisfaction?

Some of the earlier studies did in fact report less marital satisfaction or happiness in the middle years than in the earlier years of married life (Bossard & Boll, 1955; Blood & Wolfe, 1960; Feldman, 1965). Some of this reduction in marital happiness was attributed to disenchantment and boredom after many years of marriage. Pineo (1961) observed changes which occurred in marriages between the early- and the middle-years periods (up to 20 years of marriage). He found a general drop in marital satisfaction and adjustment, accompanied by losses of intimacy and reduced marital interaction. Pineo interprets these changes as being part of a process of disenchantment with marriage in the middle years. Unfortunately, Pineo did not follow the couple into the postparental period when a reversal of the downward trend in marital satisfaction may have taken place. Other studies, including more recent ones, suggest that marital satisfaction may increase during the postparental stage. Deutscher (1964) found that the quality of the marital relationship was improved or at least unchanged during the postparental period. Rollins and Feldman (1970) found that the majority of couples they studied experienced an increase in marital satisfaction after their children grew up and left home. The investigators found a curvilinear pattern of marital satisfaction over the life cycle, with high satisfaction in the early honeymoon period, followed by declining satisfaction during the childbearing and rearing periods, followed by an increase in satisfaction in the post-parental period. Glenn (1975), reviewing extensive data from six national surveys, found that middle-aged wives whose children had grown up and left home reported somewhat greater personal happiness and enjoyment of life than wives of similar age with children still living at home. And the former group of wives reported substantially greater marital happiness than the latter. In a study of the effects of the empty-nest transition on mothers, Harkins (1978) found very few consequences, and any observed had largely disappeared by the end of two years. Also, most long-term effects of the transition on the psychological well being of the mother were positive.

THE LATER YEARS OF FAMILY LIFE

THE AGING FAMILY

In reviewing the status of older people and their family life in contemporary America, Shanas (1980) points out that we tend to deprive the elderly both of responsibilities and useful functions in major social institutions. By doing this we create a kind of "role-less role" for the elderly which limits and circumscribes their activities and social relations in the community and to some extent in the family. In most areas of life, such as the marketplace and the world of work, "the only status of those aged 65 or more is that they are old" (Shanas, 1980, p. 14). Since 1900 the number of persons over 65 years of age has increased eightfold. Census figures showed that in 1979 there were more than 24 million people in the United States age 65 and over, composing 11.2 percent of the total population, as compared to about 3 million in 1900 composing 4.1 percent of the total population. (See Table 15–1.)

In the context of American family life, aging usually involves relinquishing two basic roles, the parental and the occupational. With the large increases in employment of married women, old age means that more wives as well as husbands will be relinquishing both of these roles. Thus as we look at the aging family we will be dealing with a period in the life cycle of the individual that has decreased in usefulness and prestige as it has increased in prevalence in the 20th century. It is somewhat ironic that longevity is about 70 years for men and 78 years for women in a society that glorifies youth and emphasizes the achievements of the young adult years.

Table 15–1

Population of the United States aged 65 and over, 1900 to 2020

Year	Number	Percent of total population
1900	3,099,000	4.1
1950	12,397,000	8.1
1960	16,675,000	9.2
1970	20,087,000	9.8
1979	24,658,000	11.2
1990	29,824,000*	11.7*
2000	31,822,000*	11.7*
2010	34,837,000*	11.9*
2020	45,102,000*	14.6*

* Projections
Sources: U.S. Bureau of the Census, *Current Population Reports: Special Studies* (Series P-23, No. 78); "Prospective Trends in the Size and Structure of the Elderly Population, Impact on Mortality Trends, and Some Implications" by J. S. Siegle, in P. C. Glick, *The Future of the American Family;* "Population Profile of the United States," U.S. Bureau of the Census, *Current Population Reports:* (Series P-20, No. 350); "Demographic Aspects of Aging and the Older Population in the United States," U.S. Bureau of the Census, *Current Population Reports: Special Studies* (Series P-23, No. 59).

Many elderly people remain integrated into the family

U.S.D.A. photo by Marianne Pernold

With this background let us now look at what is happening today to aging people in the American family. How are they coping with and adjusting to this final period of the family life cycle?

The eighth and last stage of the family cycle normally begins with the retirement of the husband, continues through the loss of one spouse, and ends with the death of the remaining spouse (Duvall, 1977, p. 385). The elderly couple normally continues to be "family" to their grown children, grandchildren, and often great-grandchildren. With the husband's retirement the couple faces the developmental tasks of this final stage of their lives together.

Developmental tasks of aging family members

The retired couple must seek mutually satisfactory answers to such questions as where it is best for them to live, how they will relate to each other now that they are alone, how they will relate to kin and friends, how they will adjust to reduced income, and how they will keep active as their strength and health decline in the years ahead. As she did for the previous periods of the family, Duvall (1977, pp. 390–406) specifies a number of developmental tasks facing the wife and husband in their final period of life, including the following.

Making satisfactory living arrangements. Once a couple retires they have greater freedom to live where they please. Their options may include (1) remaining in their present home, (2) moving into a smaller house, apartment, condominium, or perhaps a mobile home, and (3) moving into some type of retirement housing. In the very final years, as health fails, it may be necessary to move into a nursing home or to live with one's grown children. In recent decades more elderly who can afford to do so have been moving to warmer climates. Many are attracted by communities geared to the interests and needs of older people (Golant, 1975). In our urban society a declining percentage of the elderly live with their grown children. A widely held American value is that old people should maintain an independent household as long as they are able to do so. During the 1970s, however, this value showed signs of weakening. When nationwide samples of Americans were asked if they thought it was a "good idea" or a "bad idea" for older people to share a home with their grown children, those saying it was a "good idea" increased from 31 percent in 1973 to 40 percent in 1980, while those who thought it a "bad idea" declined from 58 percent in 1973 to 43 percent in 1980 (Davis, 1980, p. 125). (These percentages do not add up to 100 because many respondents gave qualified answers.)

Adjusting to retirement income. In most industries and some professions, such as teaching, most workers retire at or near age 65. Retirement at this age has steadily increased for American workers in the 20th century. One of the immediate consequences of retirement for most families is a substantial reduction in income. Even with some pensions and social security stipends indexed to the consumer price index, the retiree's income is not only reduced but is also subject to erosion by inflation. Thus many elderly people in the final stage of family life are apt to be faced with a reduced standard of living. However, the economic plight of old people is not nearly as bad now as earlier. The proportion of elderly below the poverty line has been falling sharply in recent years. In 1974 only 16 percent of those aged 65 and over were below the poverty line as compared to 35 percent in 1959. For the elderly living in families the proportion who were poor fell from 27 percent in 1959 to 8.5 percent in 1974 (U.S. Bureau of the Census, 1978b). Recent census data show that the proportion of families below the poverty line in 1976 was 8.9 percent for families with a head under aged 65, but only 6.1 percent for families with a head aged 65 and older (U.S. Bureau of the Census, 1979a). So there have been substantial improvements in the overall financial condition of the elderly, in spite of inflation.

Maintaining love, sex, and marital relationships. The aging couple who live alone may depend a good deal on each other for companionship as well as love and understanding. The wife can help her husband find new interests to fill his time now that he has retired. The husband can show his appreciation and devotion to his wife for all she has done over the years for him and for their children. A good marriage relationship helps satisfy most of the needs for love and companionship of the aging husband and wife (Lasswell, 1973, p. 518). Recent studies show that although there is a slowing down of sexual capacity in old age for both male and female, for many people sexual interest and gratification continues into the 70s and for some into the early 80s, and that sexual activity is beneficial to the health and well being of the elderly (Lobsenz, 1975; Martin, 1974).

Keeping in touch with other family members. As seen in Chapter 14, most Americans tend to retain ties with their relatives over the life cycle. As Duvall (1977, p. 401) says, "A two way, three generational flow of emotional and financial support between older parents and their grown children's families is general." This pattern of kinship ties between the generations is widespread across most ethnic and social class lines in the United States. As the aging couple retire from occupational roles and withdraw from other community activities, they characteristically come to enjoy more interaction with their relatives. In a sense, the process of disengagement in the community expedites reentry into the larger kinship system (Cumming & Henry, 1961: Maddox, 1968).

Keeping active and involved. There is a tendency for aging men and women to become less active in community affairs as the years roll by. This is often partly due to declining energy, poor health, reduced finances, or loss of interest. While few old folks can expect to continue the strenuous, physically demanding activities of their youth, keeping physically and mentally active is essential to their good health and well being in these later years, as studies show. One study of recent retirees found that maintaining high morale was significantly related to keeping active, especially in activities that involve helping other people (Sheldon et al., 1975). Another study of retired men in their 70s showed that those who slow down their various activities gradually, rather than abruptly, are more apt to remain happy and well adjusted in their later years (Havighurst, 1972). Authorities generally agree that remaining reasonably active, as health allows, is good for the older person's morale, health, and sense of satisfaction with life.

Disengagement

Since changes and adjustments in marriage and family relations in the final stage of the family cycle are so closely tied to changes in external statuses and roles of aging family members, it is necessary to expand our analysis to include a larger, more general view of the process of aging and the position of older people in America. One of the well-known explanations of this process of aging is the disengagement theory (Cumming & Henry, 1961).

Briefly, disengagement theory holds that with increasing age there is progressively decreasing role involvement. A major aspect of disengagement is the forfeiting of one's major life role; for the woman this has generally been her maternal role, for the man his occupational role. According to Cumming and Henry (1961, p. 14), these role losses are normally accompanied by "decreased interaction between the aging person and others. . . . His withdrawal may be accompanied . . . by an increased preoccupation with himself." Preoccupation with oneself at this stage of life sooner or later includes facing the inevitability of one's death. However, any feelings of demoralization resulting from the combination of role loss, withdrawal from social activities, and facing death tends to be only temporary, and soon gives way to a generally positive attitude toward one's disengaged state. Contributing to this more positive orientation are the facts that old age is a period of many new freedoms. (Deutscher, 1962, p. 524).

Critics of the disengagement theory argue that for many elderly the process of disengagement is not necessarily viewed positively, and that it is the active and engaged elderly who are more content, rather than the disengaged (Rose & Peterson, 1965, p. 363). Adams (1980, p. 341) suggests that the disengagement theory needs to be modified to allow for varying categories of the elderly in American society: (1) the positively oriented disengaged who are in a position to enjoy their new freedoms and who may have prepared themselves by undergoing some "anticipatory disengagement" prior to old age; (2) the negatively disengaged, who, in relinquishing the dominant roles in their lives, tend to find old age to be a period of loneliness, domestic entrapment, and bereavement, rather than new freedom; and (3) the aged who do not become disengaged at all, such as those who are self-employed and never do retire.

Both the proponents and the critics of disengagement theory generally agree that the family remains the focus of the aging person's life. That is, disengagement is *into* rather than *out of* the family (Troll, 1971, p. 281). As seen above, the elderly may be differentially prepared for this last period of their lives in the family. Why are some better prepared than others? Let us turn now to the topic of socialization for the final stage of family life.

Socialization of aging family members

A considerable reorientation is necessary for marital partners to cope with the departure of their children, retirement, disengagement, and aging. How well prepared or socialized are most Americans for these and other related aspects of the later period of life? At best, most aging American people seem to be only partially prepared for the coming of later years. This is understandable in a society that values youth, vigor, and productive roles, while taking a dim view of aging with its declining vigor and reduced productivity. Thus the socialization or resocialization needs of the elderly have been neglected—in sharp contrast to the attention given to the socialization of children and youth. Some authorities now believe that a major focus for further study of the elderly should be socialization for old age. Rosow (1967, p. 326) urges this, observing that old age

> represents a devalued, unstructured role with sharp discontinuities from middle age. Hence, the individual enters the situation with little incentive, role specification, or preparation. Effective socialization under these conditions is problematic and it is necessary to clarify both the conducive and the inimical forces at work in the situation.

Preparations for life in the final stage of the family cycle are made difficult because norms and expectations for the status-role of old age are so ill-defined in American society, and the changes from earlier status-roles are apt to be abrupt and traumatic for many. The mother whose whole life was wrapped up in her children or the man whose career meant everything may find the psychological and social adjustments required when children leave and retirement comes too much for them. They are poorly prepared for these losses unless they have additional interests and values to fall back on, and such things need to be nurtured earlier through anticipatory socialization. Many of the things that can be anticipated and prepared for have been reviewed above in our discussion of the developmental tasks confronting people in this last period of the family cycle.

Some husbands and wives are much better prepared for their senior years than others. Those with a more flexible and equalitarian orientation toward marital and family roles may find it easier to adjust to the final period of the family cycle than those with a more rigid and traditional view of marriage and family (Deutscher, 1962).

FAMILY RELATIONSHIPS OF OLDER PEOPLE

The elderly tend to be separated into two categories when it comes to kinfolk, those with kin and those without. Some old people are kinless because thay never had a marriage partner and children, or siblings, or because they have outlived their kin. Others have lots of relatives, and as elders in the "clan" they represent the apex of a pyramid of relatives spread out below them in three or four generations. Thus there are obviously great differences in the availability of kinfolk for old people to be in touch with. The proportion who are truly kinless is quite small, however (Troll, 1971, p. 265).

Proximity to children

While less is known about the extent to which parents and their adult children maintain close contact throughout the years between child-launching and old age, it is well known that toward the end of life few parents are very far from at least one of their adult children. Shanas et al. (1968) found that 84 percent of those over 65 in America live less than one hour away from one or more of their children. Residential propinquity does not, of course, guarantee either interaction or emotional closeness. Many studies show that older people prefer, when possible, to live in their own homes rather than with their children (Troll, 1971; Shanas et al., 1968; Adams, 1968; Sussman, 1965). Moving in with adult children, especially married children, is resorted to only where there is not enough money to live alone, or where health is so poor that self-care is no longer possible, or in some instances where a spouse has died. Even so, about one third of all people over 65 who have living children do live with them (Troll, 1971). So while joint households of old people and their adult children are the exception rather than the rule, related nuclear households tend to live near each other. This has been found to be particularly true among urban working-class families (Gans, 1962; Adams, 1964). When parents retire and grow older, they tend to migrate near at least one of their adult children (Troll, 1971).

Interaction with children and other kin

The evidence on contacts and interaction of the elderly with their children parallels quite closely the findings on residential propinquity (Troll, 1971; Shanas et al., 1968; Adams, 1964). Elderly parents see their adult children often, and if they live too far apart for regular visiting, as many middle-class families do, they keep in touch regularly by telephone and exchanging letters, and get together periodically for extended visiting.

In a recent study of old people in three industrial societies (England, Denmark, and the United States), Shanas et al. (1968) found that 84 percent of the American respondents had seen at least one of their children during the previous week, and 90 percent within the past month. In a study of three-generation families, Aldous and Hill (1965) found that 70 percent of the young married adults saw their parents each week, as did 40 percent of the middle-aged adults. And 70 percent of these middle-aged adults saw their children weekly. Thus the middle-aged couples tended to interact with both ascendent and descendent close relations, but more with their children than with their parents.

While the aging obviously give high priority to their relationships with their adult children, they also tend to keep in touch with their aging siblings and other relations (Cumming & Schneider, 1961). Shanas et al. (1968) found that more than one third of the elderly in their American sample had seen a brother or sister within the past week. Rosenberg (1970) found that virtually all of his working-class elderly respondents had visited with at least one relative during the previous week. Reiss (1962) found that elderly middle-class Bostonians were in contact at least monthly with one third of their relatives and one fourth of their in-laws.

The kinds of things aged persons do with their kinfolk varies somewhat by sex and social class. That sex is a factor in kinship relations has been noted by many (Aldous, 1967; Cumming & Schneider, 1961; Gans, 1962; Shanas et al., 1968). Female ties seem to be strongest. That is, mother-daughter ties tend to be stronger than mother-son ties from adulthood onward, and sister-sister ties are generally stronger than either brother-sister or brother-brother ties. Most studies show that married couples tend to live closer to the wife's parents, and interact more with the wife's relatives. Affectional ties are stronger among the women, and mutual aid flows more frequently along the female line (Troll, 1971). Older widows are more likely to move in with adult children (usually with a daughter) than older widowers (McKain, 1969; Shanas et al., 1968).

In general, social class differences in kinship relations are not as great as sex differences. While a higher proportion of visiting among working-class people is with kin, this is largely because they do less visiting altogether than do middle-class people and what they do tends to be with relatives (Adams, 1968; Sussman, 1965; Aldous, 1967). Kin relationships tend to be more sex segregated among working-class families than among middle-class families. Mother-daughter ties and father-son interactions are more commonly noted in working-class samples (McKain, 1969; Aldous, 1967). Studies show that there are some social class differences in the help patterns across the generations. In the middle class, considerable help continues to flow from aging parents to their middle-aged children, while in the working class more help goes from middle-aged children to their aging parents (Schorr, 1960; Shanas et al., 1968). Working-class aged parents are more apt to offer services to their children, while middle-class parents offer their adult children financial aid.

Are elderly people who have had children generally happier than those who have not? In a study of the effects of offspring on the psychological well being of older adults, Glenn and McLanahan (1981) conclude that having had one or more children has had no important effects on the psychological well being of older Americans in recent years, and that there is little evidence that psychological rewards are derived from the later stages of parenthood. While these findings were unexpected, they were not inconsistent with other evidence on the well being of older Americans. Other studies have shown that the frequency of interaction with offspring is virtually unrelated to the morale of the elderly (Lee, 1979; Edwards & Klemmack, 1973); and that nonkin primary relations—especially with age-peers—tend to be more satisfying to many older people than relationships with their offspring or with other relatives (Adams,

1968; Lowenthal & Robinson, 1967). Much of the interaction of older persons with their offspring and other relatives is not always pleasant and gratifying (Glenn & McLanahan, 1981). Some older people who have expected close relationships with their adult children feel disappointed and neglected (Brown, 1970).

Some parents who have expected in their old age to receive gratitude and repayment for the work and sacrifices they made for their children are likely to be disappointed. Also, intergenerational relationships may be strained by value and lifestyle differences between the elderly and their adult children, as well as by increasing dependency of the old on their children who may come to feel this as a burden (Glenn & McLanahan, 1981). In many cases older people take pride in and identify with their successful offspring, while in other cases the upward mobility of the offspring may create some social distance between them and put strains on their relationships (Stuckert, 1963b; Dyer, 1972).

Grandparenthood

Grandparent roles and relations are, of course, part of the kinship relationships we have been discussing, but grandparenthood deserves some special attention. Early marriage, the early appearance of children, and

During a person's middle and later years, the family provides nuturing and companionship

Carl Wolinsky/Stock, Boston

increasing longevity means that for more people grandparenthood starts in the middle years rather than in the later years of family life. The increase in four-generation families means that many middle-aged grandparents may themselves have living parents. So the old rocking-chair image of the grandparent seems much less appropriate today than earlier.

Robertson (1977) found the grandmother role to involve baby-sitting, home recreation, and drop-in visits, most of which were initiated by the grandchild or its parents. Since these activities generally provide pleasure without major or lasting responsibilities, many grandmothers find their role more relaxing and enjoyable than their earlier mother role.

Neugarten and Weinstein (1964), in a study of middle-class grandparents, found that most held favorable attitudes toward their grandparent-

Grandmother and granddaughter, Christmas morning

The photography of H. Armstrong Roberts

hood, deriving pleasure, comfort, and personal satisfaction from the role. (Such favorable attitudes probably reflect a social expectancy bias.) Their main difficulty seems to be facing the realization that they actually were grandparents. Both grandmothers and grandfathers saw the significance of their role in terms of being a "resource person" to their grandchildren, enjoying vicariously their achievements, and deriving emotional gratification from the relationship.

Five different styles of grandparenting were identified by Neugarten and Weinstein (1964, pp. 199–204): the formal, the fun-seeker, the reservoir of family wisdom, the surrogate parent, and the distant figure. Any particular grandparent may play one or several of these roles, depending on various circumstances.

1. The *formal grandparent* maintains clearly differentiated lines between the roles of grandparent and parent. The formal grandparent is careful not to intrude on the prerogatives of the parent, although the grandparent may provide baby-sitting services at times.

2. The *fun-seeking grandparent* relates to the grandchild in an informal and playful manner, in effect in a playmate role. Authority lines are irrelevant to the grandchild and the child's parents.

3. The *reservoir of family wisdom* grandparent serves as a resource, providing information, values, and often special skills to the grandchildren. As one young grandson was overheard describing his grandmother in awed terms to a young friend: "She's a very old lady, and she knows all about everything."

4. The *surrogate parent grandparent,* normally the grandmother, acts as a substitute for the child's actual parent, often on a routine basis for a time, as when the child is very young and its mother is employed.

5. The *distant figure grandparent* may be remote from the grandchildren, socially or spatially. Contact with the grandchildren is infrequent and fleeting, perhaps only on special family occasions and holidays.

Neugarten and Weinstein (1964) see a trend toward the fun-seeker and also the distant-figure types among the younger grandparents, while the formal type is more apt to be found among older grandparents where traditional partriarchal or matriarchal authority and age-prestige are still relevant in their relations with the younger generations.

Satisfaction with marriage and family life

Although the evidence on marital satisfaction among the elderly is not as thorough as we would wish, there are indications that many older couples are quite satisfied with their marriages, and are likely to report that their marriages are as happy or even happier than earlier (Troll, 1971; Stinnett, et al., 1970). Old age, then, does not necessarily bring marital discontent; rather, if coupled with reasonably good health and adequate economic resources, marital relations can be satisfactory for couples in the last stage of the family cycle. However, some studies have reported declines in marital satisfaction during the later years of life, particularly among the lower socioeconomic groups, and where there had not been much companionship or equalitarianism throughout the history of the marriage (Blood & Wolfe, 1960; Safilios-Rothschild, 1967). Being married seems to be beneficial for the elderly. Studies show that elderly people who are married are generally happier, better adjusted, and less lonely than other people their age who are unmarried, widowed, or divorced (Stinnett, et al., 1970).

While there have been few studies of older people's subjective satisfaction with their family relationships, there is some evidence that most elderly people, including those in nursing homes, are satisfied in this respect. Seelbach and Hansen (1980) studied samples of 151 nursing home residents and 208 others living out in the community. (Average age for the whole group was 79.8 years.) The investigators found that 88 percent of the whole group said they were perfectly satisfied with the treatment they received from their families, and 81 percent said they got as much love and affection from their families now as they did before (75 percent for the nursing-home residents and 85 percent for those living out in the community). The authors conclude that their findings show that older persons are probably satisfied with their family relations today. Caution is needed in drawing conclusions from these studies because the respondents are apt to answer in the socially desired manner.

THE POSTMARITAL FAMILY

Loss of spouse: Widowhood

Since the probability of an aging husband and wife dying at the same time is very low, the vast majority of marriages not ending in divorce will end with the death of one spouse, leaving a widowed survivor. Stated somewhat differently, a substantial proportion of the American population is going to experience widowhood, most probably in the last period of the family cycle. The probability of the wife being the survivor is by far the greatest, as we saw earlier in the chapter. (See Table 15–2.) By 1976 the difference in life expectancy of males (69 years) and females (76.7 years) was 7.7 years (Siegle, 1978, p. 11); with the death rate of males aged 65 and over exceeding that of females aged 65 and over by nearly 50 percent. In 1976, of those who have reached age 65, females will on average live for 18 more years while males will live only another 13.7 years (Siegle, 1978, p. 12). The problem of widowhood is further compounded by the practice of women marrying somewhat older men. The remarriage problem for elderly widowers is obviously far less than for elderly widows. (See Figure 15–1.)

The postmarital family, consisting of a surviving wife or husband, is not unique to the aging family, of course, but is disproportionately found in the 65-and-over age-group. The survivor has to confront the loss of

Table 15–2

Life expectancy in the United States at age 65, males and females, 1900 to 1976	Life expectancy at 65 (in years)			
	Year	Male	Female	Difference
	1900	11.5	12.2	0.7
	1940	12.1	13.6	1.5
	1954	13.1	15.7	2.2
	1968	12.8	16.3	3.5
	1976	13.7	18.0	4.3

Source: "Prospective Trends in the Size and Structure of the Elderly Population, Impact on Mortality Trends, and Some Implications" by J. S. Siegle, U.S. Bureau of the Census, *Current Population Reports: Special Studies* (Series P-23, No. 78), January 1979.

Figure 15–1

Percent distribution of male and female population 65 years and over by marital status, 1975

Source: "Demographic Aspects of Aging and the Older Population in the United States," U.S. Bureau of the Census, *Current Population Reports: Special Studies* (Series P-23, No. 59), January 1978.

a long-time spouse, and also make the many adjustments required by the shift from a married status to a single widowed status. In some ways the loss of his wife may be more difficult for a man than the loss of her husband is to a woman (Berardo, 1970; Kutner, 1956; Bock & Webber, 1972). Kutner describes the lot of the aging widower:

A life-time of close association with a woman whose complementary activities form the basis of a home now requires the most basic revision for which the widower may be wholly unprepared. If the wife was the home-maker-housekeeper, all those things upon which he depended and could anticipate in the management and upkeep [now] . . . devolve wholly upon him. The economy of convergent interests, the mutual resolution of each other's basic needs, the reciprocity of . . . well ordered roles . . . are supplanted by a solitary and often disjointed independence.

The retired widower is removed from his long-time source of self-identity: his career and his relations with his fellow workers. Then the death of his wife is likely to bring not only a loss of love, companionship, and care-taking, but also a major shift in his linkage of family, friends, and the community. Bock and Webber (1972) found that widowers frequently experience a high degree of social isolation, not only from relatives, but also from former friends, neighbors, and community organizations. They face domestic and familial roles with which they are often not familiar, and they are expected to fend for themselves. Bock and Webber (1972, p. 25) conclude that the results of widowerhood in old age can be unhappiness, low morale, mental disorders, and high suicide rates.

The picture is not necessarily a dismal one for aging widowers, however. As noted above, they have greater opportunity than widows for remarriage. McKain (1969) found that widowers tend to remarry sooner than widows (three years versus seven years after being widowed), and that many widowers marry a woman they have known for a long time, who, interestingly, often resembles their deceased wife. The new wife was generally very beneficial for the man, and the great majority of these remarriages were rated as successful.

To the elderly wife the loss of her husband may be equally grievous, of course. She must not only adjust to the loss of her lover, companion, and supporter, but also to a shift from mutual dependency and an established division of labor within the family to a new "role-less role" and to social and perhaps economic dependency on others. Bock and Webber (1972, p. 24) point out that the widow may have some advantages over the widower which help her to adjust. She will likely continue her domestic roles much as before; she is more apt to be involved in a kinship network, since kinship relations generally rely more on females than on males over the years; and the elderly widow is more likely to continue participating in church groups and other community organizations than is the widower.

There is evidence, however, that although widows do tend to sustain kinship and community contacts, many of them do not receive the kind or amount of support they need. Lopata (1978) found that "the modified extended-family network" frequently fell short of meeting the needs of widowed relatives. Adams (1980, p. 355) is of the opinion that, while the elderly generally desire autonomy, the lack of participation in a larger kin network can leave the widow in a difficult position. Even one's own adult children seem incapable of solving the support problem of the widow. Middle-class widows as well as working-class and lower-class widows are often in need of financial as well as emotional support.

Loneliness is of course one of the main problems of widowhood. (See Figure 15–2.) Among the Chicago widows interviewed by Lopata (1978) more than half said that loneliness was their greatest problem. Most of these women found that after losing their husband their new single status resulted in their being "subtly stigmatized" socially. They were excluded from social gatherings of mixed couples. Married women often regarded them with some suspicion, as though they might try to steal their husbands. It seemed to these widows that the only people they could find for friends and be at ease with were other widows. The rise of social clubs for the widowed attests to the need for companionship and social life in this population.

Adams (1980, p. 359) sees some signs of increasing willingness on the part of some aging people to experiment with alternative lifestyles when their spouse is no longer living. Some may prefer cohabitation to remarriage, both for companionship and to maintain maximum social security benefits. This would allow greater freedom and fewer legal obligations. Experimentation of this kind, often in retirement communities, may

Figure 15–2

Percent distribution of the male and female population 65 years old and over by living arrangements, 1975

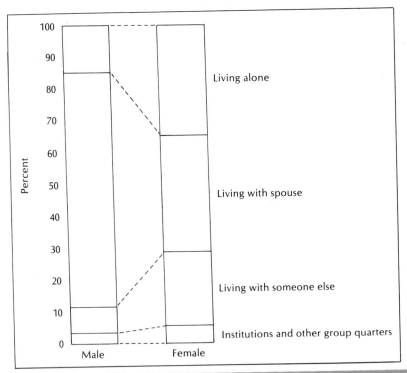

Source: "Demographic Aspects of Aging and the Older Population in the United States," U.S. Bureau of the Census, *Current Population Reports: Special Studies* (Series P-23, No. 59), January 1978.

have been learned from observing younger Americans, representing a kind of "reverse socialization" (Falkman & Irish, 1974). Given the generally conservative orientation of most of the elderly, along with the prevailing norms which support conventional relations between elderly men and women in America, it is doubtful that living together without benefit of marriage will become a widespread practice among the aging widowed in the immediate future.

SUGGESTIONS FOR COPING WITH OLD AGE

It is unfortunate but true that American society does not make it easy for us to adjust to aging. Social and psychological changes in the process of aging contain high potential for trauma, as Heiss (1968, p. 461) notes:

> [In addition to frequent] financial difficulty [are] the problems of being old in a society which values youth, the lack of an occupational function in a society which gives first place to a person's occupation . . . , [and] the usual strains attendant upon approaching death and the loss of loved ones. In America the aged have all the problems of their group, and few of the compensations to be found in more traditional societies.

Still active at 77, a grandfather rests with his grandson during harvest activities

U.S.D.A. photo by Doug Wilson

Various kinds of suggestions and some actual efforts are being made to help ease the adjustments of aging. Let us look briefly at some of these.

Better preparation for old age

It has been noted more than once that in youth-oriented America little attention has been given to preparing people for old age. What socializing agents help prepare a man for retirement, or a woman for postparenthood, or either of them for widow- or widowerhood? What institutions or agents assume the responsibility of preparing the aging person for disengagement, eventual inactivity and inevitable death?

Schools, churches, health-care organizations, the media, as well as the family, can do more to help prepare men and women for the period of life called old age—which inevitably lies ahead for the vast majority of Americans. Social scientific knowledge on aging is now being disseminated more in colleges, universities, and gerentological organizations, and through family social service agencies. Much more can be done, however.

More retirement communities

Retirement communities and various residential areas catering to the needs of the elderly have been in existence in the United States since the 1920s and are on the increase, especially in the warmer climates. This development is logical in a society where there seems to be little room for old folks to live with their adult children or other relatives. And, as noted earlier, in the face of retirement, separation from their children, and widow- or widowerhood, older people often turn to each other for companionship and mutual support. Communities for the elderly range from public housing projects to mobile home and recreational vehicle parks to leisure communities for the affluent.

Sun City, Arizona, is a good example of a successful retirement community. Started in 1960 as a development for people over age 50 with no live-in children, it has grown rapidly, and is expected to have a population of 55,000 by the early 1980s. Due partly to the success of Sun City, other developers have followed its lead and now there are a good many retirement communities in the United States. Many, but not all, are in the so-called Sun Belt. Many retired people come to see the advantages of moving into smaller dwellings in a community where maintenance and security are provided for them, along with social activities, recreation, companionship, and often health care services too.

Some communities for the elderly provide a broad array of activities. Heritage Village in Connecticut offers residents a choice of more than 70 activities, from college courses to drama groups to woodworking to volunteer community work to the usual kinds of recreation, such as golf and tennis. Most residents seem content to indulge in the leisure activities

An older couple enjoying traveling

Cary Wolinsky/Stock, Boston

available, feeling that they have "paid their dues" during their working and family-rearing years (Meehan, 1973).

Alternative family forms for the elderly

Streib (1978) points out some advantages for elderly people who are removed from their kin or no longer have any kin of joining an alternative family form such as a commune or a "family" of nonrelated senior adults. They could pool their resources and live more economically; they could share household tasks, meal preparation, and shopping; they could provide companionship, and take care of each other where necessary. Streib describes one such recent attempt to devise such an alternative family for the elderly in Florida known as Share-A-Home. This family group consists of nonrelated elderly women and men who jointly own and share a large house and divide the expenses of running the household. A salaried manager and his staff take care of the finances and are responsible for providing food, cleaning, laundry, and transportation. This is an especially good situation for a widow or widower who is no longer able to maintain his or her own household and who does not wish to enter a nursing home. A number of Share-A-Home units have spread over Florida and into neighboring states. These Share-A-Home families seem to be meeting some of the pressing needs of old folks, including (1) free choice of living arrangements, (2) close association with others who are concerned and who offer companionship and affection, and (3) the need for dignity and autonomy (Streib, 1978, p. 417).

A less formally organized alternative lifestyle developed spontaneously among the residents of Merrill Court, a housing project in San Francisco. As described by Hochschild (1973), the 43 residents (aged 60 to 80) were mostly retirees from small southern and midwestern towns who were of modest means and were very conservative. They were hardly the type to form an experimental communal lifestyle. What happened was that some residents began to meet informally for morning coffee in the housing project recreation room. This soon led to "spontaneous fellowship" among the residents, which led rapidly to all kinds of joint activities, including a Bible study group, a service club, a band which visited old folks' homes, and a workshop for homemade articles to be donated to local charities. Numerous committees were formed, and during the three years of the study Hochschild observed that most of the residents had the opportunity to chair or be in charge or some project or group activity. Feeling that they had discharged their responsibilities to their families, these elderly retirees took on responsibilities toward each other. Together they were able to work out solutions to mutual needs and problems, and lead useful and interesting lives.

Neither Merrill's Court nor Share-A-Home would suit everyone, of course. They illustrate some of the alternatives older people have for working together to meet common needs. Streib and Streib (1975) judge that true "intentional communes" are unlikely to be formed among older people because they normally want to hold onto whatever property they have accumulated, they prefer independent living units, they tend to be conservative and conventional, and they lack the energy for creating and operating an organized, communal structure.

Other assorted groups and activities for the elderly

Various programs have been created to help old people keep busy and pass their time in meaningful and useful activities, and to help improve their living situations. The American Association of Retired Persons has, for example, helped place capable retired volunteers who are specially trained by the Internal Revenue Service in providing free income tax assistance to elderly people around the country. In California a group of elderly men and women called the Gray Bears pay a dollar a year which entitles them to glean a grocery bag of leftover fruit or vegetables each week from the fields of local farmers who need their fields cleaned up after the main harvest is in.

Some American communities have Foster Grandparent programs, which employ lower-income elderly men and women to help care for institutionalized and deprived children. These foster grandparents are paid for their services, but equally important, they and their charges often develop renewed interest in life, and are drawn out of their isolation (Smith, 1973).

One of the problems with many of these work activities and community projects is that while they help improve the quality of life for older people, they do not generally meet all their emotional needs. Cavan (1974), among others, reiterates the point that people in later life continue to feel a need for an intimate relationship with someone of the opposite sex. Since there are so many more unattached elderly women than men, it has been suggested that such needs might be met through instituting polygyny. Kassel (1966) suggests that if an older man were allowed to marry two or three or more older women, this would enable many more widows to remarry. The husband and wives could pool their economic resources so all could live more comfortably. All could share the housework and lessen individual burdens. When someone got ill there would be several others present to provide the needed care. Competition among the wives for the husband's affection would be stimulating and provide incentive for keeping themselves attractive, and this would boost their morale. The husband in turn would be motivated to keep himself in good shape for the sake of his wives. Thus, polygyny could be a means for relieving the loneliness and depression of many widowed older people by providing them a better chance for remarriage.

Kassel (1966) suggested this alternative some years ago, but it still is not a realistic proposal, given existing laws (polygyny is illegal in all 50 states), and prevailing norms in America which strongly support monogamy. For the proposal to work, not only would plural marriages have to be legalized, but changes in basic beliefs would also be necessary, to say nothing of a drastic resocialization of the aged, most of whom have had long prior experience with monogamous marriage.

PROSPECTS FOR THE FUTURE

Streib (1970) predicts that most of the present trends discernible in the older population will continue into the foreseeable future. Women will continue to outlive their husbands, thus perpetuating the sex-ratio imbalance and the persistence of widowhood as a dominant feature of the elderly population.

Older people will probably continue to prefer to live separately from their adult children, although there is now some effort to reintegrate the elderly into the larger family circle. Liberalized attitudes toward divorce will likely result in more divorce among the elderly as well as among the middle aged. More of the elderly who are divorced or are widows or widowers will probably remarry, thus complicating parent-child and in-law relationships in matters of property inheritance, family assistance, and visiting.

Contacts between old people and their kin and in-laws will continue. While most old parents prefer to live alone, they tend to live near and see their children frequently, and in the middle class at least, there is a good deal of reciprocity in services and gifts, with the aging parents continuing to aid their children (Troll, 1971).

The empty-nest syndrome will probably not be a major difficulty for most women in the postparental period of life. More mothers emerita will be employed and have various extrafamily interests to help diminish the sense of loss when their children have grown up and departed. Elderly couples with sufficient financial means will find satisfaction in travel, community participation, and leisure activities, all of which can help fill the void of departed child-centered family activities.

While most older people will continue to live by themselves in their own homes or apartments until they are no longer able to care for themselves, there probably will be more housing developments and age-segregated communities available to them. Because of limited financial resources and high inflation, many elderly people who have to live on fixed incomes will continue to be an economically disadvantaged group.

Since the young and the middle aged generally control the economic, political, and legal structures in the United States, the special needs and problems of the elderly are not always given high priority. It has been argued that our society will be unlikely to do much to help the aged until they themselves become more vocal and militant in pressing their demands (Streib, 1970). In some states with large elderly populations, such as California and Florida, "gray power" is now making itself felt politically. This trend toward political action will probably continue—but not rapidly or dramatically—as the proportion of old people increases, and as more better-educated and politically aware people join the ranks of the elderly.

C H A P T E R   1 6

Prospects for the future

What does the future hold for the family? Will marriage and family survive? Will they change into something quite different, or be replaced by alternative forms of intimate relationships? In this chapter we review briefly some of the varying points of view on the future prospects for marriage and family. We will try to assess the possible impacts that the various alternative lifestyles may have on marriage and family. We will look at some predictions family sociologists are making as to what the future holds. The last section of the chapter will examine various sources of assistance and support available today, such as marriage and family counseling, family life education programs, family courts, and marriage and family enrichment programs.

WILL MARRIAGE AND FAMILY SURVIVE?
CONFLICTING VIEWPOINTS: FAMILY DISINTEGRATION VERSUS FAMILY REORGANIZATION

Debates over whether or not the family is going to survive are scarcely new. Gloomy predictions of its imminent demise may be found throughout our history. For many years the twin themes of family disintegration and family reorganization have held sway in the family literature. Twentieth-century proponents of the family disintegration viewpoint, such as

Sorokin (1937) and Zimmerman (1949), viewed with alarm family changes that had occurred since the 19th century and concluded that the American family was headed toward disintegration in the not-too-distant future. They viewed the breakdown of traditional family authority and values, and the weakening of traditional sex codes, as undermining the family institution and signaling its coming disintegration.

Other authorities, such as Burgess and Locke (1945) and Folsom (1934) interpreted the 20th-century trends and changes in marriage and family less pessimistically. They argued that the Amerian family was not disintegrating, but rather was in process of reorganizing in keeping with the broad social changes of our times. They saw the family as being in transition from its earlier traditional, authoritarian, institutional type toward a more democratic, companionship type. Family reorganization would involve its reshaping through the redefining of attitudes and values of the members—the husband and wife, the parents and children—and in the development of a new conception of the family which its members individually and collectively realize.

While the majority of family sociologists today would be more in agreement with Burgess and Folsom than Sorokin and Zimmerman, there continue to be differences of opinion among them as well as among laypersons as to the future of marriage and family in America. Concern about the "state of the American family" is being voiced by many different commentators in religious, political, and journalistic circles, as well as by social scientists. Many who view the traditional family as intrinsically valuable are dismayed at what they see happening. Increasing premarital sex, increasing divorce rates, and widening gaps between parents and their children are viewed with alarm as symptoms of family disintegration. Other observers, while also concerned with increased marriage and family disruption, tend to take a broader perspective, seeing marriage and family surviving the current, rather difficult period of change and adjustment and moving toward a more flexible structure which will provide greater personal freedom and greater opportunities for family members (Kirkpatrick, 1963; Bane, 1976a).

Still others think that marriage and family have probably outlived their usefulness, and should be replaced by alternative lifestyles (Cooper, 1971). Is this going to happen?

WILL ALTERNATIVE LIFESTYLES REPLACE MARRIAGE AND FAMILY?

As noted in Chapter 11, critics of conventional marriage and family see the nuclear family as too restrictive and inadequate to the job of meeting the goals and needs of modern Americans. Conventional marriage and family, they argue, places too many restrictions, such as sexual exclusivity, on personal freedom, and forces men and women into stereotyped sex roles. The critics argue that any security that traditional marriage and family may hold for its members is not worth the price in limitations imposed on personal freedom (Cogswell, 1975).

What do the alternative lifestyle seekers want? According to Conover (1975, p. 453), their goals and aspirations include individual autonomy, gender equality, self-actualization, openness in communication, intimacy in a variety of interpersonal relations, and sexual variety. Let us next look briefly at certain types of alternative lifestyles within which the seekers try to achieve such goals.

Types of alternative lifestyles

Adams (1973) identifies three major types or categories of alternatives to conventional marriage and family. These types are helpful in reviewing and analysing the variety of specific experiments, and in assessing their possible impact on marriage and family in the future. They are (1) *parallel alternatives,* which are external to and exist alongside of marriage and family; (2) *incorporable alternatives,* which would modify conventional marriage and family by becoming incorporated into its existing structure; and (3) *replacement alternatives,* which would actually be substitutes for conventional marriage and family.

Parallel alternatives. Such alternatives are parallel to and outside existing marriage and family patterns, for example, premarital or postmarital cohabitation or remaining single. As seen in Chapter 14, there have been large increases recently in the numbers of young women and men choosing to remain single longer before marriage. The evidence suggests that these are usually temporary rather than permanent alternatives to conventional marriage (Moran, 1972; Stein, 1975), but at any given time it can be expected that a significant proportion of American adults will be single. The sharpest rise in recent years is among women. U.S. census figures for 1979 showed that 25 percent of women aged 14 and older had never been married (U.S. Bureau of the Census, 1980b). The same report also showed there were more than 1.3 million households shared by two unrelated adults of the opposite sex, referred to by the Bureau of the Census as "unmarried couple households." It should be noted that the sharp increase in cohabitation represents a very small proportion (about 3 percent) of all adults making up married and unmarried couples who were living together in 1979 (U.S. Bureau of the Census, 1980b).

Incorporable alternatives. These alternatives aim to modify or reorganize certain aspects of conventional marriage and family without basically changing its structure. Such alternatives would range from experiments that expand the nuclear family network to include other intimate persons who would help share the family responsibilities, to open marriage and more extreme experiments, such as "mate swapping." Due to their illicit nature, it is difficult to estimate the extent of mate swapping or swinging practices. Authorities generally agree that only a tiny minority of American adults are ever involved in them (Denfeld & Gordon, 1971; Hunt, 1974). The notion of open marriage, as conceived by the O'Neills (1972), with its emphasis on equality of the sexes, role flexibility, and companionship, does appear to be a significant trend in the modification of contemporary marriage.

Replacement alternatives. These alternatives are ideologically opposed to conventional marriage and family and seek to replace them. Communes are probably the best known of these replacement alternatives. Although not new in American history, it has been during the last 15 or 20 years that the present-day varieties of communes have emerged and attracted a good deal of attention. There are many varieties, and they may be found in both urban and rural settings. Some have strong creeds their members are expected to accept; others are noncredal, relying more on personal attachments and shared interests of members. Some are primarily economic, with income and property being shared, while other aspects of life are left up to the individuals or nuclear families composing the communal group. Other communes, often strongly ideological, emphasize sharing all things. Estimates of the number of communal groups in the United States in the early 1970s ranged from 2,000 up to 4,500. With about 10 persons per commune on average, there would be not more than 45,000 people involved, which is about one hundredth of one percent of the American population (Adams, 1973). While empirical evidence is meager, estimates are that the number of communes has declined in recent years.

Group marriages, discussed in Chapter 11, bear some resemblance to certain communes. Since such group marriages are illegal and still strongly disapproved by society, it is difficult to know how many such "marriages" actually exist. Probably they are more rare than communal groups. It would seem unlikely that very many Americans will choose group marriage as an alternative to conventional marriage in the near future.

Possible effects of alternative lifestyles on future marriage and family

Will some or all of the various alternative lifestyles sooner or later replace traditional marriage and family? Or, if they are not replaced, will conventional marriage and family be fundamentally changed by the various experiments and alternative practices taking place today? Most authorities would argue that the institutions of marriage and family will survive the assaults of the alternatives (Adams, 1973; Bane, 1976a). As to the second question, it is probably too soon to say with confidence what lasting effects many of the alternative forms will have on the shape of marriage and family. Traditional marriage and family patterns are certainly undergoing changes today due to modern secular trends, including equalitarianism, feminism, and the great emphasis on individual need-satisfaction and self-enhancement. History, however, teaches us that after a spate of experimentation many of the new experimental forms tend to lose their appeal and zest and soften their most extreme or radical aspects, as is true of certain communes today (Goode, 1964, p. 5).

Which of the three categories of alternative lifestyles discussed above are more likely to survive or have any lasting effects on the future of marriage and family? Our first guess would be some of the incorporable alternatives which seek to modify traditional marriage and family but which do not aim to change the basic marriage or family structure, such as equalitarian marriage or open marriage. Second most likely to survive would be some of the parallel alternatives, such as premarital and postmarital cohabitation. Note again that these parallel alternatives do not aim to do away with conventional marriage and family or change their basic structure; rather, they offer people an optional lifestyle, which for most is only temporary. The third category of alternatives which are opposed to conventional marriage and family and seek to replace them—such as communes and group marriages—will likely continue to attract only a very small proportion of American adults in the foreseeable future. Their impact on the institutions of marriage and family will probably continue to be minimal.

It is possible that the availability of the various alternatives for those people who are not satisfied with conventional marriage and family may mean that those who *do* choose the conventional forms will be a more satisfied group than in the prealternative period of our history. Alternative lifestyles offer a safety valve for those who prefer something different.

THE FUTURE OF MARRIAGE AND FAMILY

Survival of marriage

As noted earlier, conventional marriage has come in for a good deal of criticism from several quarters in recent years. People holding traditional, conservative views are prone to decry the high divorce rates, pointing to them as evidence of a breakdown in marital stability and permanence. They may blame this on sexual immorality, early marriage of immature youth, lack of personal commitment to marriage, or lax marriage and divorce laws. At the other extreme are those who believe that conventional marriage is an old-fashioned institution that has outlived its usefulness. They argue that it is time for traditional marriage to give way to more up-to-date types of intimate relationships, some new alternative forms or lifestyles.

In spite of the gloomy views of the traditionalists who long for the good old days on the one hand and the disenchantment of the radicals on the other, there is ample reason to be cautiously optimistic as to the survival of marriage. Marriage continues to be a highly popular institution in the United States. Some authorities contend that marriage is still the most highly valued relationship in America. According to Udry (1974, pp. 1–2), "Americans believe in marriage above all. They marry earlier, remain unmarried less often, and remarry after divorce more frequently and more rapidly than people of any other industrialized nation. They look to their marriage relationship for their greatest satisfaction in life." Marriage is probably still seen as the main source of personal happiness by most of us (Campbell, et al., 1976).

In a comparison of marriage rates in 22 countries, Carter and Glick (1976, p. 388) found that in 1965 the United States had the second highest marriage rate, and that from 1970 to 1974 the United States had the highest marriage rate. High divorce rates here are accompanied by high remarriage rates, which is a pretty good indication that most who divorce are not rejecting marriage itself, but only a specific marriage partner. There is evidence that the great majority of American people, including many who advocate experimentation in alternative lifestyles, "acknowledge that for the overwhelming majority of people . . . , monogamous marriage [is] the preferred pattern" (Scanzoni, 1972, p. 156). Scanzoni predicts that monogamous marriage in America will not only survive but thrive in the coming years. Most men and women will look to marriage for their personal fulfillment, including affection, sexual gratification, and companionship. In situations where both the woman and the man are employed there is the obvious advantage of pooled resources. Two good incomes can yield a lifestyle more affluent than one good income. The majority of married couples will become parents whose children bring to them a sense of achievement, creativity, and satisfaction not available normally to unmarried men and women.

Future of marriage

While few authorities doubt the continued survival of marriage, most would agree that the conception of marriage is undergoing some redefinition. Over the past century, there has been a steady movement in industrial societies away from the older notion of marriage as primarily a means of providing economic and social security toward a conception of marriage as a means of providing love, intimacy, and companionship. It may be argued that these have become the central values of marriage today for most Americans. This long-range change has contributed to some redefinition of marriage and its permanency. The traditional lifelong commitment of marriage, at one time based on consideration of security and survival, has eroded somewhat in the face of the ascendency of the newer values of love, companionship, and the pursuit of personal fulfillment.

Also, individuals today have greater flexibility in their choices, and more reversibility once a choice has been made: There is now greater tolerance of premarital sex, pregnancies can be prevented, abortions can be obtained, and people can get divorced.

Another significant trend affecting the future of marriage is the movement toward greater equality of the sexes. The women's liberation movement is one recent aspect of this. Today women are more nearly equal to men than a generation ago not only in educational and occupational opportunities, but also in sexual attitudes and behavior. Readily available contraceptives, more liberal abortion laws, and more day-care facilities for children all represent steps in the emancipation of women from a lifetime largely confined to childbearing and rearing. One of the consequences for marriage of this greater sex-role equality is that more wives and mothers are entering the labor force, and by being more capable of supporting themselves they are apparently less reluctant than other women to dissolve unsatisfactory marriages. Thus it is likely that the divorce rate will remain high.

In sum, the trend toward equality of the sexes is conducive to some fundamental changes in marriage and family life, including expectations of companionship between the spouses, changing expectations about sexual satisfaction, equity in decision making, and numerous role readjustments.

While the great majority of people still probably enter marriage with the expectation that it will be permanent, high divorce rates suggest that many marriages are now made which clearly are not "until death do us part." The future may see more public acceptance of temporary marriages, or those that last only until the children are grown. It is uncertain just how many Americans may have reached the point of entering marriage on the temporary or experimental basis suggested by Farber (1964) in his "permanent availability" theory. Such persons, even though married, would be constantly on the lookout for someone better than their present partner, and thus remain permanently available in the marriage market. While some serial monogamy is practiced today, it should be noted that the large majority of divorced persons who remarry remain married to their second marriage partner. High remarriage rates suggest that people are not giving up on marriage itself, but rather are seeking a better marriage, or are less willing to remain in a less than satisfactory marriage.

It is difficult to see just what shape marriage of the future will take if it comes to be defined as mainly a vehicle for personal satisfaction and growth. There is some reaction already to this highly individualistic orientation. Will there be more? Will there be a resurgence of the older ideas of marital obligations, constraints, and personal sacrifices necessary to an enduring commitment? While such questions cannot yet be answered, it may be reassuring to know that marriage is still the overwhelming preference of most Americans (Roper, 1974). Bernard (1972, p. 301), an ofttime critic of marriage, still avows:

The future of marriage is as assured as any social form can be, for men and women will continue to want intimacy, they will continue to want

*Their marriage has
endured for more than 50
years*

U.S.D.A. photo by Bill Marr

to celebrate their mutuality, to experience the mystic unity which once
led the church to consider marriage a sacrament. . . . There is hardly any
probability such commitments will disappear or that all relationships between men and women will become merely casual or transient.

Survival of family

There is plenty of room to argue that the family will survive (Broderick,
1979; Bane, 1976a). Following a thorough review of historical and demographic data on the American family, Bane (1976a) predicts with confidence that parents and children living together in families are indeed
"here to stay." She finds that Americans value children and generally
share some basic views as to how a society should treat them: (1) children
should receive secure and continuous care; (2) they should not be abused

nor abandoned; and (3) they should be wanted both by their parents and by society.

In spite of family changes and adjustments required by divorce and by employment of mothers, Bane is optimistic for the future of the family. As she sees things (Bane, 1976a, p. 2):

> Arguments that modern families are failing their children usually cite rising divorce rates and the rising proportion of mothers working as evidence that children are less well cared for by their parents now than in the past. . . . In addition, statistics on falling birth rates are sometimes used as evidence that modern Americans want and value children less than earlier generations. But data on parental care, family size, and the ties between generations can be used to make a different argument, that discontinuities in parental care are not greater than they were in the past; and that changes in fertility rates may lead to an environment that, according to generally agreed-on criteria, is more beneficial for children.

Demographic materials, according to Bane (1976b), suggest that the alleged decline of the role of the family in caring for children is more myth than fact. There is evidence that parental watchfulness over children has not decreased over the past three generations, but has probably actually increased. The most important difference between children today and children of their grandparents' and great-grandparents' time is that today there are fewer of them per family. Bonds between parents and their children are strong today despite family disruptions. The proportion of children who lose a parent by death has steadily declined over the generations; while the proportion of children who live with a parent after a divorce or death of one parent has steadily gone up. Even in these times of high divorce rates and other family disruptions very few children have gone to live with relatives, or to foster homes or other institutions (Bane, 1976b, p. 105).

The increased employment of mothers outside the home has probably not materially affected mother-child relations, as we saw in Chapter 13. Although more mothers now work outside the home, and children go to school earlier and longer, neither the quantity not the quality of mother-child relations has likely changed much. Bane (1976b, p. 105) concludes that:

> The major demographic changes affecting parents and children in the course of the century have not much altered the basic picture of children living with and being cared for by their parents. The patterns of structural change so often cited as evidence of family decline do not seem to be weakening the bonds between parents and children.

Future of family

As a social institution, the family has long been a major vehicle for maximizing individual and collective security and stability. Recently, love, intimacy, and attachment have emerged as central values of family life.

Three generations gather to share the Christmas holidays

The photography of H. Armstrong Roberts

Such changes are bringing redefinitions of family roles and relationships.

One of the significant changes taking place is a redefinition of parenthood. Contrary to the older view of childbearing as an obligation, it has now become a matter of individual choice. And the growth of voluntarily childless marriages indicates that many married couples are now deciding that it is not in their interest to have any children at all (see Table 16–1). Also, many couples who do become parents are postponing having their children longer in order to do other things first. With the increasing employment of married women, those who become mothers are often confronted with pressing problems of how best to care for

Table 16–1

Proportion of married women who remain childless	*Women born in:*	*Percent childless among ever-married women*
	1846–1855	8.2
	1866–1875	11.1
	1886–1890	15.2
	1901–1905	20.4
	1911–1915	18.2
Source: Various U.S. census	1926–1930	8.6
reports on differential fertility,	1936–1940	8.3
1910–1970.	1945–	10.0 (estimated)

their children while they are at work. As single-parent families continue to grow in number, community and governmental aid programs will need to expand. Parenthood and the care of children are quite likely to become pressing issues in public policy in the United States, as they already have in many other industrialized nations.

The family life cycle is also undergoing some redefinition. As compared to earlier generations, formal education today lasts longer, young people are postponing marriage longer, the childbearing stage is shorter, and the postparental stage is longer since life expectancy is increasing.

As we noted in Chapter 6, an increasing number of young people are postponing marriage, preferring first to pursue their education, get under way in their careers, and pursue various other interests before marrying and settling down. Expanded life expectancy and preference for fewer children make it possible to defer marriage and parenthood. For some, remaining single may be regarded as a way of postponing certain obligations traditionally associated with adulthood. For many women, the growing desire to be independent and to establish their own identities and careers are good reasons for postponing marriage. It seems likely that this trend toward later marriages will continue for a while (American Council of Life Insurance, 1974).

Another change in the family life cycle is a considerably lengthened postparental or empty nest stage. Most women who marry at about 21 will have completed their childbearing period by the age of 26. The mother's two or three children will be in school when she is in her early 30s and by the time she is in her mid-40s they will be grown up and gone (see Table 16–2). As compared to her grandmother, she will be left with many more years in which to do other things, such as continue her education or seek employment. Of course, many mothers today scarcely interrupt their education or employment during their childbearing period.

The growing number of divorces at middle age suggests that more couples are now separating at about the time their children leave home. This suggests that some parents may remain married mainly for the sake of their growing children, and once the children are gone the couple

Table 16–2

Average number of children born to married women with children	*Women born in:*	*Average number of children*
	1846–1855	5.71
	1866–1875	4.55
	1886–1890	3.75
	1901–1905	3.13
Source: Various U.S. census reports on differential fertility, 1910–1970.	1911–1915	2.94
	1926–1930	3.39
	1936–1940	3.06

will separate, perhaps in the hope of finding more compatible partners with whom to spend the extended postparental years.

Few students of the family doubt that the American family has a future, but just what the future family will be like is less clear. Greater freedom and more options make greater demands on family members, and these demands and the related hazards of making choices among alternatives can be stressful. On the other hand, greater freedom of choice and more alternatives to choose from hold the promise of a richer, fuller family life for all members.

Some specific predictions regarding future marriage and family

It is always risky to make predictions in the area of marriage and family living. To make a balanced judgment regarding their future right now is certainly difficult. We are in a period of change and reaction to change. Feelings run strong on many of the issues and problems bearing on family change. Heated debates between those advocating basic changes in family structure and those opposing changes often cloud the issues and make it difficult to see what lies ahead. The data are apt to be incomplete and less reliable than we prefer; and there are many honest differences of opinion and interpretation today among students of marriage and family. However, after extensive review of the research and literature, the author believes that there is sufficient evidence or professional opinion to support the following tentative predictions (Dyer, 1979, pp. 450–451).

1. Marriage and family will survive in America, but in ever-changing forms. Changes in husband-wife relations, in parent-child relations, and to some extent in sibling relations, will be an ongoing condition of family life in the foreseeable future.

2. While the nuclear family will continue to be the predominant family unit in America, modified extended family ties will continue to be present too. That is, important ties will continue to be sustained between adult sons and daughters and their aging parents especially, and to some extent between adult siblings.

Affectional bonds between grandparents and grandchildren will continue

Elizabeth Crews/Stock, Boston

3. Monogamous marriage will continue to be the predominant form of heterosexual association in the foreseeable future. While more adults may opt to remain single longer—including those who cohabit for a time—the great majority of Americans will sooner or later marry and continue to have most of their intimate needs satisfied within conventional monogamous marriage.

4. The trend toward equalitarian marriage will continue, with wives moving toward fuller equality with their husbands in status and authority. While middle-class couples have generally taken the lead in this trend, equalitarian marriage is now spreading into the other social classes too.

5. As married women continue to join their husbands in the labor force, traditional sex-role differentiation in marriage and family will continue to decline. Families of the future will see more role-interchangeability as well as role-flexibility. Companionship or colleague-type marriages will increase. Husband-wife relationships and parent-child relationships will become even more informal.

6. Marriage partners will continue to experience many problems and situations requiring frequent adjustment efforts in the foreseeable future. In the inexorable movement toward sex role equality, many couples will find marriage an ongoing confrontation and renegotiation process. Also, greater freedom for all family members and wider ranges of choice in

Christmas Eve will remain a special family occasion

D. E. Cox/Photo/Graphics

marriage and family lifestyles will impose added responsibilities on each member.

7. Divorce rates will likely remain quite high in the foreseeable future. However, there are some indications that the recent sharp upward trend may be losing momentum, with the leveling of marriage rates, the increasing age at first marriage, and a smaller percentage of the population in the young, high divorce-risk age-groups.

8. Media and other mass culture influences will lead to increasing standardization of family lifestyles, tastes, and practices. However, there will continue to be interesting variations in marriage and family customs and lifestyles due to a continuation of certain ethnic, racial, religious, and class traditions, as well as different choices in lifestyles by some youth groups and others espousing alternative value systems.

One final note. The family as a social institution has historically been on the one hand conservative and generally reluctant to change, while on the other hand it has been adaptable and pragmatic. Marriage and family have had to adapt to strong forces and tides of social change, such as industrialization, urbanization, and secularization. The family has rolled with the punches and in all likelihood will survive all present and, we hope, all future difficulties and pressures. When we consider the strong support most other social institutions in America give the family, and the reluctance of most American people to accept radical changes in marriage and family patterns, it seems likely that a large majority of American adults will continue to prefer to live in conventional marriage and family arrangements (albeit modified and more flexible), while at the same time becoming more tolerant of others who may prefer some alternative lifestyle.

In this era of variety and change in marriage and family living, there are some husbands and wives, parents and children, and sons and daughters who, as they approach marriageable age, may be in need of counseling and help. Others seek to strengthen their marriages. Fortunately, today there is an expanding list of agencies and specialists available to provide such assistance. We will conclude the chapter with a brief review of sources of support now becoming available.

SOURCES OF SUPPORT AND HELP FOR MARRIAGE AND FAMILY

McCubbin and Boss (1980) observe that in the past decade there has been a major shift in inquiry from why families fail to why and how they succeed. Community agencies and groups are a major source of social support for families under stress, and kinship systems continue to play a major role in helping families cope.

An increasing number of programs and organized efforts to strengthen marriage and family have made their appearance in recent years. They include marriage and family counseling, marriage and family enrichment programs, family life education programs, family courts, and a variety of other agencies and activities.

MARRIAGE AND FAMILY COUNSELING

Informal marriage and family counseling has been around for a long time, tendered by clergymen, lawyers, doctors, and teachers, as they interacted with families in their main professional roles. More specialized counseling services developed as adjuncts to child guidance clinics and family welfare agencies. The first formal marriage and family counseling agencies in America, including the Marriage Consultation Service in New York City and the American Institute of Family Relations in Los Angeles, were organized in the 1930s. Scores of such agencies now function throughout the country.

Today the American Association for Marriage and Family Therapy works to upgrade professional standards and improve the services of these expanding agencies. Most AAMFT members are drawn from other professions, including social work, psychology, sociology, medicine, and the ministry. Agencies run in size from large organizations to small one-person units, and they vary considerably in their procedures and methods. Many different techniques are used, but almost all agencies try to diagnose sources of the problems the couple or the parents and their children experience, and then suggest certain kinds of treatment or therapy.

Marriage and family counseling has been criticized on a number of grounds. First, no uniform qualifying standards yet exist for marriage and family counselors. The American Association for Marriage and Family Therapy is working toward this goal of uniform standards, however. And since there is not yet a well-established body of scientific knowledge to draw on, marriage and family counseling is still more of an art than a science (Olson, 1970). Nevertheless, in spite of such obstacles, marriage and family counseling has made significant progress lately, especially under the supervision and guidance of the AAMFT.

Studies of marriage and family counselors show them to be a dedicated, generally well-qualified group who have a philosophy of "helping" (Phillips, 1970). They serve an important function in offering married couples, parents, and children an opportunity to present difficult problems to professionally trained and experienced people for counsel and guidance. Marriage counselors today tend to see their role as something beyond simply promoting marital adjustment. They try to help persons recognize the nature and sources of their problems, and will generally only help persons make decisions rather than try to tell them what decisions they should make.

FAMILY COURTS

The family court movement, somewhat similar to the marriage and family counseling effort, has been concerned with helping families overcome certain crises or serious problems. The idea of establishing special courts to handle family or domestic relation problems grew out of the juvenile court movement. The objective was to establish a court with integrated jurisdiction over all legal problems that involve members of a family. This court would be presided over by a specialist judge assisted by a professional staff trained in the social sciences. The court would use its staff and special resources to "intervene therapeutically in the lives of the people who came before it" (Kay, 1971, p. 243).

Family courts were to be empowered to handle a wide range of domestic problems, including annulment, divorce, legal separation, alimony, child custody, desertion, nonsupport, illegitimacy, and adoption. Drawing on a wide array of professional personnel, including social workers, psychiatrists, probation officers, and marriage and family counselors, the family court was intended to resolve all kinds of difficulties, offer professional guidance to marriage partners and parents, and in general help preserve marital and family ties (Kephart, 1977, p. 510).

The first family court was established in Cincinnati in 1914. While the family court movement has expanded over the years, it has seldom received the widespread support accorded juvenile courts. A few states such as California have, however, made extensive use of the family courts. The efficiency of family courts has been limited in many states by the high cost of their operation, and by the unwillingness of some communities to grant the necessary broad, jurisdictional powers to a single court. Also, many judges have been reluctant to serve in family courts (Kay, 1971).

While the family court movement has not always fulfilled the hopes originally envisioned, such courts still offer many advantages over alternatives. For one thing, an integrated family court where all domestic cases can be handled in one courtroom is generally more economical and administratively efficient than three or more different courts, each handling separated or limited domestic matters. And the family court is organized to provide varied professional help for families when they are in most need of it. With greater public support, these courts can expand their services to more families in the future.

MARRIAGE AND FAMILY ENRICHMENT PROGRAMS

Started in the 1960s, marriage and family enrichment programs are quite new compared to marriage and family counseling programs discussed above. This movement aspires to make marriage better and more rewarding for those couples whose marriages may be floundering, and also for those whose marriages are viable but not living up to their potential. Mace and Mace (1977) believe such enrichment programs can reduce the present high rates of marital failure. They see the movement as a shift from the remedial emphasis of many current marriage and family services to a "preventive concept facilitating positive growth." They see the goals of marital enhancement as marital growth, marital potential, and marital health. Modern marriage, they argue, requires "interpersonal competence," rather than the older skills found in traditional marriage and family functioning. Our changing times require this new interpersonal competence as the family moves toward the newer companionship orientation, which is based on intimacy, equity, and interpersonal interaction. Many contemporary married couples have been trying to undertake this transformation but have failed because they lacked the basic equipment, which is training in interpersonal relations. This training is what the enrichment programs aim to do (Hof & Miller, 1981).

Otto (1975, pp. 137–138) describes marriage and family enrichment programs thus:

> *Marriage Enrichment Programs* are for couples who have what they perceive to be a fairly well functioning marriage and who wish to make their marriage even more mutually satisfying. . . . Marriage enrichment programs are generally concerned with enhancing the couple's communication, emotional life, sexual relationship, fostering marriage strengths, and developing mar-

riage potential. . . . *Family Life Enrichment Programs* are for parents who have what they perceive to be a fairly well functioning family and who wish to make their family life function even better. . . . Family enrichment programs are generally concerned with enhancing the family's communication and emotional life, [and] the parents' . . . childrearing practices as well as parent/child relationships.

Marital enrichment programs became prevalent throughout the nation in the 1970s. Most are organized by educational, religious, or private agencies. Most programs involve a small group of married couples gathering for a series of weekend meeting, usually held in a church, school, or a private home. The meetings are organized and run by a qualified professional in the family field. A variety of techniques are used, such as lectures, films, reading assignments, and open-discussion sessions. Certain concepts serve as the focus, such as self-awareness, esteem building, and disclosure. For example, it has been found that if one married partner discloses an intimate feeling or thought to the other partner, the other is apt to respond in kind by also devulging some intimate feeling or thought. And the reverse is true too; when one partner is unwilling to reveal personal feelings the other partner tends to "clam up" also (Journard, 1964). It is believed that such intimate self-disclosure enhances interpersonal communication and helps each partner achieve greater self-understanding. By increasing the effectiveness of communication between marriage partners, their ability to "take charge" of their relationship is improved, and less is left to chance and to external circumstances (Miller, et al., 1975).

Although in the formative stages, these marital enrichment programs seem to hold promise. By the mid-1970s more than 200,000 couples had already participated in one or more enrichment programs (Otto, 1975). It should be noted that there is a growing concern among some professionals about possible negative effects of certain marriage enrichment programs, particularly marriage encounter weekends (Doherty, et al., 1978).

FAMILY LIFE EDUCATION AND RESEARCH

The programs discussed thus far have dealt largely with people already married. While some family life education programs are aimed at married couples and parents, the bulk of these programs are directed toward the premarital population; specifically, toward high-school and college students.

Family life education developed in the late 19th and early 20th centuries out of the ferment and change associated with declining rural life and expanding urbanism. These changes brought on or accentuated problems of marriage and family functioning. Fortunately, bodies of knowledge relevent to marriage and family living and functioning were developing in the social sciences as well as in biology, medicine, psychiatry, law, and home economics. Various organizations dedicated to the pursuit and dissemination of this knowledge arose. Such an organization is the National Council on Family Relations, founded in 1938. This is the leading organization in family life education in the United States. It publishes three widely read journals, *The Journal of Marriage and the Family, Family Relations,* and *The Journal of Family History,* in which major research and educational articles and social service activities in behalf of family life appear. It also sponsors the more recent *Journal of Family Issues.*

Today, a great many high schools and most colleges and universities throughout the United States offer one or more courses in family life education. The subject matter of the high-school courses may vary considerably from one school to another. Some courses focus on home management, nutrition, budgeting, and infant care; others cover such topics as dating and courtship, sex education, and family roles and relations. These courses, if well taught, can be very valuable to adolescents beset by the tensions and pressures of puberty and a growing awareness of the complexities of sexual and social relationships (Koller, 1974).

College courses dealing with family life may be separated into two general types: "institutional courses" and "functional courses." Actually there is often a good deal of overlap between them. The institutional course takes a broad view of the family as a social institution, dealing with such topics as the history of the family, cross-cultural variations in marriage and family structure, theories and research in mate selection, marital adjustment, and parent-child relations. Functional courses generally deal more directly with practical issues and problems of current premarital relations and marital and family relations, such as dating and courtship, sex education, marital adjustment, raising children, and in-law relationships. These functional courses, with such titles such as Preparation for Marriage or Courtship and Marriage, have become especially popular with college students in recent decades. Studies have shown these courses to be valuable for young men and women (Duvall, 1965b; Axelson, 1975).

Family life research also has expanded rapidly in recent decades. Marriage and family constitute one of the most researched fields in the social sciences today. While sociologists have taken the lead in family research, valuable contributions have come from other disciplines, including psychology, anthropology, home economics, education, and social work.

Research findings and statistic pertaining to marriage and family are regularly published by such United States governmental agencies as the Bureau of the Census, the Department of Labor, the National Vital Statistics Division, and the Women's Bureau. The majority of the vast research findings on marriage and family are published in the expanding number of professional journals devoted to family life research, education, and services, such as the *Journal of Marriage and the Family.* All family life specialists, including high-school and college teachers, marriage and family counselors, and family social workers, rely heavily on the information obtained by those engaged in family life research activities.

OTHER AGENCIES AND SERVICES

There are, of course, many other agencies and organizations, both public and private, devoted to the perservation or improvement of family life in America. In the federal government these agencies include the Bureau of Family Services, the Children's Bureau, the Women's Bureau, the Home Economic Educational Service, the Public Housing Administration, and the Social Security Administration. There are also comparable state and local public agencies concerned with promoting or protecting family well being. Private organizations include the already-mentioned National Council on Family Relations, along with the Groves Conference on Marriage and Family, the Family Service Association of America, the American Association for Marriage and Family Therapy, and numerous others (Kephart, 1977, pp. 522–523; Koller, 1974, pp. 301–315).

In conclusion, if the above evidence of public and private interest in the family is any indication of the vitality of the family in America, we may be fairly optimistic about the future. Programs and agencies for strengthening marriage and family and for helping those in difficulty are substantially stronger now than earlier (Kephart, 1977, p. 524). There is ample evidence that American people still believe strongly in marriage and family. Most Americans do get married and most manage to stay married. Children are still highly valued, and most people seem content to live in conventional family arrangements. The various alternative life-styles will probably continue to attract only a small minority of people, and it is very unlikely that any alternative lifestyles will either replace traditional marriage and family or have a critical effect on their structure or functioning. The greater freedom, rights, and expanded opportunities for women today, and the emancipation of women and men from restrictive sex roles of earlier times, means that marriage and family in the future should be based more on consensus and equity than on authority and tradition.

References

Aberle, D. F., & Naegele, K. D. Middle-class fathers' occupational role and attitudes toward children. *American Journal of Ortho-Psychiatry*, 1952, *22*, 366–378.

Adams, B. N. *The family: A sociological interpretation* (3rd ed.). Chicago: Rand McNally, 1980.

Adams, B. N. *The family: A sociological interpretation* (2nd ed.). Chicago: Rand McNally, 1975.

Adams, B. N. Can the family survive alternate life styles? *Forum*, November 2, 1973, pp. 4–8.

Adams, B. N. Isolation, function and beyond: American kinship in the 1960's. *Journal of Marriage and the Family*, 1970, *32*, 575–597.

Adams, B. N. *Kinship in an urban setting*. Chicago: Markham, 1968.

Adams, B. N. Interaction theory and social network. *Sociometry*, 1967, *30*, 64–78.

Adams, B. N. Structural factors affecting parental aid to married children. *Journal of Marriage and the Family*, 1964, *26*, 328–332.

Aldous, J. *Family careers*. New York: John Wiley & Sons, 1978.

Aldous, J. Occupational characteristics and male's role performance in the family. *Journal of Marriage and the Family*, 1969, *31*, 707–712.

Aldous, J. Intergenerational visiting patterns: Variation in boundary maintenance as an explanation. *Family Process*, 1967, *6*(2), 235–251.

Aldous, J., & Hill, R. Social cohesion, lineage type, and intergenerational transmission. *Social Forces*, 1965, *43*, 471–482.

Allan, G. Sibling solidarity. *Journal of Marriage and the Family*, 1977, *39*, 177–184.

American Council of Life Insurance. *The life cycle*. (Trend Analysis Program, Report No. 8). New York.

Amory, C. *The proper bostonians.* New York: E. P. Dutton, 1947.

Angrist, S. S., & Lave, J. R. Issues surrounding day care. *The Family Coordinator,* 1973, *22,* 457–464.

Anspach, D. F. Kinship and divorce. *Journal of Marriage and the Family,* 1976, *38,* 323–330.

Arafat, I., & Yorburg, B. On living together without marriage. *Journal of Sex Research,* 1973, *9,* 97–106.

Ard, B. N. Premarital sexual experience: A longitudinal study. *Journal of Sex Research,* 1974, *10,* 32–39.

Aries, P. *Centuries of childhood: A social history of family life.* New York: Alfred A. Knopf, 1962.

Association of American Colleges. Project on the status and education of women. October 1976. Quoted by Stencel, Sandra. Women in the work force. In *The women's movement.* Washington, D.C.: Congressional Quarterly, 1977, 37.

Axelson, L. Promise or illusion: The future of family studies. *The Family Coordinator,* 1975, *24,* 3–6.

Axelson, L. The marital adjustment and marital role definitions of husbands of working and nonworking wives. *Marriage and Family Living,* 1963, *25,* 189–195.

Bandura, A. A social learning theory of identificatory processes. In D. A. Goslin (Ed.), *Handbook of socialization theory and research.* Chicago: Rand McNally, 1969.

Bandura, A. Behavioral modification through modeling procedures. In L. Krasner & L. P. Ullman (Eds.), Research in behavior modification. New York: Holt, Rinehart & Winston, 1964.

Bane, M. J. *Here to stay: American families in the twentieth century.* New York: Basic Books, 1976. (a) Excerpt reprinted by permission.

Bane, M. J. Marital disruption and the lives of children. *Journal of Social Issues,* 1976, *32*(1), 103–117. (b)

Barry, H., Bacon, M. K., & Child, I. A crosscultural survey of some sex differences in socialization. *Journal of Abnormal and Social Psychology,* 1957, *55,* 327–332.

Bauman, K. E., & Wilson, R. E. Sexual behavior of unmarried university students in 1968 and 1972. *Journal of Sex Research,* 1974, *10,* 327–333.

Baumrind, D. Effects of authoritative parental control on child behavior. *Child Development,* 1966, *37,* 888–907.

Bayer, A. E. Early dating and early marriage. *Journal of Marriage and the Family,* 1968, *30,* 628–632.

Becker, G. E., & Michael, R. An economic analysis of marital instability. *Journal of Political Economy,* 1977, *85,* 1141–1187.

Beigel, H. G. Romantic love. *American Sociological Review,* 1951, *16,* 326–334.

Bell, D. *The coming of post-industrial society.* New York: Basic Books, 1976.

Bell, R. R. *Marriage and family interaction* (3rd ed.). Homewood, Ill.: Dorsey Press, 1979.

Bell, R. R. Marriage and family interaction (2nd ed.). Homewood, Ill.: Dorsey Press, 1967.

Bell, R. R., & Chaskes, J. B. Premarital sexual experience among co-eds, 1958 and 1968. *Journal of Marriage and the Family,* 1970, *32,* 81–84.

Bell, R. R., & Coughey, K. Premarital sexual experience among college females, 1958, 1968, and 1978. *Family Relations,* 1980, *29,* 353–357.

Bell, R. R., Turner, S., & Rosen, L. A multivariate analysis of female extramarital coitus. *Journal of Marriage and the Family,* 1975, *37,* 375.

Belsky, J. The interrelation of parental and spousal behavior during infancy in traditional nuclear families: An exploratory analysis. *Journal of Marriage and the Family,* 1979, *41,* 749–755.

Belsky, J., & Steinberg, L. D. The effects of day care: A critical review. *Child Development,* 1978, *49,* 929–949.

Bem, S. Sex-role adaptability: One consequence of psychological androgeny. *Journal of Personality and Social Psychology,* 1975, *31,* 634–643.

Benedict, R. Continuities and discontinuities in cultural conditioning. *Psychiatry,* May, 1939, pp. 161–167.

Bennett, J. W. & Tumin, M. *Social life.* New York: Alfred A. Knopf, 1948.

Benson, L. *Fatherhood: A sociological perspective.* New York: Random House, 1968.

Berardo, F. M. Survivorship and social isolation: The case of the aged widower. *The Family Coordinator,* 1970, *19,* 11–25.

Berelson, B. The value of children: A taxonomical essay. In J. G. Wells (Ed.), *Current Issues in Marriage and the Family* (2nd ed.). New York: Macmillan, 1979.

Berger, B., Hackett, B., Cavan, S., Zickler, G., Millar, M., Noble, M., Theiman, S., Farrell, R., & Rosenbluth, B. Child-rearing practices in the communal family. In A. S. Skolnick & J. H. Skolnick (Eds.), *Family in transition.* Boston: Little, Brown, 1971.

Bernard, J. *The future of marriage.* New York: World, 1972.

Bernard, S. E. *Fatherless families: Their economic and social adjustment.* Waltham, Mass.: Brandeis University Press, 1964.

Better Homes and Gardens. A report on the American family. Des Moines, Iowa: Meredith, 1972.

Bible. Saint Matthew. Chapter 19, verse 5. King James Version. Philadelphia: The National Bible Press.

Bible. Deuteronomy. Chapter 24, verses 1–2. King James Version. Philadelphia: The National Bible Press.

Billingsley, A. *Black families in white America.* Englewood Cliffs, N.J.: Prentice-Hall, 1968.

Blake, J. Is zero preferred? American attitudes toward childlessness in the 1970s. *Journal of Marriage and the Family,* 1979, *41,* 245–257.

Blau, P. M. *Exchange and power in social life.* New York: John Wiley & Sons, 1964.

Blood, R. O., Jr. Resolving family conflicts. *Conflict Resolution,* 1960, *4,* 209–219.

Blood, R. O., Jr. A retest of Waller's rating complex. *Marriage and Family Living,* 1955, *17,* 41–47.

Blood, R. O., Jr. Romance and premarital intercourse—incompatibles? *Marriage and Family Living,* 1952, *14,* 105–108.

Blood, R. O., Jr., & Blood, M. *Marriage* (3rd ed.). New York: Free Press, 1978.

Blood, R. O., Jr., & Wolfe, D. M. *Husbands and wives: The dynamics of married living.* New York: Free Press, 1969.

Bock, E. W., & Webber, I. L. Suicide among the elderly: Isolating widowhood and mitigating alternatives. *Journal of Marriage and the Family,* 1972, *34,* 24–31.

Bohannon, P. Divorce chains, household of remarriage, and multiple divorces. In P. Bohannon (Ed.), *Divorce and after.* New York: Doubleday, 1970. (a)

Bohannon, P. (Ed.). *Divorce and after.* New York: Doubleday, 1970. (b)

Booth, A. Wife's employment and husband's stress: a replication and refutation. *Journal of Marriage and the Family,* 1977, *39,* 645–650.

Bolton, C. Mate selection as the development of a relationship. *Marriage and Family Living,* 1961, *23,* 234–240.

Bossard, J. H. Residential propinquity as a factor in mate selection. *American Journal of Sociology,* 1932, *38,* 222–231.

Bossard, J. H., & Boll, E. S. Marital unhappiness in the life cycle. *Marriage and Family Living,* 1955, *17,* 10–14.

Bower, D. W. *A description and an analysis of a cohabiting sample in America.* Unpublished master's thesis, University of Arizona, 1975.

Bowlby, J. *Maternal care and mental health.* Geneva, Switzerland: World Health Organization, 1951.

Bowman, H. A., & Spanier, G. B. *Modern marriage.* New York: McGraw-Hill, 1978.

Brandwein, R. A., Brown, C. A., & Fox, E. M. Women and children last: The social situation of divorced mothers and their families. *Journal of Marriage and the Family,* 1974, *36,* 498–514.

Broderick, C. B. Damn those gloomy prophets—the family is here to stay. In B. J. Wishart & L. C. Reichman (Eds.), *Modern Sociological Issues.* (2nd ed.). New York: Macmillan, 1979.

Bronfenbrenner, U. The changing American child—a speculative analysis. *Merrill-Palmer Quarterly,* 1961, *7,* 74.

Bronfenbrenner, U. Socialization and social class through time and space. In E. E. Maccoby, T. M. Newcomb, & E. L. Hartley (Eds.), *Readings in Social Psychology.* New York: Holt, Rinehart & Winston, 1958.

Brown, R. G. Family structure and isolation of older persons. In E. Palmore (Ed.), *Normal aging.* Durham, North Carolina: Duke University Press, 1970.

Bruce, J. A. Intergenerational solidarity versus progress for women. *Journal of Marriage and the Family,* 1976, *38,* 519–524.

Bruce-Briggs, B. Childcare: The fiscal time bomb. *The Public Interest,* 1977, *49,* 87–102.

Bumpass, L. L., & Rindfuss, R. *Children's experience of marital disruption.* Discussion paper at the Institute for Research on Poverty, University of Wisconsin, 1978.

Bumpass, L. L., & Sweet, J. A. Differentials in marital stability: 1970. *American Sociological Review,* 1972, *37,* 754–766.

Burchinal, L. Trends and prospects for young marriages in the United States. *Journal of Marriage and the Family,* 1965, *27,* 243–254.

Burchinal, L. Characteristics of adolescents from unbroken, broken, and reconstituted families. *Journal of Marriage and the Family,* 1964, *26,* 44–51.

Burgess, E. W., & Cottrell, L. *Predicting success or failure in marriage.* New York: Prentice-Hall, 1939.

Burgess, E. W., & Locke, H. *The family: From institution to companionship.* New York: American Book, 1945.

Burgess, E. W., & Wallin, P. *Engagement and marriage.* Philadelphia: J. B. Lippincott, 1953.

Burgess, J. K. The single-parent family: A social and sociological problem. *The Family Coordinator,* 1970, *19,* 137–144.

Burke, R. J., & Weir, T. Relationship of wives' employment status to husband, wife and pair satisfaction and performance. *Journal of Marriage and the Family,* 1976, *38,* 279–287.

Burr, W. *Theory construction and the sociology of the family.* New York: John Wiley & Sons, 1973.

Busselen, H. J., Jr., & Busselen, C. K. Adjustment differences between married and single undergraduate university students: An historical perspective. *The Family Coordinator,* 1975, *24,* 281–279.

Butler, R. N. How to grow old and poor in an affluent society. *International Journal of Aging and Human Development,* 1973, *4,* 277–279.

Calhoun, A. W. *A social history of the American family.* (2 vols.). New York: Barnes and Noble, 1945.

Campbell, A., Converse, P. E., & Rodgers, W. L. *The quality of American life.* New York: Russell Sage Foundation, 1976.

Campisi, P. J. Ethnic family patterns: The Italian family in the United States. *The American Journal of Sociology,* 1948, *53,* 443–449.

Cannon, K. L., & Long, R. Premarital sexual behavior in the sixties. *Journal of Marriage and the Family,* 1971, *33,* 36–49.

Carden, M. L. *Oneida: Utopian community to modern corporation.* Baltimore: Johns Hopkins University Press, 1969.

Carnes, D. E. Talking about sex: Notes on first coitus and the double sexual standard. *Journal of Marriage and the Family,* 1973, *35,* 677–688.

Carter, H., & Glick, P. C. *Marriage and divorce: A social and economic study* (Rev. ed.). Cambridge, Mass.: Harvard University Press, 1976.

Carter, H., & Glick, P. C. *Marriage and divorce: A social and economic study.* Cambridge, Mass.: Harvard University Press, 1970.

Carter, H., & Pratt, W. F. *Duration of marriage prior to separation and divorce: A study based on vital records.* Paper presented to American Sociological Association, 1970.

Cavan, R. S. *Marriage and family in the modern world.* New York: Thomas Y. Crowell, 1974.

Cavan, R. S. Speculations on innovations to conventional marriage in old age. *The Gerontologist,* 1973, *13,* 409–410.

Cavan, R. S. *The American Family.* (4th ed.). New York: Thomas Y. Crowell, 1969.

Cavan, R. S. Unemployment: Crisis of the common man. *Marriage and Family Living,* 1959, *21,* 139–146.

Cavan, R. S. *The American family* (1st ed.). New York: Thomas Y. Crowell, 1953.

Chafetz, J. S. *Masculine/feminine or human.* Itasca, Ill.: F. E. Peacock Publishers, 1953.

Cheng, C. K., & Yamamura, D. S. Interracial marriage and divorce in Hawaii. *Social Forces,* 1957, *36,* 77–84.

Cherlin, A. Worklife and marital dissolution. In G. Levinger & O. Moles (Eds.), *Divorce and separation.* New York: Basic Books, 1979.

Cherlin, A. Remarriage as an incomplete institution. *American Journal of Sociology,* 1978, *84,* 638–646.

Chertok, L. The psychopathology of vomiting in pregnancy. In J. G. Howells (Ed.), *Modern perspectives in psycho-obstetrics.* New York: Brunner/Mazel, 1972.

Christensen, H. T. Scandinavian and American sex norms: Some comparisons and sociological implications. *Journal of Social Issues,* 1966, *22,* 66–74.

Christensen, H. T. A cross-cultural comparison of attitudes toward marital infidelity. *International Journal of Comparative Sociology,* 1962, *3,* 124–137.

Christensen, H. T., & Barber, K. E. Interfaith versus intrafaith marriage in Indiana. *Journal of Marriage and the Family,* 1967, *29,* 461–469.

Christensen, H. T., & Johnson, K. *Marriage and the family.* New York: Ronald Press, 1971.

Clark, A., & Wallin, P. Women's sexual responsiveness and the duration and quality of their marriages. *American Journal of Sociology,* 1965, *71,* 187–196.

Clark, J., & Kempler, H. L. Theraputic family camping: A rationale. *The Family Coordinator,* 1973, *22,* 437–442.

Clavan, S., & Vatter, E. The affiliated family: A continued analysis. *The Family Coordinator,* 1972, *21,* 499–504. (a)

Clavan, S., & Vatter, E. The affiliated family: A device for integrating old and young. *The Gerontologist,* 1972, *12,* 407–412. (b)

Clayton, R. R., & Voss, N. L. Shacking up: Cohabitation in the 1970s. *Journal of Marriage and the Family,* 1977, *39,* 273–283.

Cogswell, B. E. Variant family forms and life styles: Rejection of the traditional nuclear family. *Family Coordinator,* 1975, *24,* 391–406.

Cohen, S. E. Maternal employment and mother-child interaction. *Merrill-Palmer Quarterly,* 1978, *24,* 189–197.

Collins, J. K. Adolescent dating intimacy: Norms and peer expectations. *Journal of Youth and Adolescence,* 1974, *3,* 317–327.

Collins, J. K., Kennedy, J. R., & Francis, R. D. Insights into a dating partner's expectations of how behavior should ensue during the courtship process. *Journal of Marriage and the Family,* 1976, *38,* 373–378.

Conover, P. W. An analysis of communes and intentional communities with particular attention to sexual and gender relations. *The Family Coordinator,* 1975, *24,* 453–464.

Constantine, L. L., & Constantine, J. M. *Group marriage.* New York: Macmillan, 1973.

Constantine, L. L., & Constantine, J. M. The group marriage. In M. Gordon (Ed.), *The nuclear family in crisis: The search for an alternative.* New York: Harper & Row, 1972.

Constantine, L. L., & Constantine, J. M. Sexual aspects of multilateral relations. *Journal of Sex Research,* 1971, *7,* 204–225.

Constantine, L. L., & Constantine, J. M. Where is marriage going? *Futurist,* April 1970, pp. 44–46.

Coombs, R. H. Value consensus and partner satisfaction among dating couples. *Journal of Marriage and the Family*, 1966, *28*, 166–173.

Coombs, R. H., A value theory of mate selection. *The Family Coordinator*, 1961, *10*, 51–54.

Cooper, D. *The death of the family*. New York: Random House, 1971.

Coopersmith, S. *The antecedents of self-esteem*. San Francisco: W. H. Freeman, 1967.

Coult, A. D., & Habenstein, R. W. Closeness to non-primary relations in the American kinship system. *Journal of Comparative Family Studies*, 1972, *2*, 15–32.

Cuber, J. How new ideas about sex are changing our lives. *Redbook*, 1971, *85*, 173–177.

Cuber, J., & Harroff, P. B. *The significant Americans: A study of sexual behavior among the affluent*. New York: Appleton-Century-Crofts, 1965.

Cuber, J., & Harroff, P. B. The more total view: Relationships among men and women of the upper middle class. *Marriage and Family Living*, 1963, *25*, 140–145.

Cumming, E., Dean, L. R., & Newell, D. Disengagement, a tentative theory of aging. *Sociometry*, 1960, *23*, 102–115.

Cumming, E., & Henry, W. *Growing old*. New York: Basic Books, 1961.

Cumming E., & Schneider, D. M. Sibling solidarity: A property of American kinship. *American Anthropologist*, 1961, *63*, 498–507.

Cutwright, P. Income and family events: Marital stability. *Journal of Marriage and the Family*, 1971, *33*, 291–306.

D'Andrade, R. G. Sex differences and cultural institutions. In E. E. Maccoby (Ed.), *The development of sex differences*. Palo Alto: Stanford University Press, 1966.

Davis, J. A. *General social surveys, 1972–1980: Cumulative codebook*. Chicago: National Opinion Research Center, 1980.

Davis, J. A. *Codebook for the spring 1974 general social survey*. Chicago: National Opinion Research Center, 1974.

Davis, J. A. *Codebook for the spring 1973 general social survey*. Chicago: National Opinion Research Center, 1973.

Davis, K. Legitimacy and the incest taboo. In N. W. Bell and E. Vogel (Eds.), *A modern introduction to the family*. New York: Free Press, 1960.

Davis, K. *Human society*. New York: Macmillan, 1949.

DeFleur, M. L., & DeFleur, L. B. The relative contribution of television as a learning source for children's occupation knowledge. *American Sociological Review*, 1967, *32*, 777–789.

DeLissovoy, V. High school marriages: A longitudinal study. *Journal of Marriage and the Family*, 1973, *35*, 245–255.

DeLora, J. Social systems of dating on a college campus. *Marriage and Family Living*, 1963, *25*, 81–84.

Denfeld, D., & Gordon, M. Mate swapping: The family that swings together clings together. In A. S. Skolnick & J. H. Skolnick (Eds.), *Family in transition*. Boston: Little, Brown, 1971.

DeRougemont, D. The crisis of the modern couple. In R. Anshen (Ed.), *The family: Its function and destiny*. New York: Harper & Row, 1959.

Deutscher, I. The quality of post-parental life: Definitions of the situation. *Journal of Marriage and the Family*, 1964, *26*, 52–59.

Deutscher, I. Socialization for post-parental life. In A. Rose (Ed.), *Human behavior and social processes*. Boston: Houghton Mifflin, 1962.

Dickinson, G. E. Dating behavior of black and white adolescents before and after desegregation. *Journal of Marriage and the Family*, 1975, *37*, 602–608.

Didato, S. V., & Kennedy, T. M. Masculinity-femininity and personal values. *Psychological Reports*, 1956, *2*, 231–250.

Dinitz, S., Banks, F., & Pasamanick, B. Mate selection and social class: Changes during the past quarter century. *Marriage and Family Living*, 1960, *22*, 348–351.

Dizard, J. *Social change in the family*. Chicago: Community and Family Study Center, 1968.

Doherty, W. J., Ryder, R., & McCabe, P. Marriage encounter: A critical appraisal. *Journal of Marriage and Family Counselling*, 1978, *4*, 99–106.

Dore, R. P. *City life in Japan*. Berkeley: University of California Press, 1963.

Douvan, E. Employment and the adolescent. In F. I. Nye & L. W. Hoffman (Eds.), *The employed mother in America*. Chicago: Rand McNally, 1963.

Duberman, L. *Marriage and other alternatives*. New York: Praeger Publishers, 1977.

Duberman, L. *Social inequality: Class and caste in America*. Philadelphia: J. B. Lippincott, 1976.

Duberman, L. *The reconstituted family: A study of remarried couples and their children*. Chicago: Nelson-Hall Publishers, 1975.

Duncan, B., & Duncan, O. D. Family stability and occupational success. *Social Problems*, 1969, *16*, 273–285.

Duncan, G. J., & Morgan, J. N. Young children and "other" family members. In G. J. Duncan & J. N. Morgan (Eds.), *Five thousand American families—Patterns of economic progress* (Vol. 4). Ann Arbor: Institute for Social Research, 1976.

Duvall, E. M. *Marriage and family development* (5th ed.). Philadelphia: J. B. Lippincott, 1977.

Duvall, E. M. American laws regulating the formation of the marriage contract. In R. S. Cavan (Ed.), *Marriage and family in the modern world*. New York: Thomas Y. Crowell, 1965. (a)

Duvall, E. M. How effective are marriage courses? *Journal of Marriage and the Family*, 1965, *27*, 176–184. (b)

Duvall, E. M. *In-laws: Pro and con*. New York: Association Press, 1954.

Duvall, E. M. Conceptions of parenthood. *American Journal of Sociology*, 1946, *52*, 193–203.

Dyer, E. D. *The American family: Variety and change*. New York: McGraw-Hill, 1979.

Dyer, E. D. Upward social mobility and extended family cohesion as perceived by the wife in Swedish urban families. *Journal of Marriage and the Family*, 1972, *34*, 713–724.

Dyer, E. D. Upward social mobility and nuclear family integration as perceived by the wife in Swedish urban families. *Journal of Marriage and the Family*, 1970, *32*, 341–350.

Dyer, E. D. Parenthood as crisis: A restudy. *Marriage and Family Living,* 1963, *25,* 196–201.

Dyer, E. D. Marital happiness and the two-income family. *Southwestern Social Science Quarterly,* 1959, *41,* 95–102.

Dyer, W. G., & Urban, D. The institutionalization of equalitarian family norms. *Marriage and Family Living,* 1958, *20,* 58–68.

Eckland, B. K. Theories in mate selection. *Eugenics Quarterly,* 1968, *15,* 79–83.

Edmonds, V. H., Withers, G., & DiBatista, B. Adjustment, conservatism, and marital conventionalization. *Journal of Marriage and the Family,* 1972, *34,* 5–13.

Edwards, J. N. Familial behavior as social exchange. *Journal of Marriage and the Family.* 1969, *31,* 518–526.

Edwards, J. N., & Klemmack, D. Correlates of life-satisfaction: A reexamination. *Journal of Gerontology,* 1973, *28,* 484–492.

Ehrmann, W. W. *Premarital dating behavior.* New York: Holt, Rinehart & Winston, 1959.

Elder, G. H. *Children of the great depression: Social change in life experience.* Chicago: University of Chicago Press, 1974.

Elder, G. H. Appearance and education in marriage mobility. *American Sociological Review,* 1969, *34,* 519–533.

Ellis, A. Group marriage: A possible alternative? In G. F. Streib (Ed.), *The changing family: Adaptation and diversity.* Reading, Mass.: Addison-Wesley Publishing, 1973.

Emmerich, W., & Smoller, F. The role of patterning of parental norms. *Sociometry,* 1964, *27,* 382–390.

English, R. Beyond pathology: Research and theoretical perspective on black families. In L. Gary (Ed.), *Social research and the black community: Selected issues and priorities.* Washington, D.C.: Howard University Press, 1974.

Erikson, E. H. *Identity: Youth and crisis.* New York: W. W. Norton, 1968.

Erikson, E. H. Childhood and society (2nd ed.). New York: W. W. Norton, 1963.

Eshleman, J. R. *The family: An introduction.* Newton, Mass.: Allyn & Bacon, 1974.

Eshleman, J. R., & Hunt, C. L. *Social class factors in the college adjustment of married students.* Kalamazoo: Western Michigan University Press, 1965.

Espenshade, T. J. Raising a child can now cost $85,000. *INTERCOM, The International Population News Magazine,* 1980, *8,* 9–12.

Espenshade, T. J. Economic consequences of divorce. *Journal of Marriage and the Family,* 1979, *41,* 615–625. (a)

Espenshade, T. J. The value and cost of children. In J. G. Wells (Ed.), *Current issues in marriage and the family* (2nd ed.). New York: Macmillan, 1979. (b)

Evans, R. I. *Conversation with Carl Jung.* New York: Van Nostrand Reinhold, 1964.

Falkman, P., & Irish, D. P. *Socialization–resocialization–reverse socialization: Analysis and societal significance.* Unpublished paper presented at Midwest Sociological Society meeting, April 5, 1974.

Farber, B. Kinship and class: A midwestern study. New York: Basic Books, 1971.

Farber, B. *Family: Organization and interaction.* San Francisco: Chandler, 1964.

Farrell, W. *The liberated man.* New York: Bantam Books, 1975.

Feldman, H. The effects of children on the family. In A. Michel (Ed.), *Family issues of employed women in Europe and America.* Leiden: Brill, 1971.

Feldman, H. *Development of the husband–Wife relationship.* Ithaca: Cornell University Press, 1965.

Feldman, H., & Feldman, M. *Effects of parenthood at three points of marriage.* Unpublished paper, Cornell University, 1977.

Feldman, H., & Feldman, M. *Beyond sex-role differentiation,* Paper read at International Seminary on Changing Sex-Roles in Family and Society, Dubrovnik, Yugoslavia, June, 1975. (a)

Feldman, H., & Feldman, M. The effect of father absence on adolescents. *Family Perspective,* 1975, *10,* 21–30. (1). (b)

Ferber, M., & Huber, J. Husbands, wives, and careers. *Journal of Marriage and the Family,* 1979, *41,* 315–325.

Ferree, M. The confused American housewife. *Psychology Today,* 1976, *10,* 76–80. (a)

Ferree, M. Working class jobs: Housework and paid work as sources of satisfaction. *Social Problems,* 1976, *23,* 431–441. (b)

Fischer, C. Toward a subcultural theory of urbanism. *American Journal of Sociology,* 1975, *80,* 1319–1341.

Folsom, J. K. *The family and democratic society.* New York: John Wiley & Sons, 1934.

Foote, N. N. Matching of husband and wife in phases of development. *Transactions of the Third World Congress of Sociology,* 1956, *4,* 24–34.

Foote, N. N., & Cottrell, L. *Identity and interpersonal competence: A new direction in family research.* Chicago: University of Chicago Press, 1955.

Fox, R. *Kinship and marriage.* Baltimore: Penguin Books, 1967.

Franklin, J. L., & Scott, J. E. Parental values: An inquiry into occupational setting. *Journal of Marriage and the Family,* 1970, *32,* 406–409.

Frazier, E. F. *The negro family in the United States.* New York: Macmillan, 1957.

Freedman, M. B. The sexual behavior of American college women. *Merrill-Palmer Quarterly,* 1965, *11,* 33–48.

Freedman, R., & Coombs, L. Childspacing and family economic position. *American Sociological Review,* 1966, *31,* 631–648.

Freud, S. "Three essays on the theory of sexuality," in J. Strachey (Trans.), *The complete works of Sigmund Freud,* (Vol. 7). London: Hogarth Press and The Institute for Psychoanalysis, 1956.

Freud, S. *Group psychology and the analysis of the ego.* London: Hogarth Press, 1922.

Frieze, I. H., Parsons, J. E., Johnson, P. B., Ruble, D. N., & Zellman, G. L. *Women and sex roles.* New York: W. W. Norton, 1978.

Fullerton, G. P. *Survival in marriage.* Hinsdale, Ill.: Dryden Press, 1977.

Fullerton, G. P. *Survival in Marriage.* New York: Holt, Rinehart & Winston, 1972.

Gagnon, J. *Human Sexualities.* Glenview, Ill.: Scott, Foresman, 1977.

Gagnon, J., & Greenblat, C. S. *Life designs: Individuals, marriages, and families.* Glenview, Ill.: Scott, Foresman, 1978.

Gans, H. J. *The Levittowners: Ways of life and politics in a new suburban community.* New York: Pantheon, 1967.

Gans, H. J. *The urban villagers: Group and class life of Italian Americans.* New York: Free Press, 1962.

Gasser, R. D. & Taylor, C. M. Role adjustment of single parent fathers with dependent children. *The Family Coordinator, 1976, 25,* 397–401.

Gavron, H. *The captive wife.* London: Routledge and Kegan Paul, 1966.

Gebhard, P. H. (1971) Postmarital coitus among widows and divorcees. In P. Bohannon (Ed.), *Divorce and after.* Garden City, N.Y.: Doubleday Anchor, 1971.

Gebhard, P. H. Factors in marital orgasm. *Journal of Social Issues, 1966, 22,* 88–95.

Gecas, V., & Nye, F. I. Sex and class differences in parent-child interaction: A test of Kohn's hypothesis. *Journal of Marriage and the Family, 1974, 36,* 742–749.

Gianopulos, A., & Mitchell, H. E. Marital disagreement in working wife marriages as a function of husband's attitude toward wife's employment. *Marriage and Family Living, 1957, 19,* 373–378.

Gibson, G. Kin family network: Overheralded structure in past conceptualizations of family functioning. *Journal of Marriage and the Family, 1972, 34,* 13–23.

Glenn, N. D. Interreligious marriage in the United States: Patterns and recent trends. *Journal of Marriage and the Family.* Forthcoming.

Glenn, N. D. Psychological well-being in the postparental stage: Some evidence from national surveys. *Journal of Marriage and the Family, 1975, 37,* 105–110.

Glenn, N. D., Hoppe, S. K. & Weiner, D. Social class heterogamy and marital success: A study of the empirical adequacy of a textbook generalization. *Social Problems, 1974, 22,* 539–550.

Glenn, N. D., & McLanahan, S. Children and marital happiness: A further specification of the relationship. *Journal of Marriage and the Family, 1982, 44,* 63–72.

Glenn, N. D., & McLanahan, S. The effects of offspring on the psychological well-being of older adults. *Journal of Marriage and the Family, 1981, 43,* 409–421.

Glenn, N. D., & Weaver, C. N. Attitudes toward premarital, extramarital, and homosexual relations in the U.S. in the 1970s. *The Journal of Sex Research, 1979, 15,* 108–118.

Glenn, N. D., & Weaver, C. N. A multivariate, multisurvey of marital happiness. *Journal of Marriage and the Family, 1978, 40,* 269–282. Excerpt reprinted by permission of the National Council on Family Relations. Copyright by the National Council on Family Relations.

Glenn, N. D., & Weaver, C. N. The marital happiness of divorced persons. *Journal of Marriage and the Family, 1977, 39,* 331–336.

Glick, P. C. The future of the American family. In U.S. Bureau of the Census, *Current Population Reports.* Washington, D.C.: Government Printing Office, 1979. (a)

Glick, P. C. Future American families. *The Washington COFO MEMO II,* Summer/Fall 1979, pp. 2–5. (b)

Glick, P. C. The future of the American family. In U.S. Bureau of the Census, *Current Population Reports* (Series P-23, No. 78, pp. 1–6). Washington D.C.: Government Printing Office, 1978.

Glick, P. C. Updating the life cycle of the family. *Journal of Marriage and the Family, 1977, 39,* 5–13.

Glick, P. C. A demographer looks at American families. *Journal of Marriage and the Family, 1975, 37,* 15–26.

Glick, P. C. Marital instability: Variations by size of place and religion. *The Milbank Memorial Fund Quarterly*, 1963, *41*, 43–55.

Glick, P. C., & Norton, A. J. Marrying, divorcing and living together in the U.S. today. *Population Bulletin*. Washington, D.C.: Population Reference Bureau, 1977.

Glick, P. C., & Norton, A. J. Frequency, duration, and probability of marriage and divorce. *Journal of Marriage and the Family*, 1971, *33*, 307–317.

Golant, S. M. Residential concentrations of the future elderly. In B. L. Neugarten (Ed.), Aging in the year 2000: A look at the future. *The Gerontologist*, 1975, *15*, 61–69.

Gold, D. & Andres, D. Comparisons of adolescent children with employed and nonemployed mothers. *Merrill-Palmer Quarterly*, 1978, *24*, 243–254.

Golden, J. Patterns of negro-white intermarriage. *American Sociological Review*, 1954, *19*, 144–147.

Goode, W. J. *World revolution and family patterns* (2nd ed.). New York: Free Press, 1970.

Goode, W. J. *The family*. Englewood Cliffs, N.J.: Prentice-Hall, 1964.

Goode, W. J. *World revolution and family patterns* (1st ed.). New York: Free Press, 1963.

Goode, W. J. The theoretical importance of love. *American Sociological Review*, 1959, *24*, 38–47.

Goode, W. J. *After divorce*. New York: Free Press, 1956.

Gordon, M. *The American family: Past, present, and future*. New York: Random House, 1978.

Gordon, M. Infant care revisited. *Journal of Marriage and the Family*, 1968, *30*, 583.

Gordon, M., & Noll, C. E. Social class and interaction with kin and friends. *Journal of Comparative Family Studies*, 1975, *6*, 239–248.

Gordon, M., & Shankweiler, P. J. Different equals less: Female sexuality in recent marriage manuals. *Journal of Marriage and the Family*, 1971, *33*, 459–465.

Greenfield, S. Love and marriage in modern America: A functional analysis. In J. R. Eshleman (Ed.), *Perspectives in marriage and the family*. Newton, Mass.: Allyn & Bacon, 1969.

Gunter, J. *Roosevelt in Perspective*. New York: Harper & Row, 1950.

Gurin, G., Veroff, J., & Feld, S. *Americans view their mental health*. New York: Basic Books, 1960.

Hadden, J. K., & Borgatta, M. L. *Marriage and the family*. Itasca, Ill.: F. E. Peacock Publishers, 1969.

Haley, A. *Roots*. Garden City, N.Y.: Doubleday, 1974.

Haller, A. O. The urban family. *American Journal of Sociology*, 1961, *66*, 621–622.

Hansen, S. L. Dating choices of high school students. *The Family Coordinator*, 1977, *26*, 133–138.

Harkins, E. B. Effects of empty nest transition on self-report of psychological and physical well-being. *Journal of Marriage and the Family*, 1978, *40*, 549–556.

Harrell, J. E., & Ridley, C. A. Substitute child care, maternal employment and the quality of mother-child interaction. *Journal of Marriage and the Family*, 1975, *37*, 556–564.

Harrington, M. *The other America.* New York: Macmillan, 1963.

Havighurst, R. J. *Developmental tasks and education* (3rd ed.). New York: David McKay, 1972.

Hayes, A. *Sexual physiology of woman.* Boston: Peabody Medical Institute, 1869.

Hayes, M. P., & Stinnett, N. Life satisfaction of middle aged husbands and wives. *Journal of Home Economics,* 1971, *63,* 669–674.

Hayes, W. C., & Mindel, C. H. Extended kinship relations in black and white families. *Journal of Marriage and the Family,* 1973, *35,* 51–57.

Hefner, R., Meda, R., & Oleshansky, B. *The development of sex-role transcendence.* Preprint, 1975.

Heinstein, H. Expressed attitudes and feelings of pregnant women and their relations to physical complications of pregnancy. *Merrill-Palmer Quarterly,* 1967, *13,* 217–236.

Heiss, J. (Ed.). *Family roles and interaction.* Chicago: Rand McNally, 1968.

Heiss, J. Premarital characteristics of the religiously intermarried in an urban area. *American Sociological Review,* 1960, *25,* 47–55.

Hepker, W., & Cloyd, J. S. Role relationships and role performance: The male married student. *Journal of Marriage and the Family,* 1974, *36,* 688–696.

Herman, R. D. The going steady complex: A re-examination. *Marriage and Family Living,* 1955, *17,* 36–40.

Hess, E. H. Ethology and developmental psychology. In P. H. Musser (Ed.), *Carmichael's manual of child psychology* (Vol. 1). New York: John Wiley, & Sons, 1970.

Hetherington, E. M. Effects of father's absence on personality development in adolescent daughters. *Developmental Psychology,* 1972, *7,* 313–326.

Hetherington, E. M., & Cox, R. Divorced fathers. *The Family Coordinator,* 1976, *25,* 417–428.

Hill, C. T., Rubin, Z., & Paplau, L. Breakups before marriage: The end of 103 affairs. *Journal of Social Issues,* 1976, *32,* 147–168.

Hill, R. B. *The strengths of black families.* New York: Emerson Hall, 1971.

Hill, R. Decision making and the family life cycle. In C. Shanas & G. F. Strieb (Eds.), *Social structure and the family: Generational relations.* Englewood Cliffs, N.J.: Prentice-Hall, 1965.

Hill, R. *Families under stress.* New York: Harper & Row, 1949.

Hill, R., Foote, N., Aldous, J., Carlson, R., & Macdonald, R. *Family development in three generations: A longitudinal study of changing patterns of planning and achievement.* Cambridge, Mass.: Schenkman, 1970.

Hobbs, D. F. Transition to parenthood: A replication and an extension. *Journal of Marriage and the Family,* 1968, *30,* 294–302.

Hobbs, D. F. Parenthood as crisis: A third study. *Journal of Marriage and the Family,* 1965, *27,* 367–372.

Hochschild, A. R. Communal life styles for the old. *Society,* 1973, *10*(5), 50–57.

Hock, E. *Alternative approaches to child-rearing and their effects on the mother-infant relationship.* Columbus, Ohio: Ohio State University and Ohio Agricultural Research and Development Centers, 1976.

Hof, L., & Miller, W. R. *Marriage enrichment.* Bowie, Maryland: Brady, 1981.

Hoffman, L. W. Effects on children: Summary and discussion. In F. I. Nye &

L. W. Hoffman (Eds.), *The employed mother in America.* Chicago: Rand McNally, 1963.

Hoffman, L. W. Mother's enjoyment of work and effects on the child. *Child Development,* 1961, *32,* 187–197.

Hoffman, S. Marital instability and the economic status of women. *Demography,* 1977, *14,* 67–76.

Holmes, S. J., & Hatch, C. E. Personal appearance as related to scholastic records and marriage selection in college women. *Human Biology,* 1938, *10,* 65–76.

Hoult, T. F. *The dictionary of modern society.* Totowa, N.J.: Littlefield, Adams, 1969.

Hoult, T. F., Henzel, L., & Hudson, J. *Courtship and marriage in America.* Boston: Little, Brown, 1978.

Houriet, R. *Getting back together.* New York: Coward, McCann & Geoghegan, 1971.

Hoyenga, K. B., & Hoyenga, K. T. *The question of sex differences.* Boston: Little, Brown, 1979.

Hsu, F. L. K. *Under the ancestor's shadow.* Garden City, N.Y.: Doubleday, 1967.

Huber, J., & Spitze, G. Considering divorce: An expansion of Becker's theory of marital instability. *American Journal of Sociology,* 1980, *86,* 75–89.

Hudson, J., & Henze, L. Campus values in mate selection: A replication. *Journal of Marriage and the Family,* 1969, *31,* 772–775.

Hudson, J., & Henze, L. F. A note on cohabitation. *The Family Coordinator,* 1973, *22,* 495.

Hudson, W. W., & Murphy, G. J. The non-linear relationship between marital satisfaction and stages of the family life cycle: An artifact of type I errors? *Journal of Marriage and the Family,* 1980, *42,* 263–276.

Hunt, M. *Sexual behavior in the 1970's.* New York: Dell, 1974.

Hunt, M. *The formerly married.* New York: McGraw-Hill, 1966.

Hunt, M. *The natural history of love.* New York: Alfred A. Knopf, 1959.

Ihara, T., & Warner, R. In their own words. *People,* 1979, *12,* 87–90.

Illick, J. E. Child-rearing in seventeenth century England and America. In Lloyd deMause, *The history of childhood.* New York: Harper & Row, 1975.

Jacobson, P. H. *American marriage and divorce.* New York: Holt, Rinehart, and Winston, 1969.

Jacoby, A. Transition to parenthood: A role assessment. *Journal of Marriage and the Family,* 1969, *31,* 720–727.

Jacoby, S. 49 million singles can't be all right. *The New York Times Magazine,* February 17, 1974, pp. 11–12.

Jacoby, S. What do I do for the next twenty years? *The New York Times Magazine,* June 17, 1973, pp. 10–11.

Jaffe, F. S., & Dryfoos, J. G. Fertility control services for adolescents: Access and utilization. *Family Planning Perspectives,* 1976, *8*(4), 167–175.

Johnson, R. E. *Marital patterns during the middle years.* Unpublished doctoral dissertation, University of Minnesota, 1968.

Jones, C. A., Gordon, N. M., & Sawhill, I. V. *Child support payments in the United States* (Working paper No. 992–03). Washington, D.C.: The Urban Institute, 1976.

Jorgensen, S. R. Social class heterogamy, status striving, and perceptions of marital conflict: A partial replication and revision of Pearlin's contingency hypothesis. *Journal of Marriage and the Family*, 1977, *39*, 653–661.

Jourard, S. M. *The transparent self: Self-disclosure and well-being.* New York: D. Van Nostrand, 1964.

Kaats, G. R., & Davis, K. E. The dynamics of sexual behavior of college students. *Journal of Marriage and the Family*, 1970, *32*, 390–399.

Kadushin, A. *Single parent adoptions: An overview and some relevant research.* New York: Child Welfare League of America, 1968.

Kahl, J. *The American class structure.* New York: Holt, Rinehart & Winston, 1957.

Kanin, E. J., & Davidson, K. R. Some evidence bearing on the aim-inhibition hypothesis of love. *Sociological Quarterly*, 1972, *13*, 210–217.

Kanin, E. J., & Howard, D. H. Postmarital consequences of premarital sex adjustments. *American Sociological Review*, 1958, *23*, 556–562.

Kaplan, H. S. *The new sex therapy.* New York: Quadrangle, 1974.

Karlsson, G. *Adaptability of communication in marriage: A Swedish predictive study of marital satisfaction.* Uppsala, Sweden: Almqvist and Wiksells, 1951.

Kassel, V. Polygyny after sixty. *Geriatrics*, 1966, *21*, 214–218.

Katz, A. M., & Hill, R. Residential propinquity and mate selection: A review of theory, method, and fact. *Marriage and Family Living*, 1958, *20*, 27–35.

Kay, H. H. A family court: A California proposal. In P. Bohannon (Ed.), *Divorce and after.* Garden City, N.Y.: Doubleday Anchor, 1971.

Kempler, H. L. Extended kinship ties and some modern alternatives. *The Family Coordinator*, 1976, *25*, 143–149.

Kephart, W. M. *The family society and the individual* (4th ed.). Newton, Mass.: Houghton Mifflin, 1977.

Kephart, W. M. Occupational level and marital disruption. *American Sociological Review*, 1955, *20*, 456–465.

Kerkoff, A., & Davis, K. Value consensus and need complementarity in mate selection. *American Sociological Review*, 1962, *17*, 295–303.

King, C. E. The Burgess-Cottrell method of measuring marital adjustment applied to a non-white southern urban population. *Marriage and Family Living*, 1952, *14*, 280–285.

Kinsey, A. C., Pomeroy, W. B., & Martin, C. E. *Sexual behavior in the human male.* Philadelphia: W. B. Saunders, 1948.

Kinsey, A. C., Pomeroy, W. B., Martin, C. E., & Gebhard, P. H. *Sexual behavior in the human female.* Philadelphia: W. B. Saunders, 1953.

Kirkendall, L. A. *Premarital intercourse and interpersonal relationships.* New York: Julian Press, 1961.

Kirkpatrick, C. *The family.* New York: Ronald Press, 1961.

Kirkpatrick, C., & Kanin, E. Male sex aggression on a university campus. *American Sociological Review*, 1957, *22*, 52–58.

Klemer, R. H. Self-esteem and college dating experiences as factors in mate selection and marital happiness; A longitudinal study. *Journal of Marriage and the Family*, 1971, *33*, 183–187.

Knapp, J. J., & Whitehurst, R. N. Sexually open marriage and relationships: Issues and prospects. In R. W. Libby and R. N. Whitehurst (Eds.), *Marriage and alternatives: Exploring intimate relationships.* Glenview, Ill.: Scott, Foresman, 1977.

Knudson, D. D. The declining status of women: Popular myths and the failure of functional thought. *Social Forces,* 1969, *48,* 186–197.

Kohlberg, L. A cognitive-developmental analysis of children's sex-role concepts and attitudes. In E. E. Maccoby (Ed.), *The development of sex differences.* Palo Alto: Stanford University Press, 1966.

Kohn, M. L. *Class and conformity:* A study in values. Homewood, Ill.: Dorsey Press, 1977.

Kohn, M. L. Social class and parent-child relationships: An interpretation. *American Journal of Sociology,* 1963, *68,* 463.

Kohn, M. L., & Carroll, E. E. Social class and the allocation of parental responsibilities. *Sociometry,* 1960, *23,* 372–392.

Kohn, M. L., & Schooler, C. Reciprocal effects of the substantative complexity of work and intellectual flexibility. *American Journal of Sociology,* 1978, *84,* 24–52.

Kolb, W. L. Family sociology, marriage, education, and the romantic complex. *Social Forces,* 1950, *29,* 65–72.

Kolb, W. L. Sociologically established family norms and democratic values. *Social Forces,* 1948, *26,* 451–456.

Koller, M. R. *Families: A multigenerational approach.* New York: McGraw-Hill, 1974.

Koller, M. R. Some changes in courtship behavior in three generations of Ohio women. *American Sociological Review,* 1951, *16,* 366–370.

Kollmorgan, W. M. *Culture of a contemporary rural community: The old order Amish of Lancaster County, Pennsylvania.* Washington, D.C.: U.S. Department of Agriculture, 1942.

Komarovsky, M. Patterns of self-disclosure of male undergraduates. *Journal of Marriage and the Family,* 1974, *36,* 677–686.

Komarovsky, M. Cultural contradictions and sex roles: The masculine case. *American Journal of Sociology,* 1973, *78,* 873–874.

Komarovsky, M. Functional analysis of sex roles. In M. B. Sussman (Ed.), *Sourcebook in marriage and family.* Boston: Houghton Mifflin, 1963.

Komarovsky, M. *Blue-collar marriage.* New York: Random House, 1962.

Komarovsky, M. Continuities in family research: A case study. *American Journal of Sociology,* 1956, *62,* 42–47.

Komarovsky, M. Cultural contradictions and sex roles. *American Journal of Sociology,* 1946, *52,* 184–189.

Krain, M., Cannon, D., & Bagford, J. Rating-dating or simply prestige-homogamy? Data on dating in the Greek system on a midwestern campus. *Journal of Marriage and the Family,* 1977, *39,* 663–674.

Krantzler, M. *Creative divorce.* New York: Evans, 1973.

Kutner, B. *Five hundred over sixty.* New York: Russell Sage Foundation, 1956.

Lalli, M. The Italian-American family: Assimilation and change: 1900–1965. *The Family Coordinator,* 1969, *18,* 43–50.

Landis, J. T., & Landis, M. G. *Building a successful marriage.* Englewood Cliffs, N. J.: Prentice-Hall, 1963.

Landis, J. T., Poffenberger, T., & Poffenberger, S. The effects of first pregnancy upon the sexual adjustment of 212 couples. *American Sociological Review,* 1950, *15,* 766–772.

Lang, R. D. *A study of the degree of happiness or unhappiness in marriage as rated by acquaintances of married couples.* Unpublished masters thesis, University of Chicago, 1932. In E. W. Burgess & L. S. Cottrell, Jr., *Predicting success or failure in marriage.* Englewood Cliffs, N. J.: Prentice-Hall, 1939.

Lantz, H. R., & Snyder, E. C. *Marriage: An examination of the man-woman relationship.* New York: John Wiley & Sons, 1962.

Lasch, C. The narcissist society. *The New York Review of Books,* September 30, 1976, pp. 5–8, 10–13.

Lash, J. P. *Eleanor and Franklin.* New York: W. W. Norton, 1971.

Lasswell, M. E. Is there a best age to marry?: An interpretation. *The Family Coordinator,* 1974, *23,* 237–242.

Lasswell, M. E. Looking ahead in aging: Love after fifty. In M. E. Lasswell & T. E. Lasswell (Eds.), *Love–marriage–family: A developmental approach.* Glenview, Ill.: Scott, Foresman, 1973.

Lee, G. R. Children and the elderly: Interaction and morale. *Research on Aging,* 1979, *1,* 335–360.

Lee, G. R. Marriage and morale in later life. *Journal of Marriage and the Family,* 1978, *40,* 131–139.

Leichter, H. J., & Mitchell, W. E. *Kinship and casework.* New York: Russell Sage Foundation, 1967.

LeMasters, E. E. *Blue-collar aristocrats.* Madison: University of Wisconsin Press, 1975.

LeMasters, E. E. *Parents in modern America* (Rev. ed.). Homewood, Ill.: Dorsey Press, 1974.

LeMasters, E. E. The passing of the dominant husband-father. *Impact of Science on Society,* (Paris) 1971, *21,* 21–30.

LeMasters, E. E. Parenthood as crisis. *Journal of Marriage and the Family,* 1957, *19,* 352–355. (a)

LeMasters, E. E. *Modern courtship and marriage.* New York: Macmillan, 1957. (b)

LeMasters, E. E. Social mobility and family integration. *Marriage and Family Living,* 1954, *16,* 1–8.

Leslie, G. R. *The family in social context* (4th ed.). New York: Oxford University Press, 1979.

Leslie, G. R. *The family in social context* (3rd ed.). New York: Oxford University Press, 1976.

Leslie, G. R., & Richardson, A. H. Family versus campus influences in mate selection. *Social Problems,* 1956, *4,* 117–121.

Levinger, G. A social psychological perspective in marital dissolution. *Journal of Social Issues,* Winter 1976, pp. 34–35.

Levinger, G. Sources of marital dissatisfaction among applicants for divorce. In P. H. Glasser, & L. N. Glasser, *Families in crisis.* New York: Harper & Row, 1970.

Levitin, T. D. Children of divorce. *Journal of Social Issues,* 1979, *35*(4), 1–16.

Levitt, E. E., & Klassen, A. D. Public attitudes toward homosexuality. *Journal of Homosexuality*, 1974, *1*(1), 29–43.

Levi-Straus, C. The family. In H. Shapiro (Ed.), *Man, culture and society*. New York: Oxford University Press, 1956.

Levi-Straus, C. The principle of reciprocity. In L. Coser & B. Rosenberg (Eds.), *Sociological theory*. New York: Macmillan, 1949.

Levy, M. J. *The family revolution in modern china*. Cambridge, Mass.: Harvard University Press, 1949.

Lewis, L. S., & Brissett, D. Sex as work: A study of avocational counseling. *Social Problems*, 1967, *15*, 8–18.

Lewis, O. *La Vida: A Puerto Rican family in the culture of poverty—San Juan and New York*. New York: Random House, 1965.

Liebow, E. *Tally's corner*. Boston: Little, Brown, 1967.

Lindesmith, A. R., & Strauss, A. L. A critique of culture-personality writing. *American Sociological Review*, 1950, *15*, 587–600.

Linton, R. *The study of man*. New York: Appleton-Century-Crofts, 1936.

Litwak, E. Occupational mobility and extended family cohesion. *American Sociological Review*, 1960, *25*, 9–21. (a)

Litwak, E. Geographic mobility and extended family cohesion. *American Sociological Review*, 1960, *25*, 385–394. (b)

Lobsenz, N. M. Sex after sixty-five. *Public Affairs Pamphlet* (No. 519). New York: Public Affairs Committee, 1975.

Locke, H. J. *Predicting adjustments in marriage: A comparison of a divorced and a happily married group*. New York: Holt, Rinehart & Winston, 1951.

Locke, H. J., & Mackeprang, M. Marital adjustment and the employed wife. *American Journal of Sociology*, 1949, *54*, 536–538.

Lockwood, G. B. *The New Harmony movement*. New York: D. Appleton, 1905.

Loomis, C. P., & Dyer, E. D. *Social Systems: The study of sociology*. Cambridge, Mass.: Schenkman Publishing, 1976.

Lopata, H. Z. Contributions of extended families to the support systems of metropolitan area widows: Limitations of the modified kin network. *Journal of Marriage and the Family*, 1978, *40*, 355–364.

Lopata, H. Z. Couple-companionate relationships in marriage and widowhood. In N. Glazer-Malbin, *Old family/new family*. New York: Van Nostrand, Reinhold, 1975.

Lopata, H. Z. *Widowhood in the American City*. Cambridge, Mass.: Schenkman Publishing, 1973.

Lopata, H. Z. *Occupation: Housewife*. New York: Oxford University Press, 1971.

Lowenthal, M. F., & Chiriboda, D. Transition to the empty nest. *Archives of General Psychiatry*, 1972, *26*, 8–14.

Lowenthal, M. F., & Robinson, B. Social networks and isolation. In R. H. Binstock and E. Shanas (Eds.), *Handbook of aging and the social sciences*. New York: Van Nostrand Reinhold, 1967.

Lowrie, S. H. Dating theories and student responses. *American Sociological Review*, 1951, *16*, 334–340.

Luckey, E. B. Number of years married as related to personality perception and marital satisfaction. *Journal of Marriage and the Family,* 1966, *28,* 44–48.

Luckey, E. B. Marital satisfaction and congruent self-spouse concepts. *Social Forces,* 1960, *59,* 153–157.

Lyness, J. F. Happily ever after? Following-up living together couples. *Alternative Lifestyles,* 1978, *1,* 55–70.

Lynn, D. B. The process of learning parental and sex-role identification. *Journal of Marriage and the Family,* 1966, *28,* 466–470.

Mace, D., & Mace, V. Counter-epilogue. In R. W. Libby & R. N. Whitehurst (Eds.), *Marriage and alternatives: Exploring intimate relationships.* Glenview, Ill.: Scott, Foresman, 1977.

Macklin, E. D. Heterosexual cohabitation among unmarried college students. *Family Coordinator,* 1972, *21,* 463–472.

Maddox, G. L. Persistance of life style among the elderly: A longitudinal study of patterns of social activity in relation to life satisfaction. In B. L. Neugarten (Ed.), *Middle age and aging.* Chicago: University of Chicago Press, 1968.

Mahan, C. S., & Broderick, C. B. Human reproduction. In C. B. Broderick and J. Bernard, *The individual, sex, and society.* Baltimore: John Hopkins University Press, 1969.

Malinowski, B. *The sexual life of savages in north-western Melanesia.* New York: Harvest Books, 1929.

Martin, C. E. Aging and society study. *Sarasota Herald-Tribune,* March 1, 1974, p. 10–A.

Masters, W. H., & Johnson, V. E. *Human Sexual Inadequacy.* Boston: Little, Brown, 1970.

Masters, W. H., & Johnson, V. E. Human sexual response: The aging female and the aging male. In B. L. Neugarten (Ed.), *Middle age and aging.* Chicago: University of Chicago Press, 1968.

Masters, W. H., & Johnson, V. E. *Human Sexual Response.* Boston: Little, Brown, 1966.

Mathes, E. The effects of physical attractiveness and anxiety on heterosexual attraction over a series of five encounters. *Journal of Marriage and the Family,* 1975, *37,* 769–776.

McCord, J., McCord, W., & Thurber, E. Effects of maternal employment on lower-class boys. *Journal of Abnormal and Social Psychology,* 1963, *67,* 177–182.

McCubbin, H. I., & Boss, P. G. Family stress and coping: Targets for theory, research, counseling and education. *Family Relations,* 1980, *29,* 429–430.

McDaniel, C. O. Dating roles and reasons for dating. *Journal of Marriage and the Family,* 1969, *31,* 97–107.

McKain, W. C. *Retirement marriages* (Agricultural Experiment Station Monograph No. 3), University of Connecticut, 1969.

Mead, G. H. *Mind, self, and society.* Chicago: University of Chicago Press, 1934.

Mead, M. *Male and female: A study of the sexes in a changing world.* New York: Dell, 1970.

Mead, M. Marriage in two stages. *Redbook,* July 1966.

Mead, M. *Sex and temperment in three primative societies.* New York: William Morrow, 1935.

Meehan, T. Let the rest of the world go by at Heritage Village. *Horizon,* 1973, *15,* 16–26.

Meers, D. R., & Marans, A. E. Group care of infants in other countries. In C. A. Chandler, R. S. Lourie, & A. D. Peters (Eds.), *Early child care.* New York: Atherton Press, 1968.

Mendes, H. A. Single fathers. *The Family Coordinator,* 1976, *25,* 439–444.

Meyerowitz, J. H. *Transition to parenthood: Socio-economic variation.* Unpublished paper, 1964.

Miller, D. R., & Swanson, G. E. *The changing American parent: A study in the Detroit area.* New York: John Wiley & Sons, 1958.

Miller, S., Corrales, R., & Wackman, D. Recent progress in understanding and facilitating marital communication. *The Family Coordinator,* 1975, *24,* 143–152.

Mindiola, T. *The Mexican-American family.* Unpublished master's thesis, University of Houston, 1970.

Mirande, A. The Chicano family: A reanalysis of conflicting views. *Journal of Marriage and the Family,* 1977, *39,* 747–758.

Mogey, J. M. A century of declining parental authority. *Marriage and Family Living,* 1957, *19,* 235.

Monahan, T. P. An overview of statistics on interracial marriage in the United States, with data on its extent from 1963–1970. *Journal of Marriage and the Family,* 1976, *38,* 223–231.

Monahan, T. P. Some dimensions of interreligious marriages in Indiana. *Social Forces,* 1973, *51,* 195–203.

Monahan, T. P. Are interracial marriages really less stable? *Social Forces,* 1970, *48,* 461–473.

Monahan, T. P. Divorce by occupational level. *Marriage and Family Living,* 1955, *17,* 322–324.

Monahan, T. P. Does age at marriage matter in divorce? *Social Forces,* October 1953, pp. 84–85.

Monahan, T. P. How stable are remarriages? *American Journal of Sociology,* 1952, *58,* 280–288.

Money, J., & Ehrhardt, A. *Man and woman, boy and girl.* Baltimore: Johns Hopkins University Press, 1972.

Mott, P. E., Mann, F. C., McLoughlin, Q., & Warwick, O. P. *Shift work: The social, psychological, and physical consequences.* Ann Arbor, Mich.: The University of Michigan Press, 1965.

Moran, R. The singles in the seventies. In J. R. DeLora, & J. S. DeLora, *Intimate life styles.* Pacific Palisades, Calif.: Goodyear, 1972.

Murdock, G. P. Family stability in non-European cultures. *Annals,* 1950, *277,* 195–201.

Murdock, G. P. *Social Structure.* New York: Macmillan, 1949.

Murstein, B. Stimulus–value–role: A theory of marital choice. *Journal of Marriage and the Family,* 1970, *32,* 465–481. Excerpt reprinted by permission of the

National Council on Family Relations. Copyrights by the National Council on Family Relations.

Nass, G. D. *Marriage and the family*. Reading, Mass.: Addison-Wesley Publishing, 1978.

Neugarten, B. L., Dynamics of transition of middle age to old age adaption and the life cycle. *Journal of Geriatric Psychiatry*, 1970, *4*, 71–87.

Neugarten, B. L. & Weinstein, K. K. The changing American grandparent. *Journal of Marriage and the Family*, 1964, *26*, 199–204.

Newcomb, P. R. Cohabitation in America: An assessment of consequences. *Journal of Marriage and the Family*, 1979, *41*, 597–603.

Newson, J., & Newson, E. *Infant care in an urban community*. London: George Allen and Unwin, 1963.

Norton, A. J., & Glick, P. C. Marital instability in America: Past, present, and future. In G. Levinger & O. C. Moles (Eds.), *Divorce and separation: Context, causes, and consequences*. New York: Basic Books, 1979.

Nye, F. I. Employment status of mothers and marital conflict, permanence and happiness. *Social Problems*, 1959, *6*, 265–266.

Nye, F. I. *Family relationships and delinquent behavior*. New York: John Wiley & Sons, 1958.

Nye, F. I. Child adjustment in broken and in unhappy unbroken homes. *Marriage and Family Living*, 1957, *19*, 356–361.

Nye, F. I., & Berardo, F. M. *The family*. New York: Macmillan, 1973.

Oeser, O. A., & Hammond, S. B. (Eds.). *Social structure and personality in a city*. London: Routledge and Paul, 1954.

Ogburn, W. F. The family and its functions. In W. F. Ogburn (Ed.), *Recent social trends*. New York: McGraw-Hill, 1933.

Olday, D. *Some consequences of heterosexual cohabitation for marriage*. Unpublished doctoral dissertation, Washington State University, 1977.

Olson, D. Marital and family therapy: Integrative review and critique. *Journal of Marriage and the Family*, 1970, *32*, 501–538.

O'Neil, W. L. *Divorce in the Progressive era*. New Haven: Yale University Press, 1967.

O'Neill, N. *The marriage premise*. New York: M. Evans, 1977.

O'Neill, N., & O'Neill, G. *Open marriages: A new life style for couples*. New York: M. Evans, 1972.

Orden, S., & Bradburn, N. Marrying, divorcing, and living together in the U.S. today. *Population Bulletin*, 1969, *32*(5).

Orthner, D. K., Brown, T., & Ferguson, D. Single-parent fatherhood: An emerging family life style. *The Family Coordinator*, 1976, *25*, 429–437.

Ory, M. G. The decision to parent or not: Normative and structural components. *Journal of Marriage and the Family*, 1978, *40*, 531–539.

Osborn, R. W., & Williams, J. I. Determining patterns of exchange and expanded family relationships. *International Journal of Sociology of the Family*, 1976, *6*, 205–211.

Otto, H. A. Marriage and family enrichment programs in North America—report and analysis. *The Family Coordinator*, 1975, *24*, 137–142. Excerpt reprinted by permission of the National Council on Family Relations. Copyrights by the National Council of Family Relations.

Otto, H. A. *The family cluster: A multi-base alternative.* Beverly Hills, Calif.; Holistic Press, 1971.

Parsons, T. The normal American family. In S. M. Farber, P. Mustacchi, & R. H. L. Wilson (Eds.), *Man and civilization: The family's search for survival.* New York: McGraw-Hill, 1965.

Parsons, T. The social structure of the family. In R. Anshen (Ed.), *The family: Its function and destiny.* New York: Harper & Row, 1959.

Parsons, T. The kinship system of the contemporary United States. *American Anthropologist,* 1943, *45,* 22–38.

Parsons, T., & Bales, R. F. *Family: Socialization and interaction process.* New York: Free Press, 1955.

Patterson, G. R., Hops, H., & Weiss, R. L. Interpersonal skill training for couples in early stages of conflict. *Journal of Marriage and the Family,* 1975, *37,* 294–304.

Pearlin, I. Status inequality and stress in marriage. *American Sociological Review,* 1975, *40,* 344–357.

Peck, R. F. Family patterns correlated with adolescent personality structure. *Journal of Abnormal and Social Psychology,* 1958, *57,* 347–350.

Perleman, D. Self-esteem and sexual permissiveness. *Journal of Marriage and the Family,* 1974, *36,* 470–473.

Peterson, J. A. Anticipation of things to come. In M. E. Lasswell & T. E. Lasswell (Eds.), *Love–Marriage–Family: A developmental approach.* Glenview, Ill.: Scott, Foresman, 1968.

Petranek, C. F. *The forgotten phases of life—the postparental period of marriage.* Unpublished manuscript, 1971.

Phillips, C. A study of marriage counselors' M. M. P. I. profiles. *Journal of Marriage and the Family,* 1970, *32,* 119–130.

Piaget, J., *The language and thought of the child.* New York: Harcourt Brace Jovanovich, 1926.

Piaget, J., & Inhelder, B. *The psychology of the child.* New York: Basic Books, 1969.

Pineo, P. C. Disenchantment in the later years of marriage. *Journal of Marriage and the Family,* 1961, *23,* 3–11.

Place, D. M. Dating experience for adolescent girls. *Adolescence,* 1975, *10,* 157–174.

Pratt, L. Conjugal organization and health. *Journal of Marriage and the Family,* 1972, *34,* 85–95.

Prince, A. J. Factors in mate selection. *Family Coordinator,* 1961, *10,* 55–58.

Pringle, B. Family clusters as a means of reducing isolation among urbanites. *The Family Coordinator,* 1974, *23,* 175–179.

Proulx, C. Sex as athletics in a singles complex. *Saturday Review of the Society,* 1973, *1,* 61–66.

Queen, S. A., & Habenstein, R. W. *The Family in various cultures.* Philadelphia: J. B. Lippincott, 1974.

Rabkin, L. Y., & Rabkin, K. Children of the kibbutz, *Psychology Today*, 1969, *3*, 40–46.

Rainwater, L. *Family design: Marital sexuality, family size, and contraception.* Chicago: Aldine Publishing, 1969.

Rainwater, L. *And the poor get children.* New York: Franklin Watts, 1960.

Rainwater, L., Coleman, R. P., & Handel, G. *Workingman's Wife.* New York: Oceana Publications, 1959.

Ramey, J. Intimate groups and networks: Frequent consequences of sexually open marriage. *The Family Coordinator*, 1975, *24*, 515–530.

Ramey, J. W. Emerging patterns of innovative behavior in marriage. *The Family Coordinator*, 1972, *21*, 435–456.

Rapoport, R., & Rapoport, R. Men, women, and equity. *The Family Coordinator*, 1975, *24*, 421–432.

Rapoport, R., & Rapoport, R. Work and family in contemporary society. *American Sociological Review*, 1965, *30*, 381–394.

Raush, H. L., Barry, W. A., Hertel, R. K., & Swain, M. A. *Communication, conflict, and marriage.* San Francisco: Jossey-Bass, 1974.

Rawlins, S. Perspectives on American husbands and wives. *Current Population Reports* (Special Studies Series P-23, No. 77). Washington, D.C.: Government Printing Office, 1978.

Rebecca, M., Hefner, R., & Oleshansky, B. A model of sex—role transcendence. In D. N. Ruble, I. H. Frieze, & J. E. Parsons (Eds.), Sex roles: persistence and change. *Journal of Social Issues*, 1976, *32*(3), 197–206.

Rehberg, R. A., Sinclair, J., & Schafer, W. E. Adolescent achievement behavior, family authority structure, and parental socialization practices. *American Journal of Sociology*, 1970, *75*, 1012–1034.

Reiss, I. L. Some observations on ideology and sexuality in America. *Journal of Marriage and the Family*, 1981, *43*, 271–283.

Reiss, I. L. *Family systems in America.* Hinsdale, Ill.: Dryden Press, 1976.

Reiss, I. L. Social class and campus dating. *Social Problems*, 1965, 13, 193–205.

Reiss, I. L. Toward a sociology of heterosexual love relationships. *Marriage and Family Living*, 1960, *22*, 139–145.

Reiss, P. J. The extended kinship system: Correlates of and attitudes on frequency of interaction. *Marriage and Family Living*, 1962, *24*, 333–339.

Renne, K. S. Health and marital experiences in an urban population. *Journal of Marriage and the Family*, 1971, *33*, 341–350.

Richardson, J. G. Wife occupational superiority and marital troubles: An examination of the hypothesis. *Journal of Marriage and the Family*, 1979, *41*, 63–72.

Riemer, S. Married students are good students. *Marriage and Family Living*, 1947, *9*, 11–12.

Rivers, W. H. R. *The Todas.* New York: Macmillan, 1906.

Robertson, C. N. *Oneida community, an autobiography, 1851–1876.* Syracuse: Syracuse University Press, 1970.

Robertson, J. F. Grandmotherhood: A study of role conceptions. *Journal of Marriage and the Family*, 1977, *39*, 165–174.

Robins, L. N., & Tomanec, M. Closeness to blood relatives outside the immediate family. *Marriage and Family Living*, 1962, *24*, 340–46.

Robinson, I. E., King, K., & Balswick, J. O. The premarital sexual revolution among females. *The Family Coordinator*, 1972, *37*, 189–194.

Rockwell, R. Historical trends and variations in educational homogamy. *Journal of Marriage and the Family*, 1976, *38*, 83–94.

Rodman, H. Middle-class misconceptions about lower-class families. In A. B. Shostak & W. Gombern, (Eds.), *Blue-collar world: Studies of the American worker*. Englewood Cliffs, N.J.: Prentice-Hall, 1964.

Rogers, C. *Becoming partners: Marriage and its alternatives*. New York: Delacorte, 1972.

Rogers, C. L., & Leichter, H. J. *Laterality and conflict in kinship ties*. Paper presented at the National Conference on Social Welfare, New York City, 1962.

Rogers, E. M., & Havens, E. A. Prestige rating and mate selections on a college campus. *Marriage and Family Living*, 1960, *22*, 55–60.

Rollins, B. C., & Feldman, H. Marital satisfaction over the family life-cycle. *Journal of Marriage and the Family*, 1970, *32*, 20–28. Excerpt reprinted by permission of the National Council on Family Relations. Copyright by the National Council on Family Relations.

Roper, P. *The Virginia Slims American women's opinion poll*. New York: The Roper Organization, 1974.

Rose, A. M. Factors associated with the life satisfaction of middle-class, middle-aged persons. *Marriage and Family Living*, 1955, *17*, 15–19.

Rose, A. M., & Peterson, W. A. (Eds.). *Older people and their social World*. Philadelphia: Davis, 1965.

Rosen, B. C. Social class and the child's perception of the parent. *Child Development*, 1964, *35*, 1147–1153.

Rosenberg, G. *The worker grows old*. San Francisco: Jossey-Bass, 1970.

Rosengren, W. R. Social sources of pregnancy as illness or normality. *Social Forces*, 1961, *39*, 260–267.

Rosow, I. *Social integration of the aged*. New York: Free Press, 1967.

Rosow, I., & Rose, K. D. Divorce among doctors. *Journal of Marriage and the Family*, 1972, *34*, 587–599.

Ross, H. L., & Sawhill, I. V. *Time of transition: The growth of families headed by women*. Washington, D.C.: The Urban Institute, 1975.

Rossi, A. A biosocial perspective on parenting. *Daedalus*, Spring 1977, pp. 1–31.

Rossi, A. Transition to parenthood. *Journal of Marriage and the Family*, 1968, *30*, 26–39.

Rossi, A. Naming children in middle-class families. *American Sociological Review*, 1965, *30*, 499–513.

Rossi, A. Equality Between the sexes: An immodest proposal. In R. J. Lofton (Ed.), *The woman in America*. Boston: Beacon Press, 1964.

Roth, J., & Peck, R. F. Social class and social mobility factors related to marital adjustment. *American Sociological Review*, 1951, *16*, 478–487.

Rowe, G. P. *Patterns of heterosexual development among preadolescents*. Paper presented at the annual meetings of the National Council on Family Relations, 1966.

Rubin, I. Transition in sex values—implications for the education of adolescents. *Journal of Marriage and the Family*, 1965, *27*, 185–189.

Rubin, Z. Do American women marry up? *American Sociological Review*, 1968, *33*, 750–760.

Russell, C. S. Transition to parenthood: Problems and gratifications. *Journal of Marriage and the Family*, 1974, *36*, 294–302.

Ryder, R. G., Kafka, J. S., & Olson, D. H. Separating and joining influences in courtship and early marriage. *American Journal of Orthopsychiatry*, 1971, *41*, 450–464.

Ryder, R. G. Longitudinal data relating marriage satisfaction and having a child. *Journal of Marriage and the Family*, 1973, *34*, 604–607.

Safilios-Rothschild, C. A comparison of power structure and marital satisfaction in urban Greek and French families. *Journal of Marriage and the Family*, 1967, *29*, 345–352.

Salk, L., & Kramer, R. *How to raise a human being: A parents' guide to emotional health from infancy through adolescence.* New York: Random House, 1969.

Samenfink, J. A., & Milliken, R. L. Marital status and academic success: A reconsideration. *Marriage and Family Living*, 1961, *23*, 226–227.

Sandford, J. *Woman and her social and domestic character.* London: Longman, Green, 1834.

Savage, J. E., Adair, A. V., & Friedman, P. Community-social variables related to black parent-absent families. *Journal of Marriage and the Family*, 1978, *40*, 779–785.

Sawhill, I., Ross, H., & MacIntosh, A. *The family in transition.* Washington, D.C.: Urban Institute, 1973.

Scanzoni, J. A historical perspective of husband-wife bargaining power and marital dissolution. In G. Levinger & O. Moles (Eds.), *Divorce and separation.* New York: Basic Books, 1979.

Scanzoni, J. *Sexual bargaining: Power politics in the American marriage.* Englewood Cliffs, N.J.: Prentice-Hall, 1972.

Scanzoni, J. A social system analysis of dissolved and existing marriage. *Journal of Marriage and the Family*, 1968, *30*, 452–461.

Scanzoni, J. Resolution of occupational-conjugal role conflict in clergy marriages. *Journal of Marriage and the Family*, 1965, *27*, 396–402.

Scanzoni, L., & Scanzoni, J. *Men, women, and change.* New York: McGraw-Hill, 1976.

Schneider, D. M. *American kinship: A cultural account.* Englewood Cliffs, N.J.: Prentice-Hall, 1968.

Schneider, D. M., & Homans, G. C. Kinship terminology and the American kinship system. *American Anthropologist*, 1955, *57*, 1195.

Schoen, R. California divorce rates by age at first marriage and duration of first marriage. *Journal of Marriage and the Family*, 1975, *37*, 548–555.

Schorr, A. *Filial responsibility in the modern American family.* Washington, D.C.: Social Security Administration, 1960.

Schorr, A. L., & Moen, P. The single parent and public policy. *Journal of Social Policy*, 1979, *9*, 15–21.

Schram, R. W. Marital satisfaction over the family life cycle: A critique and a proposal. *Journal of Marriage and the Family,* 1979, *41,* 7–26.

Scully, D., & Bart, P. A funny thing happened on the way to the orifice: Women in gynecology textbooks. *American Journal of Sociology,* 1973, *78*(4), 1045–1050.

Sears, R. R., Maccoby, E. E., & Levin, H. *Patterns of childrearing.* New York: Harper & Row, 1957.

Seelbach, W. C., & Hansen, C. J. Satisfaction with family relations among the elderly. *Family Relations,* January 1980, pp. 91–96.

Sewell, W. H. Infant Training and the Personality of the Child. *The American Journal of Sociology,* 1952, *58,* 150–159.

Shah, F., Zelnick, M., & Kantner, J. F. Unprotected intercourse among unwed teenagers. *Family Planning Perspectives.* 1975, *7,* 39–43.

Shanas, E. Older people and their families: The new pioneers. *Journal of Marriage and the Family,* 1980, *42,* 9–15.

Shanas, E., & Streib. G. *Social structure and the family: Generational relations.* Englewood Cliffs, N.J.: Prentice-Hall, 1965.

Shanas, E., Townsend, P., Wedderburn, D., Friis, H., Milhoj, P., & Stehouwer, J. *Older people in three industrial societies.* New York: Atherton Press, 1968.

Shannon, T. W. *The laws of sex life and heredity.* Marietta, Ohio: Mullikin, 1917.

Sheldon, A., McEwan, P. J., & Ryser, C. P. *Retirement patterns and predictions.* Washington, D.C.: Superintendent of Documents, 1975.

Shorter, E. *The making of the modern family.* New York: Basic Books, 1975.

Shostak, A. B. *Blue collar life.* New York: Random House, 1969.

Siegle, J. S. Prospective trends in the size and structure of the elderly population, impact of mortality trends, and some implications. *Current Population Reports* (Series P-23, No. 78). Washington, D.C.: Government Printing Office, 1978.

Simon, W., Berger, A., & Gagnon, J. Beyond anxiety and fantasy: The coital experiences of college youth. *Journal of Youth and Adolescence,* 1972, *1*(13), 203–222.

Simon, W., & Miller, P. Y. *The Playboy report on American men.* Chicago: Playboy Enterprises, 1979.

Singh, B. K. Trends and attitudes toward premarital sexual relations. *Journal of Marriage and the Family,* 1980, *42,* 387–393.

Skipper, J. K., & Nass, G. Dating behavior: A framework for analysis and an illustration. *Journal of Marriage and the Family,* 1966, *28,* 412–420.

Skolnick, A. *The Intimate enviroment: Exploring marriage and the family.* Boston: Little, Brown, 1978.

Smith, B. K. *Aging in America.* Boston: Beacon Press, 1978.

Smith, C. E. Negro-white intermarriage—forbidden sexual union. *Journal of Sexual Research,* 1966, *2,* 169–173.

Smith, D. S. The dating of the American sexual revolution. In M. Gordon (Ed.), *The American family in social-historical perspective.* New York: St. Martin's Press, 1973.

Smith, M. J. The social consequences of single parenthood: A longitudinal perspective. *Family Relations,* 1980, *19,* 75–81.

Smith, W. M. Rating and dating: A restudy. *Marriage and Family Living,* 1952, *14,* 312–317.

Sorensen, R. *Adolescent sexuality in contemporary America.* New York: World, 1973.

Sorokin, P. A. *Social and cultural dynamics* (4 vols.). New York: American Book, 1937.

Spanier, G. B. Measuring dyadic adjustment: New scales for assessing the quality of marriage and similar dyads. *Journal of Marriage and the Family,* 1976, *38,* 15–28.

Spanier, G. B. Romanticism and marital adjustment. *Journal of Marriage and the Family,* 1972, *34,* 481–487.

Spanier, G. B., & Castro, R. F. Adjustments to separation and divorce: A quantitative analysis. In G. Levinger & O. Moles (Eds.), *Divorce and seperation.* New York: Basic Books, 1979.

Spanier, G. B., & Lewis, R. A. Marital quality: A review of the seventies. *Journal of Marriage and the Family,* 1980, *42,* 825–839.

Spanier, G. B., Lewis, R. A., & Coles, C. L. Marital adjustment over the family life-cycle: The issue of curvilineaty. *Journal of Marriage and the Family,* 1975, *37,* 263–275.

Spicer, J. W., & Hampe, G. D. Kinship interaction after divorce. *Journal of Marriage and the Family,* 1975, *37,* 113–119.

Spitz, R. A. *The psychoanalytic study of the child.* New York: International Universities Press, 1945.

Spock, B. *Baby and child care.* New York: Pocket Books, 1957.

Spreitzer, E., & Riley, L. E. Factors associated with singlehood. *Journal of Marriage and the Family,* 1974, *36,* 533–542.

Starr, J., & Carnes, D. Singles in the city. *Society,* 1972, *9*(4), 43–48.

Stein, P. J. *Single.* Englewood Cliffs, N.J.: Prentice-Hall, 1976.

Stein, P. J. Singlehood: An alternative to marriage. *The Family Coordinator,* 1975, *24,* 489–503.

Stencel, S. Women in the work force. In *Editorial research reports on the women's movement: Achievements and effects.* Washington, D.C.: *Congressional Quarterly,* 1977.

Stephens, W. N. *The family in cross-cultural perspective.* New York: Holt, Rinehart & Winston, 1963.

Stevenson, R. L. On falling in love. In *Virginibus Puerisque.* New York: E. P. Dutton, 1925.

Stinnett, N., Collins, J., & Montgomery, J. E. Marital need satisfaction of older husbands and wives. *Journal of Marriage and the Family,* 1970, *32,* 428–434.

Stoller, F. H. The intimate network of families as a new structure. In H. A. Otto (Ed.), *The family in search of a future.* New York: Appleton-Century-Crofts, 1970.

Stott, L. *Report on pregnancy research project at Merrill-Palmer Institute.* Paper presented at the annual meeting of National Council on Family Relations, 1952.

Stratton, J. L. *Pioneer women: Voices from the Kansas Frontier.* New York: Simon & Schuster, 1981.

Straus, M. A. Social class and farm-city differences in interaction with kin in relation to societal modernization. *Rural Sociology,* 1969, *34,* 477–494.

Streib, G. F. An alternative family form for older persons: Need and social context. *The Family Coordinator,* 1978, *27,* 413–426.

Streib, G. F. Old age and the family: Facts and forecasts. *American Behavioral Scientist,* 1970, *14,* 125–139.

Streib, G. F., & Streib, R. B. Communes and the aging: Utopian dream and gerontological reality. *American Behavioral Scientist,* 1975, *19*(2), 166–189.

Strong, B., Reynolds, R., Said, M., & Dabaghian, J. *The marriage and family experience.* St. Paul: West Publishing, 1979.

Strong, L. D. Alternative marital and family forms: Their relative attractiveness to college students and correlates of willingness to participate in nontraditional forms. *Journal of Marriage and the Family,* 1978, *40,* 493–503.

Stryker, S. The adjustment of married offspring to their parents. *American Sociological Review,* 1955, *20,* 149–154.

Stuckert, R. P. Role perception and marital satisfaction—a configurational approach. *Journal of Marriage and the Family,* 1963, *25,* 415–419. (a)

Stuckert, R. P. Occupational mobility and family relationships. *Social Forces,* 1963, *41,* 301–308. (b)

Subak-Sharpe, G. The venereal disease of the new morality. *Today's Health,* March, 1975, pp. 42–55.

Sussman, M. B. Relations of adult children with their parents in the United States. In E. Shanas & G. Streib (Eds.), *Social structure and the family: Generational relations.* Englewood Cliffs, N.J.: Prentice-Hall, 1965.

Sussman, M. B. The isolated nuclear family: Fact or fiction? *Social Problems,* 6, 333–340.

Sussman, M. B. Family continuity: Selective factors which affect relationships between families at generational levels. *Marriage and Family Living,* 1954, *16,* 112–120.

Sussman, M. B. Parental participation in mate selection and its effects on family continuity. *Social Forces,* 1953, *52,* 76–81. (a)

Sussman, M. B. The help pattern in the middle-class family. *American Sociological Review,* 1953, *18,* 22–28. (b)

Sussman, M. B., & Burchinal, L. Parental aid to married children: Implications for family functioning. *Marriage and Family Living,* 1962, *24,* 320–332.

Sweetser, D. A. The effect of industrialization on intergenerational solidarity. In R. F. Winch & L. W. Goodman (Eds.), *Selected studies in marriage and the family.* New York: Holt, Rinehart & Winston, 1968.

Taylor, P. A., & Glenn, N. D. The utility of education and attractiveness for female's status attainment through marriage. *American Sociological Review,* 1976, *41,* 484–497.

Terman, L. M. *Psychological factors in marital happiness.* New York: McGraw-Hill, 1938.

Thomas, W. I., & Znaniecki, F. *The Polish peasant in Europe and America.* New York: Dover Publications, 1958.

Thomason, B. Marital sexual behavior and total marital adjustment: A research report. In J. Himelhoch & S. F. Fava (Eds.), *Sexual behavior in Americam society.* New York: W. W. Norton, 1955.

Thompson P. A., & Streib, G. F. Meaningful activity in a family context. In

R. W. Kleemer (Ed.), *Aging and leisure.* New York: Oxford University Press, 1961.

Tiger, L. *Men in groups.* New York: Random House, 1970.

Tinker, J. N. Intermarriage and ethnic boundaries: The Japanese-American case. *Journal of Social Issues,* 1973, *29,* 49–66.

Toffler, A. *Future shock.* New York: Random House, 1970.

Troll, L. E. The family in later life: A decade review. *Journal of Marriage and the Family,* 1971, *33,* 263–290.

Tumin, M. *Social stratification.* Englewood Cliffs, N.J.: Prentice-Hall, 1967.

Turner, R. H. *Family interaction.* New York: John Wiley & Sons, 1970.

Udry, J. R. The importance of being beautiful: A reexamination and racial comparison. *American Journal of Sociology,* 1977, *83,* 154–160.

Udry, J. R. *The social context of marriage.* (3rd ed.). Philadelphia: J. B. Lippincott, 1974.

Udry, J. R. Marital stability by race, sex, education, and occupation, using 1960 census data. *American Journal of Sociology,* 1966, *72,* 203–209.

Udry, J. R., Nelson, H. A., & Nelson, R. An empirical investigation of some widely held beliefs about marital interaction. *Marriage and Family Living,* 1961, *23,* 388–390.

Uhlenberg, P. Changing configurations of the life course. In T. K. Hareven (Ed.), *Transitions: The family and the life course in historical perspective.* New York: Academic Press, 1978.

U.S. Bureau of Labor Statistics. *U.S. working women: A datebook.* Washington, D.C.: Government Printing Office, 1977.

U.S. Bureau of the Census. A statistical portrait of women in the United States: 1978. *Current Population Reports* (Series P-23, No. 100). Washington, D.C.: Government Printing Office, 1980. (a)

U.S. Bureau of the Census. Population profile of the United States: 1979. *Current Population Reports* (Series P-20, No. 350, May). Washington, D.C.: Government Printing Office, 1980. (b)

U.S. Bureau of the Census. Fertility of American women: June 1978. *Current Population Reports* (Series P-20, No. 341). Washington, D.C.: Government Printing Office, 1979. (a)

U.S. Bureau of the Census. Population characteristics: Marriage status and living arrangements. *Current Population Reports* (Series P-20, No. 323). Washington, D.C.: Government Printing Office, 1979. (b)

U.S. Bureau of the Census. Recent social and economic trends. *Statistical Abstract of the United States.* Washington, D.C.: Government Printing Office, 1979. (c)

U.S. Bureau of the Census. *Statistical Abstract of the United States.* Washington, D.C.: Government Printing Office, 1979. (d)

U.S. Bureau of the Census. *Current Population Reports* (Series P-20, No. 323). Washington, D.C.: Government Printing Office, 1978. (a)

U.S. Bureau of the Census. Demographic aspects of aging and the older population in the United States. *Current Population Reports* (Series P-23, No. 59, January). Washington, D.C.: Government Printing Office, 1978. (b)

U.S. Bureau of the Census. Fertility of American women: June, 1976. *Current Popula-*

tion Reports (Series P-20, No. 308). Washington, D.C.: Government Printing Office, 1977.

U.S. Bureau of the Census. Fertility of American women: June, 1975. *Current Population Reports* (Series P-20, No. 301). Washington, D.C.: Government Printing Office, 1976. (a)

U.S. Bureau of the census. Vital statistics, health and nutrition. *Statistical Abstract of the United States: 68.* Washington, D.C.: Government Printing Office, 1976. (b)

U.S. Bureau of the Census. Marital status and living arrangements: March, 1975. *Current Population Reports* (Series P-20, No. 287). Washington, D.C: Government Printing Office.

U.S. Bureau of the Census. *Statistical Abstract of the United States.* Washington, D.C.: Government Printing Office, 1972.

U.S. Department of Health and Human Services. Final divorce statistics, 1977. *Monthly Vital Statistics Report* (*28* 2) Washington, D.C.: Government Printing Office, 1979.

U.S. Department of Health and Human Services. *Monthly Vital Statistics Report* (*25* 1). Washington, D.C.: Government Printing Office, 1977.

U.S. Department of Labor. Bureau of Labor Statistics. Washington, D.C.: Government Printing Office, 1976. (a)

U.S. Department of Labor. *Employment and earnings.* Washington, D.C.: Government Printing Office, 1976.

U.S. Department of Labor. *U.S. working women: A chartbook.* Washington, D.C.: Government Printing Office, 1975. (b)

U.S. Department of Labor. Special labor force reports, 1970. In *The American Almanac: U.S. Book of Facts, Statistics, and Information.* New York: Grosset and Dunlap, 1972.

Vander Zanden, J. W. *American minority relations.* New York: Ronald Press, 1966.

Vreeland, R. S. Is it true what they say about Harvard boys? *Psychology Today,* 1972, *5,* 65–68.

Wakeford, G. *The heir apparent.* New York: A. S. Barnes, 1967.

Waldman, W.E., & Gover, K. R. Marital and family characteristics of the labor force. *Monthly Labor Review,* 1972, *95,* 4–8.

Waller, W. *The family.* Hinsdale, Ill.: Dryden Press, 1938.

Waller, W. *The old love and the new.* New York: Liverright, 1930.

Waller, W., & Hill, R. *The family: A dynamic interpretation.* New York: Holt, Rinehart and Winston, 1951. Copyright by Holt, Rinehart and Winston. Excerpt reprinted by permission of publisher.

Wallin, P. Sex differences in attitudes to in-laws: A test of a theory. *American Journal of Sociology,* 1954, *59,* 466–469.

Walsh, R. H., Ferrell, M. Z., & Tolone, W. L. Selection of reference group, perceived reference group permissiveness, and personal permissive attitudes and behavior: A study of two consecutive panels (1967–71, 1970–74). *Journal of Marriage and the Family,* 1976, *38,* 495–507.

Walster, E., Aronsen, V., Abrahams, D., & Rottman, L. Importance of physical attractiveness in dating behavior. *Journal of Personality and Social Psychology,* 1966, *4,* 508–516.

Walters, J., & Stinnett, N. Parent-child relationships: A decade review of research. *Journal of Marriage and the Family,* 1971, *33,* 70–111.

Wanderman, L., Wanderman, A., & Kahn, S. Social support in the transition to parenthood. *Journal of Community Psychology,* 1980, *8,* 332–342.

Warner, W. L. *Social class in America.* New York: Harper & Row, 1960.

Warner, W. L. A methodology for the study of the development of family attitudes. Social Science Research Council *Bulletin,* 1933.

Weber, M. *The Protestant ethic and the spirit of capitalism.* New York: Charles Scribner's Sons, 1930.

Weis, D. L., & Slosnerick, M. Attitudes toward sexual and nonsexual extramarital involvements among a sample of college students. *Journal of Marriage and the Family,* 1981, *43,* 349–358.

Weiss, R. S. *Marital separation.* New York: Basic Books, 1975.

Welter, B. The cult of womenhood: 1820–1860. *American Quarterly,* 1966, *18,* 151–174.

Westoff, C. F., Potter, R. G., Sagi, P. C., & Mishler, E. G. *Family growth in metropolitan America.* Princeton, N.J.: Princeton University Press, 1961.

Wheeler, M. *No-fault divorce.* Boston: Beacon Press, 1974.

White, M., & Wells, C. Student attitudes toward alternate marriage forms. In R. W. Libby & R. N. Whitehurst (Eds.), *Renovating marriage.* Danville, Calif.: Consensus Publishers, 1973.

Whitehurst, R. N. Youth views marriage: Awareness of present and future potentials in relationships. In R. W. Libby & R. N. Whitehurst (Eds.), *Marriage and alternatives: Exploring intimate relationships.* Glenview, Ill.: Scott, Foresman, 1977.

Whitehurst, R. N. Alternative life-styles. *The Humanist,* May/June 1975, pp. 23–26.

Whitehurst, R. N. Some comparisons of conventional and counterculture families. *The Family Coordinator,* 1972, *21,* 395–401.

Whyte, W. H., Jr. *The organization man.* Garden City, N.Y.: Doubleday Anchor, 1957.

Wilkenson, M. L. Romantic love and sexual expression. *Family Coordinator,* 1978, *27,* 141–148.

Williams, C. How much does a baby cost? *Redbook,* April 1976, p. 96.

Willmott, P., & Young, M. *Family and class in a London suburb.* London: Routledge and Kegan Paul, 1960.

Winch, R. F. *The modern family* (3rd ed.). New York: Holt, Rinehart & Winston, 1971.

Winch, R. Another look at the theory of complementary needs in mate selection. *Journal of Marriage and the Family,* 1967, *29,* 756–762.

Winch, R. *Mate selection.* New York: Harper & Row, 1958.

Winch, R. The theory of complementary needs in mate selection: Final results of the test on the general hypotheses. *American Sociological Review,* 1955, *20,* 552–555.

Wirth, L. Urbanism as a way of life. *American Journal of Sociology,* 1938, *44,* 20–29.

Wolfenstein, M. Trends in infant care. *American Journal of Orthopsychiatry,* 1953, *33,* 120–130.

Wollstonecraft, M. *A vindication of the rights of woman* (Rep. ed.). New York: W. W. Norton, 1967.

Wood, V., & Robertson, J. F. Friendship and kinship interaction: Differential effect on the morale of the elderly. *Journal of Marriage and the Family,* 1978, *40,* 368–375.

Wright, J. D. Are working women really more satisfied? Evidence from several national surveys. *Journal of Marriage and the Family,* 1978, *40,* 301–313. Excerpt reprinted by permission of the National Council on Family Relations. Copyright by the National Council on Family Relations.

Wright, J. D., & Wright, S. R. Social class and parental values for children: A partial replication and extension of the Kohn thesis. *American Sociological Review,* 1976, *41,* 527–537.

Yilo, K. A. Nonmarital cohabitation: Beyond the college campus. *Alternative Lifestyles,* 1978, *1,* 37–54.

Yinger, J. M. Contraculture and subculture. *American Sociological Review,* 1960, *25,* 625–635.

Zaretsky, E. Capitalism, the family and personal life. New York: Harper & Row, 1976.

Zeldich, M., Jr. Role differentiation in the nuclear family: A comparative study. In T. Parsons & R. F. Bales (Eds.), *The family: Socialization and interaction process.* New York: Free Press, 1955.

Zelnick, M., & Kantner, J. F. Sexuality, contraception, and pregnancy among young unwed females in the United States. In *Demographic and social aspects of population growth* (Vol. 1). Washington, D.C.,: Government Printing Office, 1972.

Zimmerman, C. C. *The family of tomorrow.* New York: Harper & Row, 1949.

Name index

A

Aberle, D. F., 205
Adams, B. N., 13–14, 71, 95, 97, 198, 272, 334–336, 340–343, 345, 347, 356, 360–361, 378, 380–381, 387–388, 397–398
Aldous, J., 135, 211, 213, 380–381
Allan, G., 341, 343, 346
Amory, C., 312, 344–345
Andres, D., 321
Angrist, S. S., 330–331
Anspach, D., 348–349
Arafat, I., 92
Ard, B. N., 90
Aries, P., 302
Axelson, L. J., 217–218, 413

B

Bacon, M. K., 31
Bandura, A., 33, 309
Bane, M. J., 6, 243, 396, 398, 402–403
Barber, K. E., 159
Barry, H., 31
Barry, W. A., 175
Bart, P., 186
Bauman, K. E., 84
Baumrind, D., 309
Bayer, A. E., 66

Becker, G., 209
Beigel, H. G., 57, 71
Bell, D., 5
Bell, R. R., 55, 78–79, 86, 92, 182, 189, 199–201, 230, 326
Belsky, J., 298, 322, 331
Bem, S., 47
Benedict, R., 185
Bennett, J. W., 21
Benson, L., 208, 210, 277, 300, 329
Berardo, F., 386
Berger, A., 83
Berger, B., 351
Berleson, B., 281–282
Bernard, J., 401
Bernard, S. E., 324, 328
Billingsley, A., 162
Blake, J., 282–284
Blau, P. M., 97
Blood, M., 84, 89–90, 93, 118, 121–123, 125, 133, 177–180, 247, 286, 309, 355–356
Blood, R. O., 61, 70, 84, 89–90, 93, 118, 121–123, 125, 133, 158, 161, 163, 173, 177–180, 217, 247, 286, 299, 309, 355–357, 360, 373, 385
Bock, E., 386–387
Bohannon, P., 248, 348

Boll, E., 373
Bolton, C., 114
Booth, A., 218–219
Borgatta, M. L., 97
Boss, P. G., 409
Bossard, J. H., 104, 373
Bower, D. W., 86
Bowlby, J., 222, 320
Bowman, H. A., 77, 82, 86–88, 92, 116, 132, 140–141, 260, 262–263
Bradburn, N., 218
Brandwein, R. A., 243, 244
Brissett, D., 187
Broderick, C. B., 28, 402
Bronfenbrenner, U., 308, 313, 315–316
Brown, R. G., 382
Bruce, J. A., 67
Bruce-Briggs, B., 331
Bumpass, L. L., 103, 160–161, 243
Burchinal, L. G., 103, 245, 339, 344
Burgess, E. W., 16, 19, 85–86, 89–90, 117, 121–124, 159, 161, 166–169, 194, 217, 396
Burgess, J. K., 324, 326
Burke, R. J., 218–219
Burr, W., 113
Busselen, C. K., 138
Busselen, H. J., 138

447

Subject index

This book has been set VideoComp, in 10 and 9 point Compano, leaded 2 points. Chapter numbers and titles are 18 point Compano Bold. The size of the type page is 36 by 48 picas.